Rural Athens
Under the Democracy

Nicholas F. Jones

PENN

UNIVERSITY OF PENNSYLVANIA PRESS

Philadelphia

10   9   8   7   6   5   4   3   2   1

Published by
University of Pennsylvania Press
Philadelphia, Pennsylvania 19104–4011

Library of Congress Cataloging-in-Publication Data
Jones, Nicholas F.
  Rural Athens under the democracy / Nicholas F. Jones
    p.   cm.
  ISBN 0-8122-3774-9 (cloth : alk. paper)
  Includes bibliographical references and index.
  1. Attikē (Greece)—Rural conditions. I. Title
DF261.A8 J65   2004
307.72'09385'09014—dc22   2003061794

To my grandmother
Mabel Tilford Patterson
in loving memory

Contents

PREFACE   ix

LIST OF ABBREVIATIONS   xiii

INTRODUCTION   I

1. SETTLEMENT   17

2. SOCIETY   48

3. VILLAGE   91

4. DIONYSIA   124

5. REALITIES   159

6. IMAGES   192

7. PHILOSOPHY   226

8. PARADIGMS   273

NOTES   279

BIBLIOGRAPHY   311

INDEX   327

Preface

That ancient Athens was one of the great cities in human history is, I trust, agreed by everyone, notwithstanding differences regarding the criteria by which "greatness" is to be identified and measured. As it happens, we are now living at a time when the recovery, sifting, analysis, and publication of the city's multifaceted record has reached such a level as to make possible increasingly comprehensive reconstructions and appreciations. The present study of rural Athens is confined to but a single topographically defined dimension of that record, yet one with far-reaching ramifications for our understanding in virtually every department of the city's functioning, private and public alike. But my approach, though selective, is not arbitrarily so. My goal has been to establish that rural Athens under the classical democracy of the fifth and fourth centuries B.C. constituted, or at least was dominated by, a distinct, characteristically nonurban society and culture, and then to show in rough outline how that distinct societal and cultural regime was constructed in contemporary literary (and philosophical) representations. No attempt in particular has been made to deal with the physical record, except for a few perfunctory references to secondary publications; recovery and analysis of that record is still continuing and its evaluation in any event lies well outside my experience and competence. Accordingly, my thesis is presented not as an exhaustive compilation of data but as a sort of challenge: I believe that even my partial treatment of the record is sufficient to establish the distinctiveness of rural Athens. It will remain for those who disagree to present new evidence or contrasting interpretations of the evidence examined here.

Two overarching issues, which are organically and dichotomously related to one another, are implicitly engaged by my study, the first of which is unity. Was classical Athens, whether viewed narrowly as a political entity ("the Athenians") or more broadly and socially (citizens, metics, and slaves; women as well as men; etc.) or territorially (the land of Attica), a meaningful, substantial monolithic whole? Or did "Athens" remain a loose assemblage of parts unified only nominally in rhetoric or ideology or defensively but temporarily when threatened with destruction from without?

Modern efforts to comprehend Attica in its totality have been with us for a quarter century and reflect a variety of dimensions: the topographic segmentation of Athenian territory (Traill 1975, 1986; Siewert 1982; Jones 1987); the building-block tier of segmentation into constituent demes or villages (Whitehead 1986a); temporary and shifting linkages of an economic, social, or political nature evidenced in mining leases, associational membership, or partisan alliance (many, including especially Osborne 1985b); a periodically active web of "national" cult centers bonding town and country (de Polignac 1995 [1984]); a loose nexus of associations, both urban and rural, potentially bridging existing lines of fragmentation (Jones 1999); the pan-Attic citizenship and its embedded ideology (most recently, Boegehold and Scafuro 1994, Ober and Hedrick 1996); and now the "nation" of Athens (E. Cohen 2000). But to study "Athens" in its totality and to assert its unity are of course two very different (though possibly coinciding) enterprises. These studies succeed in establishing the existence of out-reaching institutions, shared memberships, and significant linkages across Attica, but do they amount to a demonstration of a substantive *unity?*

My own just cited study of the classical association (*The Associations of Classical Athens: The Response to Democracy*), for example, while acknowledging the comprehensive reach of formally organized groups in both demographic and territorial dimensions, ends up arguing that they comprised a sort of collective reaction—and a divisive, deunifying reaction—against an urban-based democratic government. The effects, if my thesis is valid, will have been many and varied, but among them must necessarily be included the maintenance of a fundamental cleft between town and country. The present book continues this line of argument and, as such, will join forces with a by now generation-old strand of postmodernist scholarship (and the second of my two dichotomous issues), the detection and analysis of the marginalized Other or, more abstractly put, alterity. Differences of status or order, class, gender, occupation, and so on may all give rise to the perception of Otherness by the dominant center, but not until very recently has the study of alterity approached what I will argue was still another major divide (and one all the more consequential because it will have sundered the citizen body)—that between town and country. I especially have in mind Beth Cohen's edited volume *Not the Classical Ideal: Athens and the Construction of the Other in Greek Art*, and in particular Maria Pipili's essay "Wearing an Other Hat: Workmen in Town and Country." The hat that marked the countryman in contrast with his townsman counterpart was, if my thesis wins approval, only a relatively minor manifestation of a far more pervasive Otherness. My rural Athens, subject to the definitions and qualifications to be laid out in due course, may be viewed as a characterization of Attic society and culture outside the walls in terms which will have rendered it an Other from the perspective of our predominantly urban witnesses. If one were, reasonably, to ask why after all this time so fundamental a feature of Athenian society and culture could have until now escaped our attention, I would answer that because my "rustics" were dominated by a large segment of the adult male citizen "elite" they have not been subjected to the special scrutiny accorded the nonelites as defined by gender, order or rank, or ethnicity.

The book has had a long gestation, with numerous debts of gratitude incurred along the way. Recognition must begin with my home institution, the University of Pittsburgh, where preliminary versions of my work were presented to the Department of Classics, the Department of History, and several of my undergraduate and graduate classes. To Edwin D. Floyd, chair of the Department of Classics, special thanks for assisting me in the use of electronic sources, for authorizing the use of university funds for travel to a distant academic library, and generally for extending institutional and collegial support to my project. Anonymous readers saved me from errors, ambiguities, and infelicities; provided valuable additional sources and bibliography; and, perhaps most importantly, gave me an advance idea of the reception my book is likely to receive. The Department of Classics at the University of California in Berkeley graciously granted access to bibliographic materials not available to me here in Pittsburgh. I am greatly indebted to the director, Eric Halpern, and the editorial board at the University of Pennsylvania Press for agreeing to publish my book and thereby allowing it to be associated with that distinguished institution of learning.

The manuscript, save for two chapters still only in advanced draft form, was submitted to the publisher in the Fall of 2000. Publications first coming to my attention since that time, including some very recent imprints, I have attempted to incorporate in the final draft, but in the case of Edward E. Cohen's *The Athenian Nation* I think it better to postpone systematic response to some future occasion—a decision necessitated in any event by the same limitations of space that have elsewhere required me to keep citation of secondary literature to a bare minimum. Besides, my thesis, like his, needs to be set out initially in its own terms rather than in dialogue with competing acccounts of the subject.

On the wall of our bedroom above the computer on which this book has been written are two old photographs dating from the late 1800s. One is a formal studio portrait of my great-grandparents—my maternal grandmother's mother and father—and their ten children, including my grandmother herself. The other is a view of the house on the Tilford family's farm in eastern Kansas where she was raised before she moved west to Los Angeles to teach elementary school and acquired the Craftsman cottage in which I spent my childhood. Although always in my eyes the Kansas farm girl, Mabel Tilford Patterson, were she alive today, would probably find little in common with my ancient rural Athenians, but I dedicate this book to her memory anyway, with thanks for everything and especially for instilling in me a rural way of looking at things and ultimately inspiring me to explore this topic.

Abbreviations

CLASSICAL AUTHORS AND WORKS

Except in a few readily intelligible instances, I have followed the conventions of the *Oxford Classical Dictionary*, 3rd ed., pp. xxix–liv. All translations from ancient Greek and Latin in my text are my own unless otherwise indicated.

PERIODICALS

Abbreviations used are those of *L'Année philologique*, save for the usual substitution of *CP* for *CPh*, *PCPS* for *PCPhS*, and so on.

DICTIONARIES AND ENCYCLOPEDIAS

KlPauly   *Der Kleine Pauly*. 5 vols. Stuttgart, 1964–1975.
*LSJ*⁹   H. G. Liddell and R. Scott, *A Greek-English Lexicon*. 9th ed., rev. H. S. Jones. Oxford, 1940.
*OCD*³   *The Oxford Classical Dictionary*, 3rd ed., ed. S. Hornblower and A. Spawforth. Oxford and New York, 1996.
RE   Pauly-Wissowa, *Real-Encyclopädie der classischen Altertumswissenschaft*. Stuttgart, 1893–1978.

EPIGRAPHIC CORPORA, PROSOPOGRAPHIES, AND ARCHAEOLOGICAL SITE PUBLICATIONS AND HANDBOOKS (WITH MORE SPECIALIZED WORKS FOLLOWING THE CONVENTIONS USED BY SEG)

Agora III   R. E. Wycherley, *The Athenian Agora: Literary and Epigraphical Testimonia*, Princeton, N.J., 1957.
Agora XIV   H. A. Thompson and R. E. Wycherley, *The Athenian Agora. The Agora of Athens: The History, Shape, and Uses of an Ancient City Center.* Princeton, N.J., 1972.
Agora XIX   G. V. Lalonde, M. K. Langdon, and M. B. Walbank, eds., *The Athenian Agora: Inscriptions: Horoi, Poletai Records, Leases of Public Lands.* Princeton, N.J., 1991.
APF   J. K. Davies, *Athenian Propertied Families 600–300 B.C.* Oxford, 1971.

CPG   *Corpus Paroemiographorum Graecorum*, ed. E. L. Leutsch and F. G. Schneidewin. 2 vols. Göttingen, 1839, 1851.

PA   J. Kirchner, *Prosopographia Attica*. Berlin, vol. 1, 1901; vol. 2, 1903.

PAA   J. S. Traill, *Persons of Ancient Athens*. Toronto, 1992–.

PDAA   John Travlos, *Pictorial Dictionary of Ancient Athens*. New York, 1971.

PECS   *The Princeton Encyclopedia of Classical Sites*, ed. Richard Stillwell et al. Princeton, N.J., 1976.

SEG   *Supplementum Epigraphicum Graecum*, ed. since vol. 26 for 1976/1977 by H. W. Pleket, R. S. Stroud, et al.

Introduction

An Epistemological Problem

At the midwinter Lenaia festival of Dionysos in 425, Aristophanes produced the first of his extant "War" plays, *Acharnians*. The protagonist, Dikaiopolis ("Just Polis") of Cholleidai (line 406), a deme of unknown location but not one of the five demes that lay within the circuit wall, opens the comedy with a soliloquy delivered from his seat in the assembly place on the Pnyx, ending:

> O Polis! Polis! I am always the first of all to come to the Assembly and take my seat. And then, when I am all by myself, I moan, I yawn, I stretch, I break wind, I daydream, I doodle, I pluck myself, I do some figuring, looking off towards the country, lusting for peace, hating the town, but longing for my deme, which has not to this day spoken the words "buy charcoal," "buy vinegar," "buy olive oil" nor even knew the word "buy," but on its own produced everything with no grating Buy Guy in sight! And so now I have simply come prepared to shout, to break in, to abuse the speakers, if anyone touches on any topic but peace. (lines 27–39)

Two years later, in 423, at the springtime City Dionysia in Elaphebolion, the same poet's *Clouds* saw its initial production, with its foil to the philosopher Socrates an uncomprehending country man Strepsiades from the extramural deme Kikynna (lines 134, 210) now transplanted to the town, where he has married a high falutin' aristocratic lady and with her produced a prodigal son:

> Damn! She ought to die in misery, that matchmaker who put me up to marrying your mother! A sweet country life used to be mine, gathering dust, unswept, just lying around, teeming with honeybees, sheep, and olive cakes. And then I married the niece of Megacles, son of Megacles, me a country boy, she from town, pompous, pampered, a regular Koisyra. When I married her, I jumped in the sack, smelling of must, fig-crates, wool, and surpluses, she of fragrance, saffron, deep kisses, extravagance, gluttony, Cape Kolias, and the birthday goddess! (lines 41–52)

Another two years later, again at the City Dionysia, Aristophanes returned to the War with his *Peace*, whose farmer-hero Trygaios, of the country deme Athmonon (lines 190, 919), midway through the action calls upon the chorus to return with him to their plots (lines 562–563). Supplied with farming tools, they provoke Hermes' admiring comment, then this from Trygaios himself:

> Yes, by Zeus, the hoe, when it's ready to go, really shines, and the pitchforks glimmer in the sun. They'll do a fine job of clearing out the vineyard furrows! So now I too want to go to the country myself and at long last turn over my little plot with my mattock. Now, gentlemen, let us recall the old-fashioned lifestyle that this goddess once provided for us—those little fruitcakes, the figs, the myrtle berries, the sweet new wine, the violet-bed by the well, the olive trees, for which we long. Now, for the sake of these, address this goddess here! (lines 566–581)

These three passages, and the dramatic complications that they represent, are linked by strong, and significant, commonalties. Aristophanes, son of Philippos, belonged to the deme Kydathenaion (*PA* 2090; *PAA* 175685), one of the five demes entirely enclosed within the walls of Athens. Since deme-membership was hereditary, it follows that the poet's ancestors were residing in Kydathenaion when the deme system was created by Kleisthenes late in the sixth century and that, in the absence of contrary information, the family probably remained based there during the intervening century, although a passage from *Acharnians* (lines 642–644) does suggest that Aristophanes himself owned property, and inferentially a residence, on the island of Aegina. Also, the venues of the three productions were in the town, viz. the Theater of Dionysos on the southern slope of the Acropolis[1] (*Clouds, Peace*) or the Lenaion sanctuary (*Acharnians*), of unknown precise location but certainly within the walls.[2] All else being equal, finally, an urban production implies a preponderantly urban audience. Altogether, then, the three comedies are out-and-out creations of the town of Athens. Nevertheless, each of our three speakers is textually identified as hailing from a named, extramural Attic country deme. At once this paradoxical state of affairs—which is mirrored throughout virtually the entire corpus of literary representations of rural Attica—raises the question of the authenticity of the sentiments Aristophanes has placed in his speakers' mouths. Do the dramatic utterances of Dikaiopolis, Strepsiades, and Trygaios preserve a credible rural Attic voice, whether the subject be the concrete particulars of life in a country deme or, less concretely, their own perceptions of that life and of the quite different life of the town? Alternatively, as a wealth of parallel evidence extending from antiquity down to our own day would suggest, are we dealing here with an urban sensibility, with the longings or idealizing fantasies of a poet and audience long detached from the realities of life outside the walls?

The obvious solution to this difficulty would be to renew the search for evidence emanating from rural Attica itself, evidence that has not been passed through an urbanizing filter. Although it is not the purpose of this book to present previously unpublished documentation of this kind, several of the chapters are devoted to the reevaluation of material of rural origin which has long been known but, if my arguments are accepted, has not until now been sufficiently (or appropriately) appreciated. But the problem goes much deeper than merely separating distorting urban from authentic rural sources, disregarding or correcting the former, while exploiting the latter to their absolute fullest potential. The problem is also at the same time a substantive one rooted in the historically documented efforts, evidenced initially in state policy under the Peisistratid tyranny, to establish and maintain a formal boundary, albeit a permeable one, between the countryside and the town. According to the Aristotelian *Constitution of the Athenians*, the tyrant Peisistratos advanced to the poor (*aporoi*) loans which would enable them to support themselves by farming, "in order that they not spend time in the *asty* but rather be dispersed over the countryside and, moderately well off and engaged in private matters, neither desire nor have the time to take an interest in public affairs (*ta koina*)" (16.3–4); likewise, with similar purpose, he established the judges for the demes (*dikastai . . . kata dēmous*) and himself often went out into the country (*chora*) witnessing and reconciling people in dispute, "in order that they not, ignoring their tasks, come into the *asty*" (16.5).

Nor, lest there be doubts about the authenticity of these late classical reports of sixth-century events, was Peisistratos the only head of state to implement such a policy. At Erythrai, according to a fragment of the second book of Hippias' *Investigations* concerning his native city (preserved in Athenaeus 6.258f–259f), *FGrH* 421 F 1, the tyrants, locally called Fawning Dogs because of their flattering attention to the notables, after destroying their opponents and dissolving the laws, administered the affairs of the *polis*, "receiving none of the *dēmotai* within the wall; but setting up a court outside the gates, they dispensed judgments. . . ." In Kephallenia, "the son of Promnesos took power," reports a fragment of Aristotle, 611, no. 64 Rose, "and, being a hard man, did not allow more than two festivals nor (for anyone) to spend more than ten days of each month in the town (*polis*)." At Corinth, the tyrant Periander is reported by Ephoros, *FGrH* 70 F 179, and Aristotle, fr. 516 Rose (both preserved in Diogenes

Laertius, 1.98), "not to have permitted those who so wished to live in the town (*asty*)." Nikolaos of Damascus, recalling the *AthPol* text, adds, *FGrH* 90 F 58.1, that Periander "forbade the citizens to own slaves and to have leisure, always finding some task or other for them. And if anyone sat down in the agora [i.e., in town], he fined him, fearing lest they devise some plot against him." A Corinthian council *ep' eschatōn* reported by Hermippos, *FHG* III 40, fr. 16, if its domain was the *eschatia*, or hinterland, of the Corinthia, will have corresponded in design and purpose to Peisistratos's deme judges.[3] An unplaced fragment of Theopompos, *FGrH* 115 F 311, reports that certain people were compelled by the tyrants to wear the *katōnakē* (a kind of animal-skin coat) "in order that they not come into the *asty*." Lexicographers explain that the wearers of the coat would have been embarrassed by the crudeness of the garment and identify the scene as alternately Sikyon or—to return to our subject—Athens (Hesychios, s.v. [Athens]; Pollux, 7.68 [Sikyon and Athens]; Souda, s.v. [Athens]).

These fragments of ancient learning are rich in their implications. They establish the town proper, the *asty*, and with it, where present, its encircling walls as the topographical feature with reference to which a Greek state's domestic policies might be formulated and implemented in the service of the inhabitants of that town. The territories outside the *asty*, often not designated by a single comprehensive term but when so designated, the *chora*, will have been, if the *katōnakē* was in fact (as I shall argue) symptomatic, the site of a distinctive, and decidedly nonurban, cultural milieu. But these topics will be taken up in due course. The point I am making now is a methodological one: if to some significant degree the populations of the countryside were prevented or discouraged from spending time in, or even entering, the town, and if, as observed in our first paragraph, the surviving ancient literary and historical writings are the products of urban authorship, venues, and audience, how will it be possible for us to reconstruct the world of ancient rural Attica in any significant part? My stance on this epistemological issue will prove far from agnostic, for in the early years of the Peloponnesian War urban Athens was subject to an unprecedented and protracted rural presence which will have familiarized town-dwellers with the world of Attica outside the walls. Besides, we do possess authentic records of extraurban provenience and, with proper attention to the ordinary principles of source criticism, even ordinary urban witnesses may yield much that is trustworthy. But it is essential at the outset of our study to acknowledge the formidable barriers obstructing an enterprise of this nature at every turn.

Terminology and Design of the Study

Given a general interest in what was going on in the state of Athens outside the urban center, there remains the task of more clearly defining the scope of the study, for it is by no means obvious that the term used in the title of this book, "rural," is necessarily fully justified by the ancient evidence.

Some existing studies, for example, are primarily or exclusively concerned with agriculture and farming and thereby capture a very large segment of extramural spaces and populations. Thus, among modern works in the field, Alison Burford's 1993 *Land and Labor in the Greek World* gives only scant attention to nonagricultural subjects and Victor Hanson's *The Other Greeks*, which appeared two years later, is subtitled "The Family Farm and the Agrarian Roots of Western Civilization." But while of course there can be no objection to such an orientation, it remains true that, at least in the case of Athens, to study agriculture (and farming), even when broadly conceived, is not the same thing as studying the extramural countryside, the *chora*. Sanctuaries, mines and quarries, military encampments, the village and its distinctive society and culture, large (if mostly invisible) pastoral and fishing economies, and the varied manifestations of urban interaction with the country are merely the most obvious examples of topics which would remain to be examined. Conversely, as I will observe in the course of my epigraphic exploration of rural settlement in chapter 1, properties termed "*chorion* (land) and *oikia* (house)", that is, farms, almost certainly existed *inside* the walls during the later classical and hellenistic periods. And, as we shall also see in chapter 4, the festival called the Dionysia *kat' agrous*, the "Agrarian" (not, as usually rendered, the "Rural") Dionysia, was celebrated in two intramural demes, Kollytos and Peiraieus. We may thus legitimately begin to suspect that some of the farmers depicted as present in the *asty* by literary texts actually originated in nearby demes, perhaps even demes situated within the walls. But, pending the outcome of these discussions, we should at least leave open the possibility that the practice of agriculture did not neatly begin and end at the monumental boundary defining "town and country."

If one seeks for terms and definitions unmistakably indicated by contemporary ancient Greek sources, an at-first-sight attractive candidate might be the regional grouping of the demes of Attica instituted by Kleisthenes and set out in explicit detail in the *Constitution of the Athenians*, 21.4: "And he [Kleisthenes] distributed the territory (*chora*) by demes into thirty parts [i.e., the thirty *trittyes*], ten of the demes around the town (*asty*), ten (of demes) of the coast (*paralia*), and ten (of demes) of the inland (*mesogeios*), . . ." But it is clear from Traill's assignments of the demes to their respective *trittyes*, and hence their region, that this threefold partition of Attica would not serve the interests of the present study. The demes assigned with varying degrees of reliability in Traill's 1986 roster to *trittyes* of demes "around the town" come to 55, or just under 40% of the total number of demes, but only 5 of these 55 were situated inside the walls, and the big port town of Peiraieus, also walled, comprised only a single additional deme. Even allowing for the emergence of "suburban" communities in the shadow of the enceinte, it is clear that the "City" region was in fact distinctly nonurban. Thus the limitation of the study to the "Coast" and "Inland" regions would fall far short of a justifiable or meaningful design for our research.

Alternatively, the deme itself could become the object of study, and, if it did, such a study would amount to an examination of rural Attica in many of its most important dimensions. Just such an investigation was carried out with exemplary thoroughness and accuracy by David Whitehead, whose 1986 book *The Demes of Attica 508/7–ca. 250 B.C.* covers nearly every significant dimension of the Kleisthenic village within the limits of its subtitle "A Political and Social Study." Several other works deal with the deme, including most recently my own *The Associations of Classical Athens* (1999), and it is becoming apparent that study of the deme, qua constitutional entity, may be reaching the point of exhaustion. But, as will become abundantly clear, matters of importance either having nothing to do with the demes or engaging the demes in ways that even Whitehead failed fully to appreciate remain to be studied.

Aristotelian *asty*, "town," in Athens' case denotes a meaningful topographic entity, and in it and its opposing term, *chora*—not in its more general sense of "territory" encompassing all of a state's lands (as in the passage from the *AthPol* just mentioned) but in the more restricted sense of "country" in contrast with the town—we may find, I believe, a satisfactory brace of terms. "Town" and "country" are of course well worn fixtures of the academic classical vocabulary, but my reasons for preferring their use here go beyond convention and are substantively rooted in the reality of ancient Athens. At the core of that reality were the walls, beginning with Pelargikon of the prehistoric Bronze Age Acropolis, continuing with the archaic fortifications, and reaching their climax with the new system hastily constructed in 479 under the leadership of Themistocles. Despite the fact that neither the Attic countryside nor even the town of Athens in relation to its countryside are frequent topics of ancient comment, we are fortunate to have from Thucydides and the Aristotelian *Constitution of the Athenians* a series of highly suggestive notices bearing on Athenian urban-rural relations. These texts do not actually mention the walls, but they are presupposed in each case by references to *asty*, *chora*, or some other significant topographic entity:

(1) To the sixth-century tyrant Peisistratos, as noted, the *Constitution* ascribes a policy of advancing loans to the poor in support of self-sufficient farming and the institution of the *dikastai kata dēmous*, with both in whole or part motivated by a desire to keep the recipients of these services out of the *asty* (16.3–4, 5).

(2) In the wake of the formation of the Delian League, the initial imposition of tribute on the allies, and the resulting influx of large sums of money into Athens, the *Constitution* states that the politician Aristeides "advised the Athenians to take their leadership in hand and, coming in from the fields, to live in the *asty*"; "for," he said, "there would be maintenance for all, some by campaigning, some by serving as guards, some by attending to public affairs, and in this way they would solidify their leadership" (24.1). Since the first assessment is dated to the third year after Salamis, the archonship of Timosthenes (23.5), viz. 478/7, Themistocles' walls, constructed in 479 (Thucydides, 1.90–93), will have been completed by the time of Aristeides' advice to the Athenians ("and after this", 24.1). Although the story is possibly an anachronistic retrojection from conditions later in the fifth century, it does nonetheless acknowledge the pivotal significance of the walls, and the societal and cultural divide separating town and country.

(3) With the first Peloponnesian invasion of Attica in 431, Thucydides records that the Athenians began to bring in from the fields their women, children, and household furniture (2.14.1). "And the relocation proved difficult for them because many had always been accustomed to living in the country (lit. 'in the fields')" (2.14.2). "At all events, the Athenians, because of their long autonomous occupation of the countryside (*chora*) and since they, even after the synoecism (both the early and later arrivals up to the time of this war), out of habit nonetheless resided in the country (lit. 'in the fields') with their households, did not easily make the relocations, especially since they had only recently rebuilt their estates after the Persian Wars. They were depressed and took it hard, leaving their houses and the shrines—ancestral shrines which, the legacy of the ancestral state, had al-

ways been theirs—and about to change to a new way of life, each doing nothing other than leaving behind his own *polis*" (2.16.1–2). "And when they arrived in the *asty*, . . ." (2.17.1).

(4) As though resuming the Thucydidean narrative, the *Constitution* records that the Peloponnesian War broke out in the archonship of Pythodoros (432/1): "during which the People, having been shut up inside the *asty* and grown accustomed to drawing pay on campaigns, partly intentionally, partly unintentionally, began to prefer to administer public affairs themselves" (27.2). This text explicitly marks the confinement of the extramural population within the *asty* during the annual invasions of the initial stages of the War as bringing about a substantial acceptance of urban ways by the once extramural population. The implication is that, prior to the confinement, Athenians in the country had resisted involvement with the town and its institutions.

(5) The deme-judges created by Peisistratos (*AthPol* 16.5) at some point were abolished (perhaps with the expulsion of the tyrants), were reestablished in 453/2 (26.3), and finally were increased from thirty to forty after the oligarchy of the Thirty (53.1). The last cited passage adds that the *dikastai* "used to go around the demes trying cases," with the implication that they had ceased to do so no later than the fall of the Thirty in 403/2. Rhodes speculates that the judges had discontinued their travels during the closing years of the Peloponnesian War, when Dekeleia was occupied by the Spartans and the country population was confined to Athens and Peiraieus, and that after the War it was decided that they should continue to work in town.[4] But it is also attractive to associate the change of venue with the aforementioned earlier confinement during the Peloponnesian invasions and the change of orientation attributed to it by the *Constitution* (27.2).

Thus, we may conclude, the walls of Athens constituted a, indeed *the*, significant internal physical barrier defining not only the town and country spaces called *asty* and *chora* (or "the fields") but also, as these testimonies so clearly illustrate, a formidable social and cultural divide as well. Naturally, since a similar pattern of settlement prevailed across much of the Greek world, many a *polis* could effectively be studied on these terms, so this is hardly a novel position. But, for Athens, it is the documented pivotal role of the walls, above all as represented by the confinement of the country population in the *asty* during the Peloponnesian invasions of the *chora*, that renders this organization of our study particularly well justified and, in the final analysis (as we shall see), illuminating. The result of that confinement was a two-way acculturation still visible in the sources. The rural impact on the town is reflected most memorably in the "War" plays of the urban comedic poet Aristophanes, excerpts from whose *Acharnians*, *Clouds*, and *Peace* opened this Introduction. But the experience also exposed the country folk to a flow of urban influences that, to judge from the Aristotelian text quoted above (*AthPol* 27.2, no. 4), was significantly transforming and, if enduring, liable to be channeled back into the rural demes once more settled conditions had been reestablished in the countryside.

Accordingly, this book is a study of the *chora* of ancient Attica in several of its consequential aspects under the rubric of "rural" Athens. The word "rural" is of course of Latin origin, but since its noun *rus* closely approximates its companion Greek term, the adjective will I trust be an acceptable substitute for the rare and (except for classicists) unintelligible *chorikos*.[5] Since, moreover, "rural," as word, concept, and reality, is a relative term which is essentially meaningless except in relation to some urban entity, and since in any case the texts just reviewed illustrate so clearly the substantive mutual engagement of town and country, our studies will necessarily involve the town at many junctures, in fact at virtually every step of the way. Nonetheless, my purpose is to try to look at rural Athens from a rural vantage point and not, as is almost invariably the case in the existing academic, instructional, and popular literature, through a lens of urban institutions, culture, and sensibility.

Scholarly Literature and Overview of Argument

Much is already known about rural Attica, and it will be necessary to situate my project in relation to the findings of previous research. This can be accomplished by a rapid survey of recent major books and monographs.[6]

Modern study initially, and continuously to the present day, has focused on, and been organized around, the segments (constitutional or otherwise) of the Athenian state in all their aspects, archaeological, documentary, social and political, and so on. C. W. J. Eliot's *Coastal Demes of Attika* (1962), although confined to a subset of Kleisthenes' villages, represents a culmination of many years of study by early travelers, archaeologists and epigraphers. John Traill's 1975 *Hesperia* supplementary volume *The Political Organization of Attica*, a comprehensive study of the entire system of phylai, trittyes, and demes and specifically of the representation of the demes on the Council of Five Hundred, incorporates material concerning the assignment of rural demes to archaeological sites and, wherever the bouleutic quota could be determined, conveys an idea of the size of a given rural deme's citizen member population. Traill subsequently updated this work in his monograph *Demos and Trittys*, published in 1986. About this same time appeared a comprehensive study of greater Athens by Robin Osborne entitled *Demos: The Discovery of Classical Attika*, the individual chapters of which he characterized as "independent inquiries into various aspects of the relationship of town and country" (1985b, p. xii). The next year David Whitehead came out with his *The Demes of Attica 508/7–ca. 250 B.C.*, which meticulously documented the constitutionalized Attic villages in their political and social aspects. My own *Public Organization in Ancient Greece*, published in 1987, is concerned with the segmentations of territory and population across Greece, with the records of over 200 city-states dominated by a compilation of the Athenian material, including that pertaining to the rural demes. Over the years, the better documented demes have been the subjects of monographic treatments: Rhamnous by J. Pouilloux (1954), Thorikos by H.F. Mussche et al. (1975), Peiraieus by R. Garland (1987), Aixone by E. Giannopoulou-Konsolaki (1990), Atene by H. Lohmann (1992), and a forthcoming edition of the inscriptions of Eleusis by Kevin Clinton. Archaeological papers relating to some of the rural demes appeared in 1994 under the title *The Archaeology of Athens and Attica under the Democracy*, edited by W. D. E. Coulson, et al. S. D. Lambert's *The Phratries of Attica*, published in 1993, took its place as the standard study of the Athenian "brotherhood," a private association which proves to have a predominantly rural orientation. The year 1999 marked the publication of my *The Associations of Classical Athens: The Response to Democracy*, in which all the Athenian associations, including the phratries, country demes, and other extramural groups are examined with respect to their relations with the Athenian democracy.

Investigation of the rural spaces and populations of ancient Greece, especially through archaeological exploration, has in recent years added much to the institutional studies. Robin Osborne's *Classical Landscape with Figures* (1987) examines the ancient Greek countryside in terms of landform, settlement, and local economy. Rural landscape, especially as revealed by survey archaeology, is represented by T. H. van Andel and C. N. Runnels's 1987 *Beyond the Akropolis: A Rural Greek Past*, by Anthony Snodgrass and Oliver Rackham's essays in the Oswyn Murray-Simon Price collection on the Greek city (1990), by Susan Alcock's book *Graecia Capta* on Roman Greece (1993), and by various papers on environment and culture in relation to the landscape edited by Graham Shipley and John Salmon (1996). Josiah Ober's *Fortress Attica* (1985) explores Athenian land defenses in large part on the basis of topographic and archaeological field work. Scholar-farmer Victor Davis Hanson's *Warfare and Agriculture in Classical Greece* first appeared in 1983 and was republished in revised form in 1998. Integrative political roles were assigned to rural sanctuaries by François de Polignac's exploration of "the birth" of the Greek city (1984, tr. 1995), to which a number of scholars responded in a collection of essays on sanctuaries and sacred space edited by Alcock and Osborne (1994).

Rural agricultural economy has been treated in Alison Burford's *Land and Labor in the Greek World* (1993), in B. Wells's edited collection of papers *Agriculture in Ancient Greece* (1992), and in S. Isager and J. E. Skydsgaard's *Ancient Greek Agriculture: An Introduction* (1993), to which could be added quite a number of specialized studies of the cultivation of cereals, the grape, the olive, timber, and so on. "The Family Farm and the Agrarian Roots of Western Civilization" is the subtitle of Victor Davis Hanson's sweeping *The Other Greeks* (1995). Nonagricultural exploitation of the countryside is represented by J. K. Anderson on hunting (1975), C. R. Whittaker et al. on pastoralism (1988), and J. F. Healy (1978) and R. Shepherd (1993) on mining. Human responses to the rural environment are variously treated in the ecological studies of Peter Garnsey (1988, followed by his *Cities, Peasants and Food in Classical Antiquity* in 1998), R. Sallares (1991), and Thomas W. Gallant (1991). Town and country relations, chiefly in their economic dimension, are the subjects of chapters by S. C. Humphreys (1972), Moses Finley (1985 [1973]), and G. E. M. de Ste. Croix (1981) and of the John Rich/Andrew Wallace-Hadrill collection *City and Country in the Ancient World* (1991).

From this overview it will again be obvious that the study of the present topic, rural Athens, must either extend across multiple substantive and disciplinary boundaries or else, as in the present case, be significantly qualified. My subject is limited temporally to the period of the democracy, both because democracy, among Athens' various governments through the course of antiquity, potentially engaged the rural countryside in a characteristic way by reason of its apparent achievement of a relatively high degree of participation, and owing to the simple fact that it is from the fifth and fourth centuries (or more precisely, if we subscribe to the traditional periodization, 508/7 to 322/1) that we have the preponderance of our contemporary evidence (although, as will be apparent in several chapters, my

discussion will follow a continuing evidentiary record into hellenistic
times). Individual chapters further limit coverage by narrowing the field to
questions accessible through the study of texts (documentary, historical,
and literary), but more importantly because, the nature of our source materials apart, it is in these areas that we are best able to observe what I believe to be a major unrecognized, or at least under-appreciated, dimension
of the civilization of ancient Greece's first city: the fundamentally distinct
character of life in Attica outside the fortification walls.

My book seeks to address what might be described as the monolithic
model of ancient Athens. As just implied in the previous paragraph, this
"model" (which term I use with some reluctance since it may in some cases
carry with it misleading connotations) is the product of only a subset of the
scholarship just reviewed. More specialized, monographic studies naturally
often stop far short of any general characterization of the Athenian polity
as a whole; and many of the titles just reviewed, especially those of a material orientation, are of course explicitly concerned with the isolation and
description of a rural subject per se. To the contrary, the subdisciplines of
topography, archaeology, ecology, and economic history, if anything, tend
in precisely the opposite direction, that is, they tend to view a rural space
or population as a discrete entity, owing either to self-imposed limitations
of subject-matter or (as is frequently the case) in the absence of evidence
of linkage between center and periphery. Rather, the target of this investigation is the many more general scholarly, instructional, and popular writings which assert or seem to take for granted an undifferentiated "state",
"city," or "people" of Athens. But my use of term "undifferentiated" may
actually fall short of describing the actual state of affairs, for general appreciations of classical Athens, except when expressly concerned with Athenians actively engaged in farming, pastoralism or the like, often present not
only an undifferentiated, but also recognizably *urban*, "Athenian."

The tendency is visible, as we shall see in the course of our discussions, in treatments of settlement patterns, village social organization,
agricultural labor, the family, the democracy and citizen behavior, and the
reception of high Athenian culture. But sometimes the characterization is
a more comprehensive one, as a few select quotations will illustrate: S. C.
Humphreys, in her influential *Anthropology and the Greeks*, wrote that
"there was no sharp dividing line between city and countryside (*chora*) either in political status or religion."[7] Ellen Meiksins Wood, reaffirming
Humphreys's position, added that "the conceptual distinction between
town and country, or town-dwellers and countrymen, remained ill-de-

fined and ambiguous. . . . In fact, the distinction may have been even less clearly defined than Humphreys suggests, and more deeply coloured by the political unity that joined city and countryside."[8] Michael Jameson, upholding a position favoring the use of slaves for agricultural work, theorized that this additional source of labor freed the farmer to exercise his rights as a citizen in the government's urban seat.[9] Robin Osborne, in support of his view that Athenian farmers resided not on their lands but in a nucleated village-center, wrote that "The whole working of Athenian democracy demanded that the demes continued to be communities, and without modern means of communication that was effectively a demand that people continued to dwell together in villages"[10]—a line of reasoning that *mutatis mutandis* might be applied to all of Attica in respect to the *asty*, were it not for the fact that it is precisely the comparability of the "village" and the *asty* which is at issue here. Even Victor Hanson's *The Other Greeks*, the purpose of which is to rescue from oblivion "the neglected freehold farmers, vinegrowers, and herdsmen of ancient Greece,"[11] in the final analysis, as a consequence of attributing agrarian roots to Western civilization, ends up casting the countryside in a distinctly urbanizing light. As recently as 1998, an essay by Sitta von Reden investigating "the ideological work that was necessary to make Athens a single place" with respect to "topographies of civic space," finds a complex situation in which invented topographies served to contribute to "the remarkable solidarity" of the Athenians.[12] Still more recently, Edward Cohen's *The Athenian Nation*, while arguing correctly against the prevailing neat tripartite exclusive representation of Athens in terms of "orders" (citizens, metics, and slaves) and presenting in its place a more complex and multifaceted reality characterized by mobility, ambiguity, integration, and confusion, not surprisingly—given the trend of his argument—does not acknowledge adequately in my view the evidence indicating what I shall show was a fundamental cleft between town and country.[13] Only with the publication (coincidentally in the same year) of Beth Cohen's edited volume *Not the Classical Ideal: Athens and the Construction of the Other in Greek Art*—and in particular I have in mind Maria Pipili's contribution on the "Other Hat"—has formal recognition begun to be accorded to the marginalized condition of rural Athenians under the classical democracy.[14]

While it is not possible here to attempt a detailed overview of modern writings about ancient Greek civilization, it is, I think, fair to say that these widely publicized positions now constitute a sort of unchallenged *commu-*

nis opinio, especially inasmuch they appear to confirm a proposition that many appear simply to take for granted as true.

By contrast, this study will attempt to show that separation, isolation, local community, and the resulting survival of a preurban agrarian social and cultural order are rather the terms with reference to which we should view the great mass of the population of Attica. Examination of the contemporary textual record will reveal not unity or cooperation but rather a consistent state of estrangement, alienation, even hostility. Much of the underlying material basis of this rift, at least on the rural side, will be assembled in the succeeding chapters in my handling of rural settlement patterns and social organization, and, later in our study, of its specific expressions under the rubric of "realities." It will become clear that when the rural resident passed through a gate of the Themistoclean fortifications and came into contact with the dominant cultures of the intramural populations, nothing less than a thoroughgoing inversion of all that was familiar, accepted, and valued was in the offing. From my studies will consequently emerge still another variety of the Other, in this case an internal one, to be added to those species of alterity in classical Greek culture explored in recent decades.[15] And why, again, if I am right, has it taken so long for this discovery to be made? Perhaps, let me suggest, not so much because of the usual invisibility of such marginal groups (because these extramural Athenians are not invisible) as owing to the very citizen status of rural demespeople—a fact which has at once caused to be falsely bestowed upon them characteristics actually appropriate only to urbanites and, at the same time, exempted them from special consideration on the basis of gender, order, or ethnicity.

Town Versus Country

It might be thought wrong-headed to venture very far in the direction of a detached countryside on the ground that the signs of town-and-country interdependence—and of the ruralite's response thereto—are unmistakable. But some of these, such as rural demotic in combination with ownership of intramural townhouse or urban demotic or residence or political activity in combination with mining lease in southern Attica, concern only an elite with access to exceptional means of mobility, education, and social contact and so are hardly indicative of trends affecting the larger population. Nonetheless, it is precisely this evidence—evidence pertaining to a tiny upper crust of wealth, background, and privilege—which, probably for the most part unthinkingly, has constituted the basis for a monolithic culturally unified classical Athens.

To anticipate possible responses to my position, let me take up summarily with minimal documentation my views regarding those arguments which have, or might be, marshaled in favor of a unified classical Attica:

(1) Despite nearly universal comment or assumption to the contrary, the Kleisthenic organization, while segmenting and articulating all of Attica and its populations, rural as well as urban, did *not* in fact blend those component parts into any enduring unity—political, social, or cultural. The uses of the organization that actually brought citizens from town and country together were chiefly military, hence intermittent and exceptional.[16] Topographic representation in the ongoing regular constitutional organs where the organization determined participation was undercut by the portability and inheritability of the deme-affiliation and by the fact that in the case of the many boards constituted *kata phylas* no known rule required representation of City, Coast, and Inland trittys regions. Thus the democratic government could have been, and probably was, dominated by urban residents (and, at that, urban residents of long standing) notwithstanding the predominance of extramural demotics. As for the Assembly, its quorum of 6,000, which also marked an upper limit since this number appears to have coincided with the seating capacity of the cavea on the Pnyx,[17] would have amounted to only about one-fifth of a citizen population of 30,000, thereby opening up a very real possibility of domination by urban residents. The plots of those farmers who are occasionally reported by literary sources to have attended the Assembly, or to have sat on a jury panel, etc., could well, if my analysis of the security *horoi* in chapter 1 is accepted, have been situated within, or just outside, the enceinte.

(2) No evidence supports the model of the Attic association—phyle, deme, phratry, or cult group—as a mediating structure which, by design or accident, served to bring together—and so level culturally—a regionally heterogeneous membership. The phylai, despite their tripartite regional composition by trittys, were in fact dominated by their urban memberships.[18] Evidence that rural demes maintained links with urban-based fellow-demesmen, though well known, is slight; and abundant indications favor the view that the extramural deme association was highly isolated— not only from the urban center but from other demes as well.[19] Similarly with the phratries, which for the most part were regionally based outside the walls and which, like the rural demes, are sometimes known to have calved off members residing in the town. That is, urban confrères seem to have

constituted distinct, independent enclaves and, if my arguments are accepted, were served by generic cult installations maintained by the state.[20]

(3) There is no reason to believe that ruralites journeyed to Athens town and Peiraieus in order to purchase grain imported by ship. Nothing renders unlikely the natural, and more economical, reconstruction whereby the imported grain was meant for landless intramural consumers while self-sufficient rural populations produced for themselves.[21]

(4) Against any alleged unifying or integrative effects which might be ascribed to the pan-Attic religious festivals, especially the Mysteries of Demeter and Korē at Eleusis and the festival of Artemis at Brauron, it may be riposted that celebrants were often urbanites and that travel was point-to-point, bypassing the large numerical majority of typical agrarian settlements and isolated farmsteads, while in the end serving only to link urban center with an atypical isolated monumental cultic infrastructure.

(5) Evidence of farming, mining, quarrying, and other commercial activity, to the extent that that evidence consists merely of residence or home base in one (often urban) deme and holding, lease, or interest in another different (always extramural) deme does not necessarily (or even probably) establish significant linkage, much less integration or leveling, of a *cultural* nature.

(6) Similarly, exogamous marriages involving two different, sometimes remotely separated, demes might well have exerted little or no integrative effect, since they seem not to have been numerous, to have involved only relatively prosperous landowners, and to have been meant to serve only rather narrow economic purposes such as the consolidation of once unified estates or to bring about a risk-buffering protection against environmental change.

(7) "Rustics," especially farmers, who are placed by contemporary and archaizing writers and poets in and around the civic center, rather than being taken as representing a typical state of affairs, may actually have been of interest to an urban audience or readership precisely by dint of their novelty. And in any event, epigraphic evidence, as observed in chapter 1, shows that farms existed inside or just outside the walls, so whatever agrarian presence in town there was may not have reflected the totality of rural Attica. Where, finally, the very visible dramatic portrayals by Aristophanes are concerned, it is not to be forgotten that the contemporary context of the "War" comedies in particular was distinguished above all by the unprecedented confinement of the rural population within the walls of the town.

I

Settlement

State and Rural Community

ACROSS GREECE AS A WHOLE, THERE CAN BE little doubt that the articulation and organization of the countryside originated, and was thereafter maintained by a state government physically situated, in an urban seat. The most visible manifestation of the phenomenon is the segmentation of territory and population in the form of what I have elsewhere (1987) termed the public organizations, whereby rural as well as urban spaces were given boundaries and official names and the citizen members of rural communities acquired affiliations with those spaces. It is in such guise that we not infrequently can detect signs of the official administration of rural lands and peoples and deduce therefrom clues concerning their participation as constituents of the state's body politic. Across Greece, straightforward examples of segments of rural disposition with documented public functions are the *demos* (attested in eighteen city-states: Aigiale, Aigina, Athens, Chalkis, Elis, Eretria, Histiaia, Ialysos, Kalymna, Kameiros, Kos, Lindos, Miletos, Naxos, Poteidaia?, Rhodes, Stratonikeia, and Thessalonike) and the *komē* (attested in seven city-states: Argos, Lampsakos?, Lindos, Megara?, Philippopolis, Traianopolis?, and Troizen?). To these may be added localized occurrences of the *ktoina* from the Rhodian orbit (Chalke, Ialysos, Kameiros, Karpathos, Phoinix, Syme, and Tymnos), the *oiē* at Chios, and the *oba* at Sparta.[1] On such building-block "village" units were erected higher tiers of organization of the countryside. At Kleisthenic Athens, the demes were apportioned into the regionally based clusters called trittyes, and these in turn, taken three at a time, one each from the City, Coast, and Inland regions, were combined into the ten phylai. Some of the demes in their institutionalized form also constituted the component parts of regional unions organized around local cults, with the territorial locus in each of the seven known instances being situated outside the town walls.[2]

Throughout the records of the individual states in question, there are ample indications that the status of public unit was imposed from above; indeed, the mere incorporation of these rural units within statewide administrative networks hardly permits any other inference. That is, under typical circumstances an ancient Greek rural settlement or community is not to be thought of as a statutorily independent entity only casually or intermittently brought under the dominion of statewide policy or directive. Furthermore, the phenomenon seems to have been pervasive, even universal, within the confines of a single polity. Not only at Athens, with its 139 demes, but elsewhere, too, at Epidauros, Megalopolis, Elis, Lokroi Epizephyrioi, and Tauromenion, we learn from epigraphic and literary sources of the existence of dozens or scores of rural units;[3] and, since this is the kind of feature that may easily go unrecorded in the sorts of enduring records that can reach us from antiquity, similar multitudinous arrangements doubtless existed elsewhere. It would seem a reasonable inference that, if as many as 30 or 40 or more villages within the territory of a single *polis* achieved "constitutional" status, *all* or at least a high percentage of such settlements had been so institutionalized. At Athens, where alone our data are sufficient to make meaningful an argument from silence, there are very few certain or probable examples of rural settlements lacking the official status of "deme" under the regime of the classical Kleisthenic organization. Some, evidently the tiniest of hamlets, are known to have been incorporated within a larger neighboring deme (as in the case of Aphidna and its satellites); others are of only very late attestation and so may postdate the era of the autonomous democracy.[4] Where Athens is concerned, we can be confident regarding the near universality of the practice of the constitutionalization of rural settlements and their incorporation within the state.

But what do we mean by the term "settlement"? That rural territories and populations had been segmented, "constitutionalized," and thereafter regulated to some degree by a state authority implies nothing regarding disposition, that is, regarding the interrelation of such territory and population. If textual evidence is to be our guide, one might begin with Aristotle's structural account of society in the opening pages of the *Politics* (1.1.1–12: 1252a1–1253a39). Males and females mate to form households, households coalesce to form villages, and villages combine to form city-states, but only the last-mentioned, he asserts, are capable of attaining independent *autarkeia*. According to the internal logic of this agglutinative process of evolution, at each level the constituent units are analytically independent but substantively dependent entities which, once united with others of their own order or kind, are transmuted into a qualitatively distinct higher level of organization, and so on. From an evolutionary perspective, a village is the accumulated total of its households, a city-state of its villages, but functionally the larger constellation emerges as more than the sum of its parts on the score of relative degree of self-sufficiency. But did the philosopher, for much of his adult life a resident of Athens, have the city of the Lyceum in mind when he wrote this? And whether he did or not, how do the constituent elements of household, village, and city-state translate into the actual disposition of population upon the land, rural land in particular? Aristotle's discussion (like most of the relevant literary texts) is uncommunicative on all points of detail.

Determinants of Rural Residence Patterns

The settlement patterns of ancient Greece have been in recent decades a frequent topic of investigation. The fundamental question has been whether populations resided on the agricultural lands that they owned or worked, that is on "farms," or whether the primary residence was in some nucleated village, town, or city. Scholarly uncertainty on this question is reflected in the several discussions of the "farm" by Cooper (1977/78), Langdon (1990/91), Osborne (1992b), and Yoshiyuki (1993). But if we may, for the sake of argument, grant a result in favor of farmstead residence, it can then be asked if such residence was year-round or merely seasonal in keeping with the demands of an agricultural calendar; and, with regard to status, whether and to what extent these residents, permanent or temporary, comprised citizen landowners, tenants, seasonal workers, slaves, or some combination of these.

Residence patterns represent responses to a complex nexus of factors and so vary from region to region, from state to state, and, in the case of the vast and topographically varied expanse of Attica, in all likelihood from one specific locale to another. The following may, in combination, be taken as a crude approximation of that nexus and as a context for the ensuing discussion.[5]

(1) *Old versus new settlement.* To a significant degree, the rural settlement patterns of historical Greece were simply a continuation of conditions

obtaining prior to the emergence and growth of the *polis* centers. At Athens, many of the rural demes antedated the formation of the unified *polis*, to judge from archaeological remains, ancient names, and pre-synoecism historical and cultic traditions, and will have remained viable, the growth of the *asty* notwithstanding. Within the local rural community, farmers inheriting ancestral plots might choose to continue to reside on their ground even in the face of a practically more advantageous situation in town or village.

(2) *Gross topographical variation.* Nucleated settlements, whether towns or villages, presuppose the possibility of adequate communication, travel, and transport. But mountainous terrain or other barriers may work in the favor of residence on the land away from any nucleated center, as, for example, Osborne found when comparing mainland and island rural settings. Since mainland settlements often command a plain or valley system bounded by mountains or sea while many islands are simply mountains surrounded by narrow coastal plains, major village centers predominate on the mainland but on islands villages are rare and towers often prevail (towers in this case being interpreted in terms of more or less permanent farmstead residence).[6] The consequences for the variable terrain of Attica are obvious.

(3) *Size of the territory.* Since the advantages and disadvantages of farmstead vs. village residence are largely associated with the distance between residence and land (see 4, below), in smaller territories the town or village center will be correspondingly more attractive. The protection afforded by fortification walls in combination with a short commute to the fields may have made town residence attractive, as surely it did to Athenians from demes situated just outside the enceinte. But it is not clear that the same argument would apply in the case of an unfortified village center, since, in the absence of walls, the grouping of residences might render villagers even more vulnerable to attack or depredation than on widely separated isolated farmsteads.

(4) *Occupation of head of household or other resident.* "Rural" is sometimes equated with "agricultural," but the Attic population with which we are concerned will have included pastoralists, miners, quarry workers, charcoal burners, sanctuary staffs, and craftspeople of all stripes. Accordingly, the needs of a particular occupation will have variably conditioned the choice of place of residence. A nonagricultural workforce will have resided as close as possible to its work site and the population that it served. In the case of farming, by contrast, recent study by Hanson has brought to the

fore, and given renewed emphasis to, the purely practical incentives favoring on-site residence: to save time lost commuting between off-site residence and land; to make possible the sustained presence and attention required by intensive agriculture, irrigation and fertilization; to protect the land from theft, vandalism, and damage by animals; and in general to enhance the rural infrastructure.[7] All such goals would be compromised by maintenance of the household in a nucleated center, whether town or village, if that center lay any appreciable distance from the farmer's land.

(5) *Unitary versus fragmented estates.* Farmstead residence makes good sense on a continuous or consolidated holding, but would have been of questionable value in the case of an estate comprising multiple small and noncontiguous (or even distantly separated) plots. If the operation of inheritance or sale has resulted in fragmentation, with no clear advantage attaching to residence on any particular parcel, the town or village may become a more attractive option. But, as I will suggest at the close of this chapter, a compromise strategy cannot be excluded: residence on that particular *chorion* of a composite estate situated nearest to the local nucleated settlement.

(6) *Status of rural residents and duration of rural residence.* Every serious discussion of our problem raises these questions but only very rarely, if ever, with a successful attempt at their resolution. Texts are vague or entirely silent, and surface survey, or even excavation, are not likely to produce remains that can provide answers to the questions posed at the head of our discussion regarding the status (free, resident alien, or servile) or duration (seasonal or permanent) of residence outside the nucleated town or village. Residence on rural land could turn out be a function of variables not readily perceptible in the physical record and only infrequently addressed in our written source materials.

(7) *Sociopolitical regime.* When an exclusive, oligarchical regime established in an urban seat dominates affairs, there is correspondingly little reason for the outlying population to venture into the *asty*, apart from the meeting of unavoidable economic or personal needs, and so permanent residence there would be less attractive. Thus, as observed in the Introduction, the autocratic tyrant of predemocratic Athens, Peisistratos, made it a point of policy to encourage ruralites to refrain from visiting the *asty*. But democratic Athens, with its organs of government requiring a high rate of participation and urban-based compensated civic employments, exerted a centripetal pull upon the extramural population. Analogously, outlying villages provided some of the same opportunities for communal life

on a smaller scale but in a nonetheless nucleated setting. The question is not whether such attractions existed (in Athens' case, certainly, they demonstrably did), but whether or not they were sufficient to override the countervailing factors set out under the previous headings.

With these generalities in mind, we may now turn to the aforementioned textual evidence for rural settlement patterns in rural Attica:

Epigraphic Evidence for Farmstead Residence

Traditionally, scholars have looked to literary texts for any light they might shed on these matters, but their indications have proved far from unequivocal.[8] Some, written from an urban point of view, speak only loosely of the country (*chora*) or fields (*agroi*), without revealing anything about settlement patterns. Those few, now well known, passages that do seem to be informative have nonetheless proved susceptible to contrasting interpretations; for one scholar, they demonstrate that Athenian farmers did not live on their ground;[9] for another, just the opposite.[10] Archaeological excavation of various sites continues to yield valuable results, with numerous candidates for isolated "farmhouses" in Attica already published.[11] Nonetheless, much of the vast territory of ancient Attica with its 139 Kleisthenic demes remains to be explored.[12] Inscriptions, too, might be thought relevant, for not only are they contemporary and documentary but they also possess in many cases the inestimable advantage of having originated in the countryside itself. But even inscriptions, however close to the reality that is our subject, can, it now appears, be made to support quite different lines of interpretation.

Marking a major advance over Jan Pečirka's 1973 survey of "homestead farms" in Classical and Hellenistic Greece,[13] Robin Osborne in two 1985 publications argued extensively in favor of what might be called the nucleated settlement position. The book *Demos: The Discovery of Classical Attika* made the case ultimately on the basis of the peculiar nature of the sociopolitical regime and the resulting inclination of rural Athenians to reap the benefits of community life.[14] An article "Buildings and Residence on the Land in Classical and Hellenistic Greece: The Contribution of Epigraphy" reaffirmed the position by denying a residential function to buildings situated on agricultural lands, although, where Attica is concerned, "epigraphy" turned out to mean exclusively the leases.[15] Since 1985, the opposing claims of farmstead (or "homestead") residence have been reasserted but, despite Osborne's lead, with a conspicuous inattention to the evidence of inscriptions. To Osborne's book (but only incidentally the article), Merle Langdon launched a response with his succinct essay "On the Farm in Classical Attica," yet, despite the evidentiary breadth of the inquiry, with only scant reference to the epigraphic texts.[16] Victor Hanson's *The Other Greeks* has emphatically upheld the notion of the owner-occupied permanent farmstead both in Attica and elsewhere in Greece, but his discussion, too, reveals little awareness of the potential relevance of inscriptions.[17]

As a result, as things stand now, Osborne's interpretation of the Attic leases has gone unopposed, and no scholar, in support of any position, has brought into the debate what will here prove highly relevant additional bodies of epigraphic evidence—viz. the *poletai* records, the *rationes centesimarum*, and the security *horoi*. My purpose is to carry out such an investigation and, in the course of doing so, to strengthen the case in favor of farmstead residence in Attica.

Two preliminary matters. Since, first, we are dealing with written texts, it is obvious that terminology will play an important role. A review of words for real property was long ago carried out by W. Kendrick Pritchett in his study of the Attic Stelai.[18] More recently, Osborne's lexical analysis confines itself to words that might be appropriate for the description of an isolated farm, but whatever merit his comments upon individual terms for land and buildings may possess, his general conclusion must be rejected. "That, by contrast, it [the classical Attic vocabulary] has no term at all for the unit of a land with a house from which the land is worked must surely be indicative of the absence of such a unit from the countryside of Attika. Land does occur with a house associated, but this always seems to be seen as land and a house and not as a single unit, let alone as a 'farm.'"[19] Already, Langdon, who took up passage by passage Osborne's analysis of the literary record, has challenged the textual basis for so drastic a conclusion.[20] More generally, it may be objected that Osborne's position rests on a confusion between meaning and reference. Because Greek lacks a single word that *means* "farm" (that is, agricultural land with on-site residence), it is implicitly concluded that no other single Greek word or phrase could *refer* to such an entity. The speaker in Demosthenes' third speech *Against Aphobos*, 29.3, calls an agricultural property with an *oikia* and slaves an *agros* ("field"), and in the later first speech *Against Onetor*, this same property is called a *chorion* ("plot") at 30.29 and 31. The reference is to a farm, although neither *agros* nor *chorion* itself contains any notion of residence. The Athenian reality is composite, with each component separately termed and denoted both in literary narratives and in legal or documentary texts. Even though it is true that Greek lacks a specific term for "farm," this is no reason for doubting the *existence* of the thing itself.

The second matter concerns our expectations. Sources of various types, including our inscriptions, frequently mention a plot (whether denoted by *chorion* or some other term) without revealing any hint of the existence of a structure, residential or otherwise, sitting on that plot. Does this mean that, in these cases at least, the owner or other persons involved with the working of the plot necessarily resided elsewhere? To respond in the affirmative would be to overlook a fundamental feature of Athenian (and presumably generally Greek) land tenure: its tendency over time towards fragmentation, especially as the result of the workings of inheritance. Scholars acknowledge the dispersed character of Attic estates,[21] but here it needs to be emphasized that such an estate might consist of a single *chorion* with a house possibly occupied by the owner and of one or more others lacking a residential structure or at least one deserving of the appellation "primary residence." At any time, a given source may refer to one of the latter, houseless plots. Thus the question, as we shall see, is not so much whether a given plot had a "house" or not as whether, if such a "house" is attested, that "house" served a residential or some other, nonresidential purpose.

POLETAI RECORDS

The surviving records of public sales conducted by the *poletai*, collected and reedited in 1991 by Merle Langdon in *Agora* XIX, contain abundant references to landed property and to various kinds of structures. So much should be expected in view of the Aristotelian *Constitution*'s statement that the *poletai* kept records of "the lands and houses (τὰ χωρία καὶ τὰς οἰκίας) that had been inventoried and sold in the court" (47.3). Most of the items named in the inscriptions are confiscated properties put up for public auction, but a few figure in mining leases as well. Land goes by the generic *chorion*, although occasional mention is also found of *charadra*, *edaphos*, *eschatia*, *kepos*, *oikopedon*, and *pagos*. Structures, besides the common *oikia*, include its diminutive *oikidion*, *kaminos*, *klision*, *pyrgos*, and *synoikia*. Pairings of terms for land and structure, provided the surrounding text has been preserved, might in sufficient quantity tell us something about the existence or nonexistence of "farms," but the fact that they—

especially *chorion* and *oikia*—frequently occur in badly damaged contexts often leaves the matter open. Nonetheless, a half dozen or so inscriptions preserve some promising candidates:

P2 (402/1), sale of confiscated properties. At e 10–11 Langdon prints o[ἰκίαν...7....καὶ] / κῆπον without proposing a restoration of the missing text, but the presence of the "garden" suggests a farm as one possibility. Elsewhere on the stelai an *oikia* or *oikiai* are situated with reference to neighboring properties (a, b, c 7 [plural] and 14; d [2], 9–10 [Salamis], and 16), but there is admittedly no reason to suspect that such properties, including that on which the *oikia(i)* in question stood, were farm land.

cf. P4 (370/69), sale of confiscated properties. An estate located on Lemnos comprised χωρίον ἐν᾽Ομφαλίαι [ἐν ὧι ἀμπ]/[έλο]υ ὄρχοι [κ]αὶ συστὰς κα[ὶ α]ὑλὴ καὶ ἐσχατ[ιὰ.....] (8–9). No trace of a residence here, although *oikiai* do appear elsewhere on the stele (41, 48).

P5 (367/6), sale of confiscated properties and mining leases. A farm may lie concealed in the *pyrgos* and *oikia* localizing a concession at lines 74–75, if the "tower" served some agricultural purpose[22] and if it and the "house" were situated on arable, but mention of a *chorion* is lacking.

P9 (paullo ante med. saec. IV), mining leases. A reopened *metallon* is situated in fragmentary context with relation to a conjoined *chorion* and *oikia* in lines 18–19, 20–21.

P17 (350/49), sale of confiscated properties. Registered properties include an οἰκ[ίαν καὶ χωρί]/ο[ν] καὶ [κ]λισίον in Melite (20–21). Because the terms are accompanied by a single localization (from line 21), it is clear that a unified ensemble is in question. The fact that *two* structures are conjoined with the land opens up the possibility that one, the *oikia*, is residential in function, while the other, a "lean-to" or "shed," satisfied any agricultural needs,[23] although, in line with Osborne's analysis, it remains arguable that neither was meant for human occupancy.

P26 (342/1–339/8), sale of confiscated properties and mining leases. On Face B, col. III, the fragmentary line 368 is restored to record the registration of a χωρίον κα]ὶ οἰκίαν in Hagnous.

P29 (340/39), mining leases. At lines 11–12, Langdon prints τὰ χωρία τὰ [....9.....κ]/αὶ ἡ οἰκία marking the eastern boundary of a *metallon*.

While a "farm" might fit almost any of these contexts, it must be conceded that the residence-on-the-land model is not absolutely required by any of them, for, as a consequence of Osborne's work, it is clear that we cannot merely assume a residential function for the *oikia* appearing in each of the Attic examples. Nonetheless, since these estates were presumably all private properties, the possibility that the *oikia* was occupied by owner or laborer obviously cannot be excluded.

RATIONES CENTESIMARUM

The accounts inscribed in the second half of the fourth century recording a one percent tax (*hekatostē*) on the proceeds of land sales in Attica, now reedited with commentary by Lambert, preserve 144 separate items distributed over 16 fragments.[24] Given so large a number of properties, particular significance might be ascribed to any discernible pattern regarding the presence or absence of structures associated with the parcels. As it happens, in only eight instances is the mention of a structure preserved or restored, invariably in the form of the phrase χωρίον καὶ οἰκία(ν): nos. 12 (F4, lines 1–3), 13 (F4, lines 4–7), 14 (F4, lines 8–10), 15 (F4, lines 11–13), 16 (F4, lines 14–17), 34 (F6B, lines 27–31), 60 (F10A, lines 10–12), and 99 (F8B, lines 41–43).[25] In six of the eight cases, the location of the property is preserved or conjectured: Prasiai (12?, 13, 14), Prasiai or Paiania? (15), Paiania (16), and Rhamnous (99)—all demes in which the practice of agriculture is hardly to be doubted. (The sellers and the buyer in no. 34 are Sphettians; the sellers are the Thorikioi (?), one buyer a Skambonides in no. 60, but the property itself may of course in both cases be situated in still another, unnamed deme). Since in no instance is there reason to regard land and structure as distinct properties, eight prima facie cases for "farms" are thus at hand.[26] Additionally, the restored conjunction at Pallene of [χωρίον καὶ κ?]ῆπος in no. 124 (F13B, lines 2–4) unambiguously indicates some kind of agricultural activity, albeit in this instance in the absence of a structure.[27]

At the same time, while in every instance the buyers are individual Athenians, the sellers are all Athenian *corporate groups* of varying description, "territorial" (stelai 1–2) or "nonterritorial" (stelai 3–4).[28] Ownership by a group may make problematic the notion of "farm," although residence on the land by any member of that group, tenant, bailiff and slaves, etc., will be sufficient to distinguish the arrangement from the nucleated settlement model. Against my thesis, it is also entirely possible, as Lambert suggests, that the *oikia*, in line with the property's corporate ownership, was a meeting or club house of some kind,[29] but I find it unlikely that the group in question would be willing to divest itself of a structure so obviously vital to its functioning.

At all events, how do we explain the very large percentage of *choria* lacking an *oikia* or structure of any description? Several texts record the sale of *eschatiai*, understood by Lambert as outlying land in hilly areas, at least in some cases agriculturally marginal.[30] Moreover, certain descriptive words or phrases occasionally attached not only to *eschatiai* but to several of the *choria* as well are in agreement with this characterization.[31] Residence on such lands is unlikely, and for this reason, in combination with the fact of corporate rather than individual ownership, we can, I suggest, explain the general absence of an *oikia* with many of the recorded *choria*. That is to say, we are not driven by these silences to endorse the model of absentee residence by owner or laborer in a neighboring nucleated settlement.[32]

LEASES

The leasing of land with or without residential or other structures by private individuals is scarcely found in the epigraphic record of classical Athens.[33] Rather, in nearly all the examples that have come down to us, the leasing party is a corporate body—the Athenian state; or one of its segmentary divisions, a deme or phyle; or a cultic association such as one of the several groups of *orgeones* organized around a god or hero. Examination of these texts, conveniently collected (without texts, however) in D. Behrend's *Attische Pachturkunden*, Vestigia 12, München 1970, now joined by Michael Walbank's edition of leases of public lands from the Athenian Agora (*Agora* XIX, L1–16, LA 1–8),[34] reveals the not infrequent occurrence of the leasing of a *chorion* in isolation and, to the point here, of a *chorion* with an *oikia* and/or other structure.[35] Again, the question is whether, given the presence on the land of a structure, the lessee will occupy it during some or all of the period of the lease. Osborne maintains that the texts show that the *oikia* (the one consistently used term for a structure in the Attic leases) was merely agricultural in function or, at the minimum, at least not necessarily residential.[36] But the case is not, as we shall now see, a compelling one.

1) Lease of the demesmen of Rhamnous, *IG* II² 2493, 339/8. This *chorion* (6–7, [25]), the *temenos* of the goddess in *Hermeus (4–5), had previously been farmed (5–6) and, according to the terms of the present lease, will be farmed again by the lessee in conformity with elaborate guidelines (7–31). Michael Jameson reported that the full text in line 21–22, with

the addition of recent finds from Rhamnous to the *IG* text from Sounion, runs: οἰκήσει [τ]ὴν ο[ἰ]κίαν ὁ μισ[θω]σάμενος τὴν ἐπὶ / τῶι τεμένει τού- τωι ....[37] Given the rigorous requirements regarding the use of the land imposed upon the lessee, that an *oikia* should stand upon it and that he should be obligated to reside in it should not come as a surprise. But residence must be contractually stipulated because, it may be suggested, the leasing party is not the owner and may lack the customary incentive to produce the best possible yield, to guard against any depredation of the *chorion* and its infrastructure, and so on. If, as Jameson suggests,[38] the arrangement was really a quasi-liturgy, with the lessee making a *pro bono* contribution to the deme-association, such a lack of incentive would be particularly easy to comprehend. *These* are the unusual conditions, then, that make for the exceptional insertion of the clause requiring residence. What this text does not show is that such residence was *of itself* exceptional, as Osborne, arguing from his interpretation of the lease from Prasiai (no. 9, below), maintains.[39]

2) Law of the citizen *orgeones* of Bendis, *IG* II² 1361, post med. s. IV. This *nomos* (13) contains regulations for the use of the *hieron* with its *oikia* and, although no mention is made of land or farming, the explicit acknowledgment of residence by the renter is of interest. "In order that the *oikia* and the *hieron* be repaired, to spend the house-rent (τὸ ἐν[οίκιον τῆ[ς οἰ]κίας, 9) and the money raised from the sale of water on the repair of the *hieron* and *oikia* and for no other purpose, until the *hieron* and the *oikia* are repaired" (8–11) . . . "and to leave water for the party in residence (τῶι ἐνοικοῦντι) to use" (12). Such language hardly leaves any doubt on the point of the renter's occupancy of the *oikia*. Furthermore, if the occupant needs water on-site and if the sale (?) of such water (to him) is of a magnitude to contribute significantly to the maintenance of the sanctuary, such occupancy will have been continuous, very possibly for the entire duration of the rental.

3) Mediation of dispute between Salaminioi from Sounion and Salaminioi of Heptaphylai, W. S. Ferguson, *Hesperia* 7 (1938) 9–12, 69–74, no. 2; H. A. Thompson, *Hesperia* 7 (1938) 75–76; *Agora* XIX, L4b, ca. 250. The settlement concerns the disposition of the *temenos* of Herakles once "the altars and what lies beyond the railing as far as the first olive trees" have been set aside for sacred uses (8–11). Generally speaking, the plan is to divide the non-sacred properties, each *genos* receiving *choria* and an *oikia* but with certain elements to be held in common. The Sounians are to construct a new threshing floor "in the common *temenos*" of the same size as

their own, which is to belong to the men of Heptaphylai; two *oikiai* are allocated, one abutting the *temenos* to the men of Heptaphylai, another one on the east to the Sounians; gardens and "half" the well are to belong to each *genos* (18–36). "The Hale and the *agora* in Koile are to be common to both *genē*" (36–38). Two sets of *choria*, one to the east, one to the west, will be assigned to the two associations, corresponding to the location of their respective *oikiai* (38–43), with "the sacred earth" to be in the custody of the men of Heptaphylai (43–44). These *choria* were, as Ferguson explained, in accordance with the terms of the first inscription, pledged for the maintenance of the sacrifices offered by the Salaminioi from their own funds.[40] Although no direct indication is forthcoming regarding occupancy, the conjunction of house, gardens, and well on the land open up the possibility of ongoing residence on the land while under lease. According to Burford, Greek *kepoi* served "to produce the vegetables, edible herbs, and other plants useful to the household."[41] As for the well, a law of Solon allowed a person who had not found water on his own land "to take from his neighbor, filling a six-*chous hydria* twice each day"[42]—the equivalent of a single *metretes* or *amphoreus*. The very small quantity suggests that at least some wells in Attica were intended only to supply a residential household (and perhaps its "kitchen" *kepos*). Alternatively, of course, the *kepos* might have been a more substantial income-earning plot, with the well providing irrigation,[43] possibly in the absence of a household residing on the land.

The remaining texts, save number 7), constitute the basis on which Osborne mounts his case that buildings that might be referred to as *oikiai* "were not primarily residences but centres of agricultural activity," with number 9), which I reserve for last, providing what is for Osborne the clinching evidence.[44] Thus the several clauses in the following inscriptions calling for the maintenance, or allowing for the construction, of structures on the land are interpreted as referring to such an agricultural purpose. Here, however, it will be suggested that the structures are maintained or constructed precisely in order to enhance the property as a place of residence by the leasing party or his representative(s).

4) Lease of the *orgeones* of the Hero, H. W. Pleket, *Epigraphica* I (1964) 63, no. 43 (*SEG* 24.203), 333/2. Charops of Phaleron and the *orgeones* of the Hero lease τὸν [κῆπ]ον to Thrasyboulos of Alopeke at 20 drachmas each year for 30 years (1–11). Thrasyboulos may, if he wishes, build at his own expense "in the *chorion* outside the drain" (11–16). "When the time of the lease runs out, Thrasyboulos is to leave (ἀπιέναι, 18), taking the tiles and the woodwork and the doors,"[45] unless the lessors per-

suade him otherwise (16–23). We are not told what is to be built by Thrasyboulos (if he so wishes) nor whether the tiles, woodwork, and doors belong to such new construction and/or to some already existing structure.
But the inference that he will reside on the property is suggested by the
verb ἀπιέναι, a very relevant article of evidence not noted by Osborne in
his discussion of this text. Sometimes the sense is taken abstractly in the
sense of "quitting," that is surrendering of the lease, but nothing in the
present context rules out the literal, and therefore in the absence of contrary indications preferable, interpretation.

5) Lease of the demesmen of Peiraieus, *IG* II² 2498, 321/0. The terms
set out regarding the leasing of the deme's *temenē* (3) touch on the removal of mud and earth (9–11) and the cutting of timber (11); the land
(*chorion*, 11) under lease includes pasturage ((τ)/ἄλλα ἐννόμια, 12–13);
ploughing may proceed continuously for the first nine of the ten years,
only half to be ploughed in the tenth; and a crop will be produced (17–22).
At the close of the preserved text, the lessee of Halmyris is instructed, having received the *oikia* watertight (στέγουσαν) and with walls standing up-
right (ὀρθὴν), to turn it over in the same condition (22–24). It may be
suggested that the object of this last clause is to ensure that the *oikia*, having already served as the residence of the current lessee, be ready for occupancy by his successor.

6) Lease of the *orgeones* of Egretes, *IG* II² 2499, 306/5. The *orgeones*
call for the lessee "to use the hieron and the *oikiai* built upon it as [a] *hieron*" (5–7). The lessee Diognetos will whitewash any of the walls (house
walls, *toichoi*) in need of it and will build, furnish, and so forth when he
wishes (7–11). He is not to remove any of the trees upon pain of replacement in equal number (14–18). When he leaves (ἄπεισιν, 12), he will take
the woodwork, tiles, and doors, disturbing nothing else (11–14). Failure to
comply will result in his surrendering the woodwork, etc. and in the loss of
the lease (30–37). But why does the text read "when he leaves" (rather
than, say, παραδώσει ["turns over"] or ἀποδώσει ["returns"]), unless he is
actually to occupy one or more of the *oikiai*? Similarly, the clause calling
for Diognetos, when the *orgeones* sacrifice to the hero in Boedromion, "to
present the house where the *hieron* is located, opened and roofed (στέγην),
the kitchen, couches, and tables for two *triklinia*" (24–30) suggests two
things: that the house was suitably equipped for continuous residence and
that the lessee, while maintaining such continuous residence, is being required to vacate the premises on this single special occasion. Analogously,

as with text 4), the "quitting" by the lessee (ἄπεισιν, 12) should refer to his literal departure from the property.

7) Lease by the *orgeones* of Hypodektes, *IG* II² 2501, fin. s. IV. The *hieron* (1, 4, et al.) or *temenos* (4, 15, 19), like the foregoing, boasts an *oikia* (11, in fragmentary context), and, also as in the foregoing, the lessee is to make the shrine available on a single, named festival day (6–9). No reference is made to land or farming.

8) Decree of phratry Dyaleis leasing land, *IG* II² 1241, 300/299. The *chorion* called Sakinē (8–9) incorporates an *oikia*, regarding which the lease contains specific instructions: the lessee is to keep it in good repair (17–18) and he is to refrain from taking it, or any part of it, down (32–33, 40–41). Did the lessee Diodoros reside in this *oikia*? Two clues suggest that he might well have. For one, he is a Myrrhinousian (as are the two named lessors, 5–7, 12–13) and the *chorion* is located at Myrrhinous (2, 4–5) (the find spot of the stone, too, being "In vico Merenda," *IG* loc. cit.), so at least we know that he is probably not managing the property from a distance. For another, the lease requires that Diodoros cultivate the vines twice "in all seasons"; that he sow half the plot with grain, planting as much as he wishes of the fallow half with pulse; and that he tend to the fruit trees (19–25). Given such an evident ongoing need for presence on the site, residence in the *oikia* would obviously be advantageous, although he admittedly could have worked out of an existing residence in the deme, not to mention the fact that here, as elsewhere, we have no way of identifying the person or persons who will actually carry out the agricultural tasks.

9) Lease of the demesmen of Prasiai, E. Vanderpool, J. R. McCredie, and A. Steinberg, *Hesperia* 31 (1962) 54–56, no. 138 (*SEG* 21.644), ca. 350–300. A *chorion* (1–2, 7) that will produce a crop (13–16), the property comes with a number of specific items detailed from line 16 to the fragmentary end of the text. Since Osborne's case rests in large part on these closing lines and because I believe that he has misinterpreted them, I reproduce the text of the original edition:

$$[\sigma\kappa\epsilon]\acute{\upsilon}\eta\ \delta\grave{\epsilon}\ \acute{o}\sigma\alpha\ \grave{\epsilon}\text{-}$$
$$\sigma\tau\grave{\iota}\nu\ \tau o\hat{\upsilon}\ \delta\acute{\eta}\mu o\upsilon\ \grave{\epsilon}\nu\ \tau\hat{\eta}\iota\ o[\grave{\iota}]\kappa\acute{\iota}\alpha\iota\ \pi\alpha\text{-}$$
$$\rho\alpha\delta\iota\delta\acute{o}\alpha\sigma\iota\nu\ [\![\Pi[o]\lambda\upsilon\sigma[\sigma\theta\acute{\epsilon}]\nu\epsilon\iota]\!],\ \phi\iota\delta\acute{\alpha}\text{-}$$
$$\kappa\nu\alpha\varsigma\ \grave{\alpha}\mu\phi o\rho\acute{\epsilon}\omega\nu\ \chi\acute{o}\nu\delta\eta\nu : \Pi\Delta\Delta\Delta : \chi\acute{\alpha}\rho\text{-}$$
$$20 \qquad \alpha\kappa\alpha\varsigma : XXXX : o\check{\iota}\kappa\eta\mu\alpha\ \tau\grave{o}\ \mu[\ldots 7\ldots\grave{\eta}]\text{-}$$
$$\rho\epsilon\iota\mu\mu\acute{\epsilon}\nu o\nu\ \delta o\kappa o\acute{\iota} : \Pi\Pi[\ldots 9\ldots]$$

```
        [.]τες οἰκήματος εχ[ ..... 10 ..... ]
        [.]μμένον καὶ τὸ κ[...... 11 ......]
        [.]νος ἔχει τουτ[...... 13 ......]
 25     [..] : ΙΙΙΙ : καὶ επ[....... 14 .......]
        [...]στος καὶ[ ........ 15 ........]
        [....]ιστ[........ 17 ........]
        [..5..].[.........19.........]
```

Osborne asks us to believe that these lines establish the point that a structure termed *oikia* might have a nonresidential function. If this were true, then the meaning of the word *oikia* in all the many inscriptions (and other texts) under review here would potentially be affected and the case for farmstead residence that I am urging would be severely compromised. However, the alleged agricultural function of the *oikia* in line 17 depends upon Osborne's unargued assumption that to the phrase "all the pieces of equipment that belong to the deme in the *oikia*" stand in apposition the "eighty *phidaknai*" (i.e. "small pithoi"[46]) of amphorae "in the ground"[47] and "4,000 stakes" in lines 18–20, implying that the implements were housed inside. Such a use of the structure for storage, he believes, is inconsistent with the notion of residence. But the practice of modern Greek farmers illustrates how agricultural and residential functions might be combined under a single roof;[48] and even in the absence of the modern parallels, no ancient evidence precludes, or even makes unlikely, such an arrangement. Alternatively, it may be further suggested that the amphorae "in the ground" and the stakes do *not* stand in apposition to *skeuē* and so were not inside, but outside, the building. "All the *skeuē*" (16) would then be a self-contained, all-inclusive phrase designed to capture any and all articles happening to be in the *oikia* at the time, without unnecessarily specifying particular items in detail. But the amphorae and stakes, if located outside the *oikia* (and the *oikemata*), would accordingly need to receive specific mention in the lease, as in fact they do. Finally, if the *oikia* is in whole or part residential in function, the multiple(?) *oikemata* might be candidates for nonresidential uses, although the first mentioned seems to be dilapidated (20–21).

Since Osborne's case comes down to his reading of this lease, which we have now called into question, there is no longer any good reason to believe that at Athens an *oikia* in agricultural contexts was ever anything other than what it is in other contexts—a residential house (albeit one that could simultaneously be used for storage of agricultural implements).[49] Besides, scrutiny of the very inscriptions reviewed by Osborne has revealed several additional signs of occupancy of *oikiai* on leased *choria*. Two texts (nos. 4 and 6) speak of the lessee as "leaving" the property at the expiry of the lease period. Two texts (nos. 6 and 7) call for the evacuation of the premises by the lessee on a single occasion, suggesting that those premises were otherwise continuously occupied. Two texts (nos. 1 and 8) require the performance of agricultural tasks of such magnitude as to imply clear advantages to ongoing presence on the site through all or much of the year. One text (no. 3, cf. no. 2) reveals the presence alongside the house of a garden and well, thereby opening up the possibility of on-site occupancy.

The import of these findings, however, remains conditioned by the peculiar prosopographical content of the documents on which those findings are based. Some evidence is at hand from Delos that the parties entering into lease agreements with corporate bodies were relatively prosperous.[50] At Rhamnous, among the lessees are individuals who, as Jameson has attractively suggested, are probably performing a virtual liturgy on behalf of their deme-association by assuming the burden of terms of lease not necessarily attractive from a strictly business standpoint;[51] and at least one other appears among Davies' register of the liturgical class.[52] Given a wealthy lessee, it is less likely that he would personally need or choose to establish residence on leased land, even in those cases where we can be sure that it was equipped with a residential *oikia*. Such a man probably already had a permanent residence. Why should he relocate to a lease-holding for the limited period of the lease's duration? Besides, wealthy men do not do agricultural work themselves; they assign it to others and periodically pay visits to monitor their progress. Hence, again, the unusual requirement that the presumably prosperous Rhamnousian lessee reside in the *oikia* on the *temenos*-plot he will be farming. Probably more often, however, the occupants of the *oikiai* on properties such as those just reviewed will have been a bailiff (*epitropos*), tenants (whether citizen or metic), hired hands, or slaves.

At the same time, it would be wrong to eliminate the possibility of a middling lessee who views the rental of land as a money-making venture and who reduces overhead expenses by residing on the land that he is renting and working himself. Such a possibility is consistent with the fact that three, possibly four, of the identifiable lessees in our documents do not appear among Davies' register of the liturgical class (although such silence of the record of course proves nothing one way or the other)[53] and is further encouraged by the at least one case where the amount of the yearly rental payment was particularly low.[54] What remains in doubt is whether any of this holds for *owners* of farming land in Attica. For that, we now turn to our final class of documents, the security *horoi*.

SECURITY *HOROI*

A large percentage of the inscribed markers called *horoi* stood upon properties encumbered as security for debts. Typically, an intact text identifies itself as a *horos*, specifies the property or properties in question (often with the appended phrase "sold for redemption"), names the creditor(s), and closes with the amount of the debt expressed in drachmas. The *horos* was presumably erected on the mortgaged property itself (thereby making unnecessary the naming of the debtor, who continued to reside on the land, in the house, etc. and so was known to all) and served to inform other prospective lenders of the property's encumbered status. By my count, 266 different security *horoi* have thus far been published in various collections, as follows: John Fine's *Horoi* (*Hesperia* Supplement 9, Princeton 1951), ch. 1, New Horos Mortgage Stones from the Athenian Agora, pp. 1–27; ch. 2, Previously Published Mortgage Stones, pp. 28–40; Moses Finley's *Studies in Land and Credit in Ancient Athens, 500–200 B.C.* (New Brunswick 1951, revised 1985), Appendix I, The Texts of the Horoi, pp. 118–176, nos. 1–180; Appendix III, New Horoi from the Agora, pp. 182–193; Paul Millett's second appendix to the 1985 revision of Finley, The Texts of the New Horoi and Accompanying Statistical Tables, pp. xxii–xxxiii; Gerald V. Lalonde's contribution to *Agora* XIX, *Inscriptions: Horoi*, Security Horoi, pp. 37–51, nos. H73–H130, of which three, H112, 119, and 130, were previously unpublished; and thirteen new texts reported in the pages of the *Supplementum Epigraphicum Graecum* since the closing of Millett's appendix to Finley. Because Finley's catalogue of texts incorporates all of Fine's then-new texts from the Agora and Millett's appendix adds the more recently published examples in the 1985 revision of this same work, with the consecutive numbering having been preserved by inserting the new texts at the appropriate place with the addition of an "A", "B", etc. (e.g. 92A, 146B), it will be convenient to refer to these texts by Finley's numbers. The more recently published examples will be cited by reference to *Agora* XIX and to *SEG* through volume 47 for the year 1997.

The security *horoi* are overwhelmingly Athenian, since only 25 texts from outside Attica have thus far been published, namely from the islands Amorgos (nos. 8, 9, 102, 130, 154, 155, 172, 173), Lemnos (nos. 10, 103–110, 115, 190A), Naxos (nos. 131, 156, 165), Skyros (no. 111), Syros (nos. 179, 180). Among the Athenian examples, 41 are too fragmentary with respect to the identification of the property originally named on the stone to play a part in my analysis: nos. 3A, 31A–B, 37, 39, 93–95, 95A–B, 96–100, 101A–C, 127, 129A, 157, 160A, 164, 164A–C, 166–171, 171A–F, 178B, *Agora* XIX H119 and 130. One intact text does not identify the encumbered property (no. 129). One text included by Finley (no. 101C) has been re-identified by Charles Hedrick as marking a shrine.[55] Twelve texts name properties not visibly associated with arable lands or potential residential structures located on them: *ergasterion/a* (nos. 7, 91, *Agora* XIX H112), *ergasterion/a* with *andrapoda* (nos. 88–90; 166A; *SEG* 32.236 = 40.175 = 42.146)), *kaminos* and *edaphoi* (no. 92), *ke[pos]* and *andrapod[a]* (no. 178), *mylon* (*SEG* 35.136 = 39.199), and *synoikia* (no. 171F).[56] The remaining 186 texts, the subject of our study, record, broadly speaking, the hypothecation of either land (always denoted by the Greek word *chorion*) or a building (almost always *oikia*) or a combination of the two. The three major groupings break down as follows: *chorion* without a structure (66 examples), *oikia* (or *oikema*, *oikemation*) with or without other properties but without land (62 examples), and *chorion* and *oikia* with or without additional properties (58 examples). Given the generally accepted meanings of these Greek terms, we have in this record prima facie indications of the interrelationships of land and domicile, with the final category at first blush comprising farms in the familiar sense of land with on-site residence. But in order to shed greater light on settlement patterns, we will need, first, to tabulate the varying incidence of land or building or the two in combination with respect to topography, specifically on the point of intramural urban versus extramural rural locales.[57] In the end, it will be the results of the latter installment of our project, the clear patterning of the properties named in the *horoi* in relation to town and country, that will yield a conclusion firmly in favor of the model of farmstead residence. (Throughout the following tabulation, assignment of a stone with a recorded provenience to an Attic deme is based on John Traill's most recent table of assignments of demes to sites,[58] and all extramural Attic place names may be assumed to be demes unless otherwise specified).

LAND (*CHORION*) WITHOUT A RESIDENTIAL STRUCTURE

This category comprises all *horoi* marking land but without the addition of a structure that might normally be taken to have served as a residence.

urban Athens (25): 2 *ad Ilissum*, 43 Parthenon, 48 Agora, 53 Agora, 54 Athens, 55 Peiraieus, 58 Peiraieus, 60 Acropolis, 60A Agora, 66 Kerameikos, 66B–D Agora, 82B Agora, 90A Athens, 114B Agora, 122 southeast Athens, 123 north of Parthenon, 126A–C Agora, 141A Agora, 144 Munychia, 158 Athens, 175B Agora.

extraurban Attica (26): 3 Acharnai, 40 Eleusis, 42 Dekeleia, 49 Mt. Hymettos, 51 Hagnous, 52 Pelekes, 56 Erchia, 57 Eleusis, 61 Sounion, 65 Acharnai, 82A Marathon, 112 Teithras, 121 Mesogaia region, 125 Eleusis, 126 Eleusis, 126D Erchia, 126E Eleusis, 141 Anaphlystos,[59] 142 Kephale, 145 Phlya, 146 between Athmonon and Phlya, 146B Myrrhinous, 163 Hagnous, *SEG* 39.200 Halai Aixonides,[60] *SEG* 39.201 Marathon, *SEG* 43.56 Rhamnous.

no recorded provenience (15): 41, 44–47, 50, 59, 62–64, 124, 160, 174, 177, *SEG* 45.164.

From the nearly even distribution between town and country one might be tempted to infer that the hypothecation of *choria* was not significantly related to gross variations in urban or rural topography. But the actual situation may be more complex than at first meets the eye, for in none of the urban examples, including all the recently edited (or re-edited) examples from the Agora, can we be sure of the original location of the monument and hence of the *chorion* (or *choria*) in question. Self-evidently, private individuals did not own real property in the Agora, on the Acropolis, or in the Kerameikos. But from what quarters did these stones wander? Probably from no great distance, to judge from a handy (and relevant) index: of the 138 or so documents of the extramural demes, not a single example is known to have been discovered in urban Athens (or, for that matter, at any great distance from the deme center in question).[61] If various types of inscription other than *horoi* demonstrably fail to migrate from rural locations to the urban center, why should these security *horoi* have been any different?

If, then, these two dozen or so *choria* did lie near or within the fortification walls, what are we to make of properties that, in a rural situation, would naturally be assumed to be agricultural plots? It is probable, as commentators have noted, that the invariable use of the colorless generic term *chorion* masks a wide variety of real properties.[62] Pasturage, vineyards, orchards, and wood lots, as well as fields with grain crops, are all obvious possibilities. Less attractive, however, is Finley's suggestion, made on the basis of a single *horos* from Peiraieus (no. 55), that a *chorion* might sometimes be a building lot,[63] although this rendering of the word would admittedly make the recorded urban proveniences more readily comprehensible and in particular would suit the conjunction of an *ergasterion* with a *chorion* on *horos* 90A from Athens (which was published after Finley wrote). But working against the suggestion is the occasional occurrence on *horoi* from urban contexts of the term *oikopedon*: once on a restored marker from the southern slope of the Acropolis (no. 143), another time on a restored marker from the Agora reused in the wall of a modern house (no. 31A–B).[64] To judge from the word's etymology, an *oikopedon* must be the ground under an *oikos* (vel sim.), that is to say, a building lot. Another, less certain, candidate is *edaphos*.[65] Now, given the seeming consistency and conventionality of these texts, any variation in wording must be taken as significant. Accordingly, since a term (or terms) with this specific meaning was available, why would the vague *chorion*, with Finley, have been pressed into service in its place?[66]

The intramural agricultural plot, then, whatever its precise character, must remain a preferable alternative. The restoration in no. 2 of a *chorion*, a garden, and a spring adjacent to the garden,[67] however, affords the only trace of agricultural activity found in this group of *horoi*.

STRUCTURE (*OIKIA, OIKEMA, OIKEMATION*) WITH OR WITHOUT OTHER PROPERTIES BUT WITHOUT LAND

This category comprises markers of structures that, given normal Greek linguistic usage, might have served as a residence, not infrequently with the addition of some other, sometimes ancillary, property, e.g., *ergasterion/a* (nos. 87, 161), *kapeleion* (nos. 92A, 92B), *kepos/oi* (nos. 92A, 153), *kopron* (nos. 86, 86A), *lithorgeion* (no. 87), and water (no. 159). The usual term is *oikia*, but *oikema* is found in no. 81 and *oikemation* is restored in no. 86A. In none of the 57 examples is *chorion* or other word for land read or restored.

urban Athens (48): 2A Agora, 4–5 between Pnyx and Areopagos, 66A Agora, 67 Peiraieus, 67A Agora, 68 Peiraieus, 69 Acropolis, 70 Munychia, 71–72 Agora, 72A Agora, 73 Peiraieus, 73A Agora, 74A Agora, 76–77 Acropolis, 78 Athens, 78A Agora, 80A Agora, 81A Agora, 81C-D Agora, 83

Athens, 84 Acropolis, 85 Athens, 85A–C Agora, 86 Athens, 86A Agora, 87
Dipylon, 92A Agora, 92B Athens, 114 Pnyx, 114A Agora, 147 area of Pnyx,
148 north of the Amyneion, 148A Agora, 150–152 Athens, 152A Agora, 153
Athens?, 159 Athens, 161 Athens, 162 Athens, 175A Agora.

    extraurban Attica (8): 6 Eleusis, 75 Eleusis, 163A Teithras, *SEG*
41.127–129 Rhamnous, *SEG* 43.55 and 57 Rhamnous.

    no recorded provenience (6): 74, 79, 80–82, 149.

    In contrast with the even town and country distribution of the previ-
ous group of stones, nearly all the examples with a provenience are of immediate urban origin. Moreover, the octet of extraurban *horoi* is easily
explained away. Two originate in the heavily built-up sanctuary deme of
Eleusis.[68] The five examples from Rhamnous are all reported too have been
found in or around the fortress. In the no. 163A, from Teithras, the multiple *oikiai* are conjoined with a *perioikion*, evidently an encircling yard of
some kind which potentially places this example within the larger category
of "land and house" to be discussed in a moment. None of the eight, in
other words, is necessarily to be associated with an agricultural setting; in
none is there good reason to think that the occupant of the *oikia* in question was a farmer who commuted to and from his plot(s). But under more
typical circumstances, not a single *horos* marking a structure in the absence
of land is reported to have originated in extramural rural Attica. So pronounced a pattern cannot be lacking in significance.

    The absence of any mention of land in these texts was noted by Fin-
ley, who instanced in explanation the fact that under ordinary circumstances urban real estate had "little, if any, monetary value."[69] But the true
explanation may be otherwise, that it went without saying that the ground
under a structure came with it for the purposes of hypothecation. Besides,
the letter cutter, compelled to fit his text on the single face of a narrow pillar, was routinely constrained by extreme limitations of space and on occasion may have elected not to express the obvious. In any case, the
monetary value of urban lots in densely packed inner Athens could only
have reflected demand for convenient urban location in an age of primitive
modes of communication and transportation.[70] If urban real estate was in
any sense lacking in value, it would more likely have been due to the absence of the nostalgic or sentimental associations that characterized rural
agricultural and pastoral acreage. By contrast, the mere ground, invisible
and inaccessible, lying underneath a house or other structure hardly qualified for such attention.

    Something of the nature of these *oikiai* is suggested by the additional properties sometimes appearing with them, with the non-Attic island *horoi* shedding valuable additional light. A marker from Athens (no. 159) speci- fies the adjacent water supply, a valuable asset which Solon's law on water rights leaves no doubt was not enjoyed by all landed properties.[71] Two markers add a *kopron*,[72] once with an *oikemation* (no. 86A), the other time with an *oikia* (no. 86). With the *perioikion* conjoined with multiple *oikiai* in Teithras (no. 163A) may be compared the *kepoi* attending *oikiai* on markers from Aigiale (no. 9) and Arkesine (nos. 154 and 155, both restored) on Amorgos and from Athens (no. 153). These may, as noted earlier in con- nection with the lands of the Salaminioi, be domestic "kitchen" gardens at- tached to a private residential dwelling. Obviously commercial in nature, however, are the *ergasteria* associated with *oikiai* in nos. 87 and 161 and the *kapeleion* with another in no. 92B. *Oikia, kapeleion,* and *kepos* are com- bined in no. 92A from the Agora; *oikia, kepos,* and *keramos* are marked by no. 165 (with the first two terms being entirely restored) from Naxos. Nat- urally, it is not absolutely certain that such multiple properties all stood on the same ground, but if the purpose of the marker was to warn off unsus- pecting prospective lenders, the fact that the several properties were named on a single stone strongly suggests that this was the case. When it was not the case, variable locations could be specified, as in no. 87, on which an *oikia* is hypothecated with *ergasteria* "inside the wall" and with a *lithorgeion* "outside the wall." Beyond the walls, another marker, no. 14 from Vari, distinguishes an *oikia*-and-*chorion* ensemble, before which the *horos* pre- sumably stood, from a second *oikia* "in the *asty.*" The prepositional phrases, in other words, specify what could ordinarily not otherwise be inferred from the typical *horos* text. If, then, the multiple properties named on a sin- gle *horos* constituted a unified whole, it is probable, against Osborne, that at least some of these *oikiai* were residences, for water and gardens bespeak continuing presence on the site, not the occasional visit. Workplaces, pre- dictably nonagricultural in these urban settings (workshop, retail shop, kiln, quarry), will have been, in keeping with practice well attested else- where, closely integrated with the owner's or worker's residence (a con- clusion strongly urged by the presence of the garden alongside the retail shop in 92A and the kiln in no. 165).[73] Although we cannot demonstrate the residential function, the combined effect of this evidence makes the in- ference more plausible than to suppose, following Osborne's analysis of the leases, that an *oikia* was merely a storeroom, shop, barn, or the like.

All this, again, pertains to the urbanized areas of Athens, from which alone (with the exception of the eight atypical texts from Eleusis, Rham-

nous, and Teithras) we have markers for *oikiai* in the absence of any mention of land. But why, it is now time to ask, are such markers not associated with Attica outside the walls? Given the abundance of extramural *horoi*
and the consequent attractiveness of the argument from silence, the obvious answer is that an *oikia* without land (save for the ground it sat upon)
was generally not to be found in rural Attica. But before considering further this possibility, we must first examine the many instances of markers
signifying an *oikia* and *chorion* in combination.

LAND (*CHORION*) AND BUILDING (*OIKIA*)
WITH OR WITHOUT ADDITIONAL PROPERTIES

Land and building often occur as a pair, but sometimes (as we shall see)
in conjunction with other properties. The one lexical variation is the
restoration of *oikema* in no. 101A. Employing the same categories used in
the previous tabulations, we find the following topographical distribution:

urban Athens (15): 1 Athens, 18A Agora, 21A Agora, 23 Kerameikos, 26
modern Kallirhoe, 33 Athens, 35 Acropolis, 36 Pnyx, 39A Agora, 101A
Agora, 113 Peiraieus, 120 Agora, 120A Agora, 139 Areopagos, 176 northern
Athens.

extraurban Attica (35): 11 Erchia, 12 Ikarion, 12A between Laureion
district and Sounion, 13 Sphettos, 14 Anagyrous (site at modern Vari; includes an additional *oikia* "in the *asty*"), 15 modern Patissia, 16A Trikorynthos, 17 Laureion, 18 Iphistiadai, 19–20 Kephale, 22 Athmonon, 24
Sounion, 25 Ikarion, 28 Acharnai, 30 Erchia, 31 Kettos, 32 Erchia, 116 Acharnai, 117 Marathon, 118 Kephale, 119 Hagnous, 128 Cholargos, 132 Erchia, 133
Kephale, 134 Thria, 135 Erchia, 135A Ikarion, 136 Erchia, 137 Steiria, 137A
Brauron sanctuary, 138 Euonymon, 140 Ikarion, *SEG* 38.165 Aixone and
44.82 Thorai?

no recorded provenience (8): 16, 21, 27, 29, 34, 38, 39B, 175.

As with the previous tabulations, the sizable number of examples from
urban areas is compromised by the absence of even a single *horos* found in
situ and by the certainty that a privately held land or building could not
have been situated on the Acropolis, Pnyx, or Areopagos, or in the Agora
or Kerameikos. At the same time, again, any assumption of as many as 15
pierres errantes is constrained by the failure of parallel examples of stones
of known rural origin to be discovered in these same urban areas. So, as

with the isolated *choria*, it seems more attractive to imagine that these *chorion*-and-*oikia* combined properties were located within or just outside the walls, and that the *horoi* that originally marked them had been transported short distances for reuse in post-classical structures in the heart of Athens.

The fact that two-thirds of this group of *horoi* with recorded provenience are from extramural locations in Attica naturally suggests that the *chorion* is arable land and the *oikia* a house located on that land. My general reason for assuming that the *oikia* in fact stood on the *chorion* has already been given—that the single *horos* naming both properties must have visibly marked both building and land or it could not served its intended purpose. One may add the specific evidence of a marker from Brauron, no. 137A, that is restored to read "*chorion* and the *oikia* on the *chorion*." Rather than take this uniquely explicit phrase as indicating a departure from routine practice, it is easier to assume that the text makes an implicit distinction between the *oikia* situated, as was normal, on the land and some other unnamed *oikia* that happened to be excluded from this dotal hypothec. The fuller text of *horos* no. 14 from Vari marking an *oikia*, *chorion*, and an "*oikia* in the *asty*" illustrates such a disposition of properties. Moreover, where an additional property is combined on a single marker with *chorion* and *oikia*, the ensemble is consistent with farmstead residence: *choria*, *kepoi*, and *oikia* (no. 12, from the deme Ikarion); *chorion*, *oikia*, and *kepoi* (no. 12A, found "by the road between Laurion and Sounion"); *chorion*, *oikia*, and *kepos* (no. 13, from Sphettos, as restored); *choria*, *oikia*, and water adjacent to the *choria* (no. 116, from the deme Acharnai).[74] The presence of gardens and in one case of water in these examples does not absolutely prove on-site residence but it certainly suggests it strongly.[75] When the debtor undertook to mortgage property as security for his debt, he sometimes put up the natural integrated unit of land, house, garden, and, when present, water supply.

These last few examples shed light on the problem of farmstead residence in still another way. In two cases (nos. 12 and 116) multiple *choria* are conjoined with a single *oikia*. The simplest explanation is that we are dealing here with a composite estate comprising distinct plots on only one of which an *oikia* was standing. Presumably that one *chorion* with the *oikia* was the site of the *horos*. Such an arrangement would also make comprehensible the markers for a *chorion* without an *oikia* that we studied earlier. Rather than suppose the existence of an uninhabited farm with the owner

residing in a nucleated village center or even in the town, it is more economical to imagine in these cases an estate of multiple *choria* of which one
happening to lack an *oikia* had been put up as security.

Literary Evidence for Rural Residence

Does the evidence of prose narrative (that is, historical, forensic, philosophical, and related texts) confirm, or not, these seeming implications of
the inscriptions? Despite prevailing urban preoccupations and biases, references to extramural spaces and peoples are not infrequent, but nearly
every at-first-sight promising passage turns out, on closer inspection, to
be marked by an ambiguity evidently born of an absence of need to specify the particular circumstances of a person's abode. The great majority of
the texts can be grouped under three major headings:

(1) Literary texts use the word *agros*, "field," often in phrases "in,"
"from," or "to the *agros* or *agroi*" and especially where movement to and
from the *asty* is in question. Some translate "in/from/to my farm" or the
like, with the implication of farmstead residence. But this, I believe, is to
overlook the invariable *urban* perspective of these writers (and their texts):
"a field" or "the fields," from the vantage point of the town, could refer
to agricultural land with either farmstead or village residence. The probable meaning in most cases is simply that the place, place of departure, or
destination is out in "the country."

(2) Military narratives occasionally depict an invading enemy encoun-
tering agricultural laborers at work in the fields. Do such circumstances imply farmstead residence, as Hanson[76] for one has suggested? No, and
especially not in the case of rural Attica where the territories of the great
majority of the many demes were small and commuting time accordingly
short. Besides, invasions often occur at harvest time in order to inflict the
maximum destruction, and it is precisely at harvest time that we would expect every ablebodied person to be in the fields, regardless of place of residence.

(3) Neighbors are occasionally mentioned in rural contexts, but with
nearly invariable ambiguity, since "neighbor" might have reference either
to contiguous plots of land or to farms (with on-site residence) sharing a
common boundary or to adjacent domiciles in a village. What is absent in
all the examples adduced by scholars is the *explicit* assertion that a house

actually stood upon the land, thereby leaving open the possibility of residence in some nearby nucleated center. Thus:

[Demosthenes] 47, *Against Euergos and Mnesiboulos* 53: "I farm near the Hippodrome and I have been living there from childhood." Arguably, the assignment of the farmland to a location outside any named nucleated settlement and the association with that location of the permanent place of habitation indicate farmstead residence. Furthermore, with Langdon I agree, against Osborne, that the context of the speaker's remark affords no grounds for regarding this case as in any way atypical.[77] Nonetheless, it may be objected that the text's "there" is vague enough not to exclude residence in a nearby village.

Demosthenes 53, *Against Nikostratos* 4: "Nikostratos . . . was a neighbor of mine in the country (*agros*) and a man of my own age and had long been known to me. When my father died and I started living in the country (*agros*), where I now live, we now had more to do with each other since we were neighbors and of the same age." Langdon is, I believe, mistaken when he finds in the second occurrence of *agros* a clear reference to a "farm" (and likewise in a third occurrence that follows at §6).[78]

Demosthenes 55, *Against Kallikles* 23: "Before these people attempted to slander me, my mother enjoyed the company of their mother, and, visiting each other as is natural since both resided in the country (*agros*) and were neighbors and also since their husbands had enjoyed each other's company while they were alive, my mother, having gone to visit theirs. . . ." Either contiguous "farms" or merely contiguous plots with (neighboring?) houses in a village may lie behind these ambiguous words.[79]

There remain, of course, the indications of imaginative literary productions, especially drama, in which a rural residence occasionally figures. Because, however, their pertinence to the present discussion is at best indirect, I have reserved their consideration for chapter 6 under the rubric "Images." But one additional passage, though fictional, deserves inclusion here by reason of its quasi-sociological realistic orientation:

Theophrastos, *Characteres* IV, *Agroikia* : The rustic's offensive behavior is manifested when he journeys from the *agros* implicit in his *agroikia* (1) "into town" (*asty*, 15). When entertaining at home, "he calls the dog and, grabbing him by the muzzle, says 'This chap guards the land (*chorion*) and the house (*oikia*)' " (12). Since entertainment is in question, the *oikia* must be his residence (rather than, as suggested by Osborne in connection with the leases, a nonresidential structure). Since, further, the dog guards both land and house (and it is just inside the door that the rustic's words are spoken), the house must sit on that land rather than in a nucleated village center. Does the rustic own the property? Nothing in Theophrastos's vignette suggests that he does not, and the fact that the man attends the Assembly (3) proves his citizen status and so his legal capacity to own "land and house." But it is the normative, rather than particular, orientation of the scene that constitutes the true value of this text. Were Theophrastos's rustic not an easily recognized stereotypical figure, the sketch would cease to possess any comedic meaning. The implication is that a good many Attic farmers, while paying regular visits to the *asty*, were based outside the walls on farmstead residences. Even a scattering of isolated positive instances would be sufficient to overturn the nucleated settlement position, but the Theophrastian text actually goes far towards establishing the generality of the model of farmstead residence.

Not to be discounted, either, is the powerful negative evidence. Nowhere in our sources, whether documentary, historical, or literary, do we find clear indications of residence in a nucleated center of any description. Again, narratives such as those found in Plato and the orators not infrequently preserve a reference to an arrival from or departure to "the field(s)" (*agros/oi*) or "the country" (*chora*), but never from or to a *village*. Likewise, Aristophanes: among many uses of *demos*, only twice (*Archarnians* 33, 267) does it have an unambiguous extramural reference and in neither instance is the sense "village" required;[80] and, as with Plato, references to the country (involving movement or otherwise) invariably involve a locution for "field(s)."[81] Demes or other communities may be mentioned in various contexts under a proper name, but such reference obviously carries no implications with regard to residence. While, admittedly, the pattern in evidence here may simply be the product of urban inattention, it is attractive to find the explanation instead in the simple fact that Athenian landowners regularly lived on their lands, for which reason mention of "the village" per se would often have been factually inaccurate.

The Nucleated Village Center

But the principal reason for favoring the conclusion of farmstead residence is a negative one: the virtual absence of security *horoi* naming an *oikia* but not a *chorion* from outside the urbanized areas. The reason that we have no such *horoi* is, I am maintaining, simply that owner-operators lived on their farms rather than, as is widely assumed or argued, in some putative nucleated village residential center.

To be sure, the documents of the demes indicate the existence of what might justly be called public and, if you will, municipal spaces and structures: agora, stelai, theater, *dikasterion, gymnasion, palaestra*, fountain, lounge, and so on.[82] What the documents do not indicate, however, is that such communal properties actually formed a *center*, however natural such an assumption might seem. The surmise, say, that the agora represented a sort of hub of village public life must remain just that, a surmise, though a plausible one.[83] But the notion that to such a hub was attached a compact concentration of landowners' dwellings lacks support from the numerous inscriptions of the rural deme associations, in which the *oikiai*, so frequently attested in *poletai* records, leases, and security *horoi*, are hardly to be found.[84]

Still more damaging to the hypothesis of a nucleated village residential center is the fact that such a center, certainly in Athens' case, was simply not necessary. True, the territory of Attica was huge by ancient Greek standards, but this territory was partitioned by 139 Kleisthenic demes, of which only five lay within the town's circuit wall. Alison Burford's estimate puts settlements in many parts of Attica roughly ten kilometers apart, each within an area of about five kilometers' radius.[85] For adult males accustomed to walking, five kilometers out and back is an easily accepted maximum distance, and of course not all farming demesmen will have resided on plots located at the maximum distance. True, too, there is the matter of fragmented holdings to be taken into consideration. Noncontiguous, scattered composite estates have always with good reason been associated with nucleated settlement, on the theory that on the average it is more economical to live in a center than on any one of a number of scattered plots. But the demands imposed by a fragmented holding could equally well, indeed perhaps more satisfactorily, be met by an alternative strategy: the placement of the *oikia* (and other structures) of a composite estate on the *chorion* nearest the center rather than in the center itself. Residence on one's own *chorion* would also possess a clear economic advantage: it would have obviated the securing in the putative residential center of an additional parcel of land—a building lot—on which to place this hypothetical house. Although the parties to the hypothecation of property recorded on the *horoi* were generally prosperous,[86] it is still difficult to imagine why an owner-operator would have voluntarily assumed so significant an additional, and unnecessary, financial burden.

Nor does the received view gain substantial support from any attested constitutional or political requirements of deme-association membership. Yes, a prospective citizen had to be present in the village center at his own formal induction into his father's deme and, once a citizen, perhaps at that of a son (*AthPol* 42.1). Presumably, his physical presence was also required for his participation in bouleutic or other sortition (potentially, for the relatively inactive, however, a rare event, since one could serve on the Council only twice in a lifetime [*AthPol* 62.3] and since there was no known law or even ideal requiring magisterial service of any kind). All else, so far as we are informed, was elective. I am not denying that demespeople ever visited a village center (in those demes where such actually existed), only that the formal, or even informal, requirements of membership in the citizenbody and in one's deme-association somehow necessitated the maintenance of a bustling rural Attic nucleated village hub.

Against these speculative inferences must be set, of course, the ongoing results of archaeological survey or excavation as more of the deme-sites of rural Attica are systematically explored. Some of these results support the thesis argued here, for the several reported isolated "farms" and "farmhouses" will have corresponded to the *chorion*-and-*oikia* ensembles marked by many of the security *horoi* outside the walls. Rather, the question concerns compact settlement. Residential structures have been exposed in the mining deme of Thorikos,[87] but in this industrial setting circumstances will have differed from those of the typical agricultural community, since many residents obviously will not have been directly involved in farming and so the question of residing or not residing on one's land will not have arisen. More to the point of the present discussion are the reports of nucleated residential infrastructure at Erchia[88] and Halai Aixonides[89] published in 1994 in a volume edited by W. D. E. Coulson and others. Given the continuing appearance of settlements of this kind, the question, as concerns the hypothesis of the residential "deme-center," will then be one of numbers of such residences.

It is noteworthy that, given a citizen population of 30,000, a single councillor on the Council of 500 would represent 60 Athenians and that, even after we have excluded urban Kydathenaion, Melite, and Peiraieus, the sanctuary deme of Eleusis, the mining deme of Thorikos, and the fortress deme of Rhamnous, about thirty demes had quotas of five or more councillors—that is, citizen memberships of 300 or more, many of whom will have been heads of households. Excavation within the territories of demes of this size will have to demonstrate very extensive remains of domestic architecture if the proposition of the residential deme center is to be validated. Meanwhile, incontrovertible traces of isolated farm houses are long and well known,[90] and countless other *kataskeuai* may have thus far escaped detection or have been destroyed, especially if the remains have suffered the obliterating effects of deep ploughing of ancient farming sites by mechanized equipment.

Any inclination to reject the results of the epigraphic analysis must be tempered by the fact that my discussion, besides culling a few ambiguous candidates from the *poletai* records and the *rationes centesimarum* and some more or less explicit positive instances from the leases, has in the security *horoi* tapped a very substantial body of documents representing the entire expanse of Attica and covering a fairly wide span of time.[91] That 186 independent contemporary documents should not provide a single straightforward nonconforming example is of more than particular significance. Perhaps, then, we should be asking why, in demes such as Thorikos, Erchia, and Halai Aixonides, a residential property situated in a nucleated deme-center might not have been subject to the practices of hypothecation indicated by the markers discovered everywhere throughout extramural Attica. Besides, such *oikiai* (if indeed, that is what we are dealing with) are a problem for my thesis only if they were occupied by farmers whose lands lay outside the village center. Do we know this to have been true?

2

Society

IT IS IMPORTANT NOT TO OVERSTATE, or draw unwarranted inferences from, the conclusion reached in the preceding chapter, that structures normally termed *oikiai* stood on some of the *choria* of Attica and that these structures normally served a wholly or primarily residential function. This is not necessarily to say that residences were not to be found in adjacent village centers, where such existed, nor, whether or not demespeople or others resided in such a center, that that center was not a place of communal significance. But our present concern is with the description and deeper understanding of the Attic rural society that was rooted in the peculiar patterns of settlement seemingly indicated by the inscriptions and literary sources just studied. To that end, we shall begin with the rural household unit itself, then proceed to a higher, unifying tier of social organization embodied in a specifically agrarian form of personal patronage, finally returning to the role and importance of the village community.

The Attic Rural Family

While strictly speaking a "literary" work according to the generic categories of meter, diction, formulae, and so forth, the primary burden of *Works and Days* is to impart information, advice, and wisdom pertaining to agriculture (and seafaring) practiced at the level of the individual household. Taken at face value, Hesiod's text identifies the scene as Boeotia and modern scholarship puts the author's date in the mid to late eighth century.[1] What role, if any, did Hesiod's poem play in the formation of the rural culture of Attica two to four hundred years later? The question will be addressed (and with a guardedly affirmative response) momentarily, but before we reach that point, let us attempt to characterize just what it is that Hesiod endeavors to convey to his reader or (as suggested by the poem's manifest symptoms of oral composition) listener.

Following an invocation to the Muses of Pieria to sing in praise of Zeus through the poet, ending with the declaration "And I, Perses, might relate things true" (1–10), Hesiod dilates on the Two Strifes (11–26), thereby setting the stage for the fuller address of this Perses, who turns out to be the poet's brother:

Perses, may you store these things in your heart and not let the Strife that delights in evil drag your heart away from work while gawking and eavesdropping on the quarrels in the Agora. For short is the season for quarrels and agoras for him who has not laid up a seasonal livelihood of grain, which the Earth brings forth, the wheat of Demeter. Once you have a surfeit of that, then you might raise disputes and strife for the sake of another man's goods. No, you will not have a second opportunity to do so; but let us settle our dispute here with straight judgments which, being from Zeus, are best. For already we divided the estate, but you seized and carried off the greater share, honoring the gift-devouring lords, who like to judge a case of this kind. Idiots! They don't know how much more half is than the whole nor how great is the gain in mallow and asphodel. (27–41)

With this programmatic passage, as I have argued at length elsewhere (Jones 1984), Hesiod announces, then intertwines with each other, the twin themes of his poem: first, the quarrel with his brother, which, over and above any personal or legal issues involved, has occasioned Perses' neglect of productive agricultural work; and, second, the matter of work itself on which a person's livelihood, in the world Hesiod lives in, necessarily depends. That is, the real point concerning Perses is not, I maintain, that he has unfairly wrested away more than his share of the *kleros* (however urgent, outside the context of the poem, so fundamental an issue may have been), but that this dispute, a particular instance of the "quarrels and agoras" for which the season is short (30), has obstructed the acquisition of "a seasonal livelihood" (*bios . . . horaios*, 31–32). The qualification of livelihood as "seasonal," furthermore, as we shall see later in the chapter, heralds Hesiod's true theme—the practice of agriculture in its seasonal, that is temporal, aspect. Thus, as the poem unfolds, the didacticism of the *Works* is found to be tied closely not only to the *Days* proper but throughout to the central narrative as well. Hesiod does not address his advice to a rank neophyte untutored in even the most fundamental of agricultural (or maritime) practices, but rather to the listener or reader already versed in the basics but who must also command the nuances, niceties, and fine distinctions of selection, quantity, scale, and especially timing if he is to succeed. Attention to Hesiod's admonitions, that is, can make or break the householder operating on the cusp that separates a self-sufficient general prosperity from ruin.

The fundamental unit of the agrarian society laid out by Hesiod was the *oikos*, household, comprising its male head, wife, child or children, and slaves:

Bring a wife to your house at the right age, while you are not much short of thirty years nor much older. This is the right season of life for marriage. Let your wife be four years past puberty, and marry her in the fifth. Marry a virgin, so that you can teach her careful habits, and above all marry one who lives near you. But shop around in order that your marriage not be a joke to your neighbors. For a man can carry off nothing better than a good wife, but, by the same token, there is nothing worse than a bad one—a freeloader who roasts her husband without the benefit of a fire, strong though he may be, and delivers him to a savage old age. (695–705)

There should be only one son, to sustain his father's house, for this way wealth will increase in the home. But if you leave a second son, you'd better die old. Even so, Zeus can easily provide indescribable wealth to a greater number. The greater the industry and the more the hands, the greater the increase. (376–380)

First things first. Get a house, and a woman, and an ox for the plow—I mean a slave woman and not a wife, who will also drive the oxen. And make everything ready at home, . . . (405–407)

But whenever you have stored all your livelihood inside the house, I bid you to put the bondsman (*thes*) out of doors and seek out a servant (*erithos*) without children, for a servant with nursing child is worrisome. (600–603)

Let a robust man of forty drive them [the oxen], a man drawing a ration of a four-quarter loaf and eight bites for his meal, one who will attend to his work and plow a straight furrow and is beyond the age for staring at his buddies but will keep his mind on the task at hand. (441–445)

The household so constituted will provide the focus—indeed (it is almost no exaggeration to say) the sum total—of Hesiod's community. The village and, at a still higher level, the city-state, will exert only a weak influence on the *oikos*-unit and entanglements with it are to be avoided whenever possible (e.g., 493–494). At the other extreme of the continuum, while one might be tempted with Hesiod's small-holder in mind to think in terms of an "individual," it is clear that it is that person's household, not the solitary modern *ego*, which is at issue. As we shall see momentarily, it was the *oikos* which was the locus of the rivalry that visibly played so multi-faceted and corrosive a role in the interpersonal dealings not only of Hesiod's but also of our own classical Attic rural communities. What is at issue here, however, is the larger context of norms, conventions, and social mechanisms within the scope of which such rivalry constituted but one of several modes of interpersonal, or rather interhousehold, relationship.

Aristotle opens his *Politics* with a three-tiered evolutionary structural account of the origin of the city-state: From the *koinonia* of the male and the female and the *koinonia* of the free and slave arises the household (*oikia*) (1.1.6: 1252b); the first *koinonia* made up of several households for the sake of not merely daily wants is the village (*komē*) (1.1.7: 1252b); and the ultimate *koinonia* made up of several villages is the city-state (*polis*) (1.1.8: 1252b). That Aristotle intends a genuinely evolutionary process, as opposed to a mere analysis of a whole into its constituent parts, is shown by his comment that the village seems by nature to be a "colony" (*apoikia*) of the household (1.1.7: 1252b). But, where the household is concerned, we must keep in mind that forces operating in the reverse direction, emanating from both the village and the city-state, played important roles in shaping and sustaining it and in influencing the course of its future development.

Thus the village community itself, through its associational apparatus, could in various ways affect the fortunes of any of its constituent demesman families. By appointing one of its members to the demarchy (less so, in all probability, to the more specialized posts of secretary, treasurer, herald, etc.), it could raise an *oikos* to a position of enhanced authority and visibility. By favoring a *demotes* with the bestowal of rare or valuable honors, it could ennoble a household and even its descendants when the act was permanently commemorated by a publicly visible inscribed stone stele. By coming to the relief of a member in a time of crisis, it could materially affect a deme family's prosperity or even ensure its otherwise threatened survival. By the imposition of its duly authorized sanctions, such as removal from the deme's membership rolls or imposition of a fine, it could inflict that same family with disfranchisement, financial loss, or disgrace.

Beyond the village, the People, too, by their capacity to make and enforce, by the passage of decrees, the laws of the state could, with equal effect, alternately promote or constrict the fortunes of the state's households, every one of which was also a deme's household. Beginning with the domestic legislation of Solon, Athenian law provides several pertinent examples. Sons who had lost their fathers (*orphanoi*) were raised to majority at state expense, when they could begin households of their own.[2] The nubile daughters of impoverished families might be dowered by the state, thereby rescuing them from spinsterhood, helping to preserve the natal household (albeit in the female line), and contributing the wife to a new *oikos* capable of producing "Athenian" sons and daughters under the terms of Pericles' citizenship law.[3] Fathers were required to teach their sons a trade or else forfeit the legally guaranteed right of support by them in their old age, with the consequence that those sons would acquire the vocational means to sustain *oikoi* of their own.[4] Parents (and grandparents) were protected from neglect or abuse by their children, so, if nothing else, they could look forward to shelter, nourishment, and burial (not to mention protection from physical injury), matters of real concern should they continue to reside in their grown children's two or three generation household.[5] The court system stood ready to uphold a law on inheritance that identified legitimate sons, then other consanguineal and affinal relations, as rightful heirs.[6] Legitimacy itself was defined in such a way (birth to a duly betrothed, i.e., married, Athenian father and mother) that the *oikos* enjoyed a virtual monopoly as the sole venue of legitimate reproduction.[7] And so on. Given the urbanocentric manner in which Athenian legal institutions are often presented, it is easy to lose sight of the fact that all of the above interventions applied equally to distant rural households more or less permanently out of everyday contact with the seat of government in the *asty*. Thus the comprehensive modern accounts of the Greek or Athenian family in English, Lacey (1968), Pomeroy (1997), and Patterson (1998), all lack any consideration of the rural *oikos* as a distinct societal or cultural phenomenon. The "families in rural areas" in Cox's recent *Household Interests* are merely topographically grouped prosopographical data compiled with little attention to possibly contrasting urban families.[8] So the question to be confronted now is whether, in what ways, and to what extent, as a consequence (or not) of the operation of the state's laws and edicts, the households of rural Attica resembled or not their better documented urban counterparts.

Standard descriptions collect and analyze available data on betrothal, dowry, and trousseau; residence rules; reproduction; adultery; divorce and remarriage; male and female life course; domestic as well as extradomestic labor; the "retirement" and incorporation into the household of aged parents; old age itself; and other standard sociological topics. At the outset, let it be conceded that we are unable for the most part to ascertain how in detail these categories are to be mapped onto the extraurban communities of the Attic countryside. If documentary evidence is what we are looking for, we are mostly confined to the results of prosopographical study of persons with rural demotics who are known or likely to have maintained residence in the ancestral village. At best, however, these results are generally confined to Davies' liturgical—that is to say, wealthy—families and comprise a stemma, a list of public deme or city offices held, a record of properties, and any appearances in historical narratives, often over lengthy stretches of time. A compilation of this type leaves us far from the middling or lower class households in which we are also interested here; and, in any event, the limitation of the field to holders of *leitourgiai* carries with it a built-in urban bias, since the *asty* and Peiraieus were the scenes of their performance. Nonetheless, significant additional light may be shed on the rural family if we could identify some of the more pervasive factors by the operation of which such households may have come to acquire distinctively rural characteristics:

Marriage patterns. Modern research has underscored ways in which a marriage might be used by a household to gain access to farmlands situated in environmental circumstances unlike its own. Marriage so conceived would constitute (in Thomas Gallant's terminology) a species of "risk-buffering strategy." Athenian marriages outside the home deme were studied by Robin Osborne[9] and, in the train of Osborne's work, by Cheryl Anne Cox.[10] To the extent that access to arable or other agrarian concerns were factors in such marriage choices, rural matrimony would acquire distinctive characteristics over and above the conventions operating in urban settings, especially in terms of courtship, internal household dynamics, and relations between natal and marital deme.

Partible inheritance. The equal division of an estate among legitimate sons[11] might have consequences peculiar to rural settings. Once an estate had been reduced to subsistence dimensions, the presence of a son beyond the one recommended by Hesiod would inevitably result either in the unprofitable division of the land or, in order for at least one of the heirs to make a go of farming, the departure of his brother(s). Given the general inalienability of real property during our period and the resulting shortage of plots for sale, departure might well mean abandoning farming for some other income-producing pursuit. Such consequences would be of a kind or

dimension probably not regularly occurring among larger nonfarming
families in the town, where alternative occupational paths lay open. Disruption of household memberships in a rural village community will have
potentially recurred on a periodic schedule as each new generation of males
arrived at social maturity.

Mobility and visibility of women and children. Given a significant percentage of more or less isolated farmsteads (see chapter 1), but even on the
assumption of significant residential village nucleation, households in rural
environments were certainly not subjected to the same social risks—or
scrutiny—that must have typified compact urban neighborhoods. This
meant that the vigilant custody of females so graphically portrayed by
Athenian urban literature[12] need not have been maintained, at least not so
scrupulously. Thus a speech of Demosthenes records an anecdotal reminiscence of citizen women compelled during the trying times of the Peloponnesian War to become "grape-workers" (*trygetriai*), probably
involving their presence in the fields (57.45; and see below). The speaker of
another oration of Demosthenes mentions citizen women moving freely
between their neighboring country residences (55.23). Comparison of these
reports with the signs of the confinement of urban women preserved in,
say, Lysias's *First Oration*, will suffice to illustrate the difference.

Migration to the urban center. The attractions of the Big City to ruralites, especially the young and male, are a frequent theme of popular literature, especially in later antiquity. The phenomenon is happily subject to
quantification. Thanks to the inclusion in epitaphs of the deceased's demotic, study by Dammsgaard-Madsen of the large number of tombstones
of known provenience has provided clues regarding mobility. The guiding
assumption is that a person will be buried at or near the location of his or
her residence at time of death. Thus the disproportionate incidence of the
burial in urban areas of people with rural demotics demonstrates a pronounced pattern of rural migration to the *asty* (or Peiraieus), while a correspondingly low incidence of urban demotics on tombstones of rural
provenience seems to preclude an opposing outmigration.[13] The effects on
the rural household are not documented, but it is certain that the ongoing
and more or less final departure of villagers, as with the workings of partible inheritance, would have left its mark upon the morale and attitudes of
those who remained behind in the village community.

Agrarian traditions, attitudes, and values. While the distinctive features of rural culture will be reserved for discussion in chapter 5, it is appropriate to underscore here the absence in rural Attica of virtually all of

the hallmark fixtures of high urban culture. Positively put, we might characterize as distinctively rural a sense of closeness to the natural world exemplified in an interest in fertility and reproduction; a desire for economic self-sufficiency; an abhorrence but grudging acknowledgment of the necessity of manual work; an identification with a historical agrarian past; an agriculturally based but ultimately all-pervading conservatism; and a spirituality rooted in the forces affecting plant, animal, and human growth and a desire to understand and control them. A household animated by such concerns was a long way from its counterpart in town, where the intimate connection with the soil had been ruptured and food, some of it already processed, could be purchased in a market; where for self-sufficient *autarkeia* had often been substituted a dependence on disbursals of public moneys; where the drudgery of manual farm work had given way to softer urbane pursuits such as sitting on a jury, voting in an assembly, or even attending the theater; where identification with a distant "national" war of defense was regarded as a mark of an outmoded mindset; where traditional institutions and ideas stemming from the practice of agriculture were regularly called into question and ears were attuned to newfangled innovations born of economy and opportunism; and where divinities, if recognized at all, had lost many of their original natural world or agrarian associations. Such is the profound cultural cleft which we must understand if we are to imagine the Attic rural family in its cognitive and spiritual as well as in its environmental, physical, and demographic dimensions.

Philotimia and Rivalry

With this, at least rudimentary, grasp of the citizen family (and, with the addition of slaves, household) in its rural Attic situation, we can begin to explore that family in terms of its external relations. The ecological studies, such Thomas Gallant's *Risk and Survival in Ancient Greece* (1990), which departs from the premise that the household was threatened by alteration of its environment, particularly where such change involved uncertainty, are broadly concerned with all manner of "risk"—climatic, biological, social, and political—and the agrarian's strategic responses. Robin Osborne's path-breaking study of classical Attica (1985b) explored various economic and social linkages between individuals, and so between the communities of which they were members, including, in the social dimension, kin, neighbors, and demesmen. Needless to say, these two con-

trasting studies, and numerous others like them, speak directly to the
question of how our rural Attic *oikoi* interacted with one another at the
immediate boundary, village, and Attica-wide levels. But for the purposes
of understanding the as it were "culture" of the rural household, perhaps
an even more promising, but as yet unpursued, lead is represented by
David Whitehead's searching study of *philotimia*, the "love of honor."[14]
Philotimia is frequently encountered in honorific decrees as a quality ascribed to the honorand and instanced as the basis, in whole or part, for
the bestowal of the accolade. The term is relevant here, for it occurs in
many—precisely 32, by Whitehead's count[15]—of the honorific decrees of
the demes. According to the analysis, the honorand praised for his *philotimia* had redirected his otherwise self-serving pursuit of *timē* away from
himself and towards the collective benefit of his fellow deme-members.[16]
But the study leaves unanswered a pressing question relevant to our present concerns. What was the particular content of this raw or untutored
"love of honor" prior to its successful harnessing by the communal energies of the deme-association?[17] Still more specifically, what was the particular content of that *philotimia* in a rural setting?

It is surely by no accident that the narrative thread around which
Hesiod weaves his *Works and Days* concerns a rivalry—in this case, between
the author himself and his brother, Perses, over the division of their patri-
monial inheritance.[18] But the fact that Hesiod and Perses are brothers
should not be allowed to obscure the point that, with the division of the
estate, they will (or already have) become potential heads of separate
households. Furthermore, this nascent rivalry between *oikoi* is artfully exemplified on the mythical plane by the tale of the two Strifes positioned by
Hesiod at the beginning proper of his poem, following the obligatory invocation of the Muses (lines 1–10). Note that this *agōn* does not, as it might
well have, pit Strife against Harmony or Concord, but rather one form of
strife against another. For Hesiod, that Strife operates in the world is a
foregone conclusion. What is at issue is which, the Good or the Bad, will
prevail in any given situation. Bad Strife fosters evil war and battle and is
loved by no man (lines 14–16). But the Good, the daughter of Night and
Zeus, is much better for men: "She awakens even the idle to work. For a
man becomes eager to work when he looks upon another—a rich man who
hastens to plow and plant and to put his house in good order. Neighbor
vies with the neighbor who hastens after wealth. This Strife is good for
mortals" (lines 20–24). Emphasis as much as content underlies the meaning of this passage. That the full five lines should be devoted to exemplify-

ing the Good Strife specifically with reference to farming, while rivalry of potter and potter, of craftsman and craftsman, of beggar and beggar, and of singer and singer—none exclusively rural or urban—is compressed into but two (lines 24–25), unmistakably points up the Good Strife's distinctively agrarian environment. Nor can this inference be minimized on the ground that Perses' own involvement in agriculture (which is several times in evidence throughout the poem) left Hesiod with no choice, for the tale of the Two Strifes is shown by its position and by the absence of any reference to Perses or any other particular personage to be a freestanding piece of gnomic wisdom. For Hesiod, farming and rivalry are inextricably intertwined.

When we turn to historical Attica under the democracy, it is not difficult to find examples of rivalry in rural settings and to identify their underlying causes. At an early date the Athenian tyrant Peisistratos instituted *dikastai kata demous* ("judges for the villages")—"and he personally often went out into the country, monitoring and reconciling disputants, in order that they not come into town and thereby neglect their work," according to *AthPol*'s account (16.5). The nature of these disputes is not specified, but attractive possibilities are at hand. Sources of contention specific to a rural setting would include diversion of water, pilferage of crops, theft of animals or other farm property, polluting of wells, or failure to return borrowed tools or other goods. Naturally, too, the contesting of the division of a rural estate by the sibling heirs Hesiod and Perses could not have been an uncommon occurrence, since, as an estate neared the threshold of subsistence productivity, even a slight imbalance might make the difference between survival and failure. We cannot be sure what mode of division is to be imagined in Hesiod's instance, but it is certainly possible that it concerned a source of conflict frequently encountered in historical sources: the boundaries between neighboring properties.

Quarrels concerning property lines were initially conditioned by the absence of adequate surveying methods and procedures for formally recording and preserving whatever agreements or determinations had been made. Supporting this surmise is the fact that while markers (*horoi*) in comparatively large numbers have survived and are in many cases, as indicated by the inscriptions they carry, of known function, very few, if any, can be assuredly identified as defining the boundaries of private properties, urban or rural, residential or agrarian.[19] True, possible candidates may be found among the so-called rupestral ("rock-cut") inscriptions of Attica, but most of the examples thus far discovered are subject to competing interpretations.[20] Be that as it may, it is self-evident that when a boundary is not per-manently marked, and is moreover subject to incursion, obliteration, or other disturbance by farming activity, conflict is the likely outcome. If the board of *horistai* mentioned in a mid-fourth-century inscription of the deme Peiraieus (*IG* II² 1177, line 22) was concerned, as the root meaning of their title would suggest, with boundaries, we would have one good ex-ample of an institutional response to the problem at the deme level. To make matters worse, even when the location of the line was not subject to question, it remained a frequent locus of disagreement. Take, for example, the dispute narrated in the 55th speech of Demosthenes, concerned with the construction near the line of a wall which had allegedly caused runoff damage to the land of his neighbor.[21] Precisely in order to deal with dis-putes of this kind, Solon's laws had set out restrictions on a property owner's use of his land at or near a boundary. Plutarch's *Life* of Solon cites statutes limiting the planting of trees, the digging of pits and trenches, and the placement of beehives (23.6). When, in the absence of a public well, the owner had dug one on his own property and found no water, he was to have limited access to his neighbor's well (23.5). Self-evidently, such laws were established early, and presumably remained in force, because there was a need for them. At all events, apprehensions of these kinds might well be regarded as providing an additional contributing motivation, in addi-tion to those mentioned in chapter 1, for exercising the option of farmstead residence, to the extent that one's presence on the land will have greatly facilitated surveillance.

Viewed in a wider context of general Greek attitudes, furthermore, strife among rural property owners or other residents is just what we should expect. These are the people who made the *agōn* the organizational principle for some of their highest cultural pursuits, who competed with one another for *kūdos* and *timē* while discounting internal and noncom-petitive forms of achievement, and who found themselves sometimes fatally susceptible to the destructive workings of envy. Rivalry in short was all-pervasive, but for present purposes it will be well to keep in mind that the context of its operation was limited. That limited context was the funda-mental unit of property ownership and social organization and the mid-point on the Greek cultural continuum, the *oikos*. At the one extreme of that continuum, individualism as a mode of personal conduct had not yet made an appearance in this society, unless anomalously among an urban educated elite. At the other, the village-association was, as we shall see, as much a forum for the operation of a thinly institutionalized form of per-

sonal patronage as an organization possessed of significant corporate co-
hesion.[22] Rivalry in this setting inevitably meant rivalry between households.

It is here, I suggest, that we should situate the *philotimia* that, were
it not for the village-association's (as well as, at a higher level, the state's)
seemingly successful efforts to redirect it towards the accomplishment of
communal ends, would probably have made a peaceful and orderly community life impossible. Honor (*kūdos*, *timē*) could be derived from a farm
or pasture as easily as from one's illustrious pedigree or political career,
and the transgression of a property line, diversion of a stream, or theft of
a stock animal could as easily serve as a challenge to that honor as, in
modern rural Greece, such an act would challenge a man's *philotimo*. The
synonymy of the ancient and modern terms is no more accidental than is
the fact that in both cases it is a rural community which is often, if not always, the scene of its operation. Perhaps a better term, from a generally
Greek perspective, might be *philon(e)ikia*, a word which, as the *LSJ*[9] entry illustrates, confounds, and seemingly identifies, the notions of *neikos*
("quarrel") and *nikē* ("victory"), collapsing into a single lexical item the
contrasting negative and positive dimensions of rivalry. Even so, if, with
Whitehead, the concept was to be transmuted into a praiseworthy communal virtue, *philotimia* was obviously a far more suitable candidate. For
the same reason, the decrees fail even so much as to hint at the nature of
these household-centered rivalries, since to rehearse corrosive and destructive conflicts might serve only to reawaken and perpetuate them.
But, if I am right, it was the divisive real-world manifestations of the Hesiodic *neikos* which lay behind and animated a deme-association's repeated
decisions to bestow honors and rewards upon the *demotai* in recognition
of their "love of honor."

Patronage: Customary Usage and Institutional Form

RISK, THE RURAL HOUSEHOLD, AND SOURCES OF ASSISTANCE

A household sustained entirely by the production of small-holder farming
maintained a precarious existence. Even a slight shortfall might precipitate
a crisis the likely outcomes of which were, if suitable precautions had not
previously been taken, basically two: either the sale of the property and
the abandonment of farming or, potentially equally ruinous and perhaps

no more than a delaying of the inevitable, the incurring of debt on the security of the land. But what were these "suitable precautions"? Hesiod, in
the *Works and Days*, speaks directly to the point of how the agrarian
should deal with the onset of "need":

> Summon the friendly one to a feast, but let the enemy go. Above all, summon the
> one who lives near you, for if anything does happen around the place (*enchorion*),
> neighbors come ungirt, but relations by marriage (*peoi*) gird themselves. A bad
> neighbor is a disaster, just as the good one is a good blessing. He whose lot is a
> good neighbor is allotted a prize. Were it not for a bad neighbor, not even an ox
> would die. Have a fair measure be given by your neighbor, and pay back fairly,
> with the same measure or, if you can, better, in order that, if you are in need
> (*chrēizōn*, 351), you may find him sufficient later.
>
> Do not profit by base means; base profits are equivalent to ruin. Be friends
> with the friendly one, and approach the one who approaches you. Give to him
> who gives, but do not give to him who does not give. (342–354)

Multiple lines of defense against the demands of "need" earn mention in Hesiod's prescription. We might expect the first to be one's own
immediate family, but the man whose quarrel with his brother Perses affords the poem's *mise-en-scène* and whose notorious misogyny might unfavorably color his feelings towards any female members of his family
predictably disappoints any such expectation. True, wife and children are
part of the plan (376–380, 399–400, 695–705, 785–787), but the nubile *gynē*
is represented as a scheming seductress with designs on the male reader's
granary (373–375) who may roast her man alive and bring him to an un-
timely old age (698–705), while the unmarried *parthenikē* stays indoors
with her mother on a winter's day, oiling her body and sleeping in an inner room (519–526). Not a family member but rather a slave woman will
follow the oxen and put everything in good order at home (lines
405–407). As for males, one son will bring an increase of wealth in the
home, but a second will be a liability (376–377), so little additional man-
power or resources are to be found here. Nor can the agrarian, says Hesiod, count on timely assistance from his wife's relations since they, unlike
neighbors, must don appropriate dress before responding to the householder's summons. The *peoi* will not or cannot, like a near neighbor, drop
a hoe or leave the dough unkneaded in order to respond to an inlaw's
plea, but Hesiod does not tell us the reason for their dalliance. The distance to be traveled might be (and indeed has been) suggested, were it
not for the author's conflicting recommendation that the farmer wed a

girl who lives nearby (698–701). Perhaps Hesiod regarded the bonds produced by marriage to be relatively weak ones. Whatever the reason, the
preferred lines of defense reflect not consanguineal or matrimonial relations but propinquity of domicile, a principle signaled by the words "anything . . . around the place" (*chrēm' enchōrion*, line 344). It is on these
that Hesiod concentrates, for once the *peoi* have been dismissed, the text
is explicitly or implicitly concerned with the *geitones* through the beginning of a new train of thought at line 369. But because they are not, like
family members or relations by marriage, bound by culturally validated
and generally recognized ties of kinship, the farmer must assiduously cultivate reciprocating strands of obligation through the exchange of favors.

All this of course applies to the author's Askra near Thespiai in Boiotia two centuries prior to the beginning of the classical era at Athens. How
much of Hesiod's agrarian social structure fits what we know about our rural Attic demes under the democracy? One approach to an answer might
be to reopen the entire question of crisis and response across historical
Greece as a whole on a rigorous modern academic scientific footing. Notable examples are three modern Greece-wide comprehensive studies, Peter Garnsey's *Famine and Food Supply in the Graeco-Roman World:
Responses to Risk and Crisis* (1988), Thomas W. Gallant's *Risk and Survival
in Ancient Greece: Reconstructing the Rural Domestic Economy* (1991), and
R. Sallares's *The Ecology of the Ancient Greek World* (1991). But since our
focus is confined to a single specific societal regime, it will be sufficient, as
a prelude to further study, simply to interrogate the primary evidential
record of that regime. As we do so, however, a methodological point, representing a widening of the scope of the terms "risk" and "crisis," seems
to be in order: that these challenges faced by the rural agrarian need not
necessarily be the consequence of some unforeseen disruption of normal
processes and routines but could, and will here, also embrace the periodic
and so predictable fluctuations of the rural, and especially agrarian, calendar. Above all, the insistent demands of a harvest represent, in the context
of the resources of a small-holder household, a risk or crisis of sorts, especially with regard to the labor required to bring that harvest to a successful conclusion. And it is precisely on this head that the generally meager
source materials seem sufficient to point the way to a new approach. Let
us, then, return to Attica and take up one at a time the potential sources
of assistance available to our rural agrarian.

Despite Hesiod's generally negative indications (only a single son is
made available by him), the members of the immediate family are a natu-

ral supplementary labor supply, beginning with females. On this head, the
poet's model of general inactivity on the part of household members seems
to be confirmed in Attica, for the use of women for agricultural labor is
only fleetingly attested. The speaker of Demosthenes' *Against Euboulides*,
addressing the general subject of the servile acts free people are constrained
by poverty to perform, instances, as previously noted, the many town
women (*astai gynaikes*) who during the Peloponnesian War served as wet-
nurses, hired laborers, and "grape-workers" (*trygetriai*) (57.45). Old Comedy alludes to the singing of "a woman hulling barley" (Aristophanes,
Clouds 1358) and of "women winnowing grain" (Aristophanes, *Thesmopho-
riazousai* II, *PCG* III², no. 352 [339]; Nikochares, *Herakles Choregos, PCG*
VII, no. 9 [6]). Female agricultural laborers are not infrequently indicated
by specialized terms for performers of agricultural tasks, such as, in addition to the *trygetria*, the *erithos* (day-laborer), *theristria* (mower or reaper),
kalametria (gatherer of stalks, gleaner), *poastria* (weeder or grass-cutter),
and *phryganistria* (firewood-gatherer).[23] But, in several cases where these
terms are employed, it is uncertain whether we are dealing with free members of citizen households corresponding to Demosthenes' *astai gynaikes*.
Beyond Greece, Plato regards as barbarous the Thracian custom of allowing women to work in the fields (*Laws* 7.805e), and Aristotle, with reference to no particular place, echoes Demosthenes' speaker when he
observes that the poor (*aporoi*), for want of slaves, are forced to use women
and children as servants (*Pol.* 6.5.13: 1323a; cf. 1.1.5–6: 1252b on woman as
slave). Fitton Brown collected the sources on female agricultural labor
from Homer on, and explained the small part played by women in ancient
Greek agriculture in terms of three causes: (1) people resided in town,
where womenfolk remained while their husbands commuted to and from
the fields; (2) given the absence in ancient Greece of labor-intensive crops
such as cotton, rice, and tobacco, their labor was not needed; and (3) a culturally imposed deep-seated protectiveness towards women.[24] But the assumption of village residence has been challenged in chapter 1; the present
argument, prompted by Hesiod's positing of "need," presupposes a need
for additional labor, whatever the range or requirements of ancient Greek
field crops; protectiveness is rendered nugatory by the acceptance of widely
scattered farmstead residences. The inside vs. outside division of space by
gender might be invoked, although, again, in our rural setting less risk
would be incurred when a female ventured out of doors.[25] Rather, females
were probably normally preoccupied with nutritive and productive activities within or near the *oikia* (food processing, meal preparation, cloth and

garment manufacture, child-rearing, tending of gardens and stock, direction of slaves), wherein seclusion, though present, was only incidental in the rural context.[26]

So with children of the citizen household. According to Mark Golden's research, positive instances are confined to Lysias's report (20.11) that the young Phrynichos had to tend sheep while a wealthier boy was away at school in town, a dubious fragment of an unknown play of a comic poet about a boy (or slave?, Greek *pais*) shooing hens (Plato Comicus, *PCG* VII, fr. 293), a similar scene painted on a pitcher, a forensic reference to a free boy from Pellēnē put to work in a mill (Dinarchos, *Against Demosthenes* 23), and the uncertain situation of Knemon's daughter in Menander's *Dyskolos* (lines 333–334).[27] Plato's earlier utopian plan called for children to be sent into the fields to work (*Republic* 7.540e-541a), but there is little reason to find here a reflection of contemporary conditions in Attica. Under ordinary circumstances, such a paucity of positive evidence could easily be explained away with the usual arguments regarding the proclivities of urban writers, the restricted content of inscriptions, the invisibility of the nonfranchised, and so on, but Aristotle's remark about the poor being forced to use their children (and women) in place of slaves rather suggests that a negative cultural ideal is at work here. Besides, does not Theophrastos's *agroikos*, presumably typifying the Attic farmer, distrust his *oikeioi* (4.6), including presumably his own family members?

Slaves themselves, for which Aristotle's women and children (and even his ox, *Politics* 1.5.6: 1252b) are substitutes, pose major uncertainties. Michael Jameson reopened the question of agricultural slavery on the general grounds that the majority of Athenian households had one or more servile members and that slavery cannot be separated from agriculture. The increased labor requirements of intensification, diversification, and specialization were most satisfactorily met by adding a slave to the family work force (versus an increase in the farmer's own labor, or increase in the size of his own family, or hired labor) and, above and beyond the economic benefits, slave workers allowed the citizen farmer to more fully exercise his civic privileges. Slaves will always, with Jameson, have been available for agricultural work even if otherwise nominally dedicated as *oiketai* to household tasks: "if we have trouble in identifying 'agricultural slaves' in Athens it may be in part because they are everywhere. . . ." "Every Athenian was an actual or potential farmer . . . and every Athenian slave was an actual or potential farm-hand."[28] But soon after Jameson's position was seconded and reinforced by G. E. M. de Ste. Croix in 1981, the assumptions and arguments supporting it were subjected to sustained criticism by Ellen Meiksins Wood.[29] Since the debate cannot be reopened here, it will have to suffice to acknowledge with a few representative examples the explicit, however sparse, sources supporting Jameson and de Ste. Croix.[30]

Reflecting on the blessings of peace, the chorus and *koryphaios* in Aristophanes' *Peace* drop the names typical of slaves in an agricultural setting: Thratta (lines 1138), Syra (1146), and Manes (whom Syra is to call in from the *chorion*, 1146); and Trygaios later mentions the weighing out of figs for the *oiketai* "in the field" (1246–1249). Karion is one among "my *oiketai*" belonging to the farmer Chremylos in the *Ploutos* (lines 26–27). The speaker of Lysias's seventh oration identifies workers on his land as *therapontes . . . douloi . . .* and *oiketai* (16–17) and again as *therapontes* (43). At [Demosthenes] 47.53, the phrase is "the *oiketai*," at Demosthenes 55.31, "my *douloi*." The *agroikos* of Theophrastos's caricature of rusticity confides in his *oiketai* on the most important matters (4.6). By contrast with this direct testimony, inscriptions identify only persons who had probably or certainly *previously been* slaves, such as the metics of the Phyle decree, *IG* II[2] 10 and 2403, and the parties named in the manumission lists, *IG* II[2] 1554–1559+, among whom are identifiable *georgoi* and a *kepouros* (Phyle decree) and *georgoi* and *ampelourgoi* (manumission lists).[31] Jameson found here "exceptionally independent agriculturalists," whose presence "is not inconsistent with the existence of a great many more less specialized and less responsible slaves, much of whose work as that of most Athenians was on the land."[32] Nor is this weak conclusion helped by the fact that the security *horoi* recording *andrapoda* pair them with industrial establishments but never with land[33] or by our uncertainty about what proportion of the 20,000 reported by Thucydides (7.27.5) to have run away during the Dekeleian War were agricultural laborers.[34] So, while there can be no question regarding the existence of agricultural slave labor, the matter of the frequency of its use remains very much unresolved.

Servile labor, whatever motivated its use, will have imposed major financial burdens upon the citizen farmer, some of which could be avoided by opting instead for the retention of paid labor on a temporary basis.[35] Yet evidence for the hiring of agricultural labor is, as for slavery, predictably meager and scattered, however unambiguous in its import: once again the *astai gynaikes* grape-workers (Demosthenes 57.45); olive-pickers (*elaologoi*: Aristophanes, *Wasps* 712); reapers (*theristai*: Xenophon, *Hiero* 6.10; Demosthenes, 18.51); threshers (*aloōntes*: Xenophon, *Oikonomikos* 18.2; *epalōstai*: op. cit, 18.5); winnowers (*likmōntes*: op. cit., 18.2); and unspecified workers drawing wages (Xenophon, *Memorabilia* II 8.1–6, *Oikonomikos* 20.16; Plato, *Politicus* 290a; Isaios, 5.39; Demosthenes, 18.51; 53.20; Theophrastos, *Charakteres* 4.6). Since, as the *nomina agentis* indicate, most of these were seasonal workers engaged in the several stages of bringing in a grain crop, they fit the scenario of the periodic "crisis" posed by the harvest under examination here. But their use was subject to two major constraints. Such work for pay, in the case of free persons, was regarded as servile (see Demosthenes, 57.46, where the tasks performed by the "town women," including the grape-workers, are styled *doulika pragmata*) or at least befitting free but impoverished *thetes* (Plato, *Politicus* 290a; Isokrates, 14.48). The other constraint was of course financial, and it is difficult to believe that those Athenians who were driven to use their wives and children in the place of slaves or for whom an ox had to serve for an *oiketes* (and who *ex hypothesi* owned no slaves) were nonetheless able to hire workers at the regularly recurring times of peak demand on the agricultural schedule. Thus, on one end, there was resistance to hiring out oneself (or one's family members) for agricultural work and, on the other, a presumable (but unquantifiable) inability to retain such laborers when they were available.

Beyond the *oikos*, Hesiod's *peoi* are neatly illustrated in Cox's study of Athenian families contracting more than one alliance for their kinswomen by marrying their daughters into the same outside deme. Repeated choice of the same deme does suggest the sort of "risk-buffering" strategizing that is the subject of Gallant's *Risk and Survival*, particularly whenever the two demes in question were sufficiently widely separated to present contrasting constellations of risk factors, climatic, biological, social, or otherwise, and so offer insurance against local hazards. However, the fact that Cox could find, with the help of Davies' *Athenian Propertied Families*, only four positive instances of the phenomenon suggests its relative rarity, although in the case of Plato's locally endogamous betrothing of his sister, the strong possibility that the motive behind the union was the consolidation of neighboring landed estates does situate it within the realm of agricultural strategizing.[36] From the Attic grave stelai Osborne tabulated 131 instances of inter-deme marriage versus only 32 intra-deme (although 80 would have to be added if the absence of demotic meant matrimony within the deme), so the creation of exogamous affinal links was obviously common, but Osborne's own discussion illustrates how difficult it is to ascertain whether kinship, locality, or still some other consideration was the underlying motivation.[37]

What of Hesiod's *geitones* who come right away "ungirt"? However plausible the mechanics and psychology presented by the poet and however well supported by parallel traditional agrarian regimes (such as preindustrial United States), mutual assistance of the kind Hesiod seems to envision has, according to Alison Burford's study of land and labor in the Greek world, left virtually no trace.[38] In contrast with the mutual reciprocity so assiduously to be cultivated by Hesiod's reader, the actual state of affairs is perhaps better represented by the potential for discord underlying Solon's above-mentioned prescriptions regarding the placement near boundaries of beehives, trees, trenches and pits, and wells (Plutarch, *Solon* 23.6) and by the courtroom disputes preserved in Demosthenes' 53rd and 55th orations. Note, too, that Theophrastos's *agroikos* distrusts his *philoi* as well as well as his *oikeioi* (4.6). True, a neighbor might prevent burglars from carrying off the homeowner's son (Demosthenes, 47.49–61, with 61 for the *geitōn*); or one man and his wife might befriend the neighbor man and his wife, the two women paying visits to one another (Demosthenes, 55.23–24); or a neighbor might become so fast a friend as to be entrusted with the management of an estate during the owner's absence (Demosthenes, 53.4), but none of these anecdotes points to the exchange of farm labor on a periodic basis. Presumably, the factor obstructing cooperation will have been the inveterate *autarkeia* endemic to Hellenic culture and the divisive individual *philotimia*, examined earlier, which served to reinforce it.

If one's citizen farming neighbors were not available as a resource, the same may not have been true of the local free but noncitizen labor pool represented by the metics. That some metics, despite the legal disability debarring them from ownership of "land and house," engaged in farming is demonstrated by the occupational titles appended to the names of "the metics" (almost entirely restored, line 4) in the Phyle decree, *IG* II² 10 and 2403, republished with the addition of new fragments by Daphne Hereward (1952; *SEG* 12.84). Jameson counted ten *georgoi* out of 66 identifiable professions, plus a single *kepouros* (gardener) and a single *phytourgos* (nurseryman).[39] From the manumission lists belonging to the decade ca. 330–320, republished (or restudied) by David Lewis (1959), *IG* II² 1553–1561, 1564–1578, plus a new fragment from the Agora (*SEG* 18.36–50), Jameson counted 85 names with a preserved or restorable profession, of which 11 are *georgoi* and two *ampelourgoi* (vine-dressers).[40] (Additionally, at Lysias 7.10 we learn of a metic who had rented land following his manumission). Apart from the fact of manumission, the precise newly acquired status of these farm-workers is not revealed in the inscriptions, but Burford attractively suggests that they were once chattel-slave farm laborers now elevated to metic standing.[41] Perhaps surprisingly, given the nature of their work, the preponderance of these workers are identified as residing in urban demes, a datum that bears importantly on the present discussion, for town-based laborers would not have been within easy reach of most rural demes on a regular basis, although an annual harvest-time exodus with sleeping in the fields for the duration, say, remains a distinct possibility for a town-dwelling temporary labor force.

However that may be, the matter of metic residence clearly requires renewed attention, for while metics are usually typified as engaged in urban pursuits and while Whitehead's tabulation of metics' demes does indeed reveal a very large concentration in urban and suburban Athens and Peiraieus, a substantial extramural population remains and must be accounted for. For the 366 *metoikoi* of recorded deme-affiliation, the distribution by intramural or extramural deme according to my system of zones[42] follows:

Intramural including Peiraieus: Koile 4, Kollytos 42, Kydathenaion 31, Melite 75, Skambonidai 28, plus Peiraieus 69.

Inner Zone outside the walls: Agryle 6, Alopeke 31, Ankyle 1, Cholargos 1, Diomeia 1, Epkephisia 1, Keiriadai 16, Kerameis 5, Kolonos 1, Korydallos 1, Lakiadai 2, Leukonoion 1, Perithoidai 4, Phaleron 2, Thymaitadai 1, and Xypete 1.

Middle Zone: Acharnai 1, Aigilia 3, Eleusis 10, Hagnous 1, Iphistiadai 4, Kephisia 1?, Lamptrai 1?, Oa 1, Oe 1, Paiania 2?, Pergase 2, and Sphettos 1.

Outer Zone: Anaphlystos 1, Myrrhinoutta 1, Phrearrhoi 1, Rhamnous 1?, Semachidai 1, Sounion 2, and Thorikos 3.

If we overlook the several cases where the source does not distinguish between two homonymous demes (viz. Inner Zone: Agryle and Ankyle; Middle Zone: Lamptrai and Paiania), the proportion of demes with at least one recorded metic by zone is as follows: Inner Zone, 22 of 40; Middle Zone, 12 of 42; and Outer Zone, 7 of 40. When the extramural demes from the Inner Zone (16 of the 22) are included, the number of rural demes comes to 35; and to this total must be added several cases of rural Attic but non-deme residence in Kynosarges, Oropos, Pentele, and Salamis. Thus, while it is undeniable that there was a decided concentration of the resident alien population in urban demes, the extramural presence, if we count by demes, was appreciable, even after allowance is made for probable nonagricultural settings in Eleusis or Thorikos. The imbalance in *total number* of metics per deme could for all we know reflect the proportionally better documentation of the urban areas. So, clearly, metics were on hand in rural demes, but, if occupationally involved in agriculture, just what did they do? The temptation is strong to associate them with the *metikoi* and freedmen listed in the inscriptions studied by Jameson and to suppose that many were *georgoi*, gardeners, nurserymen, vine-dressers, and the like, differing only in the locations of their residences. That is to say, these laborers probably did *not* perform the tasks relating to the harvest performed by hired hands (mower, thresher, winnower, etc.), and for this reason they too are unlikely candidates for the crisis-related supplementary labor sources we are in search of.

PERSONAL PATRONAGE IN RURAL ATTICA?

Because the "needs" alluded to by Hesiod might take on a multiplicity of forms, the "crisis" presented by the increased demand for seasonal labor provides at best a test case, but it is a significant one, because such extraordinary demand was confronted by the ordinary run of Attic farms, and a consequential one, because the maneuver that could bring in the harvest could also *a fortiori* prove useful in the event of an unforeseen sudden calamity. Rather, the question that my foregoing discussion has raised is whether any of these mechanisms, singly or in combination, would have sufficed to secure the small-holder in the face of change, whether predictable or not. True, certain kinds of social acts are bound never to be recorded, and in the present case, to judge from what traces have reached us, a key factor will have been whether or not the parties in question ever entered into the sort of litigation that might have become the subject of forensic oratory. Nonetheless, a strong impression is left that the sources of assistance so far considered were either culturally disqualified or insufficiently utilized, due to cost, availability, or other factor, so as not to afford adequate protection. But one additional source, one neglected by Hesiod in consequence of his focus on the individual "friend," remains: the local village *qua* community.

A farmer's fellow villagers were probably in most cases, since they were not bound by the obligations imposed by descent, marriage, or a shared property line, relative outsiders, or even enemies to the extent that the destructive workings of *philotimia* had resulted in alienation or active

hostility. Yet whatever might have been the, as it were, normal state of affairs for these Attic villagers, there is, thanks to Whitehead's work on the
Attic demes, a strong indication that rivalry and animosity had been over-
lain by an institutionalized form of friendship, for his study of the narratives concerning Attic demespeople revealed the "semantic overlap" of
philos and *demotes*, "friend" and "demesman." [43] Thus, just as the contrac-
tion of a rural marriage may have reflected each party's consideration of the
other's environmental situation and just as relations between farming
neighbors, according to Hesiod's prescriptions, were to be a matter of
out and out favor-exchanging pragmatism, "friendship" in its rurally-
conditioned incarnation could likewise have constituted a response to the
hazards besetting the agrarian's existence.

Since Hesiod was unable to resolve the conflicts plaguing his relationships with his brother and inferentially with any female family members implicitly targeted by his stinging pronouncements, it is hardly surprising that
he also seems to have failed to exploit the resources of his community. To
the contrary, he expresses his enmity for "the gift-eating *basileis*" (lines
38–39) who threaten to favor Perses in the dispute over the division of the
estate and, personal animus aside, he is hostile to the village on cultural
grounds (if, that is, the village is implied by the blacksmith's shop at lines
493–495). Not so his brother. Presumably it is Perses who is offering the
"gifts" to "the gift-eating *basileis*" and from this it follows, nothwithstanding his brother's negative characterization of the situation, that Perses
at least has established a significant linkage, founded on reciprocity, between a household and the larger community. So, if only indirectly, the
Works and Days does preserve a memory of a specific individual's seeking
security through a reciprocal exchange relation with his fellow villagers.

But the cultivation of bonds of mutual obligation and reciprocity with
the people residing in one's own immediate community—whether family
members, affines, or neighbors—was a strategy by its very nature subject
to constricting, even self-defeating, limitations. Relatives, particularly consanguineal relatives but probably often affinal ones as well, the occupants
of farms adjoining or not far from a farmer's own small holding, and the
citizens and others that comprised the population of a rural village or ham-
let—all, given the small topographic scale with which we are here dealing,
would have tended to share the same constellation of environmental risk
factors, climatic, political, cultural, and so on. The same crisis that threatened the typical owner-operator of a typically small arable plot in all probability threatened his kin, neighbors, and fellow villagers with equally great

severity. Drought, hailstorms, insect or fungus attacks, and enemy invasion provide obvious examples of the built-in limitations of the strategy. Expressed in societal terms, dangers of these kinds uniformly threatened every inhabitant of the immediate region who was situated on the same horizontal socioeconomic stratum. For this fundamental reason, it was vitally important, as the ecological studies emphasize, for the rural small-holder to seek out and nurture a complementary set of vertical ties of reciprocity with those higher up the ladder of material prosperity, social standing, and political influence. And the evidence from Attica that, in contrast with the steady movement from rural communities to the urban areas, very few citizens seem to have relocated from one rural community to another rural community[44] strongly suggests that it was to his immediate surroundings that a rural villager looked for such "subsistence crisis insurance."

But before we can consider further this possibility, we must clear the air on a vitally crucial point—the point of socioeconomic differentiation within the village community. Acknowledgment of the presence of fellow villagers significantly more prosperous than others would have been, until relatively recently, unexceptionable and noncontroversial, but recent discussions of the comparative dimensions of farm holdings at Athens require a brief reassertion of the reality of a substantial stratification of landed wealth. Tabulation of the recorded sizes of Athenian farms by Burford has shown two things: one, the probability that most farms were in the range of 60 plethra or less; and two, that while several estates two to three times this size are recorded, no single estate is known with certainty to have exceeded 300 plethra.[45] Factors contributing to this state of affairs include the fragmentation effect of inheritance, in combination with the important additional detail, noted by Burford, that 55 plethra happens to be the smallest area that it is economically feasible to work with a yoke of oxen, the preferred complement of draught animal in use from Hesiod onwards.[46]

It is a striking fact that this range is in close agreement with the philosophers' recommendation that the largest estate be no more than four times (Plato, *Laws* 5. 744e–745a) or five times (Aristotle, *Politics* 2.4.2: 1266b [cf. 2.3.8: 1265b], citing Plato in the *Laws*) larger than the smallest. The prescriptions of these two residents of Athens may reflect, consciously or not, the prevailing conditions of their daily experience. From an ideological perspective, the data invite an evaluation in the light of the proposition that it is precisely variation in farmers' arable holdings that contributes decisively to the character, hierarchical or otherwise, of a state's sociopolitical regime. What would the result of such an evaluation be? Astonishingly, these same data have been adduced by Victor Hanson in the service of an egalitarianism rooted ultimately in an allegedly relatively uniform landed property regime.[47] While it is not possible here to weigh all the varied evidence and arguments (much of it applying elsewhere than to classical Athens) on which his conclusion depends, the question of size may be addressed. Yes, we may grant to Hanson, the approach is attractive to the historian taking into account the sharply contrasting case of ancient Rome and of other preindustrial societies and, for that matter, later hellenistic and Roman imperial Greece, but the comparison remains one of relative significance only. For one thing, mere acreage alone, as Hanson himself would be the first to concede, does not settle one way or the other the issue of value, for variations in quality of land, such as fertility and depth of soil, vulnerability to predation (fungal, insect, human, and otherwise), proximity to markets, and so on, must be considered. But even granting for the sake of argument the usual "all else being equal," it remains true that a factor of four or five, where relations between land owners are concerned, is a substantial variation, particularly if we assume, as we must, that those at the lower end of the spectrum are operating at the break-even level. When the *autourgos* independent farmer is faced with a crisis, chances are that his fellow villager with a farm four or five times the size of his own will possess the resources not only to weather the storm but also to provide relief for those less fortunate than himself. And this is not even to consider the strong likelihood that owners of the larger estates generally possessed wealth disproportionately greater than comparison of acreages might suggest. The three largest known estates were owned by Phainippos, son of Philostratos, of Kolonai (*PA* 13978; see *APF* 14734, with pp. 553–554 on the estate); Alkibiades, son of Kleinias, of Skambonidai (*PAA* 121625; *APF* 600, with p. 20 for the estate at Erchia); and Aristophanes, son of Nikophemos, of unknown deme (*PA* 2082, *PAA* 175475; see *APF* 5951, pp. 201–202, with p. 202 on his extensive properties over and above his lands). These examples show that a larger estate might be a concomitant of significantly greater property holdings across the board. That an egalitarian ideology was ever observed outside the urban center of a democratic polity is suspect enough in itself, but surely the internal dynamics of a rural agrarian community could not have failed to reflect so marked a variation in arable land and other property holdings.

From these indications it is clear that for the typical small-holder confronted with a crisis, a potential source of relief resided in the wealthier members of his own rural community. If an institutionalized and enduring social form for the provision of such relief is the object of our search, a promising candidate is at once suggested by the parallel experiences of other preindustrial agrarian economies, ancient Italy in particular. Scholars in quest of linkages between rich and poor under such conditions have often opened up the question of the existence of an ancient Greek patronage system. Some form of linkage, it seems, must have been available in any event in order to explain the apparent relative stability of the village communities in Attica (where, for example, vestiges of the functioning of Kleisthenes' demes are still to be found nearly 900 years after their creation). The model is a familiar one. The threatened poor needed the secure rich in order to survive the pressures of both periodic increased demand and unforeseen calamity and to reestablish themselves under future more settled conditions; for support in disputes or formal legal proceedings; and in general whenever (as was often the case) they were compelled to deal with adversaries, legitimate or otherwise, more powerful than themselves. The few rich needed the many poor for their agricultural labor-power (especially on a seasonal basis when even a permanent resident force of slaves might not be adequate); for their political support as voters in elections, referenda, and trials; and for their indispensable role, through visible displays of social deference, as advertisers of the social hierarchy and their own place within it. Circumstances in Greece appear to have been ripe for the emergence of patronage, and its flourishing in nearby Italy somewhat later under similar conditions is strongly encouraging. Yet it is one of the more notorious enigmas of Greek history that very little direct evidence for patronal institutions seems to have reached us and, to judge from the silence on the matter in recent comprehensive discussions of reciprocity, the consensus would seem to be that they simply did not exist in classical Athens.[48]

Perhaps the most perplexing element of this silence of the sources concerns terminology, since no well established vocabulary, corresponding, say, to the standard Latin words for the elements of patronage, is in common use. The noun *pelates* is glossed by imperial Greek writers as *cliens* (Plutarch, *Romulus* 13.7, cf. Dionysios of Halikarnassos, 1.83.3); and despite the contrasting etymologies (the Greek means "one who approaches;" the Latin, "one who heeds"), the scattering of classical uses of the word does seem to support Rhodes' statement that in prose its meaning is one who is dependent on or works for another[49]—a sense that would be most appropriate in our rural setting. Attic *prostates* denotes the citizen "patron" of a resident alien, but one of the two parties was not a citizen (whereas we are concerned here with relations among citizen *demotai*); and in any event the Athenian *prostates* was involved with formal constitutional and legal matters, not with the sorts of basically economic and social/political issues that are respectively the concerns of the Roman client and patron.[50] However, analogously with *pelates/cliens*, at least one imperial Greek writer understood *prostates* as *patronus* (Plutarch, *Romulus* 13.3 and 7; *Marius* 5.4), and Millett found a classical text in which *prostateia* resembles the patronage of one citizen by another (Xenophon, *Oeconomicus* 2.3, 5–6, 7–9).[51] From this evidence I would conclude not that appropriate terminology did not exist (for it did, with classical examples at that), but that for the most part the terms were not used or may even have been deliberately avoided.[52]

If we grant as an hypothesis the existence of a classical Athenian patronage system, a possible explanation for the extreme rarity of the words for "patron" and "client" is suggested by the experience of the Roman world and in particular is prompted by Richard Saller's discussion of the relative frequency of the language of social subordination in inscriptions versus its comparative absence in literary writings. Inscriptions were set up by clients, who, as recipients of favors, were expected to publicize those favors through the expression of their gratitude and thereby to exalt the social superiority of the benefactor. By contrast, literary works, and especially the formal published letter, were the products of leading members of the Roman aristocracy, but for them such explicit references to their own or their clients' rank would be read as "a tactless advertisement" of one's own personal superiority and of the relative inferiority of the client.[53] At Athens, it is precisely the class of putative "patrons" who are responsible for the surviving literary evidence on which we are primarily dependent for our knowledge of class interrelations in the Attic countryside; and so, if these Athenians behaved like Romans, their silence would be comprehensible. Accordingly, we could understand how an institution fundamental to the functioning of Attic rural society could have escaped notice by the authors of over 100 surviving courtroom speeches, by the topical observations of contemporary life in Old Comedy, and by the sources of the scholiasts and lexicographers whose jottings on just such matters have come down to us in great quantity. But what about the Attic inscriptions? Does not Saller's reasoning require that they document the "language of subordination"? That, in contrast with universally held opinion, they in fact do we shall see shortly.

Discussions of the possible existence of a form of patronage in Greece have always focused upon a single ancient textual tradition which, though isolated, does seem unequivocally to indicate patronal practices in a small Attic deme around the middle of the fifth century: *AthPol* 27.3:

For Kimon, since he owned property worthy of a tyrant, first performed the common liturgies in splendid fashion, and then sustained many of the (i.e. his) *demotai*. For any of the Lakiadai who so wished could approach him each and every day and receive what was necessary for a comfortable livelihood (*ta metria*); and, as well, all his fields were unfenced, in order that anyone who wished might enjoy the produce.

A somewhat fuller version, differing from the Aristotelian account by making the Athenian people, not the demesmen of Lakiadai, the beneficiaries of Kimon's largess, is attributed by Athenaios (12.533a–c) to the tenth book of the *Philippika* of Theopompos (378/7–ca. 320), *FGrH* 115 F 89:

Kimon the Athenian posted no guard over the crop in his fields and gardens, in order that those who wished of the citizens might enter and gather fruit and take whatever they wanted of what was in the plots. And then he made his house common to all; and he always provided an inexpensive dinner for many people, and the poor of the Athenians used to enter and dine. He attended to those who each day asked something of him, and they say he always led around with him two or three youths with small change on them and ordered them to give it away whenever someone approached him with a request. And they say that he made contributions for burials. And he also did the following many times: whenever he saw one of the citizens poorly clothed, he would order one of the youths accompanying him to change clothes with the man. From all this, he enjoyed a high reputation and was first among the citizens.

Finally, Plutarch, expressly drawing on the *AthPol* and silently incorporating numerous details from Theopompos, produced in his *Life* of Kimon a somewhat embellished pastiche of both sources while alertly observing that Aristotle had indicated Kimon's fellow demespeople, not the Athenians at large, as the recipients of the donations:

(10.1) And already being wealthy, Kimon spent the *ephodia* from his campaign, which he believed he had earned honorably from the enemy, even more honorably on the citizens. He removed the fences from his fields, in order that it be possible for strangers and those in need of the citizens to take from the crops without fear. And every day he put on a dinner at his home, frugal to be sure but adequate for many, to which any who wished of the poor might come and have a maintenance without trouble, now at leisure for public affairs alone. (2) But Aristotle says [*AthPol* 27.3] that it was not for all Athenians but for his *demotai* the Lakiadai that he prepared the dinner for anyone who wished. And well dressed young cronies attended him, each of whom, if any of the older town residents (*astoi*) in shabby clothes chanced upon Kimon, would exchange cloaks with him. This practice left an impression of majesty. (3) And these same young men, carrying a great quantity of coin, approaching the more dignified of the poor in the Agora, would quietly slip small change into their hands. Such subjects the comic poet Kratinos appears to have had in mind in his *Archilochoi* (*PCG* IV Cratinus, fr. 1) (4, six lines of verse). (5) And again, Gorgias of Leontinoi says that Kimon earned money in order to spend it, and spent it in order to be honored; and Kritias, who became one of the Thirty, prays in his *Elegies* for "the wealth of Skopadai, the great-mindedness (*megalophrosynē*) of Kimon, and the victories of Arkesilaos of Lakedaimon. . . ." (6) But proclaiming his house [in the *asty*?] a public town hall for the citizens, and in the country (*chora*) providing for strangers to take and enjoy the first fruits of the ripe crops and all the fine things the seasons bring, after a fashion he brought back to life the fabled communism of the time of Kronos.

It is possible, with Wade-Gery and others, that the ultimate source of both the Aristotelian and Theopompan stories is Kritias, whose verses are cited by Plutarch (10.5),[54] in which case the tradition would not only be classical but Attic as well. But Attic, in this case, does not have to mean "urban," for even when Kimon and his retinue operated in the Agora, the *megalophrosynē* is that of the *grand seigneur*'s personal largess, not that of the democratic politician operating through the machinery of a democratic legislative system. That in any event these texts, or rather this single tradition, record a genuine practice of patronage has been accepted by Moses Finley,[55] David Whitehead,[56] and Paul Millett.[57]

Since our concern is with specifically rural society, it is especially gratifying to note the situation of the deme Lakiadai outside the walls to the northwest, beyond Kerameis and Boutadai, half the way to Mt. Aigaleos. The deme's small size—bouleutic quota two, implying a citizen population of only 120 when all Athenians numbered 30,000—also makes it a plausible setting for a "patron's" undertaking to offer free produce, meals, clothing, and cash handouts to all his fellow demesmen on a regular, continuing basis. Given such small numbers, we may legitimately think in terms of a "personal" face-to-face species of patronal relations in contrast to the democratic institutionalized form later to emerge in the town of Athens. But by what good fortune have we this, and only this, isolated positive instance? The answer is simple—the fame of Lakiadai's illustrious *demotes*, Kimon.[58] Except for such a celebrity among its members, it is highly unlikely that a little village would attract the attention of an historian, since its affairs will have justifiably have been regarded as too far removed from the mainstream of city-state affairs. Nor were the smaller demes themselves even likely to have produced records which might stand some chance of reaching us. About 91 of the 139 demes, including Lakiadai, lack even a single inscription that may be assigned to the local village-association, and among these 91 are numbered the great majority of the 73 with a quota of two or fewer (all of which, significantly for our study, were situated outside the walls).

Reciprocity of the kind still practiced in Lakiadai in Kimon's time certainly bears little relation to the forms of social welfare which were provided by the central government later in the fifth century. Particularly striking was these programs' relatively greater accessibility to those who happened to be in the vicinity of their disbursal—namely, the town. Thus, paying work was available from time to time on government-sponsored building projects, but in the classical period at least these were all confined to the Acropolis and its environs. Government service was compensated, too, but again only for those within comfortable reach of the seat of government in or near the Agora. Expenditures on the poor in the form of festivals, including the dramatic choregies, were spatially concentrated in the urban center, in the case of the choregy in the Theater of Dionysos, in the case of the Panathenaia in and about the Agora, and so on. Manifestly, these aptly characterized forms of "community" or "municipal" patronage differed in essential ways from what we see in Kimon's case. For one, again, while the dimensions of a small deme like Lakiadai might make possible mutual familiarity among all residents, a similar personal relationship between "patron" and "client" will obviously not have obtained in the Big City. For another, the sorts of largess engaged in by Pericles and his "radical" democratic successors were exclusively and conspicuously urban by virtue not only of the locus of their disbursal but also of their specific content. The *AthPol* partially substantiates the latter point at the close of the story about Kimon, where the big man of Lakiadai is contrasted with his eventual urban counterpart and successor: "Now Pericles' property was not sufficient for such expenditure and he took the advice of Damonides . . . to distribute to the people (*hoi polloi*) what belonged to them, and so he introduced a daily payment to the jurors" (27.3). Put this way, the point is about *degree* of wealth, but the amount of money involved may merely be a consequence of the fact that, whereas Kimon was dealing with a small village community, Pericles aimed to influence all of citizen (urban) Athens.[59] Thus, *AthPol*'s report may actually concern a more fundamental contrast between traditional rural agrarian practices, involving (inter alia)

access to a rich demesman's fields, and the practices soon to be characteristic of the *asty*, involving (inter alia) pay for jury service.[60]

The general absence of positive evidence for the sort of arrangement
ascribed to Kimon's Lakiadai constitutes a substantial silence that goes well
beyond the mere avoidance of an offensive language of subordination discussed above. At best, if explicit textual evidence is sought, one could cite
the several liturgies in the demes, which generally took the form of a choregy and which, like their better known urban counterparts, did constitute
a sort of patronage on the part of the wealthier members of the village
community.[61] Except for these, the only positive examples for the sort of
personal patronage under review here are the two reported by Whitehead:
the speaker at Isaios 9.18 who claims that no demesmen of Halai Araphenides could be found to testify against Thoudippos; and at Lysias 16.14,
Mantitheos's declaration of his intention to supply two of his fellow demesmen with *ephodia* of thirty drachmas each.[62] Neither of these exchanges,
expressed or implied, approaches the level of Kimon's massive and continuing largess. Elsewhere, on Millett's showing, Isokrates presents in his *Are-
opagiticus* (32–35) a nostalgic encoded apologia for the idea of patronage,
while Menander's *Heros*, dramatically placed in the deme of Ptelea, por-
trays patronage in the form of debt-bondage.[63] But these scattered testimonies are hardly adequate recognition of so fundamental a social
institution on the scale demanded by classical Attica. Given as many as a
hundred or more genuinely rural demes, the patronal exchanges involving
a large majority of Athenian citizens, among them (like Kimon) members
of a social and political elite, should have left their mark on the record.
Why do we not learn more about these practices, if only in an indirect, implicit form?

One possible answer, of course, is that "Kimonian" patronage had
ceased to exist. Millett argued this is in fact what happened, when, in 462,
the "democratic revolution" led to the development and extension of
democratic institutions, with "private patronage on a grand scale" being
absorbed and rendered extinct by various forms of public subsidy.[64] Alternatively, one could invoke the mode of giving by the rich going by the
modern neologism "euergetism," to be distinguished from patronage by
its ostensibly voluntary nature, although in the classical Athenian case it is
clear that the most conspicuous form of such "giving," the liturgy, was neither wholly voluntary nor without expectation of reciprocation—that, in
other words, patronage had resurfaced in altered form.

But a third, quite different, approach is arguable: that, while the effects of the democratic ideology adduced by Millett did indeed flourish in an urban setting, Kimonian style patronage survived in rural communities but in a form that has left no record or, if it has left a record, that is difficult to recognize for what it is. Could such a case be made, one could appeal to the phenomenon of "disguised patronage," one of the four types recognized by Blok and cited by Saller in his study of Roman personal patronage.[65] On this approach, admittedly a weak one, it could be suggested that the ostentatious munificence socially approved under an aristocratic regime had been driven underground by the rise of a dominant democratic ideology and thereafter operated only "under the table." Such a hypothesis is weak because, since no supporting evidence, only surmise, is involved, it is incapable of confirmation or refutation. Fortunately, the alternative approach, that personal patronage did survive, but in a hitherto unrecognized form, does appear to be tenable.

I will argue that the effects of the rise of the democratic ideology invoked by Millett remained a mainly urban phenomenon and that in rural demes, certainly in ones as far removed from the *asty* as Kimon's Lakiadai, the old ways survived, indeed survived by many years, the "revolution" of 462 and its aftermath. The sources recording this hard-to-recognize personal patronage are, in accord with the latent implication of Saller's observations on Roman usage, precisely inscriptions. For it is inscriptions, again, since they record the acts of a democratic mass corresponding to Saller's Roman underclass, which may preserve the "client" 's patronally mandated expression of his relative social inferiority and of his "patron" 's corresponding superiority. The inscriptions in question are the decrees of the demes themselves, an epigraphic dossier long known to specialists and repeatedly studied but not yet, if I am right, fully understood. The reason they are not fully understood is that a rural practice has been submerged in an institution—procedures, form, and terminology—imported from, or more likely imposed by, an urban central government.

The urban institution by which I believe rural Attica patronal practice has been disguised is that of the granting of honors by the *demotai*. The potentially relevant evidence is by the standards of our topic relatively copious. Among the 157 inscriptions emanating from a deme-association, all but 12 of which are assignable to a specific identifiable deme,[66] no fewer than 94, or about 58%, can be identified with certainty or probability as honorary decrees,[67] and of the 94 only 4 belong to intramural urban demes.[68] Since the deme-associations, to judge from the surviving epi-

graphic harvest, could also record on stone decrees not related to the conferral of honors, sacrificial calendars, leases, accounts of various kinds, lists
of names, boundary markers, and so on, that 58% of all surviving documents should record or reflect the bestowal of honors leaves no doubt
about the importance of this activity. Several features of the process, furthermore, fit a reasonable model of patronal exchange. Easily overlooked
because it is so obvious, the mere fact that these decrees, with their often
elaborate clauses setting out the honorand's benefactions, summations of
the honorand's character in laudatory language ("excellence," "justice,"
"love of honor" and the like), and a seemingly full catalogue of the honors bestowed, were, at considerable associational expense, engraved on
stone, and displayed in a conspicuous venue tells us that we are observing
something more than mere archival record-keeping. Skillfully executed and
(when accompanied by relief sculpture[69]) artistically accomplished, these
decrees constitute the single most important, not to say informative, relic
of many an Attic deme.

But it is the identity, or rather social-political profile, of the honorands
that provides the first really suggestive clue. According to Whitehead's
prosopographical researches reported in his book of 1986, the count of individuals honored by their own or another deme stood at that time between 113 and 116, and of these (setting aside nine demarchs) "almost
three-quarters" could be assigned "some sort of personal or family background of prosperity and/or activity either in the deme or outside it or
both."[70] The significance of this statistic was not lost on Whitehead. Noting the presence among the honorands of clusters of relatives by birth or
marriage suggesting the preeminence of a few prominent families, he characterized these families as *domi nobiles* and underscored their vital contribution to the deme-associations' well being.[71]

Nonetheless, this same illuminating discussion, however secure its evidential basis, does not fully exploit the deeper significance, and specifically
the possible elements of reciprocity, explicit or latent in these associational
transactions. To mention another obvious and therefore potentially unap-
preciated dimension of the honoring procedure: the persons passing the
decree were the whole, or some subset, of the duly enrolled *demotai;* that
is to say, in the case of a rural deme, the ordinary run of farmers whose
lands (as we saw) might have been exceeded in scale by a factor of four or
five by those of the party they were likely to be honoring. While, unfortunately, no honorary decree preserves information regarding the count for
or against the passage of the motion, the *lex sacra* of Lower Paiania, a large

deme with a bouleutic quota of 11, gives the association's quorum as 100 of the demesmen.[72] A number this high suggests a broadly-based participation by a sizable percentage of resident villagers. On the usual assumption that the bouleutic quotas are a reliable guide to the actual citizen populations of the several demes, and given an aggregate Athenian population of 30,000, 11 members on the Council of 500 would imply a village association membership of 660 citizens. Naturally, the number actually in attendance on any given occasion requiring the quorum may have exceeded that number by far; the 100 merely constitute the absolute minimum of citizens required in order to do business. Since, then, there is no reason to suspect that what was true of Lower Paiania around the mid-fifth century was not true of other demes at this or other times, we are entitled to contemplate the possibility of a reciprocal exchange between a wealthy, political, and influential honorand and the mass of rank-and-file resident village demesmen.

But it is the record of the benefits conferred by the honorand and the occasional (but pointed) acknowledgment of the party(ies) so benefited that present us with the telltale clues about the nature of these transactions (as I have called them). The decrees preserve references to the staging of sacrifices (*thysiai*);[73] the holding of deme-association liturgies, the *choregia*,[74] the gymnasiarchy,[75] and "the Pyrrhic dancers;"[76] partially overlapping with the *choregia*, the staging of the *heortē, pompē,* or *agōn* of a particular deme's celebration of the (Rural) Dionysia;[77] the erection or repair of communal structures, especially ones of cultic function;[78] and the filling of a financially onerous deme magistracy. The context of these benefactions is generally cultic, and to the extent that animal sacrifices or other distributions were involved, the donor's generosity will have contributed to the immediate material well-being of the grateful *demotai*. These were not empty, self-aggrandizing gestures or showy acts of conspicuous consumption designed merely to enhance the prestige of the donor.

It is the asymmetry—so fitting to a patronal context—embodied in material munificence and laudatory reward revealed by the texts of the documents, however, that I wish to underscore. Not infrequently, the point is made that the benefactions were bestowed at the honorand's personal expense.[79] Since, given the usual catalogue of benefits and their specific ascription to the party being honored, so much might seem to have gone without saying, the fact that the obvious is nonetheless mentioned may have served to point the contractual nature of the exchange. At the opposite, receiving end of the exchange, at first glance seemingly otiose

phrases or clauses make the point that the benefactions were expressly intended to work to the betterment of the deme or the *demotai*.[80] But why
say this, unless to point the fact that praise, crown, statue, and so on are
being offered in reciprocation not for disinterested civic-mindedness but
for the honorand's promotion of the interests of the very party responding
with the conferral of honors? Furthermore, the motivating clauses of the
decrees routinely cite the "goodness" of the benefactor, his "excellence,"
"justice," and so on. Such language is not to be dismissed as mere verbiage,
although it is true that vague or illusive phrases might have been intended
to mask details of the honorand's actions that for reasons unknown to us
the deme-association deemed better not to set out in permanent written
form.[81] Rather it may, on the Roman model, be interpreted in terms of the
inferior party's expected public display of social deference. An ostentatious
bestowal of complimentary accolades might *in and of itself* have simultaneously served, above and beyond a crown or subsidized sacrifice or other
material reward, as a form of reciprocation.

If I am right, the reader might expect some of the honorand's benefactions to bear the stamp of a rural community through their addressing
of concerns specific to an agrarian (or pastoral) economy. As it happens,
several signs of just such a tendency are preserved in the decrees. According to a decree of the demesmen of Eleusis, Xenokles of Sphettos, over and
above his contributions of a cultic nature, saw to it that, by the construction of a stone bridge at his own expense, "the residents of the suburb and
the farmers be secured."[82] A decree from Ikaria (the formulaic "Decreed
by the Ikarians" is restored in line 1) honors the demarch, with the broken
context containing the words ". . . good crops were produced over the entire countryside,"[83] presumably with respect to some action or effort on
the part of the honorand. Something about (the honorand's distribution
of?) "the portions of the crops" can be read in a fragmentary decree from
Rhamnous moved by a Rhamnousian (and, therefore, with certainty a decree of the *demotai* named in line 8).[84] A fragment of an honorary decree
assigned to Sphettos preserves, near the close of the summary of the honorand's benefactions, a contextless reference to "the people dwelling
around (the deme-center?)."[85]

Whereas in these cases the honorand is normally a member of the
community of *demotai*,[86] in several others he is a statewide Athenian military officer. From the site of ancient Aixone, a decree honoring Demetrios
of Phaleron characterizes the war as having broken out "in the countryside" (*chora*, line 6) and states that he restored peace "for Athenians and

the countryside" (*chora*, lines 9–10).[87] Similarly, a fragmentary decree from
Eleusis perhaps honoring a general (the name is not preserved) may originally, if correctly restored, have cited the honorand's efforts to secure "the
safety of the ground and of the citizens living on it."[88] Less conjecturally,
the decree of the Eleusinians of about the same date honoring the general
Aristophanes of Leukonoion states that "he took care that the crops be
brought in from the countryside in safety."[89] From Rhamnous again, honors for the general Epichares cite his tending to the crops (lines 8–9), his
efforts "that the harvest be safe for the farmers" (line 11), his care of the
vineyards (lines 11–12), and so on.[90] A generation later, a second decree of
the Rhamnousians, granting honors to Dikaiarchos of Thria for garrison
duties, in like fashion states that "he took care of the guarding of the fort
and of the rest of the Attic countryside" (lines 15–17) and cites his loyalty
to each and all alike "who had removed their cattle to safety on account of
the war, offering salvation and assistance for any purpose anyone sum-
moned him" (lines 19–20).[91]

    Admittedly, it is true that in these latter cases it is impossible to deter-
mine whether the military official in question was merely following orders
or, as might be expected on the patronage model, had voluntarily cultivated
the good will of the host deme-association by deliberately and self-con-
sciously serving the agrarian (and economic) interests of its rural citizen
members. Be that as it may, on either understanding of the situation the
demesmen evidently thought that reciprocation in the form customary under normal circumstances (that is, involving a member of the association)
was entirely appropriate. A general, that is to say, could be treated as though
he, too, were a member of the host deme, even though in each instance the
decree itself provides the explicit evidence that he was not.

    Throughout, it is notable that in several cases the honorand's inter-
vention involved the "crops," although the circumstances in question can
only be imagined. But to the extent that a routine harvest, with its extraordinary labor demands, is at issue (as opposed to special conditions imposed by warfare), the epigraphic record affords some confirmation of my
initial enlarging of the notion of agrarian "crisis" to include the periodic
and predictable agricultural event alongside the rarely occurring and un-
foreseeable calamity addressed by the ecological studies.

    Some further, indirect corroboration of the reconstruction comes
from a perhaps unexpected quarter, namely the documents of the phyle-
associations.[92] These number just over fifty, but an even higher percentage
than in the case of the demes—in fact, all but two or three—are decrees,

and of the decrees a large majority are of the honoring type. What is of interest here is the general dissimilarity between the honorands cited by the
two associations. Among the honorands of the phylai are an unexpectedly
large number of *phyletai* who had filled posts, or served in liturgies, in the
arena of statewide politics in the town of Athens. These men were honored, as I have argued, because they had put their positions in the Athenian government to use in service of their fellow tribesmen who, since their
interests seem to have been "represented" by the honorand, could be
viewed as his constituents.[93] By contrast, no such officer is to be found
among the far more numerous deme honorands, save the thesmothete of
the year 329/8 crowned by his demesmen (the Epieikidai) on a statue base,
IG II² 2837 (and any significance this exception might possess is reduced
by the simultaneous presence of the Boulē and his fellow magistrates as co-
honoring parties of his phyle, and by the fact that the stone was discovered
in Athens ["Athenis ad viam Apollinis," *IG*], far from the deme-center of
the Epieikidai). Conversely, the matters of rural interest that we have just
found in the deme honorary decrees are entirely absent from the decrees
of the urban-based phyle-associations. The granting of honors by both
phyle and deme, it is clear, is wrapped up with matters pertinent to the associations' contrasting vital interests, respectively urban and (in significant
part) rural. *Phyletai* used their honor-bestowing machinery to exert influence in the domain of central Athenian institutions. Extramural *demotai*
used theirs, it now seems, in the promotion of interests traditionally pursued in an agrarian setting within the framework of personal patronage.

   Democratic ideology, argues Millett, was inimical to the idea of personal patronage, for, whereas Athenian thinking upheld egalitarianism, patronage by its very nature was an asymmetrical relationship between a
superior and an inferior party, with the former dominating the latter. For
Millett, patronage was minimized, concealed or disguised, criticized or
ridiculed as shameful. At best, a semblance of patronal forms could be
found in the subservient *kolax* flattering his prosperous potential benefactor or in the friendly-loan societies called *eranoi*,[94] but even so, patronage,
now "a minor social phenomenon," maintained only a "vestigial and peripheral existence."[95] The cause of this development was not, Millett is at
pains to emphasize, ideological objections, for, given sufficient economic
pressure, any amount of such objections could have been overridden, but
rather the deliberate measures taken by democratic politicians to under-
write the economic independence of the poor, which removed the need for
wealthy patrons of the Kimonian stripe.[96] Measures of this kind had had a

long history. Peisistratos's offering of loans in support of farming (*AthPol* 16.2) and his establishment of the traveling deme-judges (16.5) were reasonably taken by Finley as weakening the aristocracy's traditional hold on the rural communities. Similarly, later, when in 453/2, under Pericles, the apparently defunct *dikastai kata demous* were reinstituted.[97] With Millett, we could add Aristotle's proposal that, to rescue the multitude from extreme poverty, revenues be collected into a central fund, to be distributed in amounts large enough for "ownership of a plot" or, failing that, for capital "for trade or farming," among other plans (6.3.4: 1320a–b), if we could be sure he had Athens in mind.[98] All these measures seem to have been aimed at patronal structures in rural communities, but if they were, there is little reason to think that they were successful. According to the evidence and arguments set out above, personal patronage had indeed remained very much alive in some of the demes situated far outside the walls of the *asty*. But this fact can be appreciated only when one reads the demes' public decrees, as we have, in the terms appropriate to their content and implicit purpose.

By way of putting in perspective my model of rural personal patronage, it is important to underscore factors which made well nigh impossible the existence *in the town* of the variety of patronage that I have just ascribed to extraurban demes. Chief among the ways in which the urban environment threatened the survival of the traditional forms was the presence there of vastly more powerful potential patrons embodied in the workings of democratic institutions—voting assembly, bill-moving politician, or ambitious holder of a liturgy.[99] No rural large-holder transplanted to the *asty* could expect to compete with urban politicians on the town's terms. Nor could he, when seeking the advantages of an urban residence, reasonably expect that his position in the home community would remain unaffected. Physical presence on an ongoing basis was required in order to learn of and respond to dependents' requests and complaints, to maintain surveillance over wayward members of the flock, to make visible demonstrations of one's economic or social potency, and to mete out favors on the spot and in a timely fashion. A wealthy landowner from a rural deme might establish residence in town only to discover not only that he was now without the services of the *clientela* back in the village but that conditions did not favor the building of a new one either. The *asty* of a populous city-state simply did not afford conditions conducive to the formation or nurturing of face-to-face ties of mutual reciprocity, certainly not on the terms presumably familiar within tiny rural communities. And, after all, it was in the countryside, not the town, that subsistence-level small holders faced the sorts of unpredictable (or predictable) crises that might prompt them to enter into a condition of dependency upon a more powerful benefactor. But the resources of a major city-state, especially a wealthy one like Athens, could effectively remove the threat of crisis from an ordinary person's everyday concerns.

To conclude, the available evidence would seem to satisfy all the necessary conditions required by the assumption of a system of personal patronage in an agrarian community: the presence of a wide range of risks threatening significant damage or loss; sufficient socioeconomic stratification (evidenced first of all in widely varying acreages) as to make possible an asymmetrical mutual dependency between superior and inferior parties; the potential for the ongoing duration of such relationship to the extent that residence or regular presence in the home community was maintained; the face-to-face interaction of the parties concerned within the often diminutive citizen deme-associations; and the conferral of benefits demonstrably of interest to a prospective rural clientele in response to which the demesmen will have reciprocated in an asymmetrical but nonetheless appropriate fashion. So portrayed, our Attic rural patronage will have occupied a middle ground between the purely unmediated reciprocity ascribed to Kimon and the Lakiadai and the mass, anonymous institutional functioning of the central government of Athens, by combining the customary personal face-to-face interactions characteristic of such often tiny agrarian communities with the institutionalized forms of the deme-association's "constitutional" apparatus.

Communal Activity in the Deme-Association Center

The notion of a deme or village "center," though a fixed element in virtually all studies of this kind, is, as we saw at the close of the preceding chapter, without textual foundation, epigraphic or literary. Prose sources preserve references of movement to and from "the field(s)" or to and from a specific deme, which is sometimes given by name, but nothing is ever said about a "center," whatever might be the corresponding Greek locution. Rather, the deme/village center seems to be the product of the observation and occasionally the excavation of an occupation site associated with a specific Attic deme by reference to epigraphic finds, significant public architecture, or topographical clues from ancient writings. But let us assume for the time being that in an appreciable number of cases there actually was such a thing. What we would still need to discover is the roles played by such a center in the life of the village. What were its more or less permanent fixtures? In what numbers and with what frequency was it the scene of visits by members of the community? What village institutions might have focused in it significant communal activities? To what extent did the ideology—the assumptions, attitudes, and values—that we might ascribe to rural villagers contribute or not contribute to its vitality as a locus of rural culture? The evidence may be grouped under six headings:

Assemblies. At Athens, the assembly of the deme-association went by the Greek for the place of its convening, *agora*. The term is now attested at or for Aixone, Besa, Eleusis, Erchia, Halai Aixonides, Otryne, Peiraieus, Skambonidai, and Sounion.[100] But in fact, even in the absence of the term, a meeting of some sort must be assumed for every deme from which we have a decree or other collective act of the *demotai*. Since the *agora* was by definition open to all members of the village-association, every rural household including a citizen will have been able to participate. But actual attendance is predictably difficult to establish. An unpublished inscription from Kos records a count of 248 votes in the deme of Halasarna,[101] but since we cannot even guess at the total membership of the association, it is not possible to estimate the percentage of participation. Again, an inscription from the Attic deme of Paiania sets the quorum at 100;[102] and of the two homonymous demes going by this name, ours must be Lower Paiania with a bouleutic quota of 11.[103] Given that the quotas approximately represent the actual citizen population, then, when the number of Athenians stood at 30,000, the 11 Paianians on the Council of 500 will have represented a deme membership of 660. So, under these conditions, the quorum will have represented about one-sixth or one-seventh of the registered demesmen. The speaker of Demosthenes' celebrated narrative of a meeting of the demesmen of the Attic deme Hagnous in the 57th oration *Against Euboulides* says that 73 of the demesmen took the oath before voting (57.9). Since the deme's quota was 5, implying a membership of 300 when the Athenian population stood at 30,000, about one-quarter will have attended despite the long walk of 35 stades to and from the meeting place in town for those residing in the deme (57.10). At the same time, this meeting's extraordinary circumstances (a review of the deme's membership rolls) disqualifies it as in any way typical. Elsewhere, in the absence of a textual account, the known or probable use of a theater for meetings in those villages possessing one (see below) might suggest wide participation, but we have no actual example of an *agora* held in a *theatron*. And what of frequency? At Aixone, the isolated attestation of a "regular meeting" (*agora kyria*) in *IG* II^2 1202, lines 1–2, suggests a plurality of meetings, some of them not "regular," but even with this evidence before him Whitehead, after a full review of the record for the Attic deme's *agora*, could nonetheless remark that a deme might get by with a single assembly a year.[104] Given the wide range of business documented by the combined records of all 139 demes, this might make for a very tight schedule if a single deme transacted every item on the composite agenda.[105] So, while it is true that in no instance is more than a single meeting in a given year attested for any Attic deme, we should leave open the possibility of more frequent convenings of the assembly.

Theaters. From literary, epigraphic, and archaeological evidence we learn of the existence of a *theatron* in nine demes (Acharnai, Aixone, Eleusis, Euonymon, Halai Araphenides, Ikarion, Peiraieus, Rhamnous, and Thorikos), to which may be added several others on the basis of grants of *proedria* (Anagyrous and Myrrhinous), choregic dedications (Aigilia and Painania), and the staging of dramas at the Dionysia (Kollytos).[106] The existence of a theater in or near a village center should, according to its dimensions, imply a proportionately low or high level of involvement in the community's organized life, although we can never be sure just who—male or female, free or slave, etc.—was in attendance at any function not strictly limited to official members. Attested functions include the announcement of honors previously voted by the *demotai* in the *agora*[107] and stage performances of various kinds, especially including the activities associated with the *agōn* of Dionysos.[108] Frequency becomes the issue once again, but except for the known annual period of the Dionysia and of other cultic celebrations recorded on *leges sacrae*, all specifics predictably elude us.

Other communal structures. Besides the omnipresent cultic facilities (altar, shrine, temple, etc.), isolated epigraphic sources preserve a record of a *krēnē* and *palaistra* with *apodyterion* at Kephisia[109] and a *leschē* at Aixone.[110] Structures of various types were built or maintained by benefactors of the deme, as we learn from the survival of the decrees bestowing honors upon them.[111] All such communal structures in various ways presuppose significantly widespread and repeated use. If archaeological discoveries could only situate them in a nucleated "center," we could speak with greater confidence about their presumable communal significance. Stelai engraved with the transcripts of associational business were widely and frequently erected in or near the agora, theater, shrine, or other spot

explicitly or presumably situated in the village center.[112] Stelai imply a significant readership, even if the "readers" included illiterate or semi-literate
farmers or shepherds listening to the spoken reading of an educated fellow-
villager. That the stelai were meant actually to be read (as opposed to serving a merely archival purpose) is shown by the occurrence of clauses in
honorary inscriptions announcing that any future benefactors will be similarly awarded,[113] although this same evidence points to the targeting of the
message to the few people wealthy enough to bestow a praiseworthy favor
upon the village community.

Cult activities of the village-association. Sacral events recorded for individual Attic extramural demes range from the omnipresent sacrifice
(*thysia*)[114] through the "dramatic contest" (*agōn*),[115] "festival" (*heortē*),[116]
"dinner" (*hestiasis*),[117] "all night" celebration (*pannychis*),[118] "the Pyrrhic
dancers" (*hoi pyrrhichistai*),[119] and others. The assumption of a generally
high level of frequency is prompted by the famous *lex sacra* of Erchia,
which in its preserved text calls for 59 rites over the course of the year.[120]
Since animal sacrifices normally issued in the distribution of meats to the
participants, a visceral (as well as social or strictly religious) motive for attendance was presumably often present. The *lex* from Attic Skambonidai
reveals that resident aliens were welcome on at least one occasion;[121] and
varied testimonies, literary and epigraphic, put beyond doubt the regular
presence and active participation of females of the citizen class.[122] The case
for a significantly active village association is perhaps strongest here, in the
domain of cult.

The operation of patronage. Above, I have argued in favor of a form of
patronage adapted to the peculiar economic and institutional setting of the
rural agrarian village. From the specific content of decrees (e.g. the personal circumstances of a mover or honorand) it is evident that villagers of
substance and political experience must often have been present in their
deme assembly-places. It may be, then, that a patron's base of operations
was the village hub, although visits to his isolated farmstead (see chapter 1)
are equally imaginable, especially wherever animals, produce, agricultural
implements and so forth were involved.

Village ideology. No attempt will made here to tackle this complex
topic (it is reserved for my discussion of "realities" in chapter 5), except to
note some of its possible components. Whitehead, as we saw, has related
the frequently observed practice in honorary decrees of praising the honored party's *philotimia* to concerted efforts to promote village solidarity.
With this principle were in competition, as we saw in our discussion of

philotimia and rivalry, individualistic self-aggrandizement, the insistent demands of the household, and the higher goals of the city-state. All told, it
is clear that the claims of the village faced an uphill battle against the forces
threatening its disintegration, and by no means was a victory, or even domination, by the village a foregone conclusion. To complicate matters still
further, even within his rural setting an ancient Greek villager's thinking is
held by Victor Hanson to have been susceptible to the ideological lure of
a "new rural identity," "rural" or "agrarian chauvinism," "quietism," or
"aloofness in the fields." [123] Whatever the importance of the village as a
municipal center, by no means could it be said that a rural Athenian's engagement with it was undivided, nothwithstanding the determined promotion of a communal *philotimia*.

Conclusion

Our examination of rural society has out of necessity been concerned
only with the elites at the top of the city-state's hierarchy of statuses. This
necessity is one dictated by the laws of the state of Athens. Only citizens,
except under rare special circumstances requiring legislative action by the
People, could own land or the structures sitting on that land—that is, to
use the term justified by our analysis in chapter 1, a farm. Only citizens
might be members of a village-association, since such membership was
nothing more or less than a localized subset of the larger membership in
the state's citizen caste. Patronage, the principal subject of this chapter,
will have been largely, if not entirely, a matter of relations between citizens, for only a citizen was likely to accumulate sufficient wealth or to
acquire sufficient influence (by dint of his constitutionally provided opportunities for political advancement) to play effectively the role of patron; and, at the opposing end of this asymmetrical but mutually
beneficial arrangement, only a citizen (by dint of his constitutionally provided capacity to vote in an election, sit on a jury, or, to the present
point, participate in his village-association's public life) was in a position
to reciprocate that patron's largess.

At the same time, it is likely that Attic rural society was significantly
integrated across lines of gender, economic class, and constitutional status. The hints in this direction that have emerged from the foregoing
presentation have been few but tantalizing. Women of the citizen class
might venture outdoors to a neighboring farm to visit female neighbors;

actively participate as officers and worshippers in the cultic functions of their village-associations; and, albeit under duress, engage in paid agricultural labor outside the home. Their children, likewise statutory minors, similarly participated in rural cult life and, again under the press of poverty, could perform the tasks otherwise left to slaves. Slaves themselves remain a question in their rural agricultural settings, at least in terms of the numbers involved and their distribution over households rich and poor, but with the metics at least we have in the evidence of the deme-affiliations certain indications of their presence across the full expanse of rural Attica. Other rural groups, of variable legal status but probably not citizens in most cases, will have included herders of various descriptions, fishers, charcoal burners, itinerant field laborers, the personnel of rural cult centers, and village-based artisans. Also, at any given time the countryside will have witnessed the presence or visits of pilgrims and other travelers, ambassadors, peddlers, brigands, runaway slaves, and beggars. Most of these categories of rural denizen are known from textual records so fleeting that no attempt can be made, at least not here, to reconstruct their place in Attic rural "society."

3

Village

THE FOREGOING ATTEMPT TO OUTLINE SOME of the structural components and internal dynamics of ancient Greek rural society is dependent upon crude approximations of socioeconomic stratification; the testimony of a much earlier, non-Attic, and poetic witness; and (in the case of personal patronage) the implications of a foreign (ancient Roman) paradigm. Accordingly, it is evident that to a real extent our model of Attic rural society partakes of an ideal or typical characterization which, given the additionally complicating variations across Attica in topography, local economy, proximity to the *asty*, and so on, may or may not correspond in detail to the conditions obtaining in any single village community. To put it in Aristotelian terms, the preceding chapter more nearly cleaves to the typifying tendencies of the *Politics* than to the particularistic and empirical case-by-case approach of the 158 *Politeiai*. By way of remedy, what we need to do is to examine a sample of the individual deme communities in the hope that we can thereby gain an appreciation of the Attic village in its particularity.

Forty-eight of the 139 deme-associations can be identified as the sources of over 150 epigraphic documents, all certainly or with high probability originating at the site of the deme in question.[1] Not all documented demes, however, meet the criteria of relevance of the present study. The 48 demes with at least one inscription include four of the five intramural demes (Kollytos, Kydathenaion, Melite, and Skambonidai, but not Koile) as well as the port town Peiraieus, the mining deme Thorikos, the sanctuary deme Eleusis, and the garrison demes (in addition to Eleusis) Phyle, Rhamnous, and Sounion. None of these, clearly, falls within the parameters of a typical rural community as defined in this work. And of the 38 remaining, just four are represented by an epigraphic record sufficiently voluminous and informative to permit an attempt to characterize the in-

ternal doings of an individual village community in its own right: Acharnai, Aixone, Halai Aixonides, and Teithras.

Acharnai

With a bouleutic quota of 22, Acharnai was by far the largest of the Attic
deme-associations in terms of citizen members; indeed, its quota exceeds
that of the next largest deme, Aphidna, quota 16, by nearly 38%. For this
reason alone, there is considerable attraction to Traill's division of Acharnai into two distinct demes which, continuing to share the name in common, would have occupied ground in the area of modern Menidi several
miles north of Athens in the foothills of Mt. Parnes: the larger on the site
at Menidi proper and assigned to the Inland trittys of Oineis (quota
15/16?), the smaller on a site southwest of Menidi and assigned to the City
trittys of the same phyle (quota 7/6?).[2] As for visible physical remains, C.
W. J. Eliot reported in the *Princeton Encyclopedia of Classical Sites*, published in 1976, that, while in the early 19th century vestiges of "a considerable town" could still be observed 1 kilometer to the west of Menidi,
foundations of buildings were as of his writing not observable.[3] Five security *horoi* from the site(s) have thus far been published: Finley nos. 3
(*chorion*), 28 (*chorion* and *oikia*), 65 (*chorion*), 116 (*chorion* and *oikia*), and
SEG 39.200 (*chorion*).[4] Mention will be made below of the probable fate
of the Temple of Ares and Athena Areia, which is widely believed to have
stood in Acharnai prior to its relocation to the Agora in town.

Whatever the disposition, the combined citizen population of greater
Acharnai was enormous, even outsized, to judge by the standard of the
bouleutic system. Accordingly, Kirchner's list of demesmen totaled 422,
and Davies' roster of members of the propertied class includes 37 Acharnians. To put the matter in a perspective relevant to the concerns of this
book, the quotas of all five intramural demes taken together totaled only
27. Swollen by large numbers of metics, visitors from abroad, and slaves
(over and above many resident non-*demotai* citizens), the population
within the walls at any given time exceeded by far that of any rural district,
but the demographic center of the citizenbody lay outside the walls to the
north in the direction of this rural settlement.

Nor is the matter of Acharnai's size confined to the quota and its constitutional implications and consequences. Thucydides, in the course of
narrating the first Spartan invasion of Attica in the summer of 431, says that

Archidamos halted his advance at Acharnai, "the largest settlement of the demes of Attica (as they are called)" (2.19). The historian goes on to observe that the Acharnians were "a big part of the *polis*," "for their *hoplitai* stood at 3,000" (§20). If all these hoplites were citizens, this figure would represent 10% of a population of 30,000 (in comparison with the 4.4% implied by its 22 members in the Council). But, while scholars are agreed that Thucydides' number is too high,[5] it is equally clear that the author, with his customary tendentiousness, may have exaggerated in the service of a point: that Archidamos's strategy turned on his calculation of the number of Acharnians who had taken refuge within the walls.[6] That number was large enough, he felt, that when the demespeople saw that their properties were about to be ravaged, they would be able to "incite the whole people to battle," with a predictable favorable outcome for the Peloponnesians. If, on the other hand, they did not sally out, he would be able to plunder the plain (including the deme's lands) at will and even advance to the walls of the town, because the Acharnians, deprived of their possessions, would no longer be eager to run risks on behalf of the possessions of others—indeed, precisely because of Acharnian resistance, *stasis* would beset their deliberations (2.20.4). As things worked out, Pericles' policy of nonengagement prevailed, for he refused to convoke the Assembly or to permit any other gathering, confining his response to the dispatch of cavalry to prevent the ravaging of the fields near the *asty* (2.22.1–2). As a result, the Peloponnesians took leave of Acharnai and proceeded to plunder "some of the other demes between Parnes and Mt. Brilessos (i.e. Pentelikon)" (2.23.1). Was it the presence of large numbers of Acharnians within the walls that, once Acharnai itself had been ravaged, had allowed so sacrificial a policy to prevail?

Six years later, in 425, Aristophanes produced his *Archarnians*, and the chorus of demesmen is represented as implacably hostile to the Spartans, eager for war, and anything but unwilling to run risks in battle. Even if the bellicosity of the Acharnians has been exaggerated in order to create a foil for the peace-making efforts of the protagonist Dikaiopolis, the demesmen's warlike propensities cannot be entirely a figment of the playwright's imagination. So, the Acharnians who, in 431, had persuaded Pericles (or had been persuaded by him) not to engage the invaders in defense of Attic farmlands, are now, in 425, found champing at the bit to do that very thing. Six years under such volatile conditions is a long time, and when one takes further into account the loss of Pericles' charismatic leadership, it is understandable how such a change of attitude might have occurred. But since the volte face does raise the question of the Acharnians' political profile, there is good reason to review what else we know from ancient sources about these demespeople.

Because only a few miles of level plain stood between the deme and the appropriately named "Acharnian" Gate,[7] it is likely that at all times, in peace or war, Acharnians were frequent visitors to the *asty*. A rough index is afforded by the tombstones of Acharnians published in *IG* II²: of a total of 77 (nos. 5778–5854), only 12 (nos. 5787, 5788, 5797, 5800, 5809, 5817, 5830, 5842, 5846, 5848, 5852, and 5853) have a recorded provenience at or near the site(s) of the deme. And given the population numbers just reviewed, even a modest percentage of the deme's population could have made a significant and palpable impact on life within the walls. No wonder, then, that literary sources preserve a vivid impression of the villagers—"a collective impersonal stereotype of the Acharnian character," as Whitehead summed up the situation.[8] That "stereotype" is embedded in a number of poetical texts, including but not limited to the chorus of Aristophanes' play.[9] For present purposes, suffice it to say that it appears to have been rooted in two images. A fragment of an unknown comic poet preserves the salutation of an Acharnian as "oaken" (*druinos*) and "unfeeling" (*anaisthetos*), with an alternative spelling of the former given by lexicographers as the compound *dryacharneus*, "oak-Acharnian."[10] These terms are variously interpreted as "wild" (*agrioi*), "hard of mind" (*skleroi*), and "not to be softened" (*atenktoi*). The other image is preserved in the proverbial *Acharnikoi onoi*, "Acharnian donkeys," glossed as "of the big and sluggish."[11] From these slight but pithy hints Whitehead abstracted "the proverbial wild men, as tough and unyielding as old oak."[12] The inference is plausible and seemingly supported by Aristophanes' ascription of formidability to the Acharnian womenfolk (*Lysistrata*, lines 61–63; *Thesmophoriai*, lines 562–563), but when we come to the Aixonians and Teithrasians later in this chapter, we shall find that similar qualities were ascribed to their women as well, suggesting that "toughness" was regarded as a generic quality of rural demeswomen and not therefore to be confined necessarily to any specific country deme. Accordingly, I suspect that a more specific meaning is to be found in the case of Acharnai, a meaning that is more literally bound up with this deme's historical experience, to wit, with the demesmen's activity as charcoal-burners and sellers of their product in the town.

Thucydides does not, within the scope of his brief narrative, specify "the possessions" of the Acharnians ravaged by the Lacedaemonians. But if Aristophanes' text is interrogated, two answers are implied by the words or acts of the chorus. One, their vineyards have already been destroyed (as would be expected, since the production followed upon repeated annual invasions of Attica); Dikaiopolis himself, in an effort to empathize with the Acharnians (he himself is a demesman of Cholleidai, line 406), remarks that he too has lost a vineyard (line 512). Two, as evidenced by Dikaiopolis's parody of a scene from Euripides' *Telephos* (lines 204–625), the Acharnians fear for the (future) loss of their charcoal production (see especially lines 333–334). The difference between the two sources of the deme's livelihood is vital for our understanding of the Acharnians' corporate personality, as represented by Aristophanes. Vineyards, once destroyed, are gone for many years; a vineyard does not recover between annual invasions.[13] But Dikaiopolis' threat to slay the scuttle of charcoal (lines 325–337) makes no sense unless the audience is expected to assume that production, despite the recurrence of invasions, remains a viable possibility. For the play's dramatic present and future, the chorus is therefore above all to be seen as *anthrakeutai* (see especially lines 178–185, 211–218, 665–675). May we find, then, the meaning of "oak-Acharnian" in the wood that was the raw material of their industry? And the "Acharnian donkeys"? If the charcoal had to be transported any considerable distance, draught animals would normally be required, but a less pedestrian reading would make the Acharnians themselves the donkeys. Because charcoal is extremely light by volume, a full load of maximum carryable weight, once upon a person's shoulders, could easily leave the impression that it was being transported by a beast of burden. A likely recollection of the scene (although the Acharnians are not mentioned by name) is preserved in a fragment of an unidentified speech by the orator Andokides preserved in *Souda*, s.v. *skandix*:

For let us not ever witness again the charcoal-burners coming out of the mountains into the *asty*, and sheep and cattle and the wagons and little women . . . , and old men and workers in armor! Nor may we have again to eat wild greens and chervil![14]

From the reference to "workers in armor" it is clear that the passage might be assigned to the years of the Acharnians' enforced incarceration within the walls described by Thucydides, but it would be rash to preclude the occurrence of similar scenes under more peaceful conditions. It may be suggested that the presence in town of such figures was a familiar feature of the urban scene and that the abhorrence of that presence expressed by Andokides' speaker was characteristic of the Athenian urban sensibility.

Contrary to the impression possibly left by both Thucydides and Aristophanes, the sight of *rus in urbe* is accordingly not to be dismissed as merely the freakish and fleeting consequence of a foreign invasion of the countryside.

Now, if, in contrast to the point of view of these literary witnesses, we want to recover the Acharnians' own perception of themselves and of their community, we must turn to the epigraphic finds from the deme itself. Technically speaking, the oath taken by the Athenian ephebes and the oath of Plataia, since both were on display at Acharnai (*SEG* 46.143), belong here, but our concern is with documents in the name of, and pertaining to, the Acharnians themselves.

(1) Decree concerning construction of altars for Ares and Athena Areia, ca. 340–335. L. Robert, *Études épigraphiques et philologiques* (Paris, 1938) 293–296, reedited by G. Daux, *Charisterion . . . Anastasios K. Orlandos* I (Athens, 1964) 87–90 (*SEG* 21.519):

When Leon was priest, decreed by the Acharnians, Kalliteles, son of Stesios, made the motion: In order that the altar of Ares and Athena Areia be constructed in the best possible manner, since the god [Apollo at Delphi] replied that it is more agreeable and better for the deme of the Acharnians and the Demos of the Athenians to construct the altars of Ares and Athena Areia in order that the affairs of the gods be piously disposed towards the Acharnians and the Athenians, decreed by the Acharnians: Since the selected persons and the architects declare the cost of the construction, to declare the sum the demesmen think right for the construction of the altars, in order that no impediment to the construction arise before the sacrifice of the Areians [i.e. Ares and Athena]. And in order that the person advancing the funds receive reimbursal. . . .

(2) Two decrees honoring deme-association officers, 315/4. G. Stainchaouer, *AE* 131 (1992) [1994]: 179–193 (*SEG* 43.26):

Decree A. Diogenes, son of Naukydos, made the motion. Since Phanomachos, the treasurer during the archonship of Praxiboulos [315/4], performed all the sacrifices to the gods and the heroes on behalf of the demesmen during his year and took care of the Dionysia well and honorably with the demarch Oinophilos, has made a *phiale* weighing one mina of silver in accordance with the law, has rendered account of everything under his administration to the city and to the demesmen within the timeframe mandated by the laws of the city and of the demesmen, has turned over to the Acharnians the cash remaining in his care from the housekeeping-fund to the amount of 329 drachmas, upon the completion of his audit was found to have carried out his duties as treasurer with justice, and has administered well and honorably all the matters that the Acharnians assigned to him: resolved by the Acharnians, to praise Phanomachos, son of Nikodemos, of Acharnai and to crown him with a crown of olive in recognition of his honor-seeking and justice towards the demesmen; and that the secretary of the demesmen engrave this resolution on a stone stele and erect it in the sanctuary of Athena Hippia; and that the treasurer pay out [20] drachmas for the engraving of the stele and render account to the demesmen.

Decree B. Diogenes, son of Naukydos, made the motion. Since the demarch Oinophilos and the treasurer Phanomachos and the superintendent of the Dionysia well and honorably have taken care of the sacrifice to Dionysos, the procession, and the contest, and administer all else on behalf of the demesmen in accordance with the laws: resolved by the Acharnians, to praise the demarch Oinophilos, son of Oinophilos, and the treasurer Phanomachos, son of Nikodemos, and the superintendent Leon, son of Theon, and to crown each of them with a crown of ivy, and that the demarch announce these crowns at the contest of the Dionysia in Acharnai, that the demarch Oinophilos engrave this resolution on a stone stele and erect it in the sanctuary of Athena Hippia, that the treasurer Phanomachos pay out 20 drachmas for the engraving and render account to the demesmen, and that the honorands and their descendants be granted privileged seating in the first bench for all time at the contest of the Dionysia in Acharnai.

(3) **Decree regarding payment for sacrifice from receipts of theater, ca. 300.** *IG* II[2] 1206:[15]

. . . and his . . . each and every year the secretary and the demarch, whoever happen to be in office at the time, [to pay out] 20 drachmas from the moneys being collected from the theater. But if the [sc. moneys from the] theater are [insufficient] . . . , the demarch and the treasurer, whoever happen to be in office at the time, are to pay out to them the written sum for the sacrifice out of the housekeeping-fund of the demesmen. That the secretary in conjunction with the demesmen engrave this resolution on a stone stele and erect it in the sanctuary of Athena Hippia, and that the demarch [—]enes pay out to them for the engraving of the stele 20 drachmas and render account to the demesmen.

(4) **Decree granting honors to a priestess, ca. 300.** *IG* II[2] 1207:

[name lost], son of [—]okles, of Acharnai made the motion. Decreed

by the demesmen, since the priestess [name entirely lost] has set up dedications to [Athena] Hippia . . . a couch . . . cash. . . .

**(5) Thank offering to Ares and the Roman emperor Augustus,
time of Augustus. *IG* II² 2953:**

[Good luck.] When Apollophanes, son of [name lost], [was priest]
and Theoxenos, son of Demetrios, and [name lost], son of [Apo]llonios,
were stewards and [name lost] was the eponymous archon of the city, the
community of the Acharnians in recognition of . . . [dedicate this] thank-
offering to Ares and Sebastos [i.e. Augustus]. . . . [—]os, son of Diognetos, of Acharnai, made this.

The references in these inscriptions to physical structures within the
boundaries of the deme have long been studied in the light of the results
of archaeological investigation. The inscriptions imply a shrine to [Athena]
Hippia (no. 4) and actually mention a theater (no. 3), the latter presumably the scene of the deme's own Dionysia (no. 2, A and B), but neither
shrine nor theater has yet been located. Not so with the remaining epigraphically attested structure. Our decree no. 1 contemplates the construction at Acharnai of altars of Ares and Athena Areia. From Roman times,
perhaps 350 years later, the *charisterion* to Ares and Augustus (no. 5), which
was reported to have been discovered at Menidi and in any event mentions
"the community of the Acharnians," records the deme's thanks for some
unspecified benefaction. Homer Thompson's reconstruction of the sequence of events lying behind these articles of evidence now enjoys wide
acceptance. Remains of a large temple were discovered in 1937 near the
middle of the Agora and identified as belonging to Ares on the strength of
Pausanias's itinerary (1.8.4; *Agora* III, no. 117). Unambiguous signs that
the temple had been moved to its present location prompted a search for
its original site, with our two inscriptions (nos. 1 and 5) settling the matter
in favor of Acharnai, despite the absence of remains on the ground. Pausanias, who visited Acharnai around the middle of the second century A.D.,
mentions neither Ares nor his temple in his description (1.31.6), but the
classical altars of Ares and Athena Areia (no. 1) would appropriately have
stood before a temple dedicated to the war god. After the building had
fallen into disrepair, it will have been moved from Acharnai to the Agora
by Augustus, in gratitude for which the demesmen responded with the
thank offering (no. 5) for "a timely rescue operation."[16] Thus, ironically,
the one physical structure from Acharnai that we can identify by name is
known from its remains not in the deme, but in the town of Athens.

"The Dionysia" attested in inscription no. 2 are of course the so-called "Rural" Dionysia celebrated by certain of the demes in evident coordination with the several Dionysian festivals in the town. According to decree B, the Acharnian version comprised a sacrifice (*thysia*), procession (*pompē*), and contest (*agōn*), the final item with reference to dramatic competition. The festival will receive full attention in chapter 4 in the larger context of its celebration throughout Attica. From a variety of sources (especially, but not limited to, Pausanias, 1.31.6), we also learn of Acharnian observance of Amphiaraos (?), Apollo Agyieus and Erithaseos, Ares, Artemis, Asklepios (and Asklepiastai), Athena Hippia and Hygieia, Dionysos Melpomenos and Kissos, and Herakles.[17] Although no *lex sacra* from the deme has survived, it is apparent that the Acharnians maintained a full calendar of internal associational cultic activities on their own ground and did not simply depend upon the parallel offerings in the nearby civic center of Athens.

Despite the unprecedented imperial intervention, the Acharnians' installations and activities are much in keeping with the records of the other demes, and the same may be said concerning personnel: demarch, secretary, treasurer, priest, priestess, temple stewards, and the ad hoc board of persons "selected" for a specific task. Also unexceptionable are the award of honors, accounting procedures, and cutting and erection of stone stelai. The financing of a major project through the advancing of funds by a wealthy member of the association (no. 1) is a familiar procedure which, in line with the approach taken in the preceding chapter, is best regarded as but one manifestation of rural community patronage. Not visibly connected with private largess, however, the raising of funds (in this case, to pay for a sacrifice) from a theater (no. 3) is not exampled elsewhere among the rural demes. At Peiraieus, the theater is let out by the deme,[18] and such could have been the case here in Acharnai as well, but the sale of tickets for performances is not to be ruled out. Chapter 4 will review the scattered but clear evidence for itinerant producers, actors, and spectators circulating among the various demes during the season of the Rural Dionysia. As for Acharnai, likely candidates for visitors are urban dwellers, whose path out the Acharnian Gate and a half dozen or so miles by road to the deme would have reversed the direction of the apparently frequent visits by the *anthrakeutai*.

Unusually for a deme-association, the Acharnians are repeatedly identifiably engaged outside their own proper boundaries, the charcoal-sellers in the *asty* being merely the most memorable examples. According to inscription no. 1, approval for the altar(s) had been sought from Apollo at

Delphi, whose response included reference to the People of the Athenians in addition to the deme itself, suggesting a cooperative arrangement between deme and Demos. At home, the treasurer is called upon to render account both to the state and to the demesmen and within the constraints of time mandated by the laws of Athens as well as those of the demesmen (no. 2, A). The references here to the *polis* illustrate and underscore the dependence inherent in Acharnai's status as a deme community. Mention has been made of the erection on the deme's ground of the Ephebic Oath and the Oath of Plataia. Early in Imperial times, the *koinon* of the Acharnians tenders thanks not only to the god but also to the emperor in an inscription displayed in the deme (no. 5), while in the Agora the re-erected temple of Ares will palpably announce the rural deme's continuing urban presence. Thucydides and the inscriptions preserving the bouleutic quotas inform us of Acharnai's great relative size among the demes, but it may be that a more striking feature is the sustained and significant evidence for its symbiotic relation with the town.

Aixone

Aixone is, excepting certain of the garrison encampments, the most plentifully epigraphically documented of all 139 demes. Nonetheless, all the eleven substantial preserved inscriptions emanating from the village-association fall within the space of a single generation in the second half of the fourth century, viz. between 345/4 and 313/2, so our dossier may well not be representative for all of classical antiquity. Epigraphic productivity (and perhaps survival, as well) in any case seems, to judge from the stones so far discovered, to be a function of size. Aixone was one of the larger demes, with its bouleutic quota of 11?[19] placing it behind only Acharnai (22) and Aphidna (16) and with Kydathenaion (11/12), Lower Paiania (11), and Eleusis (11?). Again, the average quota of a deme represented by at least one inscription is 5.42 versus the average quota of all demes of 3.59 councillors. But this does not explain the extreme chronological constriction.

However that may be, given the deme's size it is not surprising that its center has been located with some certainty. Strabo (9.1.21: 398) ordered the coastal demes from Phaleron to Sounion as follows: Peiraieus, Phaleron, Halimous, Aixone, and Halai Aixonides. According to the results of Eliot's careful study, the deme's territory was defined by the sea and Hymettos to the west and east and by natural features bounding the territories of Halimous and Halai Aixonides to the north and south respectively.[20] Physical remains document the occupation of the area from Mycenaean through Geometric, Classical, and Roman times,[21] and Eliot, working from the original find places of our inscriptions, placed the main settlement in the neighborhood of the church of Hagios Nikolaos.[22] The eventual spreading (or movement) of the settlement to the coast may be connected with the neighboring Anagyrasians' fame for red mullet (*orphōs*, "great sea-perch," *LSJ* [9] s.v.) witnessed by the Athenian comic poet Plato's *Syrphax*.[23] Since Eliot's 1962 publication, the deme in all its aspects has been treated by E. Giannopoulou-Konsolaki, *Glyphada*, Athens 1990 (*SEG* 40.287) and again by A.P. Matthaiou in *Horos* 10–12 (1992–1998) 146–169 (*SEG* 46.8, with 149, 154, 173, 247, and 314). The latter study reviews the evidence for the location of Aixone at modern Glyphada (including the findplaces of inscriptions and the accounts of early European travelers), restudies and classifies the epigraphic record, notes that the theater has yet to be found, and reopens the question of the precise location of the deme's center (or centers). A security *horos* from the site marking a *chorion* and *oikia*, *SEG* 38.165, figured in our study of farmstead residence in chapter 1.

The following roster of texts represents finds reported through *SEG* 47 (for 1997), excluding small uncommunicative fragments such as *SEG* 46.149, 247 and 314.

(1) Sacred law on the perquisites for various priestesses, ca. 400. *IG* II² 1356 (*LSCG* no. 28), supplemented by new fragment: *SEG* 46.173:

[Perquisites for _ _ _] . . . a half-hekteus of wheat: 3 obols: a kotyle of honey: 3 obols: three kotylai of olive oil: 1 drachma, 3 obols: firewood: 1 1/2 obols: for the table, a ham, a side of hip-joint, a half-portion of tripe.

Perquisites for the priestess of (the) Heroine: 5 drachmas: the skins from the Heroina (?), the entire singed adult victim: 3 obols: the distribution of meats, a half-hekteus of wheat: [3 obols]: a kotyle of [honey]: 3 obols: three kotylai of olive oil: 1 1/2 obols: firewood: 2 obols : and for the table, a ham, a side of hip-joint, a half-portion of tripe.

Perquisites for the priestess of Dionysos Anthios: 5 drachmas: the skin of the adult victim: and for the table, a ham, a side of hip-joint, a half-portion of tripe.

Perquisites for the priestess of Hera: 5 drachmas: the skin of the entire singed adult victim: 3 drachmas: the distribution of meats: [a half-hekteus of wheat: 3 obols] : a kotyle of honey: 3 obols: three kotylai of olive oil: 1 1/2 obols: firewood: [2 obols]: and for the table, a ham, a side of hip-joint, a half-portion of tripe.

Perquisites for the priestess of Demeter Chloe: 5 drachmas: the distribution of meats: a half-hekteus of wheat: 3 obols: [a kotyle of honey: 3 obols] : three kotylai of olive oil: 1 1/2 obols: firewood: 2 obols: and for the table, a ham, a side of hip-joint, a half-portion of tripe.

[Perquisites for the priestess of _ _ _]a : 5 drachmas: the skin of the adult victim, the distribution of meats, a half-hekteus of wheat : 3 obols [a kotyle of honey: 3 obols: three kotylai of olive oil: 1 1/2 obols : firewood : 2 obols : and for the table, a ham, a side of hip-joint, [a half-portion of tripe . . .].

[Perquisites for the] priestess: 5 drachmas : [_ _ _] 1 drachma : [a kotyle] of honey: 3 obols [_ _ _] a chous of wine [_ _ _].

(2) Lease of land and associated decree of the demesmen, 345/4. IG II² 2492; SIG³ 966; RIJC I, no. XIIIbis; Pleket, _Epigraphica_ I, no. 42; Behrend, _Pachturkunden_, no. 25:

On the following terms the Aixonians leased the Phelleis plot to Autokles, son of Auteas, and Auteas, son of Autokles, for forty years, at 152 drachmas each year, on the condition that [sc. that they make use of the land] farming and in any other manner they wish. To pay the rent during the month Hekatombaion, but, if they do not, the security will go to the Aixonians both from the crops from the plot and from everything else belonging to the party not paying. Nor is to be permitted to the Aixonians either to sell or to lease to anyone else, until the forty years run out. And if enemy troops debar access or destroy anything, one half of the proceeds from the plot are to go to the Aixonians. And when the forty years run out, the lessees are to turn over half of the land without a crop on it and whatever trees are on the plot; and the Aixonians are to bring in a vine-dresser for the final five years.

The time of the lease of the Demetrian crop [i.e. grain] begins with Euboulos's archonship, that of wood-cutting with the archon after Euboulos. The treasurers under the demarch Demosthenes are to engrave the lease on stone stelai and to set them up, the one within the sanctuary of Hebe, the other in the lounge, as well as markers on the plot itself no smaller than two tripods on each side.

If an extraordinary war levy on the land to the city should occur, the

Aixonians are to pay it, but if the lessors contribute, the contribution is to be counted against the lease.

Any earth removed in an excavation no one may deport except back on to the plot itself.

But if anyone makes a motion or puts to the vote anything contrary to this contract before the forty years run out, he is to be liable to the lessees on a charge of injury.

Eteokles, son of Skaon, of Aixone made the motion. Since the lessees of the Phelleis plot, Autokles and Auteas, agree with the Aixonians to cut down the olive trees, to select men who are, with the demarch and the treasurers and the lessee, to sell the olive trees to the person offering the most. They are to calculate half the interest on the moneys accrued at the rate of a drachma [sc. per mina per month, i.e. at a 12% annual rate] and subtract (this amount) from the lease and to engrave on the stelai the reduced amount of the lease. The Aixonians are to take the interest on the money [raised from] the price of the olive trees. The party buying the olive trees is to cut them down whenever Anthias brings in the crop in the archonship after Archias's before the plowing. They are to leave stumps not less than a palm's length [in height] in the spaces around the trees marked by potsherds, in order that olive trees as fine and large as possible grow up during these years. The following were selected to sell the olive trees: Eteokles, Nauson, and Hagnotheos.

(3) **Decree granting honors to** *syndikoi,* **ca. 330.** *IG* II² 1197:

(traces including names of honorands of which the last-named is) . . . Leophilos, son of Eudi[kos]. The demarch in office on each occasion is to summon them to the preferred seating [sc. in the theater], and they are to have the same awards (all that are given in accordance with the law) as the *syndikoi* headed by Laches, in order that others too seek honor, knowing that they will receive acts of gratitude from the demesmen. The demarch Philotheros is to engrave this resolution on a stone stele and erect it in the theater.

(4) **Decree granting honors to** ?*hieropoioi* **of ?Hebe, ca. 330–320.** *SEG* 46.154:

. . . (remains of at least three names with patronymic) [well] and honorably took care of the festival (*heortē*) to (Hebe? Hera?). Decreed by the *demotai* to praise them and to crown each of them with a golden crown of 500 drachmas in recognition of their justice and love of honor towards the [*demotai*]. To inscribe this resolution on a stone stele and [erect it . . .].

**(5) Decree granting honors to two *choregoi* of the deme, 326/5. *IG*
II² 1198:**

Philoktemon, son of Chremes, made the motion. Since the *choregoi* of
Chremes' archonship, Demokrates, son of Euphiletos, and Hegesias, son
of Lysistratos, well and honorably performed the *choregia* for the Aixonians, to praise them and crown them with a crown worth eight (?) drachmas in recognition of their seeking of honor and of their service to the
demesmen. And the demarch Dorotheos and the treasurers are also to give
them ten drachmas from the income of the demesmen for a sacrifice. The
demarch Dorotheos is to engrave this resolution on a stone stele and erect
it in the theater, in order that those about to perform the *choregia* for the
Aixonians know that the deme of the Aixonians will honor those seeking
honor on their behalf.

**(6) Decree concerning the leasing of pasturage and procedure for
settlement of disputes pertaining thereto, 326/5. *IG* II² 1196:**

Face A. (traces) . . . court, and the . . . and the demarch Dor[—] . . .
to the *hieropoioi*, that . . . well . . . and the demarch to render judgment . . . to the parties having paid and to the party not having paid the
price of the pasturage-rights. But if any of those owing wish to resort to
arbitration to the demesmen concerning what they owe, having sworn
prior to entry into the court to conduct the arbitration in whatever way it
[the arbitration] is likely to be as just as possible, that the arrears be de-
ferred until the demesmen render judgment. They are to swear that, whenever they resort to arbitration, to abide in whatever the demesmen resolve
and render payment . . . of their own or tender their own securities to the
demesmen. But whichever of them do not abide nor pay what they owe
nor, taking their sureties, deposit other such ones, untouched, in their
place, nor . . . they wish to refer to arbitration concerning these things . . .
and the *syndikoi* and . . . (the) demarch with the *syndikoi* . . . to the demesmen as much . . . but if any of these things . . . introducing into a court . . .
to the demarch. . . .

Face B. . . . to decide . . . and I shall not rescind any of these things—
neither I myself nor, with my knowledge, any of my people, unless the
demesmen resolve to sell the pasturage-rights. And for the future time I
shall reveal to the demesmen if I am aware of anyone doing any of these
things in the fields. If I swear honestly that the foregoing is true by Zeus,
by Poseidon, by Demeter, many good things are to come to me; but if I
should swear falsely, the opposite. The . . .

(7) Decrees granting honors to religious officers, 320/19. *IG* II²
1199:

Philaos, son of Chremes, made the motion. Since the allotted *hieropoioi* for the sanctuary of Hebe justly and honorably took care of the sacrifice to Hebe and to the other gods to which they were supposed to sacrifice and have rendered an account and audit, to crown each of them with a crown of olive—Anticharmos, son of Nauson, Nearchos, son of Chairigenes, Theodotos, son of Aischron, Aristokles, son of Kalliphon—in recognition of justice and seeking of honor with respect to the demesmen. The demarch serving after the archonship of Neaichmos is to engrave this resolution on a stone stele and erect it in the sanctuary of Hebe. And to praise also the *sophronistai* and crown each of them with a crown of olive: Kimon, Megalexis (?), Pythodoros, son of Pytheos, and the herald Charikles in recognition of their seeking of honor in connection with the all-night celebration (*pannychis*). And to praise also the priest of the Herakleidai, Kallias, and the priestess of Hebe and Alkmene and the archon, Kallisthenes, son of Nauson, and to crown each of them in recognition of piety and seeking of honor with respect to the gods. And to engrave this resolution on a stone stele and erect it in the sanctuary of Hebe.

(8) Decree granting honors to two *choregoi* of the deme, 317/6. *IG* II² 1200:

Philoktemon, son of Chremes, made the motion. Decreed by the demesmen, since the *choregoi* during Demogenes' archonship, Leontios, son of Dion, Glaukon, son of Kallikrates, well and honorably served in the *choregia* for the Aixonians, to praise them and crown each of them with a crown worth 500 drachmas in recognition of seeking of honor. . . .

(9) Decree granting honors to Demetrios of Phaleron, 317–307. *IG* II² 1201:

Gods. Aristokrates, son of Aristophanes, made the motion. Since Demetrios, son of Phanostratos, of Phaleron is a good man with respect to the Demos of the Athenians and the deme of Aixonians and, when war broke out in the countryside, and Peiraieus and the *asty* were divided on account of the war, serving as ambassador, reconciled Athenians and brought them back together again and worked out peace for Athenians and the countryside and, chosen superintendent by the Demos of the Athenians, passed laws that were good in the interests of the city. Later, . . .

(10) Decree granting honors to two members of the deme-association, 313/2. *IG* II² 1202:

When Theophrastos was archon, in the regular meeting. Decreed by the Aixonians, Glaukides, son of Sosippos, of Aixone made the motion. Resolved by the Aixonians, since Kallikrates, son of Glaukon, of Aixone and Aristokrates, son of Aristophanes, of Aixone are good and honor-seeking concerning the deme of the Aixonians, to praise them in recognition of excellence and justice with respect to the deme of the Aixonians and to crown each with a golden crown worth 500 drachmas. The funds for the crowns are to come from housekeeping from the remaining moneys of the archonship of Theophrastos, and the demarch Hegesilaos and the treasurers are to give to them the funds for the crowns. An announcement is to be made at the comedies of the Dionysia in the theater at Aixone, that the deme of the Aixonians crowns them in recognition of excellence and justice with respect to the deme of the Aixonians and the communal properties (*ta koina*) of the Aixonians. And the demarch Hegesilaos and the treasurers are to engrave this resolution on a stone stele and erect it in the theater in Aixone.

(II) Decree granting honors to two *choregoi* of the deme, 313/2. N. Kyparissis and W. Peek, *MDAI(A)* 66 (1941) 218–219, no. 1:

Gods. Glaukides, son of Sosippos, made the motion. Since the *choregoi* Auteas, son of Autokles, and Philoxenides, son of Philippos, well and honorably served in the *choregia:* Decreed by the demesmen, to crown each of them with a golden crown worth 100 drachmas in the theater at the comedies after the archonship of Theophrastos, in order that the other *choregoi* about to serve in the *choregia* seek honor too, and that the demarch Hegesilaos and the treasurers also give to them 10 drachmas for a sacrifice, and that the treasurers engrave this resolution on a stone stele and erect it in the theater, in order that the Aixonians always stage the Dionysia in the best manner possible.

Generally speaking, it is clear from our documents that the finances of the deme were significantly bound up with the productive land enclosed within its boundaries. The lease of arable (no. 2) and the document concerning pasturage (no. 6) speak explicitly on this head, for both, over and above details regarding the land itself, are basically concerned with the association's financial interest in the income-producing capacity of these corporate holdings.

The inscription *IG* II^2 2492 (no. 2) is richly informative regarding the leased property, the uses to which it will be put, and arrangements for its exploitation by lessees. To be collected over the lengthy period of forty years, at an annual rate of 152 drachmas, the fees will provide the association with a guaranteed significant income for a generation and more. The crops themselves (along with other, unspecified valuables) will be surety against payment of the rent and, should the lessee fail to pay, will be seized against back payment. Specific language is added to the contract to protect the association in the event of enemy invasion, to guarantee maintenance of the trees, and by various means to ensure that the land will be readied for letting out again immediately upon expiry of the lease. An addendum provides guidelines for the carrying out of the lessee's decision to cut down the olive trees, once again with the express purpose of protecting the present and future interests of the association. Nor are the interests of the lessees neglected. The plot may be farmed or be put to any use they choose. Grape vines are already, or will soon be, growing on it. The olive trees are at the time of closing of the agreement mature enough to possess significant value as wood. Given such a range of produce, these must have been among the more productive lands within the deme. Whether the same was true, however, of the "pasturage" (with its attendant fees and rights, collapsed under the single Greek term *to ennomion*) which is the subject of the somewhat later decree (no. 6), is not revealed by our text.[24] What does come across emphatically is the association's concern with legalities, specifically with the securing of its right to collect a contracted rental fee on its properties and its willingness to proceed to arbitration, then to the courts, in order to enforce the terms of the lease. Note again, too, that the oath preserved fragmentarily on Face B calls for the party swearing to "reveal to the demesmen if I am aware of anyone doing any of these things *in the fields*." Evidently, the scope of the village-association's vigilance was not only determined but far-reaching as well. But why such vigilance? Much is to be said for the view that it was real holdings such as these, put out to rent, that comprised a major source of income for a deme-association's corporate activities. But rentals, it is clear, were not the only such source.

Given Aixone's large size, it is not surprising that we learn of several demesmen of wealth. Over against the 223 Aixoneis catalogued by Kirchner in his *Prosopographia Attica*, eleven demesmen were identified as members of the liturgical class in Davies' *Athenian Propertied Families*.[25] Among these are two famous Athenians, the pupil of Plato and namesake of a dialogue, Lysis (II), son of Demokrates (I) (*PA* 9574; *PAA* 617405) and the distinguished general Chabrias, son of Ktesippos (I) (*PA* 15086). But our interest is less in famous individuals than in the local community. Nat-

urally, it is to be expected that some upper-class families will eventually migrate elsewhere—thus the family of Kallippos (I), son of Philon (I) (*PA*
8065; *PAA* 559250). From the fact that all but one of the family's tombstones were found in Peiraieus, Davies inferred "that by the first half of the
fourth century the family interests were no longer centered in the family
deme and were bound up in some way with the commercial life of the
port." [26] The tombstone of Lysis and of a son, Timokleides, was set up, to
judge from its find-spot, in or near the deme of Xypete, southwest of the
town, according to its editor, Ronald Stroud;[27] and the gravestone of his
daughter, Isthmonikē, and apparently her husband, a demesmen of Paiania, *IG* II² 7045, was found built into the Dipylon Gate. The question for
us is, were there Aixonians of substance who maintained a base or foothold
of some sort in the village, while (as in the cases of both Lysis and
Chabrias) certain of their fellow demesmen pursued their fortunes in an urban setting? As it happens, unambiguous indications that there were are at
hand:

(a) Of the 52 tombstones of Aixoneis collected in *IG* II², viz.
5403–5454, at least five were discovered in or near the deme or along roads
leading to or from the deme: 5417, 5430, 5448, 5453, 5454. Two more recently published conforming examples are *SEG* 12.169a (near Glyphada)
and 18.97 (at Glyphada).

(b) While Plato's dialogue finds Lysis in Athens (in approximate
agreement with the provenience of the tombstone just mentioned), Davies
inferred from a passage in that same text, 205c-d, that "the family held a
hereditary priesthood of the cult of the Herakleidai within the family's
deme Aixone." [28] This is the priesthood held by the Kallias (presumably a
member of the family) who is praised in our no. 7, *IG* II² 1199, lines 23–24.
Maintenance of a cult, and priesthood, in Aixone should entail residence,
if only temporary or involving only certain members of the family, within
the deme as well.

(c) Although Chabrias's international military adventures took him far
afield, a lost speech of Hypereides (fr. 137 Jensen) reports a mansion which,
if (as Davies finds probable) the scene of his victory celebrations in 374
([Dem.] 59.33–34), was "perhaps" situated at Cape Kolias.[29]

(d) Kallippos (I), son of Philon (I), whose family connections with
Peiraieus were mentioned above, produced a son Philon, among whose
own four sons was Philokrates, named on a gravestone (*IG* II² 5448) found
north of Hagios Nikolaos on the road to Vari. Since such a provenience lay
within the territory of Aixone, Davies inferred that "[p]erhaps a family

arrangement left Philokrates in possession of such of the family property as lay in the deme, . . ."[30]

From the inscriptions, it is clear that the association's institutional infrastructure was of sufficient magnitude to make desirable the ongoing presence of village patrons. Cult, as often, is to the fore. Beside the priesthood of the Herakleidai in no. 7, the priestess of Hebe and Alkmene is honored alongside him in the same inscription, and no. 3 calls for the erection of stelai within the sanctuary (*hieron*) of Hebe and "in the lounge" (*leschē*) (lines 23–24). The *lex sacra IG* II² 1356, our no. 1, now, as a consequence of the discovery of a new fragment at Glyphada (*SEG* 46.173), reassigned by Matthaiou to Aixone from Halai Aixonides, is concerned with the specification of perquisites of at least six priestesses including, where all or part of a divinity's name is preserved, the Heroinē, Dionysos, Hera, Demeter Chloē, plus one other largely lost but certainly female divinity. Since all the divinities preserved are either female or, as in Dionysos's case, female in orientation, and since only priestesses, but no priest, occur, it is entirely possible that the intact *lex* dealt exclusively with a cult apparatus devoted to the girls and women of the deme. But the general point to be made is that the deme was well endowed with sacral sites, personnel, and events.

By contrast with this assiduous attention to Aixone's *demotides*, a character in the urban dramatist Menander's *Kanēphoros* could, evidently with reference to a well-known stereotype, refer to "some ill-spoken old woman" as "Aixonian on both sides."[31] According to literary sources, the Aixonians were well known for their contentiousness.[32]

This leaves the still undiscovered theater, the scene of the comedies staged at the ("Rural") Dionsyia attested by two of the decrees (nos. 10 and 11) and of all the productions—whether comedic, tragic, or rhapsodic—supported by the deme's several and apparently oft-rewarded *choregoi*. Appropriately enough, the theater will be the scene of the erection of stelai honoring *choregoi* and announcing the association's commitment similarly to honor any future such benefactors (nos. 3, 6, and 11). Besides the Dionysian *agōnes*, associational cultic functions mentioned by the texts are the sacrifice for which two honorands were on two different occasions voted 10 drachmas (nos. 5 and 11), the festival (no. 4, *heortē*), and the "all-night celebration" (no. 7, *pannychis*). While any kind of quantification is entirely beyond us, it is difficult to resist the hunch that cultic activity, with its attendant elements of entertainment and consumption, was a prominent aspect of this village-association's calendar. The scene of that activity was the

deme itself, whether shrine or theater or other communal space. And
among this festive calendar's supporters and organizers were the notables
who had maintained a base in the ancestral village, if they were not permanent residents, and who undertook the onus of priesthood and choregy.

The *choregoi*, and their activities, mentioned in several of the decrees
demand special mention here, for it will be observed in chapter 4 that
Aixone is one of the very few ordinary Attic rural demes (that is, once we
have excluded anomalous cases such as Peiraieus, Eleusis, Thorikos, Rhamnous, and so on) for which theatrical productions are securely recorded.
Perhaps significantly, each of the three inscriptions concerned with the
choregia cites two *choregoi* (nos. 5, 8, 10, and 11), but the nature of that significance is quite unclear. Was the object to divide a burden too great for
one demesman? Or was the privilege eagerly sought, requiring that multiple *choregoi* be assigned to each single production? Still another possibility
was put forward by Whitehead. He noted that our nos. 10 and 11, moved
in the same year by the same man, each honor a pair of Aixonians, the latter two identified as *choregoi*, the former two not so identified but with the
announcement scheduled to be made "at the comedies of the Dionysia."
Because there could be only one winning play, it occurred to him that one
pair were the winners (namely, the two individuals designated *choregoi* in
no. 11), the other two "defeated in competition by Auteas and Philoxenides
but nonetheless thanked and rewarded by their grateful fellow demesmen
as the men who *proxime accesserunt*."[33] But this ingenious argument contains a fatal flaw: Whitehead's winners will receive crowns worth 100 drachmas, the losers crowns worth 500 drachmas! Perhaps we should reverse the
order of finish. I prefer, however, to underscore the fact that the recipients
of 500-drachma crowns are *not* identified as *choregoi*, a fact which, in combination with passage of the two decrees in the same year, strongly suggests
that their benefactions took some other form. Announcement "at the
comedies" may prove nothing about the nature of that service if, as is
highly likely, the Dionysia was the premier communal event on the Aixonian calendar and therefore a fitting occasion for all manner of pronouncements. After all, the somewhat earlier decree no. 3 (ca. 330) calls for the
bestowal of *proedria* on persons, viz. *syndikoi*, not connected with dramatic
production, and for the erection of the stele carrying the decree in the theater. Inferentially, a gathering in the theater on the occasion of the
Dionysia was not strictly limited to the staging of the dramatic productions.

Aixone is one of three demes—the others are Eleusis (*IG* II² 2971) and

Sphettos (*SEG* 25.206)—known to have honored Demetrios of Phaleron with an inscription, so to that extent a certain formulaic quality might be expected in these perhaps not entirely spontaneous accolades. Nonetheless, it remains notable that the war (for the ending of which Demetrios is above all being honored by the Aixonians) is stated to have broken out "in the countryside" and that the eventual peace is represented as accruing to the benefit of the "Athenians and the countryside." Are these merely un-premeditated allusions to the scene of conflict, or are we to find here a deeper, and more pointed, meaning? Neither the Eleusinian nor the Sphet-tian text, though both are intact, contains any such language. May I sug-gest that in these twin mentions of the *chora* we are to recognize the agrarian perspective and interests of the demesmen whose letting out of arable and pasturage, by the chance survival of two inscriptions, is known to have so visibly contributed to their communal welfare? From the in-scription concerning pasturage (no. 6), the oath, besides binding the swearer to personal compliance with its specific terms, also requires him to turn over to the demesmen anyone he finds violating the terms of the de-cree *en tois agrois*, "in the fields" (no. 6, face B, lines 13–16). The preposi-tional phrase perhaps neatly encapsulates the Aixonians' agrarian orientation. These villagers saw themselves as the occupants of the coun-tryside, not (as a contemporary urbanite might have portrayed them) as residents of a suburban community dependent on the *asty*.

Halai Aixonides

Apparently by accident, another Attic deme relatively well represented in the epigraphic record is Aixone's immediate neighbor to the south, Halai Aixonides, substantial in size of population (its quota was six) and, like Aixone, assigned to the coastal trittys of Kekropis. Again as with Aixone, this deme falls within the scope of C. W. J. Eliot's *Coastal Demes of At-tika*, where is set out the evidence establishing both the extent of the deme's territory and the probable location of its village center. Bounded on the north by a line running from south of Voula towards Hymettos, Halai was limited on the west by the sea, on the east by Hymettos and its spur, and extended southwards to Vouliagmene and Cape Zoster.[34] Eliot placed the village center at Palaiochori between Voula and Vouliagmeni, a site with surface remains from the archaic to Roman times, but with a concentration of sherds from the Classical and Hellenistic periods.[35] Excavations of the site reported since Eliot's date of publication have yielded extensive remains of architecture. For the reports, see (in modern Greek) "Observations on the Domestic Form of the Attic Demes" by Giorgos Stainchaour[36] and, with reference to our deme alone, "The Deme of Halai Aixonides" by Ioanna Andreou[37] in the volume edited by W. D. E. Coulson and others under the title *The Archaeology of Athens and Attica under the Democracy* published in 1994.

The name of our deme, like its homonymous fellow deme on the opposite eastern coast, Halai Araphenides, evidently commemorated "saltworks" (Greek, *halai*), with the compound meaning "the Aixone salt works."[38] The implication would seem to be that, prior to the setting of the deme boundaries, Aixone's domains had extended further to the south. Menander wrote a play, now lost save for its title, called *Halaieis*, but the deme in question is not Aixonides but Araphenides,[39] so no help on this (or any other) point is to be found here. As with Aixone, the deme's rich lapidary harvest is (where datable) confined to the late classical period, with a total cessation of surviving datable texts after ca. 300. For new fragments, see now G. Steinhauer, "Demendekrete und ein neuer Archon des 3. Jahrhunderts v. Chr. aus dem Aphrodision von Halai Aixonides," *MDA(A)* 113 (1998) 235–248.

(1) Sacral accounts, ca. 400. P.D. Stavropoullos, *AE* 1938, pp. 23–25 (*SEG* 12.52):

(10 lines of traces, including [*dem?*]*archon* at line 3) . . . treasurer of sacred moneys . . . was secretary . . . they handed over . . . drachmas . . . treasurer of sacred . . . ?number of drachmas, 3 obols . . . Timarchos . . . the co-magistrates. . . . [—]stratos was secretary . . . they handed over. . . .

(2) Decree concerning auditing procedure (*euthynai*) for officials of deme, 368/7. *IG* II² 1174:

Euthemon made the motion. In order that the communal properties [*ta koina*] be secure for the demesmen and that the demarchs and the treasurers give the *euthynai*, decreed by the demesmen: That the demarchs and the treasurers deposit in the box the account of the receipts and expenditures according to each month, since the (officers) of Nausigenes' archonship are on their own voluntarily depositing their account by month. In the following year, to conduct the *euthynai* before the month Metageitnion from the records in the box but not from other (records). To write up this resolution and erect the stele in the agora. And let the demarch bind by oath the *euthynos* and his assessors to conduct the *euthynai* in accordance with the resolution posted in the agora. And if . . . and (if) they do not execute the *euthyna* in accordance with this resolution. . . .

(3) Decree requiring oaths to be administered to deme officials and others, ca. 360. *IG* II² 1175:

Astyphilos made the motion. Concerning the matters Nikomenes is voicing: Decreed by the demesmen [_ _ _] . . . of Euthemon. . . . In order that in the future no such thing occur in the deme. That the demarch Nikostratos and the treasurers and the priests and the priestesses take the oath.

(4) Statue base recording a dedication, ca. 360. *IG* II² 2820:

The persons chosen by the Halaieis to make the statue for Aphrodite, crowned by the demesmen, made the dedication to Aphrodite. (24 names with patronymic). Praxias, son of Lysimachos, of Ankyle made (this).

(5) Decree granting honors to priest of Apollo Zoster and his four assistants, ca. 360. K. Kourionotes, *AD* II (1927–1928) 40–41, no. 4, improved by W. Peek, *MDAI(A)* 67 (1942) 9–10, no. 7:

Decreed by the Halaieis, Hagnotheos, son of Ekphantides, made the motion. Whereas Polystratos, having become priest of Apollo Zoster, is well and piously and in a manner worthy of the god occupying the priesthood, has exceedingly honorably outfitted the sanctuary, has decorated the statues in cooperation with the persons chosen by the demesmen, has taken care also of the sacrifice of the Zosteria according to ancestral custom, and has rendered account of his superintendence to the demesmen: Accordingly, on account of all these things, to praise the priest of Apollo, Polystratos, son of Charmantides, of Halai and to crown him with a crown of laurel in recognition of his piety and justice; and to praise also those selected with him for the superintendence of the sanctuary and to crown each of them with a crown of laurel: Theodotos, son of Theodotos, of Halai; Lischeas, son of Phileriphos, of Halai; Pantakles, son of Sokrates, of Halai; Hagnias, son of Milesios, of Halai. And to engrave this resolution and erect it in the sanctuary of Apollo. The treasurer is to pay out whatever expense is incurred and is to render account to the demesmen. Halaieis (honor) Polystratos. Halaieis (honor) those selected (with Polystratos).

(6) Fragments of decrees concerned with cult of Apollo Zoster, ca. 350–300. K. Kourionotes, *AD* II (1927–1928) 42–43, nos. 6–7, improved by W. Peek, *MDAI(A)* 67 (1942) 8–9, no. 6:

Kourionotes, no. 6. . . . for the Halaieis, and chosen . . . to Apollo. Accordingly, in recognition of all these things to praise . . . because he is a good man concerning the deme of Halaieis . . . of Phrynichides . . . in recognition of seeking of honor . . . of Apollo Zoster. And to praise . . . and crown him with a golden crown worth 500 drachmas. . . .

Kourionotes, no. 7. . . . the sanctuary . . . given . . . [—]skai shared . . . to render thanks . . . for the Halaieis to choose . . . the crown . . .

(7) Fragment of decree concerned with cult of Apollo Zoster, ca. 300. K. Kourionotes, *AD* II (1927–1928) 41–42, no. 5, improved by W. Peek, *MDAI(A)* 67 (1942) 10, no. 8:

. . . that the demarch engrave this resolution on a stone stele and erect it at Halai in the sanctuary of Apollo Zoster. Whatever expense is incurred, (to render account of it) to the demesmen.

(8) Security horos. Found between Pnyx and Areopagos. No date. Aixonides or Araphenides? *IG* II² 2761b (*SIG*³ 1195; Finley 1952, no. 5):

Marker of a house pledged to the Halaieis, 200 drachmas.

From these (and a few additional literary) sources, considerable information may be garnered concerning, first, the cults of the deme-association. Appropriately, these cults included one of Poseidon, for Athenaios (6.297e) ascribes to the Halaieis a curious sacrifice of a tunny fish to that god. Stephanus, commenting on *Zostēr*, glosses the term as an isthmos of Attica, where Leto shed her clothing and bathed in the lake. "Here," he continues, "the Halaieis sacrifice to Leto and Artemis and Apollo Zosterios."[40] A temple of Apollo Zoster, and near it a priest's house, were excavated and identified by Greek archaeologists during the 1920s and 1930s.[41]

The cult is documented by the largely uncommunicative decrees, or fragments thereof, discovered in the excavations at Vouliagmene by Kourionotes, our nos. 5–7. The primary concerns are, as often in sacral texts of this kind, with personnel and funding. The accounts (no. 1) mention a treasurer of sacred moneys, secretary, and co-magistrates in the course of a few fragmentary lines concerning transfer of funds. The intact decree from Vouliagmene (no. 5) honors the priest of Apollo Zoster and four fellow demesmen for their attention to the sanctuary (outfitting of the *hieron*, decoration of the cult statue, performance of the sacrifice of the Zosteria, etc.). The two fragments nos. 6 and 7, identifiably honorary, may have been of a similar character. Evidently, the cult of Apollo was central to the deme's associational life and, as such, its continuing vitality depended upon the good will and dedication of its priestly officers no less than upon a steady stream, and orderly administration, of sacral moneys.

A somewhat different aspect of cultic administration may be reflected in the enigmatic beginning of the motion recorded in *IG* II² 1175 (no. 3), for there is reason to believe that the declaration that "no such thing" is to occur in the deme has to do with some matter of cultic administration.[42] Similar concerns but ones explicitly outside the cultic sphere are a matter of consideration in the well-preserved *IG* II² 1174 (no. 2), which details the procedure of *euthynai* for the review of the tenure of deme-association officers. The object of these measures is baldly declared in the preamble: "In order that the communal properties be secure" (followed paratactically by the introduction of the proper subject of business, the *euthynai*). From these two documents one might infer that the stability of this association was, or was perceived to be, vulnerable to disruption from within the association. A breach of religious propriety or the embezzlement of corporate funds might throw the deme's affairs into disarray, if, as suggested in the previous paragraph, it was in cultic functions that the villagers found the organizational nexus of their communal life.

Such concern with proper procedure is relevant to the question of the competing claims of communal welfare and individual ambition discussed in our examination of *philotimia* and rivalry in chapter 2. Strict regulations were evidently necessary in order to protect the *koinonia* of the village from the depredations of a personal "love of honor." So it is with respect to his *philotimia* that the honorand in no. 6 is praised and crowned "because he is a good man concerning the deme of Halaieis. . . ."

Besides the potential for sacrilege, peculation, or other outrage, what else can we say, on the positive side, about the internal forces driving and sustaining this village association? At the deme level, such matters usually remain well beyond our knowledge, but in this case we have some valuable clues in the composition of the body of 24 demesmen "chosen by the Halaieis to make the statue for Aphrodite" who, after being crowned by the demesmen, dedicated no. 4 to the goddess. If we may supply as a suppressed premise the assumption that "making" a statue in fact means paying for it, they may justly be characterized as benefactors of the village-association. The clues reside in the prosopographical backgrounds of these benefactors: Whitehead found that eighteen of the twenty-four are otherwise known as active in the deme or outside it, and that as many as sixteen may reasonably be identified as relatives of one another by either birth or marriage.[43] Public service of this kind involving a cluster of natal and affinal relations, in combination with the degree of prosperity implicit in the provision of a statue, suggests again the existence of an upper crust of influential notables—the personal "patrons" whose existence and importance were affirmed in the previous chapter. And when, furthermore, their generosity was reciprocated by a crowning and the erection of a dedicatory text carrying all twenty-four names in full, they received, as the Roman model might prompt us to expect, a cherished acknowledgment of their superior places in the community.

Did our two dozen Halaieis reside in the village, or were they in whole or part urbanites who merely visited the home-base on sacral or other important occasions? A single security *horos*, *SEG* 39.200, records the hypothecation of a *chorion* but without an accompanying *oikia*. Over against the 292 Halaieis listed by Kirchner in *Prosopographia Attica*, of which he identifies 31 as of the phyle Kekropis (i.e. as Aixonides), Davies' roster assigns seven Athenians to our deme,[44] one of whom is relevant here. If [Phil]ippos Athe[n]ippou (line 20) is the same man as the Philippos of Halai who purchased two plots in the deme for four talents ca. 350–325 (*IG* II^2 1598, lines 37–41),[45] this would be a strong indication of a significant local presence on the part of at least one dedicator. From Palaiochori (Eliot's candidate for the deme center), the choregic inscription *IG* II^2 3091 records victories in the names of Epichares (lines 1–2, 7–8) and Thrasyboulos (lines 3–6). Although present scholarly opinion favors the view (against Kirchner) that the victories belong to the town's Lenaia or Dionysia (rather than the "Rural" Dionysia, held in the deme),[46] the erection of the stone in the village would nonetheless establish an alternative yet equally viable local presence for the two *choregoi*. Whether town-dwellers or residents of the village, the triumphs of holders of Athenian liturgies, even if the productions had taken place in the *asty*, seem to have been viewed as reflecting favorably upon the home community and as something in which the Halaieis could take some justifiable pride. The pull of Athens would in this case not have extinguished the village's sense of its own importance or worth, despite the clear evidence for urban relocation suggested by the find-spots of the many epitaphs of Halaieis: Among the 75 tombstones of Halaieis printed by Kirchner (*IG* II^2 5455–5529/30, all unaccompanied by modifier), only two, nos. 5522 and 5525, from the vicinity of Cape Zoster, with certainty originate from the site of our deme, while most other Aixonides, where a provenience is recorded, seem to have been buried in Athens or Peiraieus and environs.

Teithras

A deme-association of average citizen membership with a quota of four, Teithras is securely placed on the basis of epigraphic finds at Pikermi far to the east of Athens and assigned by Traill to the coastal trittys of Aigeis.[47] The deme seems to have made only a scant, but arguably telling, impression on contemporary Athenians. The comic poet Theopompos (fl. ca. 410–ca. 370) linked Teithras with dried figs (*ischades*),[48] and, if merely an allusion to a distinctive local agricultural product, the association is unremarkable. But Aristophanes knew the fresh fruit (*sukon*) as slang for *pudenda muliebria* (*Peace*, line 1350), which opens up the possibility of an urban dramatist's making obscene humor at the expense of a distant rural village.[49] Aristophanes, at *Frogs* lines 475–477, recalling his characterization of Acharnian women mentioned earlier, seems by his phrase "Teithrasian Gorgones" to imply something negative about their womenfolk, for Hesychios, commenting on this phrase, glossed "Teithrasian" as "harsh" and "rough."[50] By this point we are accustomed to the ascription of rudeness to country folk, but it may be more particularly suggested here that the pejorative characterization was (again) prompted by the relative remoteness of the village and by the participation of rural women in outdoor agricultural work that that remoteness made possible.

All five of our texts originate on the deme-site at Pikermi:

(1) **Fragment of a ritual calendar, ca. 400–350. J.J. Pollitt, *Hesperia* 30 (1961) 293–297, no. 1 (*SEG* 21.542; Sokolowski, *LSCG Suppl.* no. 132):**

FACE A: 7 drachmas. On the fourth of Boedromion. . . . To Zeus. . . . 17 drachmas. A male sheep. . . . 1 drachma, 2 obols. Perquisites. On the fourth of the waning month. Four drachmas. To Athena a sheep. . . . To Zeus preliminary sacrifices . . . a milking pig, . . . Perquisites (traces). *FACE B:* (traces) . . . drachmas . . . ten . . . adult (victim). . . . adult (victim) (traces).

(2) **Two decrees concerning the leasing of land, ca. 350. Originally published by H. Möbius, *MDAI(A)* 49 (1924) 1–13, no. 1, improved by A. Wilhelm, *APF* 11 (1933–1935) 189–200 (*SEG* 24.151), reprinted by H. W. Pleket, *Epigraphica I: Texts on the Economic History of the Greek World*, Textus Minores 31 (Leiden, 1964) no. 41; Behrend, *Pachturkunden* no. 24; *Agora* XIX, pp. 156–157:**

Euthippos was demarch. Decreed by the Teithrasians, Eudikos made the motion. In order that the communal property (*ta koina*) be secure for the demesmen and that (the) Teithrasians know the existing and future states of affairs, the demarch is to engrave (the names of) all people who have on each occasion leased any of the communal properties. Decreed by the Teithrasians, Pandios made the motion. Since Xanthippos is a good man with respect to the communal properties (*ta koina*) of the Teithrasians, voted by the Teithrasians to lease to Xanthippos the plot at Teithras (on which neighbors . . . and the hero shrine of Epigonos (?), and on the south the Herakleion and the plot of the hero Datylos and the sanctuary of Zeus), for all time both to him and to the heirs of Xanthippos on both sides. And it is to be permitted to Xanthippos to use the plot as he has wished, and to the heirs of Xanthippos, paying . . . to the Teithrasians each year. But if enemies in wartime cause damage for the one holding the plot, (he) is to pay to the Teithrasians half of whatever he takes from the plot, but if he declines, to be released from the lease for better fortune. To place the stele in the Koreion and to engrave the names of those leasing the plots on each occasion and the leases, (indicating) how much each has agreed to pay, but, if anything has been written previously in opposition to this decree, to expunge (it) from the stele. Three men in the presence of the demarch are to engrave, in addition, that the Teithrasians release [from these terms] the parties leasing for all time. And (it is) the Teithrasians (who) are to lease the plots on each occasion. And the lessees are to render to the Teithrasians the payment each year and are to pay the extraordinary war-tax on their behalf to the city. And they are to pay the rents to the demarch in office on each occasion during the month Elaphebolion . . . things leased . . . these just as . . .

(3) **Record of leases, ca. 350.** H. Möbius, *MDAI(A)* 49 (1924) 1–13, no. 2 (*SEG* 24.152); *Agora* XIX, p. 157:

The lessee Andrares, son Pytheos, of Teithras has leased [name of property lost]. The lessees Antias of Teithras and Euthynos of Oe have leased the plot Phelleos in Teithras. The lessee Apollodoros, son of One[. . .], of Teithras has leased a plot in Teithras, and from this point for all time (?) it has been leased.

(4) **Decree honoring Euthippos for underwriting a statue, ca. 350.** H. Möbius, *MDAI(A)* 49 (1924) 1–13, no. 3 (*SEG* 24.153):

Blepyros made the motion. Since Euthippos well and justly took care of the statue and made it bigger than he had agreed and prepaid the money, resolved by the Teithrasians to praise Euthippos and to wreathe him with a wreath of olive and to turn over to him a mina of silver out of the deposited silver, and to engrave this resolution on a stone stele and erect it in the Koreion.

(5) **Decree honoring the deme's four councillors of the year 331/0 or 330/29. E. Vanderpool,** *Hesperia* **31 (1962) 401–403, no. 3 (***SEG*** 21.520);** *Agora* **15, no. 45:**

Decreed by the Teithrasians, [name lost] made the motion. To crown each of the *bouleutai* of the year of Arist[. . .]'s archonship with a gold crown, since they well and zealously took care of the sacrifices and all other matters which the demesmen had bidden. The following were the (four) *bouleutai:* [remains of four names]. To engrave this resolution on a stone stele and erect it in the. . . .

The Teithrasian dossier, though small in volume, is varied enough to approximate a cross-section of the official public activity of an Attic deme: a cult calendar with schedule, victims with prices, and perquisites (no. 1); documents pertaining to the leasing of associational land (nos. 2 and 3); and decrees honoring benefactors, in one case a donor without title (no. 4), in the other (uniquely for a deme) statewide public officials selected from the membership of the village-association (no. 5). To these may be added the security *horoi* from the site, Finley nos. 112 (*chorion*) and 163A (*oikiai* and *perioikion*), already studied in chapter 1 in relation to farmstead residence. Because the dated texts are nearly contemporaneous (falling in or near the middle third of the fourth century), a combined interpretation is clearly warranted.

As elsewhere, benefactors, in one case a demonstrably wealthy one, are found playing roles in sustaining the communal life of the deme-association. Euthippos's underwriting of a statue (no. 4) is a straightforward case, but the presence of additional candidates may lie concealed in the two mid-fourth century leases (nos. 2 and 3). Because the lessee of the estate in no. 2, one Xanthippos, is acknowledged to be "a good man with respect to the communal properties of the Teithrasians" (lines 6–8) and because this fact is given as the reason for the demesmen's favorable vote approving the lease, it is likely, as Michael Walbank has speculated, that the lease is a virtual liturgy. That is to say, his "goodness" resides precisely in his willingness to undertake the lease of "the communal properties." The tenant, as Walbank puts it, has undertaken to pay, in the form of rent, a sort of annuity to the deme.[51] To describe the situation in the societal terms introduced in chapter 2, Xanthippos could be seen as one of the "patrons" of the Teithrasian community, if we could only be sure that he was a Teithrasian, a probability somewhat undercut by the presence of the lessee from Oē in no. 3.

Specifics concerning the wealthier members of the deme are, as it turns out, in short supply. Versus the 52 Teithrasioi compiled by Kirchner in *Prosopographia Attica*, Davies' catalogue in *Athenian Propertied Families* cites only one Teithrasian (3510) among the 779 known members of the liturgical class.[52] But instead of concluding that there was no significant wealth in this deme, it is perhaps suggestible that the village's energies had been directed inwards in the pursuit of self-preservation rather than towards the town where the record of the holding of a liturgy or other evidence of "propertied" status was far more likely to be preserved. True, again, one of the lessees in no. 3 was a demesman of Oē, but all three of the others named were men of Teithras.

Still, while the membership and bounty of this distant coastal community may have remained concentrated in the ancestral settlement, it does not follow that links with the urban center, or with the central government housed in that center, were entirely lacking. Of the six tombstones of Teithrasians published by Kirchner (*IG* II² 7533–7539), the recorded proveniences are Acropolis (7537), Kerameikos (7533, 7539), near the Ilissos (7534/5), Peiraieus (7538), and Salamis (7536), clear indications of an urbanizing out-migration. Significant in a different way is inscription no. 5, a decree of the demesmen crowning four *bouleutai* of the (immediately preceding?) year, "since they well and zealously took care of the sacrifices and all other matters which the demesmen had bidden" (restored). Elsewhere, I have argued that this innocent-looking accolade actually conceals a form of representative government.[53] The *bouleutai* are of course the deme's "representatives" in the Council of Five Hundred in Athens, their number determined by the system of bouleutic quotas. But, if so, whose sacrifices are these? And just what were these "matters" to which they had attended at the bidding of the demesmen? Given the centralized role of the councillors (if nothing else, the Council's *bouleuterion* was situated on the west side of the Agora square), activities at the deme center itself would seem to be ruled out. Accordingly, I concluded that, if the venue of their activities was the town, the four Teithrasians, acting on behalf of the their fellow demesmen back in the village, had served as true "representatives" of the constituency from which they had been selected.[54] Thereby, a degree of Attica-wide unity imposed from above in the form of a body of councillors selected from all 139 village-associations according to a system of population quotas could coexist with the isolation otherwise indicated for some of these remote rural communities. The Teithrasians might at once remain village-based *and* dispatch their quota of councillors to Athens with instructions to promote the *demotai* in the arena of Athenian politics.

Three Models

No small selection from the 35 percent of demes for which at least one inscription survives could possibly be taken as representative of all of rural Attica. Rather, the goal of this chapter has been to take a detailed look into the internal affairs, from the rural village's own perspective and in its own language, of a small number of communities, even if, were the full truth known, they might prove untypical. But perhaps it would be well now, in closing this exploration of the particular community, to essay a general conclusion by combining with it the results of our discussions of historical Attic rural settlement and society in the preceding two chapters. Such a conclusion can be expressed in the form of three analytically distinct (but not necessarily mutually exclusive) models:

(1) *Relatively unorganized assemblage of individual households.* In *Associations of Classical Athens*, I marshaled multiple lines of argument in favor of the relative isolation of the demes, both in regard to each other and especially in regard to the urban center.[55] Chapter 1 of the present work has taken the theme of isolation still further by building a case in favor of farmstead residence throughout extramural Attica. Chapter 2 has maintained that these same *oikoi* were the loci of a potentially ruinous competitiveness in order to neutralize which the deme-associations cultivated an ideal of corporate *philotimia*. Additionally, the parallel case of modern rural Greece would suggest, not a unified community, but rather households divided by rivalry and intense competition for comparative advantage, with honor and prestige, not "community spirit," being the operative social dynamics.[56] Accordingly, it is a real question whether, and to what extent, the household units comprising rural Attic settlements did or did not create and uphold a meaningful degree of communal solidarity.

(2) *Cohesive, internally focused community acknowledging the priority of village over individual and household.* Alternatively, rivalry and competitiveness, though present, are not allowed to overwhelm the expression of group commonalties or the pursuit of shared goals. Socially, the community might be bound together internally by the patronal reciprocities we explored in chapter 2. Institutionally, the community will have been de-

fined and maintained by the formal structures of the deme-association in evidence throughout the epigraphic records of our four selected demes. This model would be especially appropriate wherever physical separation from the urban center precluded or impeded regular participation in the communal activities of the *asty*, with the intensity of communal vitality varying directly and proportionally with the distance of travel, communication, or transport.[57]

(3) *A "bedroom" community of functional urbanites.* By contrast with the preceding model, physical proximity to the urban center might cause a reorientation of village life—political, economic, cultural, or emotional—away from the rural nucleus itself towards the *asty*. Thus, this model differs from the preceding only in respect to the situation, within the village or outside it, of the locus of activity and group identification. Where the centripetal pull of the town predominates, individual village households will develop independent parallel lines of engagement with it, perhaps to the general neglect of mutual village-based ties with fellow demesmen.

These models are to be regarded only as analytical constructions, not as actual descriptions of any particular deme, since some demes could have partaken of more than one orientation depending upon their particular circumstances. Acharnai, given the unambiguous literary testimony for the presence of its demesmen in town (albeit under the press of the Lacedaemonian invasions), may have borne the imprint of the proximity of the town (3), while distant Teithras probably remained relatively more isolated from the *asty*, their urbanizing members severing ties with the ancestral community (2). But here, clearly, we are dealing not with alternatives but with a continuum of gradations reflecting relative access to, or isolation from, Athens. So, too, with (1) versus (2), for rather than the domination of one of the poles over the other, it is perhaps wiser to think in terms of opposing tendencies, one or the other predominating in keeping with the weakness or vitality of the deme-association in each case. But on the side of village solidarity, one could appeal to a scattering of indications of frequency of, or high participation in, village associational functions: from Lower Paiania, a quorum of 100 representing nearly one-seventh of the citizen population;[58] from Erchia, a cult calendar calling for 59 (preserved) sacrifices for the year, to be held for the benefit of a citizen membership of no more than 360;[59] and, similarly, from one of our own four demes, Aixone, a staff of at least seven priestesses each devoted to a distinct village divinity (text no. 1, ca. 400). While the case for farmstead residence suggests that the preponderance of the agrarian population resided on the land rather than in any (unsubstantiated) residential nucleated center, allowance will obviously have to be accorded the architectural remains uncovered at Erchia, Halai Aixonides, and elsewhere. And, whether residential or not, the municipal roles of the center indicated by assemblies, theaters and other communal structures, cult activities, the operation of patronage, and village ideology are manifest. Thus the case for model (2) seems to be a strong one provided that farmer residence is not assumed to be a necessary component of village nucleation. But it still remains to consider perhaps the best known (and understood) such communal event of all, the Rural Dionysia, and this is the subject of the following chapter.

4

Dionysia

THE FESTIVAL AT ATHENS CALLED (erroneously, I shall argue) the "Rural" Dionysia is unique in that it is the only festival known (a) to have been celebrated in two or more demes and (b) at the same time to have been paralleled by another festival or festivals in the name of the same divinity held in town under the aegis of the Athenian state. Are these two facts interrelated? And, if so, what is the significance of that interrelation for our understanding of rural Attica?

That we can learn as much as we do is owing to the survival of several pertinent literary sources and especially a comedic representation of the festival in Aristophanes' *Archarnians*, of a few relevant pictorial representations in vase-paintings and sculpture, and of a large number of inscriptions emanating from the concerned communities themselves. Despite, however, the predictably intense scholarly attention that has been given to this record, a number of important issues remain to be addressed or to be addressed from new evidential or methodological perspectives. What is the evidence for the name of our Dionysia, and does that evidence really support the conventional characterization of its orientation? Do we know the identities of all the demes in which the festival was celebrated, or have some escaped detection? Did all demes celebrate the Dionysia or only a few and, if a few, on what basis? Do certain primitive features of the festival or of the events associated with the festival, which seem to comport so poorly with the well-known dramatic and choral competitions, justify, with recent scholars, the inference that we are actually dealing with two different Dionysia? What were the specific events of the program, and what was their sequence? Did the festival so constituted conform to the otherwise general insularity and consequent particularity characteristic of the Attic demes? What was the status of a given deme's celebration with respect to its own non-demesmen residents, to neighboring demes and other Athenians, and to the state of Athens as a whole? Some of these questions are new, some old, but to all I propose to suggest answers that will significantly enhance our understanding of village culture, over and above any light they may shed on the matter of rural-urban relations touched on in my initial paragraph.

My discussion departs from, and inevitably builds upon, the works of previous scholars, beginning with the comprehensive accounts of Deubner (1932)[1], Pickard-Cambridge (1962 and 1968)[2], and Whitehead (1986).[3] Since Whitehead's treatment, our knowledge has been advanced by Henrichs's look at Dionysos from the perspective of town and country (1990), by Cole's examination of the Dionysiac procession in the context of cities other than Athens (1993), and by Habash's comparison of the two festival scenes in Aristophanes' *Archarnians* (1995).[4] My findings will in the main be in agreement with the views expressed in these and other studies. What will distinguish my approach, apart from the posing of some new questions, is my sustained attention to the inscriptions which, except for the detailed expositions of Pickard-Cambridge and especially Whitehead, have not received much attention, despite the fact that these texts (in contrast with a passage from Plutarch or Aelian) are contemporary and, even more importantly, originate in the very communities in which the festival was celebrated. It is the epigraphic record that, as will be seen, again and again permits new insights into previously neglected major aspects of our Dionysia.

Name and Orientation of the Festival

"Rural Dionysia" is a long-established name for the festival among classicists using English, but it will be revealing to review the rather tenuous basis for the adjective. The several Athenian festivals called *(ta) Dionysia* are regularly distinguished by modifying words or phrases,[5] and in the present case the Greek traditionally rendered "rural" in English merely conforms to this larger pattern. At Aristophanes' *Archarnians*, lines 202 and 250, Dikaiopolis is made to refer to the festival he is organizing as *ta kat' agrous Dionysia*. Aeschines' *Against Timarchos* alludes to the performance of comedies in *ta kat' agrous Dionysia* in the intramural deme of Kollytos (1.157). Theophrastos's character sketch *Adoleschia* offers as an example of garrulity the man who observes that *ta kat' agrous Dionysia* take place in Posideion (3§5). Plutarch remarks at *Moralia* 1098b on the raucous behavior of slaves "making the rounds whenever they make a

meal on the Kronia or celebrate *Dionysia kat' agron.*" From these and perhaps now lost sources, scholiasts and lexicographers of later times pick up
and reproduce the phrase.[6] This leaves only one text, an apparently nonconforming one, to be accounted for. At *Republic* 5.475d, Plato writes of
people who, desiring to hear each and every chorus, "run around *ta
Dionysia*, missing neither those [sc. Dionysia] *kata poleis* nor those *kata
komas.*"[7] No reference is made to Athens, although Plato's city of citizenship and residence is presumably to be included among the *poleis*.
However, "villages" at Athens are called *demoi*, not *komai*, so on this head
the fit with our festival is not as precise as one would expect had the author had our Dionysia in mind.[8] Be that as it may, nothing about Plato's
sentence in any way suggests that he is using technical, or even well-
established informal, nomenclature. Thus the modifiers rendered "rural"
with respect to Athens' Dionysiac festivals seem always to incorporate a
prepositional reference to fields or a field. Accordingly, the English word
"rural," the applications of which extend far beyond the practice of agriculture implicit in the Greek word for "field,"[9] seems to be an inexact,
and potentially misleading, artifact of modern scholarship. Had such been
the meaning of the Greek, the phrase would have run something like *ta
kata choran Dionysia*.[10]

The point is not without significance for our study, because among
the Athenian demes for which the Dionysia are attested are two, Kollytos
and Peiraieus, which were situated within the town walls and therefore
hardly "rural" in any customary sense of that term. Their example shows
that gross topography does not underlie the organization of the festival, at
least not as the primary point of differentiation. Rather its basis is "fields,"
that is, farming, and farming may be practiced even within the walls, in
close proximity to urban settlements, and indeed by persons who are otherwise citified in their situation, habits, and attitudes. Our few but unambiguous literary depictions of the festival, notably that in Aristophanes'
Archarnians, show *ta kat' agrous Dionysia* to have been a celebration of a
specifically agricultural, or agrarian, economic regime, life, and culture.
Dikaiopolis, the central figure in this celebration, himself alludes to the cutting of his grapevines by the invading Lacedaemonian army (line 512). By
contrast, a true *rural* festival in an ancient Attic context would at once have
*ex*cluded intramural communities and *in*cluded pastoral, montane, and
maritime communities. But our Dionysia preserves no trace of having been
a festival of herders, woodcutters, charcoal burners, quarry workers, miners, or fishers. Therefore, the attested names for the festival might better

be rendered the Agrarian Dionysia, as though the Greek had stood in the analogous adjectival form *ta agroika Dionysia* or, taking a hint from Demosthenes, *ta arouraia Dionysia*.[11] The town versus country dichotomy, which underlies virtually every modern discussion of the subject, is accordingly only of secondary significance in comparison with the festival's primarily *cultural* orientation.

The literary sources do not of course exhaust our ancient evidence for the nomenclature of the festival. The many inscriptions originating in the demes themselves—often the only source of information in a given case—without exception speak simply of *(ta) Dionysia*. Since, then, the phrase *kat' agrous (agron)* is never found in a source emanating from the demes for which the festival is attested, it may be suggested that the phrase reflects the point of view of our literary writers—namely, the town of Athens. So much is clearly indicated by the eighth speech of Isaios when the speaker states that his putative maternal grandfather "always took us *eis Dionysia eis agron*" (§15) from a point of departure that may be inferred to have been in the *asty* (see below, under Phlya). By contrast, it would probably not have occurred to the demesman or woman residing in a village to distinguish the local celebration of the festival from the town's by reference to "fields" (or a "field"), especially if, as suggested by the primitive character of certain of its features, the Dionysia was originally of an agricultural orientation and only later, once introduced into an urban environment, came under the influence of a population removed from the practice of farming. But in the end, the use of the urban phrase *kat' agrous (agron)* proved to be the only the most superficial of the symptoms of the town's impact upon this ostensibly agrarian religious festival.

Distribution of the Festival over the Demes

Pickard-Cambridge's detailed account, originally published in 1953 and later reissued in a second edition by Gould and Lewis in 1968, refers by name to a total of twelve demes: Acharnai, Aigilia, Aixone, Anagyrous, Eleusis, Ikarion, Kollytos, Myrrhinous, Paiania, Peiraieus, Phlya, and Rhamnous, plus the non-deme Salamis.[12] The latest detailed study, Whitehead's *The Demes of Attica*, published in 1986, found that "some degree of evidence can be found relating to the festival in as many as fourteen different demes (as well as in Brauron and Salamis);" his list comprised all of Pickard-Cambridge's demes with the addition of Halai

Araphenides and Thorikos, plus the non-deme Brauron alongside Salamis.[13] My study, however, will now show the number to be considerably higher—nineteen—through the addition by various routes of Cholleidai, Euonymon, Hagnous, Lamptrai, and Sphettos.

But a more fundamental point turns on Whitehead's elusive phrase "some degree of evidence," for it acknowledges the assumptions involved in arriving at these rosters of demes allegedly observing "the Rural Dionysia." To begin, all authorities assume that the literarily attested *ta kat' agrous Dionysia* and the epigraphically attested *(ta) Dionysia* are one and the same event. The present study endorses this assumption on the strength of the identification of the "fields" in the literary references to the former festival with the actual fields in the demes the inscriptions of which attest the latter and, more particularly, in light of the agreement between Theophrastos (3.5) and inscriptions from Hagnous, Peiraieus, and Thorikos (see below) that the festival took place in the month of Posideion. But in more pressing need of explanation is the fact that among the 19 demes in my roster, for only 14 is the one or the other festival name attested. On what basis is the addition of the five others justified? Simply stated, the presence of dramatic or choral competitions. The link between the festival (when named) and dramatic and choral *agones* is repeatedly and amply illustrated by my roster below. Aeschines (1.157), for example, ascribes comedies to *ta kat' agrous Dionysia* of Kollytos; and, where we are dependent on epigraphic sources, some aspect of stage competition (*agōn*, tragedy, comedy, *choros, choregoi* and *choregiai, proedria*, etc.) is attested in the great majority of the demes for which the Dionysia is independently documented. Thus Aigilia, Myrrhinous, Paiania, and Sphettos, in the absence of a reference to the festival, all merit inclusion by reason of an attestation of some element of these *agones*. Another deme, Euonymon, qualifies on the strength of the physical remains of a theater, even in the total absence of a written mention of the festival, of competitions, and indeed of the theater itself.

The inference is further strengthened, moreover, by powerful negative evidence. There is not a single example from the demes of a dramatic or choral production, in any of its manifestations, in association with a specific event other than our Dionysia, with a divinity other than Dionysos, or at a time other than the time of our midwinter rite in Posideion. True, the *agōn* of the festival of Artemis called Tauropolia is found at Halai Araphenides (see below), but the inscription preserves no trace of the activities elsewhere associated with the Dionysiac festival. Were we to judge from what our sources, especially the inscriptions, tell (or do not tell) us, we might conclude that the theaters were primarily, even exclusively, devoted to just this festival. Naturally, a *theatron* might have non-agonistic uses, but the meeting of the deme-association's *agora*[14] is the only category of such use that can be illustrated from the sources. Generally speaking, the prevailing absence of any alternative occasion for dramatic or choral *agones* among a considerable body of documentation from a total of 48 different demes[15] provides what is, in my estimation, the decisive contributing argument favoring the extrapolations underlying the rosters of demes presented by my predecessors and now by myself.

Because no work, recent or otherwise, contains a full case-by-case catalogue of the demes celebrating our festival, and in order to work into the discussion (and justify) the five new examples absent from the latest published list (namely, Whitehead's), I will present here *seriatim* the relevant testimony. Each name is followed by a numeral in parentheses indicating the deme's bouleutic quota according to Traill's latest published figures,[16] the significance of which will become apparent in due course. The roster, with its citation and renderings of texts, will then provide the basis for my detailed discussions regarding the disposition, content, and schedule of the festival and for my concluding characterization of its place in the larger setting of Athens and Attica.

Acharnai (22).[17] Two twin *choregiai* in dithyramb,[18] with accompanying *didaskaloi*, are recorded by the early fourth century monument *IG* II² 3092. The attribution to Acharnai is guaranteed by the prosopographical references assembled in Kirchner's commentary and the pertinence *ad Dionysia agrestia* previously established by Brinck's dissertation *de choregia* (*IG*, ad loc.). Two decrees of 315/4, *AE* 131 (1992) [1993] 179–193 (*SEG* 43.26), make repeated references to the festival in the course of bestowing of honors. In the first, the *tamias* is stated to have "well and [honorably] supervised the Dionysia" with the demarch (A, lines 5–7). In the second, the three honorands—the demarch, the *tamias*, and the epimelete of the Dionysia (B, lines 1–3)—are recorded to have "well and honorably supervised the *thysia* to Dionysos and the *pompē* and the *agōn* . . ."; the demarch is to announce the crowns "at the *agōn* of the Dionysia at Acharnai" (B, lines 12–14); and they and their descendants are to have the privilege of *proedria* in perpetuity "at the *agōn* of the Dionysia at Acharnai" (B, lines 19–22). *IG* II² 3106 (s. IV), from the site at Menidi, records a dedication following victories *ad certamina agrestia . . . festis rusticis* (Brinck, Kirchner) in the *[kyklios] choros* (i.e., dithyramb) and comedy, with flute player

and [*didaskalos*] appended. *IG* II² 1206 (fin. s. IV), referred to Acharnai by
Koehler with reference to the restored mention of the shrine of Athena
Hippia at lines 15–16 (comparing 1207, line 4), concerns the raising of rev-
enues for a *thysia*, in the first instance from the theater (lines 4–7).

Aigilia (6). A father and his two sons, victorious as *choregoi*, dedicate
to Dionysos the statue and the [altar] in *IG* II² 3096 (ante med. s. IV a.).
Early authorities cited by Kirchner suppose the senior honorand had discharged his choregy *Dionysiis agrestibus*. The reported findspot in the village of Kalybia south of the village of Markopoulos,[19] along with the
identification of the second son with the secretary *kata prytaneian* of
343/2 from Aigilia (*IG* II² 223, lines C 1–2; 224, line 2; 225, lines 4–5), se-
cures the attribution to the deme.

Aixone (11?). Decrees of the Aixoneis praise and crown men who had
served commendably as *choregoi: IG* II² 1198 (326/5), 1200 (317/6), and
MDAI(A) 66 (1941) 218–219, no. 1 (313/2). No. 1198 calls for erection of
the stele "in the theater" (lines 21–22). The last mentioned text decrees that
the honorands be crowned "in the theater at the comedies after
Theophrastos's archonship" (lines 3–6) and again calls for erection of the
stele in the theater with the addition "in order that (the) Aixoneis always
stage (the) Dionysia in as fine fashion as possible" (lines 11–12). *IG* II² 1202
(313/2), though not visibly concerned with the *choregia*, calls for announcement of the honors for two benefactors "at the comedies of the
Dionysia at Aixone in the theater" (lines 14–16) and instructs the demarch
and *tamiai* to erect the stele "in the theater at Aixone" (lines 18–21). The
acephalous *IG* II² 1197 (ca. 330) preserves (as restored) the injunctions that
the demarch in office at any given time summon the honorands to the
proedria (lines 9–11) and that he erect the inscribed stele in the theater
(lines 18–21).[20]

Anagyrous (6). The fragment of a decree bestowing honors *IG* II²
1210, from the village of Vari, associated with virtual certainty with the
deme of Anagyrous,[21] preserves a reference to the crown after which the
IG text is restored to read: "and let him have *proedria* at the *agōn* of
tragedies whenever they stage the Dionysia, and let the demarch summon
him to the *proedria*."[22] A choregic monument of the fifth century from the
area assigned to the deme on external prosopographic evidence, *AE* 1965
(1967), pp. 163–167, commemorates a victory with Euripides as *didaskalos*,
but the editor inclined to refer the victory to the urban Dionysia. A verse
inscription from near Vari of the following century, *IG* II² 3101 (post med.
s. IV a.), records a victory at the Dionysia—"a *kosmos* for the deme"—in

the "sweet-laughing *choros*," taken by Wilamowitz to refer to comedy (*IG*, ad loc.). Both the actual dedicator and his father (whose ivy wreath figures in the poem) were taken by Kaibel to be *Dionysiis agrestibus victor* (*IG*, ad loc.), but the Dionysia in question might conceivably have been, as with the preceding example, a town festival.

Cholleidai (2). The hero of Aristophanes' *Archarnians*, Dikaiopolis, upon the conclusion of his private peace treaty with the Spartans, declares at line 202: "I'll go inside and conduct *ta kat' agrous . . . Dionysia*." The participle *eisiōn* ("entering," representing, as often with the participle in construction with a finite verb, the main idea) is, with Starkie, to be referred to the "house" on the proscenium which is doing double duty for Dikaiopolis's town and country residences.[23] The chorus of Acharnians pursues him over hill and dale (line 235). Starkie supposed that they are led some miles from Athens and that, although there is no change in scene, the spectators were to imagine that the original stage setting on the Pnyx in town has been transformed into "the country parish" of Dikaiopolis.[24] Similar transformations of scene have more recently been proposed by Dover, Dearden, and Fisher.[25] Dikaiopolis in fact tells us at lines 266–267 of his song to Phales that he has entered "*the* deme," i.e. his own deme. At this location ensues an aborted celebration of the festival, again identified by Dikaiopolis as *ta kat' agrous Dionysia* at line 250. What, then, is the identity of this "country parish"? At line 406 Dikaiopolis, at Euripides' door, declares "I, Dikaiopolis . . . *Cholleidēs*, am summoning you!" True, as Starkie explains, the caller wishes to ingratiate himself with Euripides, *ho cholopoios*, and so, in accordance with frequent Aristophanic practice, he is equipped with punning demotic.[26] But the presence of the pun does not negate the hero's dramatic membership in the deme Cholleidai and the latent implication, now first appreciated by the audience, that his Dionysia had been celebrated at its (unfortunately for us) still unknown (though extramural) location.[27]

Eleusis (11?). The choregic inscription from Eleusis *IG* II^2 3090 records a victory by two *choregoi* in comedy with Aristophanes as *didaskalos;* the appended "second victory" in tragedy gives Sophocles as *didaskalos*. Pickard-Cambridge argued that the reference is to "a festival or festivals at Eleusis" and, on the supposition that his "production" (lit. "teaching" of the chorus) is to be taken literally, that "Sophocles and Aristophanes must both have gone to Eleusis, and the festival there will have been of importance, even if the plays were not first performances."[28] A fragment "In museo Eleusinio," *IG* II^2 3100 (med. s. IV), seems to have recorded a

choregic victory in comedy, while the scrap *IG* II² 3107 (s. IV) fails to preserve the genre of competition. Seven other texts, all found at Eleusis, are
decrees recognizing various benefactors with honors including *proedria*
(*IG* II² 1185, med. s. IV; 1186, med. s. IV); *proedria* in the deme of the
Eleusinians with the demarch summoning the honorand to the *proedria*
(1187, med. s. IV); summons of the honorand by the demarch . . . just as
for the others to whom the deme has granted *proedria* (1189, 334/3);
proedria in the theater whenever the Eleusinians stage the Dionysia (1192,
fin. s. IV, restored); *proedria* with summons by the demarch just as for the
others to whom *proedria* has been granted (1193, fin. s. IV); and *proedria*
with summons by the demarch enforced by a 100 drachma fine for failure
to comply (*Hesperia* 8 [1939] 177–180 [= 1194 + 1274 + new fragment], ca.
300). Announcements of honors are to be made "at the tragedies of (the)
Dionysia in Eleusis" (1186); "at the *agōn* of tragedies in the theater at Eleusis" (1187); "at the *agōn* . . . of (the) Dionysia" (1189); and "at (the)
Dionysia in the tragedies" (1193). The stele is to be erected "in the theater
of the Eleusinians" (1185, restored) or "in the Dionysion" (1186). But the
most informative single text, 1186, honors two Thebans, of whom the first
mentioned, with his students, "when the Eleusinians were holding the
Dionysia, proved energetic and zealous towards the gods and the *demos* of
the Athenians and of the Eleusinians, in order that the Dionysia be as fine
as possible and, providing at his own expense two *choroi* (i.e. dithyrambic
choruses[29]), one of boys, one of men, contributed to Demeter and Korē
and Dionysos" (lines 6–14). From a later era, a state decree of 165/4, *IG*
II² 949, recognizes a demarch who had (as restored) ". . . at the Dionysia
sacrificed to Dionysos and conducted the *pompē* and . . . , and also staged
the *agōn* in the theater . . ." (lines 31–33).

Euonymon (10). For a theater, see Whitehead 1986a, p. 219 with note
255 and the references collected there; and, more recently, Wiles 1997, pp.
29–30, with detailed description and photograph.

Hagnous (5). *IG* II² 1183 (post a. 340), now reassigned from Myrrhinous to Hagnous by Traill,[30] contains a directive [to transact business?]
"on the 19th of the month Posideion . . . concerning (the) Dionysia, . . ."
(lines 36–37). With Wilhelm, the festival had already occurred earlier in the
month and the meeting was designed to deal with resulting financial and
administrative matters;[31] with Lipsius, the meeting was preliminary with
the festival following after the 19th (*IG*, ad loc.). The reference to
Posideion in either event guarantees the text's pertinence to the *Dionysia
agrestia*.

Halai Araphenides (5). A decree of the Halaieis, identified by the provenience as Araphenides,[32] *AE* 1932, *Chronika*, pp. 30–32 (ca. 350), honors one Philoxenos for his *choregia* of the *pyrrichistai* (choruses of Pyrrhic dancers) and for discharging well "all the liturgies in the deme" (lines 1–7). Announcement will occur "at the *agōn* of Tauropolia" (lines 13–20); and he will have *proedria* in all the *agōnes* that the Halaieis stage, with the herald issuing the summons (lines 20–24). A still unpublished decree of 341/0 announced at *Ergon* 1957, pp. 24–25 (= *PAAH* 1957, pp. 45–47) is reported to have mentioned *agōnes* celebrated at the Dionysia in Halai.

Ikarion (4/5). Athenaios (2.40a–b) asserted that both comedy and tragedy were invented in Ikarion, and while the validity of the assertion cannot be tested here, it is of interest that it is from this very deme that the earliest of our documents, *IG* I[3] 253 (ca. 450–425) and 254 (ca. 440–415?), originate. The first records accounts, including those of Dionysos; the second concerns the deme's *choregia*, with references in fragmentary contexts to tragedy (lines 9, 21, 34), the *protochoroi* (lines 15, 17)[33], and "the *choros*" (line 35). One decree of the demesmen, *IG* II[2] 1178 (ante med. s. IV), honors the demarch who had "well and justly staged the *heortē* and the *agōn* for Dionysos" (lines 6–8); another, *Hesperia* 17 (1948) 142–143, no. 1 (*SEG* 22.117; ca. 330), calls for erection of the stele "in the Dionysion" and announcement of the crown "at the tragedies of (the) Dionysia" (lines 8–9). The rest are dedications, all discovered "at the Dionysion": by the *epimeletai* of the restoration of a statue to Dionysos (*IG* II[2] 2851, s. IV); by a victor to Dionysos with *didaskalos* (3094, init. s. IV); by three *choregoi* (a father and his two sons) victorious in tragedies (3095, ante med. s. IV a.); by three victors (3098); and by a *choregos* victorious in tragedies (3099, med. s. IV).

Kollytos (3). Aeschines, 1 *Against Timarchos* (345 B.C.) 157, in the course of his attack upon his adversary alludes to the performance of comedies in Kollytos at *ta kat' agrous Dionysia*. Demosthenes, 18 *de Corona* (330 B.C.) 180 (cf. 262 and 267), assails Aeschines by allusion to his one-time poor theatrical "crushing" of the part of Oinomaos in Kollytos. At §242 the onslaught resumes with the intended insult *arouraios Oinomaos*, by which the speaker targets the *agrarian* orientation of the deme festival in which the part was acted. While Demochares, nephew of Demosthenes, according to an ancient *Life* (p. 4.27–36, cf. 5.19–20 Martin-Budé), ascribed the drama to the otherwise unknown *tragodopoios* Ischander, Hesychios, s.v. *arouraios Oinomaos*, says it was Sophocles' play *Oinomaos*.

Lamptrai (5 or 9). A fragment of an honorary decree of an unidenti-

fied phyle from the Acropolis, *IG* II² 1161 (fin. s. IV), calls for announcement (of crowns?) "at Lamptrai . . . at the Dionysia" (restored; lines 4–5).
It is not possible to determine whether the deme is Upper Lamptrai
(bouleutic quota 5) or Lower Lamptrai (bouleutic quota 9) and thus
whether it was the larger or smaller of the two (or both?) that hosted the
festival.

Myrrhinous (6). The preserved closing lines of the decree *IG* II² 1182
(med. s. IV) open with the grant of "*proedria* . . . in all the spectacles,
which the Myrrhinousians stage" (restored; lines 2–4).[34]

Paiania (1 or 11). The dedication *IG* II² 3097 (med. s. IV a.) records
the victory as *choregos* in tragedy by Demosthenes, son of Demainetos, of
Paiania.[35] Whether we are dealing with the upper (bouleutic quota 1) or
lower (bouleutic quota 11) deme is not ascertainable.

Peiraieus (8?). Variously termed *ta Dionysia, ta Dionysia ta Peiraika*,
and the *Peraia*, the festival is sporadically documented over a long period
and with repeated acknowledgment of state intervention.[36] Thus the law
moved by Euegoros declaring a moratorium on the taking of pledges and
seizing of property during certain festivals lists the festivals in question, beginning with "the *pompē* to Dionysos in Peiraieus and the tragedies and
comedies" (Demosthenes 21 *Against Meidias*, 10). No mention of *choros*
occurs in the law or elsewhere in connection with our Dionysia, but
[Plutarch], *Lives of the Ten Orators* 842a, credits the statesman Lykourgos
with instituting an *agōn* in honor of Poseidon at Peiraieus comprising "not
fewer than three *kyklioi choroi*."[37] *AthPol* 54.8 states that the demarch of
Peiraieus stages the Dionysia and appoints the *choregoi*. According to
Aelian, *Varia Historia* 2.13, Socrates went down to Peiraieus when Euripides, "the poet of tragedy," was competing there. Accounts record the sale
of skins from the festival (*IG* II² 1496 [334/3], col. IV, lines a70–73), the
performance of sacrifices by the generals (op. cit. [331/0], lines d144–145),
and contributions to a sacrifice by the Eleusinian *epistatai* (*IG* II² 1672
[329/8], line 106). A decree of the Peiraieis (line 32) of 324/3, *Agora* XIX,
L 13 (*IG* II² 1176+), sets out terms for the leasing of the theater, but, although the grant of *proedria* figures in the fragmentary text (lines 11, [13],
16), no reference is made to the Dionysian festival.[38] Later in the fourth
century, a decree of the People, *IG* II² 380 (320/19), calls for the *agoranomoi* in Peiraieus to level and prepare "the roads and streets" where the
pompē for Dionysos (as well as for Zeus Soter) will take place (lines 19–23,
25–32, 34–40). A state decree of 307/6, *IG* II² 456, calls for the *apoikoi*
(lines 7, 14) of Kolophon in Athens to be given "*th[ea]*"—evidently special

seating of some kind—at *ta Dionysia ta Peiraika* (lines 32–33). The intact decree of the Peiraieis *IG* II² 1214 (ca. 300–250) bestows on the honorand the privilege of *proedria* in the theater "whenever the Peiraieis stage the Dionysia" (lines 19–21), with instructions for the honorand's introduction into the theater by the demarch (lines 22–25) and provision for announcement by the herald in the theater "at the *agōn* of tragedies" (lines 28–33). After a long silence, following a revival dated ca. 120 B.C. by Garland,[39] state decrees honoring the ephebes exhibit some of the language, if not the former substance, of the classical festival.[40]

Phlya (5?). The speaker of Isaios, 8 *On the Estate of Kiron* (between ca. 383 and 363) in support of his case that he is the child of the testator's daughter, observes: "And not only were we invited to such rites [i.e. the aforementioned sacrifices], but he [Kiron] also always took us to the country to the Dionysia, and we viewed the shows with him, sitting by his side. . . ." (§15–16). Since Kiron owned land in the deme of Phlya (§35), this was in all likelihood the scene of these Dionysia, to which he (with the speaker in tow) repaired from the one of his two *oikiai* in the *asty* in which he used to live (loc. cit.).[41]

Rhamnous (8). Honors from the mid-third century, *SEG* 22.120, bestow *proedria* at the Dionysia and call for announcement by the herald at the *agōn* of the Dionysia (lines 5–7, with some restoration). An earlier inscription dated s. IV (?), *IG* II² 3108, is restored to record the dedication by a Rhamnousian *choregos* victorious in comedies. In the fully preserved *IG* II² 3109 (init. s. III), from Rhamnous, the Rhamnousian dedicator registers his victory "in boys and men" while gymnasiarch and (in a later addition to the stone) in comedies while *choregos*. Kirchner's commentary cites Isaios, 2.42 on the gymnasiarchy in the deme and notes Brinck's observation that at the time the text was inscribed the *choregia* had already been abolished in Athens, thereby ensuring reference to the festival in the deme.

Sphettos (5). A fragment of a stele found at Philati and perhaps to be assigned to Sphettos, *SEG* 36.187 (ca. 350–300), is restored in lines 10–11 (with the crucial intervention of an *SEG* editor, Ronald Stroud) to read "(at let him have) *proedria* in the theater . . . alongside the priest of Dionysos, . . ."

Thorikos (5). The calendar *SEG* 26.136 (ca. 400–350), now reedited from autopsy by G. Daux, *AC* 52 (1983) 150–174, schedules the Dionysia for the month of Posideion (line 31). A decree of the Thorikioi dated epigraphically ca. 400, *SEG* 34.107, mentions "three *choregiai*" in broken context (line 5). Another fragment, from the excavations of the deme site and dated to the fourth century, *SEG* 40.128, preserves similarly broken references to *choregiai* and *choregoi* (lines 4, 9), comedy (lines 2, 5–6), and tragedy (line 6).

To these examples from the Kleisthenic constitutional demes may now be added evidence from two other Attic communities:

Brauron. Scholia on Aristophanes, *Peace*, line 874: "And in Brauron, a *demos* (sic) of Attica, (were) many prostitutes. And there the Dionysia used to be staged too, and in each deme, in which they were drunk . . . and, while drunk, they used to grab many prostitutes."

Salamis. *AthPol* 54.8 records that the archon on Salamis stages the Dionysia and appoints the *choregoi*. An inscription recording a victory in the "*choros* (i.e. dithyramb[42]) of boys," *IG* II² 3093, is dated epigraphically to the early fourth century B.C. After a long interval, announcement of a crown "at the tragedies of the Dionysia in Salamis, whenever they first occur" (apparently following a hiatus) is enjoined at *IG* II² 1227 (131/0), lines 30–32; of a crown "at the *agōn* of the tragedies of the Dionysia in Salamis" at 1008 (118/7), line 82; and of a crown "at the [new] *agōn* of tragedies of the Dionysia in Salamis" at 1011 (106/5), line 58.

At the outset of our study we reviewed the evidence for the name of the supposedly "rural" festival and found that the fuller formulation preserved in literary sources consistently identified it in terms of "fields." We can now appreciate the significance of that finding, for three of our nineteen demes might well be thought of as conspicuously urban in character.

The case of Peiraieus is straightforward in this regard. The port town was enclosed within the Themistoclean Walls. With reference to the festival, a state decree, *IG* II² 380 of 320/19, calls, as we saw, for the preparation of "roads and streets" for the passage of the *pompē* of Dionysos. But however urban Peiraieus may have been, it nonetheless retained traces of an agricultural orientation. The *horos IG* II² 2623 marked a boundary of something belonging to the Peiraieis, but while Kirchner had restored "boundary [of the *chora*]" in lines 2–3, my own examination of the squeeze at the Institute for Advanced Study in Princeton has eliminated this restoration and offered "boundary [of the land]" in its place.[43] A *locatio* of the demesmen of Peiraieus, *IG* II² 2498 (321/0), sets out terms for the leasing of a *chorion* (line 11), with clauses concerning the removal of mud and earth and the cutting of timber (lines 9–11), pasturage (lines 12–13), and with elaborate instructions for ploughing and fallowing (lines 17–22). Security *horoi* from Peiraieus record the hypothecation of *choria* without

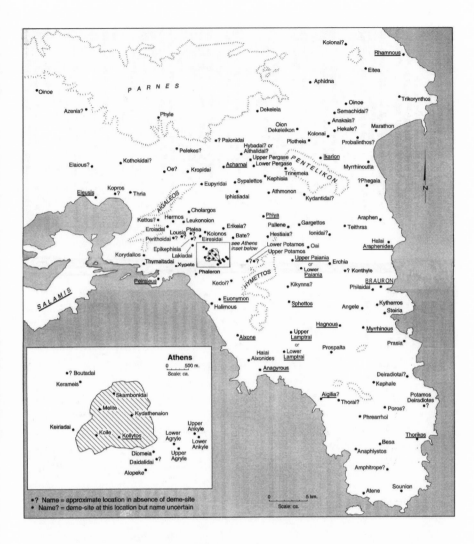

Map 1. Demes (with Brauron and Salamis) celebrating the Dionysia. The following demes are of unknown location and accordingly do not appear on the map: Acherdous, Auridai, Cholleidai, Eitea (Akamantis), Epieikidai, Eroiadai, Hamaxanteia, Hippotomadai, Krioa, Oion Kerameikon, Otryne, Pambotadai, Phegous, Pithos, Sybridai, Themakos, and Tyrmeidai. Modified from Nicholas F. Jones, *The Associations of Classical Athens: The Response to Democracy* (New York: Oxford University Press 1999), figure 3.1, "The Demes of Attica," used with permission of Oxford University Press.

structures (Finley 1985b, nos. 55 and 58); and of a *chorion* with an *oikia* situated on it, that is, a farm (Finley 1985b, no. 113). Plainly, Peiraieus town, though enclosed within the walls and hardly "rural" in the customary sense of that term, did possess sufficient "fields" to justify the phrase *ta kat' agrous Dionysia*.

The same applies to Kollytos, one of the five demes within the classical circuit wall. The "rural" character of the deme's Dionysia was queried by Whitehead, although his basis for doing so was not stated.[44] To be sure, the boundaries of the deme, were they known with precision, would probably have enclosed considerable infrastructure, for archaeologists assign the so-called Industrial District to the southwest of the Agora area either to it or to its contiguous neighboring deme, Melite.[45] No epigraphic or other written evidence of fields or farming in Kollytos itself (as for Peiraieus) survives, but the security *horoi* and two general considerations strongly indicate the practice of agriculture in this (and the other) intramural demes. Among the security *horoi* are many that, though lacking a specific authenticated provenience, are associated with the town of Athens or with specific locations within the walls, viz. the Agora, Acropolis, Parthenon, and so on. Some mark the hypothecation of single *choria* (about a score of examples),[46] others *choria* and associated *oikiai* (about a dozen examples).[47] Since not all such stones could have wandered from extramural locations, this evidence points unambiguously to farming in and about the five intramural demes, Kollytos among them. Besides, as is well known, fortification walls are laid out, as at Athens, not simply in order neatly to enclose a built-up inhabited area, but with reference to topography, with the occasionally detectable result that significant unoccupied areas are incorporated within the enceinte. And, in any event, arable land, like a water supply, must have been regarded as a strategic necessity in the event of siege and may therefore have by conscious design been included within the fortifications. If there is a question about Kollytos, it concerns the venue of the dramatic productions attested by Aeschines and Demosthenes, but even if a stone *theatron* were to be assumed, the absence of visible physical remains should not be surprising in this continuously occupied and built-over area.

Eleusis, too, might be thought less rural than urban in view of its large bouleutic quota (11?), significant number of resident statutorily landless metics,[48] and thriving sanctuary of Demeter and Kore, but in fact its agricultural orientation is explicitly attested. Security *horoi* from the deme record the hypothecation of single *choria* (five examples[49]), although, perhaps by accident, we have no instance of a plot with a residential structure

on it. But "the people occupying the suburb (*to proasteion*) and the farmers" are mentioned in a decree of the Eleusinians from Eleusis of the year
321/0, *IG* II² 1191, lines 19–20. There can be no doubt concerning the pertinence of the formulation *kat' agrous* to this deme otherwise far better
known, in antiquity as today, for its architectural development.

With these three major apparent exceptional cases accounted for, we
may proceed to a more comprehensive characterization of our nineteen
demes. We would like to know of course the answer to a question often
raised by commentators but to this point left unresolved: Did all demes celebrate the festival in some fashion or do we have in our slender evidentiary
record an approximation of the original state of affairs?[50] Initial hints are
suggested by a mapping of the nineteen demes in question according to
John Traill's most recent assignments (see Map 1). One is struck by the
fairly even distribution over the entire expanse of Attica, no major district
being without at least one deme for which the festival is attested and, except perhaps for Hagnous and Myrrhinous, no concentration of demes
with the festival in a single constricted area. Naturally, such a distribution
is consistent with the hypothesis that all demes celebrated *ta kat' agrous
Dionysia* and with the surmise that we have a random selection of the total record, but another characteristic of our demes, their relatively large
size, prompts a different line of approach. Given Traill's numbers for the
bouleutic quotas, the nineteen demes average 7.47 councilors versus an average of 3.59 councilors for all 139 demes, or over twice the average.[51] Sev-
enteen of the 19 exceed the average. Sixteen of the 36 demes with a quota
of five or more or 44%, eight of the 16 with a quota of eight or more or
50%, are on our roster versus a total rate of attestation of 13.7% (19 of 139).
To be sure, larger demes tend to be better represented in the epigraphic
record, the average quota of the 48 demes with at least one document in
the name of its association being 5.42 versus the average of 3.59,[52] but this
small imbalance hardly accounts for the pronounced tendency towards
large size in evidence here.

It is not difficult to imagine why the festival should have been held
with greater frequency in the larger demes. The specific components of the
festival, above all the procession (*pompē*) and competitions (*agōnes*), entailed the presence of significant numbers of people. By its very nature, a
procession requires numbers, both as participants and as onlookers. But it
is with the competitions that size is seen to be an operative factor. For only
four of the nineteen (Cholleidai, Hagnous, Lamptrai, and Phlya, each a
case where slight or nonexistent epigraphic or literary testimony provides

no support for an argument from silence) is an attestation of *chorēgia*, *agōn*, *proedria*, comedy, tragedy, or *choros* or physical remains of a theater lacking. Stage productions require numbers and even if an actor or a *didaskalos* was a non-demesman (see the final section), the choruses of men and boys will presumably have been drawn largely from the home deme population. Greater numbers, too, will also have enhanced the prospects of finding wealthy demesmen able and willing to shoulder the responsibilities of the *choregiai* that alone made such choral presentations possible. But it is of course the necessity of attracting an audience for the productions so frequently mentioned or implied in the inscriptions that all but settled the matter in favor of the larger demes. Would a full-scale Athenian drama, even if not the work of an Aristophanes, Sophocles, or Euripides, have been put on before an audience of villagers whose nominal adult male membership stood at only 40 or 60 demesmen?[53]

An audience, in turn, presupposes a venue providing adequate seating and viewing—that is, a *theatron* of some sort. There are nine demes— Acharnai, Aixone, Eleusis, Euonymon, Ikarion, Peiraieus, Rhamnous, Sphettos, and Thorikos—for which physical, epigraphic, or literary evidence directly attests the existence of a theater.[54] For seven of the nine is preserved some sort of explicit textual reference to the Dionysia entirely independent of the evidence for the theater, while for the two others (Euonymon and Sphettos) the general absence of epigraphic material leaves their cases open. Theaters and the Dionysia, in other words, go together. Again, as I have already observed, save for the convening of the deme's *agora*, specific evidence is not forthcoming of any other uses to which a *theatron* was, or could have been, put. Thus, again, the inclusion in my catalogue of Euonymon, despite the absence of an attestation of the festival or of any of its associated events. Nor, contrariwise, does the seeming—but only seeming—negative evidence regarding theaters work against this conclusion. Demes with epigraphically attested *theatron, proedria, agōn*, dramas, or *choros*, it is true, have not in several cases yet produced physical remains of an orchestra or cavea. But a *theatron* might have been nothing more than a well-positioned slope with extemporaneous staging arrangements erected, and broken down, come the month of Posideion. Even where modern structures do not cover the site or where modern farming practices have not destroyed or scattered the ancient remains, the "theater" might well have left no traces to be discovered.

To bring our discussion to its conclusion, these considerations strongly suggest that *ta kat' agrous Dionysia* were celebrated exclusively, or nearly exclusively, in the larger demes. Of the 90 demes with a quota of three or fewer councillors, only two, Cholleidai (2) and Kollytos (3), appear in our roster and they are special cases, since the candidacy of Cholleidai depends upon the combination of widely separated passages in an imaginative literary work, and Kollytos, situated as it was within the walls, could draw upon an enormous non-*demotai* urban population for its audiences. For the others, it is unlikely that any ever staged the festival. About one case at least we can be sure on this point. At Erchia, a deme of moderate size (quota 6/7), the nearly intact *fasti* SEG 21.541 not only do not include a Dionysia but are also lacking even a single entry for the month Posideion, the month of its celebration elsewhere.[55]

No one could seriously suggest, of course, that we now have all, or nearly all, the demes celebrating the festival, but it could be, if my arguments are valid, that the demes lacking by accident of production or preservation of records an attestation of *ta Dionysia* were also ones with large populations, such as extraurban Alopeke (bouleutic quota, 10), Anaphylstos (10), Aphidna (16), Kephale (9), Marathon (10), Phaleron (9), and Phrearrhoi (9). Intramural Kydathenaion (11/12) would be another possibility, were it not for the fact that it would have had to compete with nearby (and also intramural) Kollytos. However, of these demes, only for Marathon have we evidence of the worship of Dionysos.[56]

Granting the monopolization of the festival by a relatively few widely spaced demes, various arrangements allowing participation by non-festival demes might be imagined. Might the smaller demes have cooperated with one another in order to amass the resources, financial and human, that seem to have been required for the staging of the festival? But the likelihood of this ever having happened is severely compromised by the consistent silence of the epigraphic record of the deme-associations vis à vis any mode of inter-deme involvement. Regarding cult matters (often the subject of formally inscribed deme association acts), only a single example of inter-deme cooperation has reached us: a decree of tiny Kydantidai (quota 2/1) and Ionidai (also 2/1) dated 331/0, SEG 39.148 (= 41.71), honors the *kolokratai* and the priest of Heracles for their superintendence of the rites of the hero, presumably conducted jointly by both associations (probably at Kydantidai, since all three honorands have this demotic and none the other). Furthermore, besides the general absence of more documents of this kind, the likelihood of cooperative arrangements is also undercut by the fact that certain of the demes promulgated exclusionary policies prohibiting participation by outsiders in their associational rites.[57]

Formal cooperative schemes were therefore probably rare. But even in
their absence, the mere presence of an outsider in the deme's theater may
have been viewed with less alarm, for ancient sources explicitly record that
actors, *didaskaloi*, and spectators participated in or viewed the Dionysian
agōnes in demes other than their own (see the final section). Perhaps, then,
to return to a specific case mentioned earlier, Erchians wishing to participate in a Dionysia "in the fields," lacking a festival of their own, will have
traveled to the nearby larger deme of (Lower?) Paiania (quota, 11) or to the
somewhat smaller Halai Araphenides (quota, 5) on the coast. Besides, a
mercenary motivation on the demes' parts may be suspected in some cases,
since inscriptions from two demes, Acharnai and Peiraieus, document the
raising of revenues from their theaters.[58] That these income-producing
venues should have been closed to all but demesmen (and perhaps their relations) seems unlikely on the face of it. Larger demes staging the festival,
therefore, may not only have played host (as we already know they did) to
the demesmen (and non-demesmen) of other demes and indeed of Athens
itself, but they also may have done so on a scale that was sufficient to com-
pensate for the absence of the festival in the demes of their guests. The distribution of our demes over the expanse of Attica (see Map 1) suggests as
a simple intuitive model a large local center with a theater catering to
neighboring smaller demes, with occasional visits from the town.

The Events of the Festival and Their Sequence

From the sources cited thus far we learn quite a bit about the events of
the festival, and on their basis it should be possible to reconstruct the festival's program in an event-by-event sequence and thereby fill a conspicuous gap in the present secondary literature. But because still other
activities, not mentioned to this point, have been or could be claimed for
the Dionysia on the strength of external testimony, it will be well to consider their candidacy before venturing further. Method is crucial. By what
criteria might a given activity be ascribed to the festival? First, obviously,
association with Dionysos, then, secondly (and no less obviously), specific
association with the celebration in the month of Posideion. The second
criterion is made necessary by the ample evidence for the observance of
the god in the demes in contexts lacking any discernible link with the festival: structures: Dionysion, *temenos, hieron,* and *oikia*;[59] a statue dedicated to Dionysos;[60] sacrifices to Dionysos;[61] funds in the name of

Dionysos;[62] and various divine epithets of the god—Anthios, Kissos, Lenaios, and Melpomenos.[63] At Erchia, the cult calendar *SEG* 21.541 lists two sacrifices to the god, one on 2nd Anthesterion (Γ, lines 42–47), the other on 16th Elaphebolion (Δ, lines 33–40), but none, as noted above, in Posideion. Besides Erchia, the demes which are indicated by the above observances of the god but which lack specific attestation of the festival are Gargettos, Halai Aixonides, Kerameis, and Marathon.

To commence the reconstruction of the program, our two criteria must be applied to the confused and confusing evidence coming under the head of *askoliasmos*. To put the matter simply, it is now clear, thanks to the disentangling of the ancient evidence by Latte in an article published in 1957, that not one activity (as previously thought) but two activities are in question: one, a game in which the participants attempted to jump onto and remain atop an inflated and greased *askos* (hence, according to Latte, the ancient false association with *askoliasmos*); the other, the true *askoliasmos*, involving various modes of hopping on one leg (that is, *askoliazein*). The question for us is which of the two games, if either, was part of the Dionysia. The beginning of an answer is to be found in a bit of post-classical learning, attributed to Didymos, variously reproduced in the scholiast on Aristophanes, *Ploutos* 1129 (where a form of the verb *askoliazein* occurs) and the lexicographers Harpokration (codex Marcianus Gr. 444),[64] Pollux, 9.121 (p. 180.20–27 Bethe), and Souda α 4177 (I, p. 385.7–25 Adler). Proceeding on the basis of the mistaken belief in a connection with *askos*, the notice (hereafter, for convenience's sake, represented by the scholiast) brings the verb into relation with an otherwise unknown festival Askolia, "in which they jumped on *askoi* in honor of Dionysos," followed by a note glossing Askolia as "a festival (*herotē*) of Dionysos."[65] The Askolia may be a phantom,[66] but the scholiast seems sure of the association between the god and *askoi*, a linkage elsewhere unambiguously affirmed by an oft-cited literary text. Virgil's second *Georgic* at lines 380–384 runs: "Because of no other fault a goat is slaughtered on all the altars for Bacchus and old plays mount the stages; and the sons of Theseus put up prizes for cleverness amidst the villages and crossroads and, happily amid their cups, in soft meadows leapt on greased skins."[67] A somewhat later writer of the Roman era, L. Annaeus Cornutus, in the course of describing a sacrifice of a billy goat to Dionysos, partially replicates Virgil's testimony when he writes ". . . and skinning it (sc. the goat), the young farmers in the Attic villages jump on to the *askos*."[68]

This evidence, furthermore, establishes the second crucial point, the

connection between this Bacchic wine-skin game and the *Dionysia kat'
agrous*. Virgil (with partial corroboration from Cornutus) expressly links
Bacchus, rural spaces, the wine-skin game, and plays on stages; the scholiast, although a reference to anything "rural" is lacking, Dionysos, the
wine-skin game, and the theater. With regard to the final item, the theater,
the scholiast provides explicit testimony—testimony quoted by Latte but
passed over by both Pickard-Cambridge[69] (although he does quote the
scholia in part) and Whitehead[70] (although he cites the scholia without
quoting them): "And they used to place in the middle of the theater inflated and greased *askoi*, leaping onto which they would slip. . . ."[71] The
scholiast goes on to quote as an illustration Euboulos (*Amaltheia, PCG* V
Eubulus, 7(8); frag. 8 Hunter): "And, in addition, placing an *askos* in the
middle, jump and all laugh together at those falling down!"[72] The significance of this fragment for our purposes turns on the interpretation of the
words *eis meson* ("in the middle"). Hunter discerns a reference to the
movements of the game itself,[73] but is difficult to resist a rapprochement
with the scholiast's "in the middle of the theater." The "middle" of the
theater will presumably have been the orchestra. A particular venue is in
any case to be preferred over Virgil's poetic "soft meadows" and Cornutus's vague "Attic villages." To be sure, Latte had linked the mention of
the theater with theories on the origins of drama, and Hunter on this basis urged that the reference to the theater not be pressed,[74] but in fact this
detail must be taken at face value unless and until it is overturned by positive evidence. The upshot is that the combined effect of our testimonies is
to situate the event in our Dionysia and to narrow the specific setting to
the scene of the agonal productions so abundantly documented in our
other sources.[75] At the same time, the genuine *askoliasmos*, the hopping on
one leg, remains unplaced, for the scholiast's information on jumping is
brought into relation with Dionysos only via his comments on *askoi*. But
just as *askoi*, if understood to be wine-skins, are at home with a celebration
of Dionysos (even if it is in Posideion, a time of no particular significance
for viticulture), hopping, which might have been viewed as serving to
awaken the earth from its winter slumber or more particularly to acceler-
ate the growth of autumn sowings, would be perfectly appropriate to a
midwinter fertility rite.[76] The *askoliasmos*, too, could have been played "in
the middle of the theater," but without new evidence we shall never know
for sure.

Be that as it may, a still more important implication follows: that, contrary to the views of Whitehead[77] and (more recently) Habash,[78] there

were *not* two differing versions of the Dionysia, one organized around a theatrical *agōn*, the other incorporating ancient ritual activities rooted in agriculture. Rather, however diverse the origins of its several components, the festival seems to have integrated those components into a single, unified program that, to judge from available indications, may have differed little from deme to deme.

We may now turn to the question of the larger framework of the festival's program. Necessarily, since no source appears to preserve a full bill of fare, our reconstruction will represent a composite pastiche of our data from all nineteen demes (with Brauron and Salamis kept in mind for their comparative value). Such a method is justified, first, by the numerous visible commonalities across the demes (especially involving events surrounding the *agōnes*) and, second, by the likelihood, to be revisited in my final section, that the several demes independently imitated a shared exemplar in the City Dionysia of Athens.

A succinct summation of the festival is embedded in an honorary decree from Ikarion, *IG* II² 1178, lines 7–8: "for Dionysos, the *heortē* . . . and the *agōn*." Plutarch, in a passage that may or may not pertain to Athens, isolates the former element: "The ancestral *heortē* of the Dionysia in antiquity was conducted in a popular and cheerful manner, an *amphoreus* of wine and a grape branch, and then someone used to lead a billy goat, another person followed carrying a wicker basket of dried figs, and to cap it all (was) the *phallos*."[79] The details of this concise *précis* are highly suggestive. The *amphoreus* of wine may have something to do with the wineskin game just discussed, either (with less likelihood) providing a liquid filling for the *askoi* or, with our scholiast, serving as the prize for the winner of the game.[80] The *klēmatis*, rendered here grape branch, is of uncertain relation to the first term in the conjunction of "the *klēmatis* and the *pompē* of Elaphebolion" in a late Hellenistic state decree (*IG* II² 1043 [38/7], lines 31–32), but it is difficult to accept that there is no connection. I shall suggest later a possible association with the so-called palm branch illustrated in the Hagios Eleutherios frieze believed by Deubner to depict our festival. But we can be more confident that Plutarch's billy goat is a sacrificial animal and the basket of dried figs an offering of some kind.

A procession (that is, the *pompē* implicit in Plutarch's verb), sacrifice, a celebrant carrying a basket, a phallos bringing up the rear, all in an atmosphere of simple jocularity, are the essential elements of the celebrated passage in Aristophanes' *Acharnians* wherein the protagonist Dikaiopolis conducts, or rather begins to conduct, *ta kat' agrous Dionysia* (lines

237–279, with 202 and 250 for the festival's name). Although these proceedings are interrupted by the sudden entry of the chorus at line 280, the passage is nonetheless invaluable in that it preserves for us a contemporary portrayal of our festival in an extramural deme, which we have taken to be Cholleidai in keeping with Dikaiopolis's demotic.[81] Dikaiopolis himself glosses *ta kat' agrous Dionysia* as "sending the *pompē* and sacrificing with the *oiketai*" (lines 248–250), but the scene, taken as a whole and reduced to its essentials, embodies a more detailed articulation: (1) the *euphemia* or proclamation of silence (lines 237, 241); (2) the *aparchai* (line 244) comprising the ladling of soup over the cake by Dikaiopolis's daughter (lines 245–246); (3) Dikaiopolis's prayer to Dionysos that the whole be received favorably (lines 247–252); and (4) the *pompē*, incorporating basket-bearer and phallos, ritual *aischrologia*,[82] and the singing of a hymn to Phales (lines 247–279 passim). The procession will be led by the basket-bearer (Dikaiopolis's daughter, line 242), followed by the two slaves with the phallos (lines 259–260), with Dikaiopolis himself bringing up the rear singing the *phallikon*, his rendition of which occupies the remainder of the vignette (lines 263–279). But where is the victim corresponding to Plutarch's billy goat, the animal widely associated with the god in sacrificial contexts?[83] Starkie supposed that the basket-bearer's basket (line 244) contained inter alia the sacrificial knife (*sphagis*), and that Dikaiopolis tells her to set the basket down so that the knife may be produced for the sacrifice.[84] Stage properties not mentioned in the text, at the minimum the knife and a victim (perhaps Plutarch's billy goat), would have to be assumed. Alternatively, one could with commentators, as suggested in the outline above, continue to take the cake as surrogate victim and the ladling of the soup over the cake as the *aparchai* enjoined by Dikaiopolis.[85]

Besides these literary portrayals of Plutarch and Aristophanes, the *pompē* is epigraphically attested in the large demes of Acharnai, Eleusis, and Peiraieus, although, with the exception of the very late appearances of the ephebes in the port town, no further details are forthcoming. But concerning the *thysia* we are better informed. Mention has already been made of the several attested shrines of the god in various demes, and the dedication of (a statue and) an [altar] to Dionysos at Aigilia, *IG* II[2] 3096, preserves an example of the actual scene. At Peiraieus, the scale of the proceedings was sufficient to justify the sale of skins and the recording of the transaction in *IG* II[2] 1496, lines 70–73 and 144–145.[86] At Acharnai, the decree *IG* II[2] 1206, lines 4–12, calls for the raising of 20 drachmas for a *thysia* from "the money collected from the theater" or, failing that, from the general fund. From the same deme, the second of the twin decrees of 315/4, *SEG* 43.26, states that the honorands "well and honorably supervised the *thysia* to Dionysos and the *pompē* and the *agōn*" (lines 1–6). Much later, a state decree of 165/4, *IG* II² 949, honors the demarch of Eleusis for his *thysia*, the *pompē*, . . . and "the *agōn* in the theater" (lines 30–34). Besides providing additional documentation on sacrifices, these latter two inscriptions are particularly valuable in that they illustrate an otherwise undocumented linkage of sacrifice, procession, and "contest"—and in the identical order at that.

But before proceeding to that "contest," a note is required concerning the scale of the festival, a topic into which the inscriptions afford very little insight. Aristophanes' comedic *pompē* had comprised only four people, namely Dikaiopolis, his daughter, and the two *oiketai*, but at the same time the text hints at more substantial dimensions. Dikaiopolis's mother will watch "from the roof" (line 262), presumably the top of the *skēnē* now imagined to be a structure in a village center through which the celebrants are supposed to be progressing. Dikaiopolis warns his daughter that among the crowd (line 257, probably with a gesture in the direction of the audience) are people who may "nibble away" her gold jewelry without her knowing it. Furthermore, Dikaiopolis's erotic musings, with reference to his daughter at the close of the prayer (lines 254–256) and throughout the phallic hymn (lines 263–265, 271–276), are echoed by Plutarch's characterization of the *pompē* as "popular and cheerful." Elsewhere, Plutarch writes of "the wailing and the uproar" of slaves under the influence of "pleasure-seeking and tastelessness."[87] All this would be very much at home in a deme like Peiraieus where, it will be recalled, a state decree (*IG* II² 380) called for the preparation of the "roads and streets" for the *pompē* for Dionysos. Aristophanes' rooftop spectator, crowd, and pickpockets may well have struck a respondent note in an audience on the Acropolis more likely to have attended the festival in the port town or in intramural Kollytos than in Dikaiopolis's own minuscule rural village of Cholleidai.

To resume my thread, it is tempting to infer that the linkage of sacrifice, procession, and contest found in the inscriptions also corresponds to the actual order of events. Given a festival limited to a single day, might the celebrants, following the completion of the sacrifice, have formed the procession, which, having made the rounds of the deme community, then led itself and any onlookers into the agonal venue, in many cases a *theatron*? Support for the bare sequence of events is forthcoming from the program of the City Dionysia. According to Pickard-Cambridge's reconstruction, the preliminaries reenacting the advent of Dionysos from Eleutherai included a sacrifice; on the first day proper, the 10th of Elaphebolion, came the *pompē*, in conjunction with which occurred the sacrifice of a bull and other victims; then, beginning on the 11th, the dramatic productions continued for three days (during the Peloponnesian War) or four days (before and after the Peloponnesian War).[88] Assumption of an analogous sequence in the demes is encouraged by the view, shared by several commentators, that, although the festival's primitive features may have originated in the countryside, the dramatic *agōnes* were an invention of the town only later to be imitated in the demes.[89] Such imitation would certainly have extended to the ordering of the program.

The following proceedings, although summarily termed simply "the *agōn*" in the primary sources, if viewed compositely across the full record of all our demes, actually comprised a number of different events, the sequence of which may be reconstructed with some confidence.

Once the spectators were in place, the recorded event likely to have come first was the *proedria*, the summoning of persons previously honored by the deme to their privileged seating in the front row. The summons proper (signaled by forms of the verb *kalein*) was executed by the demarch (at Aixone, Anagyrous, Eleusis, and Peiraieus) or the herald (at Halai Araphenides). One imagines an appropriately grand and stately entrance in full view of all in attendance. Examples of the throne-like backed chairs survive only at Ikarion[90] and Rhamnous,[91] but the inscriptions—though not those of these two demes—attest *proedria* at Acharnai, Aixone, Anagyrous, Eleusis, Halai Araphenides, Myrrhinous, Peiraieus, Rhamnous, and Sphettos.

With the seating of the dignitaries, the next official act will have been the announcement, recorded for Acharnai, Aixone, Eleusis, Halai Araphenides, Ikarion, Lamptrai, Peiraieus, and Rhamnous, plus Salamis. At Peiraieus and Rhamnous, the speaker is specifically (and appropriately) identified as the herald. Where so stated, the announcement concerns the previous crowning of the honorand (and so undoubtedly included some of those persons already seated in the *proedria*), but in one instance, at Aixone, an inscription calls for the crowning *itself* to take place "in the theater at the comedies" (*MDAI[A]* 66 [1941], 218–219, no. 1, lines 3–6). This case is also unusual in that here alone the announcement is attached to the comedies, whereas elsewhere, when dramas are mentioned, it is always the *agōn* of tragedies or simply tragedies (Eleusis, Ikarion, and Peiraieus, plus Salamis). The anomaly, previously unnoticed, adds force to the suggestion of Pickard-Cambridge, based on the choregic record, that comedy alone was contested in this deme.[92] But in other demes, it may have been felt that the announcement of the association's highest honors was more at home with the solemn seriousness of the tragedies. Alternatively, an explanation having to do with the program is also available: that tragedy came first and so was naturally preceded or otherwise attended by the ceremony marking the climax, and end, of the series of preliminaries. In any event, contrary to Whitehead's suggestion that the proclamation incorporated the crowning ceremony itself,[93] the announcement will have been a distinct item, as its technical terminology, the presence in two instances of the herald, and the explicit language required at Aixone when the actual crowning *was* intended all clearly suggest.

The term *agōn* occurs in the inscriptions of seven demes: Acharnai, Anagyrous, Eleusis, Halai Araphenides (of the Tauropolia), Ikarion ("for Dionysos"), Peiraieus, and Rhamnous, plus Salamis, and is regularly specified as either "of (the) Dionysia" or "of tragedies."[94] Nowhere, oddly, is the contest in comedy modified by this term, viz. *agōn*, although when comedy *is* mentioned, it, no less than tragedy, is subject to "victory." However that may be, comedy (*komodoi*) figures in various contexts at Acharnai, Aixone, Anagyrous?, Eleusis, Kollytos, Peiraieus, Rhamnous, and Thorikos. Tragedy (*tragodoi*) is thus far attested at [Anagyrous], Eleusis, Ikarion, Kollytos ("Oinomaos"), Paiania, Peiraieus, and Thorikos, plus Salamis. Both are attested for the same deme in five, possibly four, instances: Anagyrous?, Eleusis, Kollytos, Peiraieus, and Thorikos. A third event, usually denoted *choros* and with Pickard-Cambridge to be identified as dithyramb, is found at Acharnai (with comedy), Anagyrous? (with comedy? and tragedy?), Eleusis (with both comedy and tragedy), Halai Araphenides ("the *pyrrichistai*"), Ikarion (with tragedy), Peiraieus (with both comedy and tragedy), and Rhamnous (with comedy), plus Salamis (with tragedy). Choral performances may also be more generally indicated for Athens by Plato's remark, quoted earlier, regarding people "running around" the Dionysia in order to hear "each and every chorus" (*Republic* 5.475d). Except for the fact that *choros* is never found as the sole attested event, we have no clues as to just where the dithyramb, when contested,[95] came in the agonal program. We must rest content with the possibility that tragedy, because it alone is known to have been accompanied by the announcement, stood first after the preliminary sequence of summons, *proedria*, the announcement of crowns and possibly other previously bestowed honors or, exceptionally, an actual crowning itself. To invoke again the parallel evidence of the City Dionysia, a passage from Aristophanes,

Birds, lines 786–789, seems to show that in 414 the (three) tragedies were performed in the morning, to be followed by (the single) comedy during the afternoon of the same day.[96]

No mention has yet been made of the two games which, although viewed by previous scholars as activities distinct from the *agōnes*, it was suggested above were really part of them to the extent that they seem to have been held in the *theatron*. Again, the *amphoreus* of wine carried in Plutarch's *pompē* may somehow represent the *askos* on which the contestants were to teeter and/or have served as the eventual winner's prize. The appropriateness of the activity to Dionysos has been underscored in a recent review of drinking games by Lissarrague, who finds in it "a worthy homage" to the god.[97] While the status of the one-leg hopping game *askoliasmos* remains enigmatic, it is tempting to speculate further that both it and the wine-skin game were fitted around or in between the major agonal productions. Either or both would have served well to relieve the tensions created by tragedy, or to amplify and continue the raucousness of comedy, or to punctuate the lyric splendor of the dithyramb. A *kōmos*, possibly reflected in Dikaiopolis's address of Phales as "fellow komast" (line 264), might make sense here too for the same reason, but despite earlier scholars' belief in its inclusion in the festival, no trace of it has appeared in our survey of the primary sources.[98]

But still another candidate remains, one suggested by the two fighting-cocks pictured on the well-known Hagios Eleutherios calendar-frieze in Athens, which, though of late Hellenistic or Roman Imperial date, is widely regarded as relevant to classical Athenian arrangements. In the panel corresponding to Posideion, the month of our festival, three judges are sitting behind a table on which rest five crowns, while before the table appear a palm frond and the two cocks.[99] Whereas earlier scholars had held, as I will suggest now, that the figures represent an actual *Hahnenkampf*, Deubner rejected this view on the basis of stylistic incompatibility with the remainder of the frieze and insisted that the cocks were merely "ein Sinnbild des Agons."[100] But a cockfight, even if inappropriate in more formal venues of the town, would be very much at home in a rural agrarian setting. Moreover, the appropriateness of fighting cocks to the dramatic stage is now vividly illustrated by the "Getty Birds" depicted on a vase first published in 1985. The figures were initially referred by Green to Aristophanes' *Birds*, but Taplin made a case that they in fact represent the *agōn* of the Just and Unjust Logoi in the *Clouds*, a position more recently reaffirmed and strengthened in an appendix to *Comic Angels*.[101] The decisive point is ornithological: as Taplin observes, the Getty birds are domesticated chickens (*alektryones*), better known in Athens as fighting cocks than as laying hens and entirely out of place among the wild species of Aristophanes' chorus.[102] The wider context has been supplied by Fowler's amply documented demonstration that cockfighting was a common pursuit at Athens and that cocks were associated with all agonistic contests and especially those of the theater.[103] If a make-believe cockfight could be put on the stage before an audience in the City Dionysia, then the real thing may well have not been out of place in Aixone, Halai Araphenides, or Phlya. At the very least, it is clear that the Getty pot must force a reappraisal of Deubner's symbolic interpretation.

At all events, entr'actes of such sorts would make perfect entertainment sense in a festival that had begun with the ribaldry and low humor of Dikaiopolis's procession. Perhaps it was such viscerally entertaining performances that lie behind the phrase "in all the spectacles" restored in a decree from Myrrhinous, *IG* II² 1182, lines 2–3, and again in the provision for "spectacle" (*th[ea]*) at *ta Dionysia ta Peiraika* in a state decree, *IG* II² 456, lines 32–33, in Isaios's use of the verb *theorein* (8.16), and in the term *theatron* itself. Language of this kind, with its slant towards the visual, seems to suggest something more than the dramatic and choral-specific *"agōn."*

Since our inscriptions make frequent reference to victories by *choregoi*, and indeed since it is the expressed purpose of many of our inscriptions precisely to commemorate such victories, it follows that the *agōnes* had ended with some sort of judgment and declaration of the winners, but no written record of such judgment or declaration has reached us. All we have is the above-mentioned frieze panel, with its depiction of judges, cocks, and palm frond. If the cocks are not literal contestants in an *agōn* of their own, they may symbolize (with Deubner) that in tragedy, comedy, or dithyramb. No less speculatively, the frond may be distantly related to the *klēmatis* carried in the procession described in the passage from Plutarch (527d) discussed earlier; in any case, again with Deubner, the branch signifies "den Sieg."[104] After the decision(s) had been reached by the judges, the likely final act of the festival will have been the placing of the crowns upon the heads of the victors.

But, having reached this point, we may still wonder about the duration of the festival from its inception to this climax. Late hellenistic epigraphic testimony has ephebes on hand in Peiraieus for four days,[105] but the general uniqueness of the port town's arrangements and the late date render this datum doubly irrelevant to our present concerns. Dikaiopolis,

at the close of his phallic hymn, declares to Phales that, if he drinks with
them, "in the morning" he will gulp down the cup of peace when the
drinking bout is over (lines 276–278). Such attainment of the leader's
hoped-for goal suggests that the festival will have ended and that its dramatic length will thus have been no more than one full day since it began.
But if a single twenty-four-hour period was sufficient time in tiny Cholleidai, the threefold *agōnes* of tragedy, comedy, and dithyramb in Eleusis must
surely have run into multiple days. No generalization, clearly, is possible.

No less problematic is the question of the composition of the audience. Aristophanes put Dikaiopolis, his daughter, and two *oiketai* in his
pompē and Dikaiopolis's mother on a rooftop as a spectator. I see no objection to the surmise that the groups symbolically represented by these
dramatis personae also viewed the agonal productions with which the festival continued in a *theatron*. Plutarch, in one of the two passages quoted
above (1098b), asserts that "the *therapontes*" (again, like Aristophanes'
oiketai, slaves identified by function rather than status) participated in the
festival, although, if Aristophanes is his source, the assertion may possess
no independent value. But, specific literary texts apart, a more general set
of circumstances is operating here as well. The *agōnes*, as we have just seen,
were the scenes of the announcements of the previous conferral of crowns
voted by the several associations of *demotai*—that is, the adult male citizen
hereditary memberships—of this or that deme. As I have argued, the ver-
bal iteration of an already bestowed honor would make little sense if the
audience of the announcement were no different from the group that had
previously voted and bestowed the praise, crown, or so on in the deme's
agora.[106] Therefore, an audience of wider composition seems likely—
women, children, slaves, and probably also metics and non-*demotai* citizens. Besides, the seating capacities of the better preserved or known
theaters at Thorikos[107] and Peiraieus[108] exceed by far the adult male citizen
member numbers indicated by these demes' bouleutic quotas.

The Dionysiac Festival Beyond the Deme

Now that we have rejected the notion that each and every deme might
have staged its own Dionysia, and indeed have suggested that the festival
was mostly confined to a relatively few larger demes, it is natural to wonder whether Aigilia, Ikarion, Myrrhinous, and the others opened up their
winter Dionysiac festivals to outsiders, including but not limited to Athe-

nians whose demes lacked the festival. That this sometimes happened has long been known. Aeschines, a demesman of Kothokidai (*PA* 354; *PAA* 115030), had acted in a dramatic production in Kollytos; and Demosthenes describes him as a hireling of two actors called the Baritones (*barustonoi*, 18.262, cf. 267), evidently a troupe possibly traveling to other locations as well. Aristophanes, a demesman of Kydathenaion (*PA* 2090; *PAA* 175685), was *didaskalos* in comedy at Eleusis. Sophocles, a demesman of Kolonos (*PA* 12834), was, according to the same choregic text, *didaskalos* in tragedy at Eleusis, and, if the *tragodopoios* of Aeschines' *Oinomaos*, at Kollytos as well. Euripides, a demesman of Phyla (*PA* 5953; *PAA* 444585), produced in Peiraieus and, if a choregic text of the fifth century from Varkiza (*SEG* 23.102; 26.225) belongs to Anagyrous (where the festival is fragmentarily attested) and if the occasion in question is the Dionysia, in a second deme other than his own. Nor is the phenomenon confined to actors and playwrights. To illustrate a philosophical point, the Athenian Plato (whose deme, let it be noted, was Kollytos [*PA* 11855], the scene of *ta kat' agrous Dionysia*) at *Republic* 5.475d, as we saw earlier, writes of unidentified persons "running around" the Dionysia, "leaving out neither those (sc. Dionysia) in the *poleis* nor those in the *komai*," the latter term with obvious reference to our festival. Similarly, the *therapontes* said by Plutarch (1098b) to have participated in the *Dionysia kat' agron* are described as *periontes*—"making the rounds."

From these particulars certain implications seem to follow. For one, commentators are surely correct in concluding that the several festivals could not have been held on the same day in Posideion. The closest a source comes to a precise date is an inscription from Hagnous placing the subject of the Dionysia on the deme association's agenda, thereby suggesting to commentators that the festival was scheduled alternatively later or earlier than that day, the 19th of Posideion. The Thorikos calendar simply gives the month, although admittedly this is a general striking feature of the calendar as a whole.[109] Given the weather in Greece at this time of year, it may be suggested further that the schedule was flexible, each deme waiting for a day or days suitable for an outdoor procession and open-air dramatic performances. But such an arrangement might well have resulted in many or all demes settling on the same few days, and in any event would of course have impeded any advance planning to visit the festival demes in a predetermined sequence.

For another, and more significantly, such circulation of actors, playwrights, and audience in and out of individual demes points up the unusual, indeed unique, place of our festival in local Attic village society. When measured against a general background of insularity and exclusion, it represents a conspicuous exception to the otherwise prevailing isolation of the deme community.[110] Furthermore, interdeme movement of this kind also plays a dynamic role, for it may account in part for another striking feature of our record of the festival, the general homogeneity of structure, content, and nomenclature from one deme to another—again in contrast with a marked trait of the Attic deme, its pronounced particularity.[111] Hardly any trace is to be found of the odd institution, practice, or name that in other contexts so often bestow a mark of local distinctiveness.

If the Dionysia transcended the limits of the individual deme staging the festival, the fact that the state government had become, or eventually became, involved as it evidently did is not at all surprising. The case of the atypical Peiraieus, as we have seen, is well documented in this regard. The law of Euegoros, cited by Demosthenes 21.10, prohibited the taking of pledges and the seizing of property during certain named festivals including "the *pompē* to Dionysos in Peiraieus and the comedies and tragedies." A state decree (*IG* II² 380) calls for preparation of the roads and streets for the procession. Another such decree enjoins the *apoikoi* from Kolophon to be given (as restored) "viewing," presumably special seating of some kind, at *ta Dionysia ta Peiraika* (*IG* II² 456, lines 32–33). The state's generals on one occasion in the late 330s are found conducting the sacrifices (*IG* II² 1496, lines d144–145). Financial interventions extend from the collection of moneys raised by the sale of skins of sacrificial victims (*IG* II² 1496, lines a70–73), to the contribution to the expenses of a sacrifice by the *epistatai* of the Eleusinian Mysteries (*IG* II² 1672, line 106), to the prohibitions on financial transactions in the aforementioned law of Euegoros (Demosthenes, 21.10). Exceptionally, the deme itself maintains control over the theater, early in the fourth century turning its administration over to contractors (*Agora* XIX, L13 =*IG* II² 1176+), while later in the century the *architekton* is found in charge (*IG* II² 456, lines 32–33, restored). But we can be sure that the festival in Peiraieus in all its major aspects remained, directly or indirectly, under the control of Athens through the person of the demarch, the association's chief officer, for he, entrusted with the administration of the Dionysia, including the appointment of *choregoi*, was, unlike his colleagues in the demarchy, appointed by lot by the People (*AthPol* 54.8).

Elsewhere, evidence for the role played by the demarch is sketchy but nonetheless suggestive and in keeping with Whitehead's characterization of his mediating role in transmitting state policy to his village constituents.[112] At Acharnai, in one decree the demarch is recorded to have cooperated with the *tamias* in supervising the festival; in the second, he and the *tamias* and the epimelete of the Dionysia are found supervising the *thysia* to Dionysos, the *pompē*, and the *agōn*, and it is he who is to announce the crowns at "the *agōn* of the Dionysia." At Ikarion, the demarch stages the *heortē* and the *agōn* for Dionysos. Minor roles are recorded at Aixone (with the *tamiai*, to erect the stele in the theater), Anagyrous (to summon the honorand to *proedria*), and Eleusis (to summon the honorands to *proedria*). Outside the deme system proper, the *archōn*—the officer paralleling the deme's demarch—of Salamis stages the Dionysia and appoints the *choregoi* (*AthPol* 54.8). Since the demarch, to judge from surviving evidence, is, in Whitehead's words, "the only post which may legitimately be assumed to have existed in all one hundred and thirty-nine demes,"[113] it is an attractive, though unverifiable, inference that he played similar roles in other demes as well.

Less overtly, and on a larger scale, the state's hand seems to be implicit in the fact, brought out by critics, that, given the attested scheduling of the Dionysian festivals in the demes (in Posideion[114]) and the town (Lenaia in Gamelion, Anthesteria in Anthesterion, City Dionysia in Elaphebolion), it was possible for a person to participate in both the local and general Athenian celebrations.[115] The beneficiaries would have included not only demespeople eager to join in the town's Dionysia without passing up the home celebration but also deracinated urbanites who wished, without foregoing the urban festivals, to return to the ancestral deme (the deme, let it be remembered, that continued to be represented by their inherited *demotikon*) for the local village Dionysia. Was this calendric compatibility the product of conscious planning? We cannot be sure. It is natural to speculate, given the grandeur of the Lenaia, Anthesteria, and City Dionysia, that the object was to prevent the general neglect and decline of the deme festivals, but by no means is it evident that the latter were incapable of competing with the town. The productions of major playwrights, among them Sophocles, Euripides, and Aristophanes, were commemorated on monuments erected in deme locations, and, while in at least one case it is likely that an inscription placed in a rural deme celebrated victories won in the town,[116] there are no a priori grounds for doubting that a tragedy, comedy, or dithyramb, albeit not necessarily a first performance, might have been staged in a deme's *theatron*.[117] The chorege will have valued the attention of his fellow demesmen, and a large audience in a stone theater at Peiraieus, Ikarion, or Rhamnous was surely deserving of a major effort by a major playwright. So, while an Athenian did not in all probability have to choose between the claims of one's village home and of one's city-state, many may have been content to remain in the home deme for their Dionysia. Such circumstances would help make comprehensible the fact, noted by Mikalson, that the Dionysia was the most widely attested festival of the Attic countryside.[118] Perhaps, then, it was the urban festivals which were being spared neglect through any such manipulation of the festival calendar.

Must we conclude, in the light of these actual or seeming interventions, that this state of affairs was the product of Athenian governmental policy? No, for the law of Euegoros appears positively to preclude any notion of Attica-wide regulation. While specifically naming the festival in the "super deme" Peiraieus (to which, moreover, as we have just seen, much of the remaining record for state involvement pertains) and while naming a series of urban festivals (Lenaia, City Dionysia, and Thargelia), no reference, explicit or otherwise, is made to the Dionysia *kat' agrous* by this or any other locution.[119] Except for the expected mediating roles played by the demarchs, it is arguable that the situation we have found was the product of actions taken independently and spontaneously by the several deme communities. Larger demes undertook to construct theaters because only they could marshal the material resources to do so, only they could supply choregoi sufficiently numerous to produce plays and choral odes, and only they could muster audiences worthy of such productions. At the same time, these demes (like all demes), as a consequence of their contacts with the urban center produced by governmental, military, and economic necessity, were inevitably exposed to the influence of the high cultural productions of the town and were thus in a position, if so inclined, to introduce dramatic or choral *agōnes* into what had once been a purely agricultural midwinter fertility festival. The uniformity of form and content that we find from deme to deme may just as likely, that is, be the product of parallel imitations of a common exemplar as of imposition of the urban paradigm from above. But even if, as it seems, the local communities, extramural as well as intramural, had come under the spell of the town, enough remained of the original agrarian roots of the Dionysia, exemplified in the procession and possibly in theatrical entr'actes, to demonstrate for us the continuing expression of those less sophisticated impulses. And although the contests in tragedy, comedy, and dithyramb were, as the famous names among their *didaskaloi* prove, of urban origin or inspiration, the mere fact that these works could be produced (as premieres or otherwise) in a local theater speaks emphatically to the vitality of those communities.

Conclusions

It is now time to sum up the results of our study in the form of a series of propositions:

That, in keeping with the evidence for the name of the festival and as exemplified by its specific content, *ta kat' argous Dionysia* was fundamentally an agrarian affair designed to celebrate the culture of an agricultural community and, since it was not (as the word "rural" has always implied) strictly tied to locale, could be held even in intramural settings.

That, as suggested by the distribution and bouleutic quotas of the demes (now increased to nineteen in number) certain or likely to have celebrated the festival, the Dionysia was probably confined to widely spaced larger demes, usually or always ones with theaters, with an expected audience including resident non-*demotai* (women, children, non-demesmen citizens, metics, and slaves) as well as persons from neighboring smaller demes and the town.

That the more primitive activities associated with the festival, which recent scholars have thought incompatible with the more urbane dramatic and choral *agōnes*, were in fact integrated into the program to the extent that they were part of the procession or were with varying degrees of probability held in the theater.

That the program, when all sources are combined to produce a single, composite whole, comprised, in order: sacrifice and procession (including *euphemia, aparchai*, prayer, and phallic hymn); *proedria;* announcements; *agōnes* in tragedy and/or comedy and/or dithyramb (with tragedy coming first) preceded, punctuated, or followed by entr'actes comprising (with varying degrees of probability) the wine-skin game, the one-leg hopping game (*askoliasmos*), and perhaps cockfights; decisions by judges; and announcement and crowning of winners.

That, as illustrated by the movement of actors, *didaskaloi*, and audience, the individual festivals were not constrained by the insularity otherwise typical of the demes and, as illustrated by the several shared specific features of the program, do not evidence the particularity also typical of the demes.

That such commonalities, however, are not to be understood in terms of a uniform design imposed by the People in Athens but rather as parallel imitations of a common exemplar undertaken independently by the several deme-associations. Nonetheless, the fact remains that the dramatic productions in particular cannot be regarded as homegrown expressions of agrarian (whether extra- or intramural) village culture when in fact they were a once-yearly special event catering in part to an extra-village (and, indeed, urban) itinerant audience.

5

Realities

THIS AND THE FOLLOWING CHAPTER undertake a comprehensive portrayal of what we shall provisionally (and loosely) term rural "culture" in its respectively factual ("realities") and representational ("images") modes. Since much attention has already been given to the realities of rural life under the rubrics of settlement (ch. 1), society (ch. 2), the individual village (ch. 3), and the local "rural" Dionysia (ch. 4), these topics will be treated in summary form. Much of the residue will be taken up here, not with the (vain) hope of achieving full coverage but rather in the continuing pursuit of establishing the fundamental "otherness" of extramural Attica.

A more serious, methodological problem concerns the use of source materials in the two chapters. When does a given source speak for "reality" and when for "image"? Even a "documentary" inscription executed and displayed in a rural village might come under suspicion regarding its purpose and function, as we shall see momentarily when we turn to the matter of literacy. But still more problematic are those written sources which are conventionally called "literary" but misleadingly so, because that one term both masks important distinctions and rather prejudges the character of these writings on the side of imaginative "artistic" production. Few would ascribe genuine literary qualities to the *Constitutions* ascribed to Aristotle and the "Old Oligarch," or to Athenaios's *Deipnosophistai*, or to the fragments of ancient learning preserved in various scholia or lexicographical writings, yet each (and other writings like them) make significant contributions to our knowledge of Attic rural culture. But because they are factual, or at least so purport, works of this kind must stand apart from those self-declared creations of the imagination the purposes of which do not necessarily include accurate historical or contemporary portrayal. With acknowledgment of ascending degrees of remove from the real world, may be set here comedy, especially the extant comedies of Aristophanes (Old)

and Menander (New); the relevant *scripta minora* of Xenophon; the character sketches of Theophrastos, and (falling outside the chronological
range of this study) the post-classical *Letters* of farmers and fishermen of
Aelian and Alkiphron. The methodological problem they present is
whether the content of these writings, even the ones of demonstrable
Athenian authorship and publication, is to be exploited as *erga* or *logoi* or
both. My approach, in brief, is one dictated by the assumption (yet a well
grounded one, I believe) that even a work of vivid imagination cannot, if
it purports to represent reality, depart too far from that reality which is its
base without lapsing into mere pointless and unentertaining fantasy or
silliness.

This assumption will allow me to use the selfsame writing, viz. Aristophanes' *Peace* or Theophrastos's *Agroikia*, in two different, contrasting,
ways: at the level of the incidental detail which forms the setting or context as it were of the author's imaginative flight of fancy, true literary works
may be utilized as sources of "realities," while their imaginative core—exaggeration, parody, distortion, or other Tendenz—will fall on the side of
representation, the subject of our concluding chapter. "Image" does not of
course condemn a representation to falsehood, but what it does do is leave
open the possibility, indeed the likelihood, of the proposition with which
this work opened—that the artistic productions of urban authorship presented in an urban setting to an urban audience may have significantly
transformed the rural reality.

Settlement, Residence, and Mobility

Chapter 1 reopened the question, or rather set of interconnected questions, concerning the place (farm or nucleated center), duration (seasonal
or year round), and status (free, resident alien, or slave) of agrarian residence in rural Attica. The epigraphic evidence was found to favor residence in an *oikia* on the land itself, while leaving open the matters of
duration and status. Literary testimony appeared consistent with this result; and as for the archaeologically attested village (i.e. Kleisthenic deme)
nucleus, no evidence, literary, epigraphic, or even archaeological, precludes the typification of this center as monumental, administrative, and
ceremonial but not necessarily residential. But movement between farm
and village center probably varied greatly depending upon the particular
deme's corporate vitality (expressed inter alia in the convening of its

agora, its cultic calendar, and the existence and use of a *theatron*), while movement to and from the town will likewise have varied greatly according to distance, competition from the village, and economic necessity, among other factors (see chapter 3, at the end, for three suggested models of deme-and-town relations).

Patronage: Big Man, Crisis, and Reciprocation

In Chapter 2, following a review of the anciently attested sources of farm labor, I considered the possibility that they might have proved inadequate to meet the demands of an unforeseen crisis or even of the periodic and predictable peak labor demands of planting, harvest, pruning, etc. The documented substantial variations in size of land holdings by individual Athenians (not to mention other forms of wealth possessed by those same individuals) would have allowed for, or even necessitated, I argued, the emergence of patronal reciprocal relations between a Big Man and smallholder citizen landowners. Evidence for such reciprocal exchanges was found in the honorary decrees of the deme-associations.

Agricultural Labor: Family, Class, and Gender

According to the prescriptions of Hesiod's *Works and Days*, field work, where indicated, is generally left to males; and, away from the farm, it is the *aner* whose tasks in winter time are threatened by "the blacksmith's seat and warm lounge" (493–495). But ploughing is not left entirely to males, for a female "purchased, not married" is to follow the oxen (405–406). Where free females are concerned, the *parthenikē* stays indoors on a winter's day with her mother, bathing, anointing herself with oil, and taking to bed in an inner room (519–525); and the female *pygosto-los* poking around your granary (373–375), since her status is not specified, may with West be "your wife, your neighbour's wife, or a slave." [1] Given the prevailing misogynistic tone of his presentation of females in both the *Works* and the *Theogony* (witnessed above all by the Pandora myth), however, it is doubtful how far these patently prejudicial vignettes may be pushed.

Discussion in chapter 2, departing from the assumption of a (Hesiodic) *oikos* of conjugal pair, few children, and minimal slave workers, proposed that cultural ideals discouraged field work by wife and children, noted the fleeting indications of the use of slaves in agricultural capacities, denied the extensive use of itinerant work gangs, and speculated that the presence of metics as tenant farmers has been underestimated. Literary sources at all events find males in the fields, yet, contrary to an expectation arising out of evidence for the seclusion of females in an urban setting, occasionally reveal the apparently socially approved movement of women outside their homes. Demosthenes preserves a litigant's report to the effect that two citizen mothers regularly visited each other "as was natural (*eikos*) since both resided in the country (*agros*) and were neighbors and also since their husbands had enjoyed each other's company . . ." (55 *Against Kallikles* 23), from which it is a legitimate inference that such visits were rendered "natural" by the country setting but would not have been "natural" had the two residences been in an urban area even if the women were neighbors and their husbands were friends. To this especially valuable normative statement we may also add the scattered testimonies regarding female agricultural labor and laborers reviewed in chapter 2, provided that we keep in mind the non-citizen or at least uncertain status obtaining in several cases. For what it is worth, Aristophanes' Praxagora from her location in town declares that she thinks that "other women" will come "directly from the fields (*ek tōn agrōn*), to the Pnyx" (*Ekklesiazousai*, 280–282), again suggesting not only visibility and mobility but also the exercise of such freedoms presumably (given the demands of the play's plot) in the absence of males.

Rural female visibility, furthermore, is arguably reconcilable with the ambiguous statement of the speaker of Demosthenes' *Against Euboulides* (57.45) characterizing as "servile" (*polla doulika pragmata*) the use of free *astai gynaikes* as vineyard workers during the Peloponnesian War. But just what aspect of the arrangement was "servile" for these last-mentioned women? As usage in town might suggest, the mere fact that they were, in defiance of convention, out-of-doors and so visible to strangers, especially, one would presume to be the point, strange males? Or was it the work itself (whether normally done by males or, if by females, females of lower status)? There can be little doubt but that it was the work itself. For, as we have seen and shall continue to see throughout, agricultural labor was typically associated with slaves—in actual practice (chapter 2), in literary portrayals (chapter 6), in utopian schemes (chapter 7); it was beneath not only free women but also all women and men of free (and *a fortiori* citizen) status. And because it was agricultural work in which the charge of servility adhered, we are relieved of the necessity of looking to visibility *tout court* as the sole explanation for the Demosthenic testimony.

Hesiod, the Seasons, and Seasonality

The goings and comings of the rural population, whether free or slave, male or female, young or old, were subject to still another variable, particularly where agriculture was concerned: the time of the year, the *horai*, the "seasons." The point might be thought self-evidently true, perhaps not even requiring mention in the case of a rural regime dominated as it was in this case by the practice of agriculture and pastoralism, but, as we shall see in a moment, things were quite otherwise in the town, and it has been the town that has occupied center stage in the discussion of this as of so many other matters.

The particulars of the calendar, the schedule, day or night, early or late, were taken up by the agricultural writers throughout classical Greek and Roman antiquity and, in modern times, have been treated in detail by scholars, most recently in the ecological studies. There should be in fact nothing in the least problematic or debatable about the flat-out proposition that the "natural" passage of time governed the working lives of the agrarian population and that what governed a working life in a labor-intensive environment such as this one probably had comparable effects in the non-working aspects of rural society and culture. Barring positive evidence for the intervention of alternative schedules from elsewhere, rural existence should be expected to reflect the march of the seasons across the board. That it in fact did is evident first of all from the text, or rather the oral traditions represented by that text, which we shall momentarily conjecture remained in circulation (in some sense of that term) in classical Attica and which were represented *in primis* by the *Works and Days* of Hesiod. Elsewhere I have taken up at length the detailed interpretation of the poem under the title "Perses, Work 'in Season,' and the Purpose of Hesiod's *Works and Days*," arguing that, despite the superficial signs of divided purpose and even inconsistency, its diverse subject matter is organized around the primary theme of work, and that work is conceptualized in terms appropriate to the farmer's (and sea-trader's[2]) pursuits as properly done "in season," specifically in conformity with Hesiod's own agricultural (and maritime) calendar.[3]

Thus the *Erga* emerge not as a personal moralizing message to a

brother in the wake of a dispute over the division of an inheritance nor, at
the other extreme, as a tract on the abstract notion of Justice, but rather as
a more general and less abstract series of admonitions on the importance
of timing, above all in respect to the seasons.[4] While Hesiod's reader is told
the basics about setting up a small-holder farming household, the emphasis is consistently upon the nuances of selection, quantity, and above all
timing, for it is "season" (*hora*) and "seasonal" (*horios*) that figure as the
author's principal operative terms—the niceties of detail that can make or
break a man poised, as the subsistence farmer was, on the brink of ruin.
Seasonality in its literal agrarian senses is enlarged, furthermore, into a general preoccupation with propriety, as shown initially by the application of
the leading terms themselves to other, non-agrarian contexts. Thus, for example, when the *horaios* man, who is not far short of or much beyond
thirty years, takes a wife, this marriage is *horios* (lines 695–697). When propriety is expressed in quantitative rather than temporal terms, the allied
word *metron* is employed with reference to the measurement of grain into
vessels (600), to the "measure" of the ages of bulls (438) or humans (132),
to the "measures" or rules of the sea (648), and, in the cultural sphere, to
the "measured" movement of the tongue (719–720). If you expect to fill
your barns, you must order your *erga* "in measure" (306–307). Reciprocal
relations are brought into play as well, for if you expect to find security in
your neighbor, "have fair measure given to you by him, and pay back fair,
with the same measure, or better, if you can" (349–351). In the *Days* propriety is expressly brought into relation with the same calendar with which
the *Works* had dealt in agricultural terms. And at line 694 the universal ap-
plicability of the notion is spelled out in so many words, here invoking still
another term from the vocabulary of propriety, *kairos*: "Keep watch on
measures (*metra*)—due proportion (*kairos*) is best in all matters."[5]

Whether or not the people of classical rural Attica adhered to seasonal
agrarian calendars is not at question here, for of course they did. Rather the
question is, first and preliminarily, did the town and its populations similarly observe those calendars rooted in their agrarian past and (outside the
main conurbations) present; and, secondly, to what extent, if at all, did any
urban disturbances of the traditional modes of the articulation of time
manage to penetrate Attica beyond the walls. While, apart from the urban-
influenced official promulgations of the deme-associations we have little
from the villages to work with, the indications regarding practice in the *asty*
are plentiful. Several areas of apparent rural vs. urban variation are at hand:

(1) *Physical environment.* True, not all of the spaces within the walls

were built up with permanent infrastructure; in chapter 1, for example, we reviewed the epigraphic evidence for plots, even farms, within or in the near vicinity of the central fortification. To be sure, the Acropolis-Agora complex and Peiraieus town were thickly occupied by buildings, monuments, and pavements, but even so late reports of plantings have reached us.[6] Landscaping, however, is not to be confused either with wild nature or with the economically driven practices of the agriculturist.

(2) *Artificial, regulated supply of foodstuffs and other agricultural products.* As in cities of the modern world, produce from rural regions, in its raw or processed forms, was made available to Athenians in centralized markets throughout classical antiquity. So again, as with the artificially constructed physical environment, an urbanite could easily lose touch with the ebb and flow of seasonal variation. In Athens' case, the abnormality was exaggerated under the fifth-century empire by the influx of foreign goods (famously remarked by Pericles in the Funeral Oration, Thucydides, 2.38.2), supported by a legislature acting in various ways to regulate supply and prices in the face of seasonal (as well as political or military) fluctuation.

(3) *Use of a civil calendar out of phase with the natural world.* In contrast with a purely natural lunar calendar and with the festival calendar wherein each of twelve (or, in a leap year, thirteen) months was named after a festival occurring within it, classical Athens also observed for governmental legislative purposes a third, "prytany" calendar. At least in Aristotle's day, the year was divided into ten *prytaneiai* of 36 (the first four) or 35 (the last six) days each, the *prytaneia* being the term of service of the 50 *bouleutai* representing one of the ten phylai in the Council of Five Hundred (*AthPol* 43.2). Although from the fourth century both the festival and prytany calendars commenced on the same day, viz. the first new moon after the summer solstice, and although in later times the preambles of official inscriptions sometimes identify the day with an equation of the dates according to the two systems, it is obvious that the "civil" calendar constituted a sharp break with contemporary agrarian time-reckoning.[7] True, its uses were confined to "official" governmental acts, but precisely the fact that they were official constituted a weighty challenge to a natural scheme of reckoning according to phases of the moon.

(4) *Disruption of agrarian schedules by military operations.* Invasions of an enemy's lands were regularly timed to coincide with harvest season, in order thereby to wreak maximum damage through destruction of crops.[8] Synchronization of agriculture and warfare represented the urban

invader's ultimate assault upon the ways of the agrarian countryside. The very time when the rural population was to have been deployed to its greatest capacity in the reaping of the fruits of agricultural labor instead became the time when that population was depleted of its able male workforce in order either to attack another population's harvestable crops or to defend its own.

(5) *Theorizing of science and philosophy.* As though to rationalize or even to validate the degenerative effects of these developments, the speculations of proto-scientists, philosophers, and sophists wore away at the traditional agrarian worldview by offering mechanistic causal explanations in place of divine governance and, more generally, by promoting a cultural relativity that robbed the otherwise dominant and unquestioned "natural" ordering of the world of its special status.

Diet

Much attention has been given of late to the subject of food in classical antiquity, but to a great extent the orientation of such studies has centered on an upper class, and therefore predominantly urban, set, with specific attention to the symposium, the gourmet feast, cookery and cookbooks, and so on.[9] This urban bias reflects, as usual, the authorship, subject-matter, and readership of the sources, but in the case of Greece, and particularly classical Athens, it is not clear that its operation is as distorting as one might initially expect. Across Greece the ancient diet evidenced a consistent pattern: a base comprising cereals (wheat and barley, although the consumption of the latter by humans is problematic), legumes, olive oil, and wine; meat (especially in the form of sacrificial animals) and fish (including shellfish) at irregular intervals depending upon availability; milk processed in the form of cheese; vegetables grown in gardens (onion, garlic, radish, etc.), fruits (figs, grapes, apples, etc.), and various seasonings. Within this characteristically Hellenic framework, no gross variation correlating with town or country situation is easily discernible—or to be expected since, after all, the town-dweller's food came from essentially the same source as the farmer's. But of course we would like to know more regarding not only rural vs. urban variation but also any specifics differentiating one rural region, settlement, or household from another. Literary sources are sometimes helpful when they mention particular foodstuffs in association with particular Attic demes, although one has always to keep in mind the very real possibility of distorting stereotyping.[10] Otherwise, any further refinements are likely to be forthcoming only from the recovery of physical remains such as pottery finds sufficiently inform- ative to indicate culinary function; planting sites betraying the ancient identities of tree, vine, or field crop; and seeds, spores or other botanical remains. Ecological studies by Peter Garnsey and others have already done much to map out the place of food as "a biocultural phenomenon,"[11] but with only occasional attention to any significant cleft between urban and rural practice, at Athens or elsewhere.

Nonetheless, despite the present general lack of specificity, it will be helpful I think if we can isolate some of the factors on which, in the case of rural Attica, significant variations between town and country might de- pend—variations which, had we better source materials, would be imme- diately visible and comprehensible. The quartet of partially overlapping dichotomies that follow are offered only as analytical tools and are merely intended to provide a context for the fleeting details of our classical (and especially post-classical) literary record. Again, save the self-evidently non- conforming first item, they are all predicated upon the same dietary base briefly sketched above.

Wild versus products of agriculture. Through gathering, hunting, or fishing, ruralites presumably will have had access to native vegetation, wild game, and fish. If urban dwellers were to consume such food, its presum- able source in many cases would have been the central market. The latter part of this proposition might be tested against the literary references for particular commodities for sale in the Agora collected in *Agora* III, pp. 193–206, but they present a mixed picture. Fish (nos. 640–647, pp. 195–196) and birds (nos. 653–654, pp. 197–198) are represented, while "meat etc." (nos. 648–[658], pp. 196–197) does not include game. Note, however, with regard to the last item, the goods brought to the Agora by the The- ban in Aristophanes' *Archarnians,* lines 860–958.

Constraint versus choice. "It was the rustic poor who approached closest to omnivorousness, but under constraint rather than through de- liberate choice."[12] Country people consumed whatever was at hand—and when and where it was at hand. By contrast, the urban markets of Peiraieus and the Agora will have attracted foodstuffs from so wide a range of topo- graphical and climatic environments as to nullify the effects of local varia- tion, including seasonal ones, which normally governed the diets of self-sufficient rural communities. Hesiod in the *Works and Days,* I have ar- gued, sets great store by the admonition to do things "in season," and this

precept will have had obvious predictable consequences for the availability
of foodstuffs. Contemporary American *nouvelle cuisine* makes a virtue of
the use of seasonal produce, but for the isolated rural district of ancient
Greece it was a harsh and probably unwelcome necessity of life.

Farm-produced versus procured in city. Farmers are sometimes depicted in literary sources procuring foodstuffs in town: Trygaios will buy
some salt fish "for the farm" (*eis agron*) before heading home to his plots
(Aristophanes, *Peace*, 562–563, with Olson's note on 563); and Theophrastos's farmer, after first inquiring about the price of the same product (as
well as that of hides), does the same (4.15; and cf. 6.9 on *ta tarichopolia*).
Aristophanes' *Archarnians* depicts a Megarian coming to the Agora in
Athens and exchanging what he represents as piglets (actually they are his
two female children) for garlic and salt (729–835) and a Theban peddling
herbs, wild birds, small game, household items, and Copaic eels (for which
Dikaiopolis offers sprats from Phaleron and a quintessentially urban commodity, an informer packaged in ceramic, the latter to be put to various
uses at home) (860–958). But the fact that these special cases involve foreigners should not be allowed to obscure the fundamental distinction between the raw produce of the wild *chora* and the commodities for sale in
the Agora: that the latter were in large part *processed*: flour, preserved fish
(again), cheese, wine, and the like. Wheat could be milled, olives pressed,
grapes fermented on the farm, but it remains probable that urbanites had
easier and more varied access to foods in processed forms compared to
country folk, especially those out of easy reach of the Agora.

Farm-produced versus imported from abroad. "On account of the
greatness of our city all things from every land come to us, and it falls to
us that the goods produced right here are harvested with no greater homegrown enjoyment than the goods of other peoples" (Thucydides, 2.38.2).
However hyperbolic, these words ascribed to Pericles' *Funeral Oration* do
add a dimension of variation transcending any obtaining between more
typical town-and-country regimes. Grain ships certainly (and presumably
others carrying imports of all kinds) made port at the harbors immediately
below the town, and it was there—and there alone within Athenian territory—that cargoes were off-loaded. No organized attempt was made to
convey the grain or other commodity to other destinations in Attica,
whether by sea or any other means of conveyance. Elsewhere I have suggested that the great bulk of at least the grain never went beyond these urban districts, while extramural communities normally relied upon local
production.[13] Accordingly, variations of quality, freshness, price, ease of

availability, etc., must be added to those more straightforward ones having to do with the specific identity of the goods in question.

The extent to which these factors actually resulted in significant variations between rural and urban diets will come down in significant part to the particular evidence of the literary sources, especially comedy and satire, which of course cannot be examined in detail here. At a higher level of generalization, John Wilkins, writing under the rubric "comedy on the countryside and agriculture," attempts to close, or at least to minimize, the division between urban and rural with a view to understanding the seemingly "hybrid" nature of comedy.[14] But whatever might have been the truth about the Attic comedic stage, the reality of food—the "discourse" of which is Wilkins's subject—might I suspect turn out to be one of difference, not of hybridity. With due allowance for a common dietary and culinary menu of grains, meats, oil, and wine, and with admission that the eating habits of some urbanites and some ruralites will have resembled those of their opposite numbers on significantly numerous occasions, differences between town and country of some consequence *did* almost certainly exist—once, that is, we realize, as the foregoing discussion has proposed, that it is not only a matter of particular foodstuffs (or dishes) but also of additional, quite different modes of variation.

Clothing

Where dress is concerned, as with foodstuffs, one would expect an agrarian population to make use of local products and thereby possibly set itself apart from the practices of urban dwellers. The clothing to be worn by the dirt farmer had been prescribed by Hesiod in the *Works* (536–546); and two preclassical poetic sources from outside Attica set the stage for what is to come in the age of the city-state:

Theognis (Megara, ca. 640–600), lines 53–56:

Kyrnos, this *polis* is still a *polis*, but the people are different—people who previously knew neither acts of justice nor laws, but who wore out skins of goats (*doras aigōn*) on their sides and who dwelt outside this *polis* like deer. And now they are *agathoi* . . .

Sappho (Mytilene on Lesbos, ca. 650–600), fr. 57:

And what country girl (*agroïōtis*) casts a spell on your mind . . . dressed in a country jerkin (*agroïtin . . . spolan*) . . . and not knowing how to pull her rags above her ankles?

Returning to Athens, it is possible to recognize at least five, possibly six, different articles of clothing which may securely be associated with Attica outside the walls, while being found in the town only rarely or under special circumstances.

Pilos. One, the *pilos*, has recently been studied by Maria Pipili under the title "Wearing an Other Hat: Workmen in Town and Country."[15] To be distinguished from the skullcap, "the countryman's pilos" is defined as "a rustic hat probably made of wool, fur or animal skin (sheepskin or goatskin) which was obviously necessary to protect people working in the open air from harsh weather conditions; . . ." Pipili underscores the hat's rudeness; collects examples from vase painting showing it being worn by hunters, farmers, a woodcutter, herdsmen, and fishermen and boatmen; and identifies its function as a marker of inferior social status in contrast with more "respectable" individuals. Some of the depictions are mythological but all have relevance to practice in contemporary living Greek society. Pipili contrasts her *pilos*-wearers with "respectable" *citizens*,[16] but in fact none of her evidence precludes the possibility that some of her subjects are themselves citizens, however rude, inferior, or marginalized. Thus Aristophanes' Strepsiades, a farmer from the country deme Kikynna, is represented as having forgotten his dogskin cap (*kyneē*) when he left home (*Clouds*, line 268).[17]

Katōnakē. As we saw in the Introduction, Theopompos, *FGrH* 115 F 311, and lexicographers preserve a tradition that at Athens (and Sikyon) the tyrants forced people to wear a lowly garment called the *katōnakē* in order that the wearers be too embarrassed "to come into the *asty*" (Hesychios, s.v. *katōnakē* [Athens]; Pollux, 7.68 [Sikyon and Athens]; Souda, s.v. *katōnakē* [Athens]). Etymologically, the word seems to be derived from *katō* "below" and *nakos* "fleece," suggesting with the lexicographers an *himation* (?) with a fringe of sheepskin (Hesychios, Moreis) or a thick woolen garment with fleece stitched to the bottom edge (Pollux) or simply a skin (*diphthera*) bordered with fleece (Souda, s.v.; Schol. Aristophanes, *Ekklesiazousai* 724).[18] But it is not so much the garment itself as the status of those who wore it that is at issue. Aristophanes[19] makes the citizen woman Lysistrata typify the Athenians under the tyrants as wearing *katōnakai*, whereas later the Spartans, after liberating the city, dressed the

Demos in a *chlaina* again (1149–1156). The Athenian Praxagora, wife of a citizen, associates the *katōnakē* with slaves in the urban setting of the *Ekklesiazousai* (lines 721–724). At Sikyon, the 33rd book of Theopompos's *Historiai, FGrH* 115 F 176 (and likewise, Menaichmos, *Sikyonika* fr. 2 M), recorded that certain [slaves] were called "*katōnakē*-wearers;" and the lexical sources reaffirm its servile associations (Schol. Aristophanes, *Ekklesiazousai* 724). Finally, on what authority we do not know, the wearers of the garments at Athens thereby prevented or discouraged from entering the *asty* under the tyrants are expressly identified as *politai* by Souda—a linkage which, if true, would help immensely my case for a rural Athenian "other." However this may be, the *katōnakē* remains identifiably extramural.

Spolas. At Aristophanes, *Birds* 933–935, Peisetairos asks a slave (?) to remove his *spolas* and *chiton*. He then hands the *spolas* to the (Pindaric) poet, who proceeds to soliloquize that, wandering apart from his people among Scythian nomads, he now possesses no "weaver-agitated" garment but "goes inglorious on his way—a jerkin (*spolas*) without a *chiton*" (941–945).[20] A fragment of Sophocles, *Aias the Lokrian*, "of a spotted dog, . . . Libyan *spolas*, leopard-bearing skin" (fr. 11), reaffirms the foreign association and (non-woven) animal-skin material. Scholiasts and lexicographers identify the *spolas* as an outer corselet of leather, sometimes worn in warfare (Pollux 7.70, et al.), the military use being illustrated by Xenophon, *Anabasis* 3.3.20 and 4.1.18. A specfically Attic rural association, however, admittedly seems to be lacking.

Sisyra. Still another kind of animal-skin coat, sometimes doubling as a blanket, the *sisyra* is found across a wide spectrum of Athenian classical writers including Aeschylus (Tetralogy 20, play A, fr. 158a), an unknown Attic comic poet (*FCG* adespota, fr. 206, line 1), and Aristophanes (nine occurrences in the intact plays[21]). Among the last-mentioned, at *Wasps* 1138, Philokleon, evidently punning but with unclear meaning, declares that a garment being handed to him by Bdelykleon is "a Thymaitid *sisyra*"—i.e. from the Attic deme Thymaitadai, situated on the coast north of Peiraieus and west of the *asty*. Whitehead asks "Is this a colorful way of saying 'rustic'?"[22]

Diphthera. ". . . a jerkin made from unprepared animal skin and worn chiefly by rustic males such as farmers and herdsmen,"[23] *diphthera* has an occurrence of particular relevance to our concerns at Aristophanes, *Clouds*, lines 71–72. Strepsiades, recalling conversations with his haughty aristocratic town wife concerning the rearing of their son, declares that he had said to him that (after he had grown up) "whenever you are driving goats from The Rocks, like your father, wearing a *diphthera*, . . ." Later in the play, Strepsiades identifies his deme as Kikynna (134, cf. 138), tentatively placed by Traill east of Hymettos at a site north of Sphettos.[24] Strepsiades, furthermore, is not only a citizen, but a citizen of means at that.[25]

Trochades. Finally, and sixthly, the Edict of Diocletian of A.D. 301, *IG* II[2] 1120, line 12, lists "rustic male *trochades*" (partially restored), *trochades* being glossed by Hesychios s.v. as "sandals (made) from goat skin." Though late, the evidence may bear on the classical age, given the resistance to change of rural cultures.

Why garments of animal skins? On-site availability of skins produced by stock may be a large part of the answer. The cost of a mantle of goat skin was estimated by Losfeld at one-eighth to one-fourth that of an *himation* of wool, and with Pierre Waltz may be added the factor of reduced hand labor required for preparation.[26] But it was an economy purchased at significant social cost. Allusions by Athenian writers to the wearing of animal-hide clothing by uncivilized non-Greek peoples could only have served to create, or to reinforce, the impression of savagery. With the visible (or perceived) crudeness, furthermore, was linked what was, for the free Greek, an even more objectionable association: with slaves and servility. Savagery and servility are hardly qualities that modern scholars have taught us to associate with the Athenian citizen class, urban or rural. But even the prosperous citizen farmer Strepsiades may fondly contemplate the day when his free-born legitimate son will literally follow in the footsteps of his goat-herding, skin-wearing father. Not surprisingly, the records of sale of the property of the Hermokopidai (i.e. of a prosperous urban set) contain amidst several entries for clothing no item such as those just reviewed.[27]

To combine these implications, it would seem that, even for an Athenian citizen under the classical democracy, to be rural was to be uncivilized, to be rural was to be as good as a slave—at least in the estimation of urban writers and their urban readerships. The urban, the civilized, the truly free wore garments woven from wool on a loom, by contrast. And there can be no doubt that, to a very real and appreciable degree, the clothes made the Athenian. In a "shame" culture ruled not by inner realities but by externals and their appearances, the differences will have been instantly perceived— and have set the tone for any interaction with the town-dwelling population. Any country person—and, again, I include here the free and citizen along with the slave—clad in an animal-skin jerkin venturing through the gates will have been instantly recognized and marked as an inferior "other." When the Old Oligarch comments that in Athens "the Demos is no better clothed than the slaves and the metics" (*AthPol* 10), he may have been referring at least in part to a just such a situation. That is, when a citizen farmer from Kikynna (and a citizen of means at that) came to town dressed in a goatskin, he could not be distinguished from the lower-class persons who routinely wore such garments in town as well as in the country.

Music

All aspects of "culture" in the narrower, particular sense of that term might be suspected to have a distinctively "country" expression, but in order for a specific cultural artifact found in or associated with rural Attica to be distinguished from a contrasting urban expression we usually need explicit literary testimony to that effect. So much is forthcoming in the case of "music," viz. song with or without instrumental accompaniment. The chorus of *Archarnians* invokes the Muse to "come to me, your fellow demesman, bringing a rousing, tuneful, more rustic (*agroikoteron*) song" (664–675). Praxagora in *Ekklesiazousai* calls upon her female confederates, soon to be dressed in their husbands' clothing and wearing false beards, to set off, leaning on their canes and singing an old man's tune, mimicking the manner of the rustics (*tōn agroikōn*)" (266–279). Various types of "country" song, not necessarily Attic, figure in the roster compiled by Athenaios at *Deipnosophistai* 15.618c–620a.

Speech, Orality, and Literacy

As with their dress and general deportment, the countryman or woman venturing into town brought along their distinctive speech, but whereas one's rustic clothing might be temporarily exchanged for more urbane garments and a bath might wash away the smells of the animal pen or freshly manured field, that same person's speech—syntax, diction, inflection, and so on—was unlikely to undergo any convincing transformation. As a consequence, those urban-based writers whose works have come down to us presumably had ample opportunity to observe, characterize, and (it seems) denigrate their rustic counterparts' use of the Greek language. Plato, as we shall see in chapter 7, is particularly harsh in his assessments of the behavior, deportment, and particularly speech of the *agroikoi*. And, consistently with this bias, in his account of antediluvian Athens in the *Kritias*, the population remaining after each prehistoric destruction is said to have comprised "unlettered mountain people" (109d; cf. *Timaios* 22e and 23b). But, biases apart, what, if anything, do we know of the actual character of rural Attic speech? While renderings of dialect in the comic poets, especially Aristophanes, of persons from other city-states (and often humble and even identifiably rural persons at that) reveal a sensitivity to variations in the use of Greek by sometimes ordinary people,[28] it is unexpectedly difficult to identify specifically rural (as opposed to merely non-Athenian) speech.

Nonetheless, a scattering of comment (as opposed to actual examples) leaves no doubt about the distinctive quality of rural Attic. While town language became more refined and affected under the influence of the sophists (Aristophanes, fr. 205), rustics were expected to speak like rustics (*PCG* VIII Adespota, *947; 694Kock; cf. Aristophanes, *Ekklesiazousai* 241–244). Accordingly (and to adduce a specific example), the proverbial "ox standing on one's tongue" as an explanation for halting speech may with Ehrenberg allude to "a countryman's inhibitions" in the face of such formidable urbanity.[29] But the really telling testimony comes from Sextus Empiricus, *Against the Grammarians* 1.10.264: "For many, they [the grammarians] say, are fashions [of speech], one of the Athenians, another of Lacedaemonians; and, again, among Athenians the old fashion is different, the present fashion altered. Nor is the fashion the same of those in the country (*kata ten agroikian*) and of those residing in the town (*en astei*). To which point the comic poet Aristophanes [fr. 685] says:

> διάλεκτον ἔχοντα μέσην πόλεως
> οὔτ᾽ ἀστείαν ὑποθηλύτεραν ‹τ›
> οὔτ᾽ ἀνελεύθερον ὑπαγροικοτέραν ‹τ›

> (him) having the middle dialect of the *polis*,
> neither the rather feminine and urbane (dialect)
> nor the unfree and rather rustic (dialect) . . .

To the femininity of the town is opposed not the masculinity of the countryside but rather its absence of freedom. To be *agroikos* is to be servile. When we turn to the utopian prescriptions of the philosophers in chapter 7, we shall see that agrarian labor was routinely assigned to slaves. Where variation in *dialektos* is concerned, the implication is that rural Attic speech was utterly lacking in any trace of cultivation, refinement, or taste. This testimony is isolated yet, contrary to the favorable or at least neutral impression left by speakers of identifiably rural Attic origin on the comic stage, it is unambiguous on the point of a distinctive rural "reality."

Beyond this broad and characteristically pejorative urbane characterization, it is not possible to describe Attic rural speech in any detail. But more progress might be made if we were to consider the matter of the writing and reading of the written word—that is, literacy.

Any attempt to pose and answer the question concerning the level and extent of literacy of rural Attica during the classical (or any other ancient) period must now, in view of the high degree of sophistication to which the subject has been brought by among others W. V. Harris (1989) and Rosalind Thomas (1989 and 1992), begin by defining one's terms. How is literacy to be defined? What types and degrees of literacy can be recognized, and how are they detected and measured? How did the use of writing come about? What are its uses and purposes? Exactly what, particularly concerning the levels of literacy, is implied by the existence and promulgation of various modes of writing, inscriptions, accounts, honorary decrees, laws, announcements, ostraka, and all the rest? Were these texts actually meant to be read, or did they have some other purpose and function? And similarly concerning literacy's companion term, orality, comparable questions may be raised, and to them may be added the complicating matter (one as it turns out very germane to the present case) of how in the more complex circumstances such as we encounter in classical Athens literacy and orality interacted synergistically with each other. Sophisticated though the new approach(es) may be, however, the recent literature reveals little interest in literacy as it pertains to the countryside per se.[30]

Building on Harris's work in particular, my approach will depart from a methodological observation regarding the *onus probandi* differentiating the opposing camps championing relatively high or low literacy rates for the classical *polis*: that that burden rests squarely on the shoulders of the proponent of any appreciable degree of competence in reading and writing beyond the unquestioned attainments of an elite urban intellegentsia. Too often, undoubtedly under the influence of an almost oppressively visible written record of Attic governmental, judicial, historiographical, and literary pursuits, it is the other way around, and the proponent of illiteracy or (better, because positively put) orality is thrown on the defensive and expected to produce proof of literacy's absence. But in fact, as Harris convincingly argues, none of the preconditions necessary for the emergence of a genuine widespread literacy are to be found, even when one confines one's attention to the better documented urban scene—not to mention the *a fortiori* case of the countryside.[31] To wit: the nonexistence of any formal, institutionalized educational system; the absence (and therefore, given the copious quantity of surviving relevant sources, nonexistence) of any societal ideal favoring the acquisition or practice of literacy; and, concurrently with the latter, the highly probable survival into at least the fourth century and possibly to the end of antiquity and beyond of orality in all its complex manifestations. Rural Attica under the democracy produces no village school, no itinerant teacher from the town or elsewhere, no discernible tradition of at-home schooling. Thus, as I shall argue, the palpable reports or physical traces of writing (and hence of reading) from the Attic countryside must be seen in a context other than one of a generally prevailing ability to read and write.

By its very nature, the operation of orality will normally leave no direct traces and at best will be discernible only indirectly in the surviving written record. Homer's poems themselves were to enjoy a continuing vogue among Athenians—presumably rural as well as urban—but a work sharing the "oral" qualities of the *Iliad* and the *Odyssey* yet of a more specifically rural content and orientation might allow a more promising approach. Such a work is Hesiod's *Works and Days*, exploited in chapter 2 in our reconstruction of rural Attic society (and just considered in the present chapter in connection with seasonality). To see the poem's relevance here, it is appropriate to observe that the opening third of the text, ostensibly addressed to the poet's wayward brother, Perses, and the kings, is rich in a variety of traditional forms, viz. myth, parable, allegory, and proverbial maxims; and that the poem as a whole, but particularly these traditional elements, may with Martin West be placed in a wider context of wisdom literature extending all the way back to Sumer.[32] Presumably, barring some totally undocumented role played by the Mycenaean Greek Linear B script or other (to us) unknown writing system, transmission to Hesiod's time was effected by exclusively oral means. Study of the text by G. P. Edwards and by West himself has, in any case, revealed (in West's words) "the habits of the oral poet."[33] To be sure, the *Works* is not orally composed and transmitted verses in their raw form, a mere transcription of a nonliterate oral performance, but rather the hybrid product of a lettered reworking and amplification of a received tradition. Nonetheless, an essentially oral poem preserving the traits that facilitated (and once written down, still reflect) its creation and survival in the absence of a writing system could enjoy a continuing currency among the *agrammatoi* under an otherwise literate regime—and particularly so an oral poem primarily concerned with agriculture when the setting in question, as here, is a rural one.

From the vast testimonia assembled by Rzach and later corrected and amplified by West,[34] it is clear that Hesiod's poem continued to be cited, and cited frequently, in later Greek antiquity. Several of the writers in question are Athenians or non-Athenians residing in Athens of the classical era: Aeschines,[35] Aristotle,[36] Plato,[37] and Xenophon.[38] Several of their citations of the *Works* represent, as would be expected in the case of an urban writer dealing with generally nonagricultural topics, the poem's gnomic or otherwise traditional content; and it is precisely that gnomic content in combination with the extreme brevity of most of the texts that strongly suggests recollection from memory, that is from the oral tradition. Aeschines, by way of prefacing his "recitation" of lines 240–247, observes: "for he [Hesiod] says somewhere [Greek *pou*—evidence that no written text is being used?, cf. Xenophon, *Memorabilia* 2.1.20], teaching the masses and advising the cities not to accept the evil ones among the demagogues, . . . but I will recite the verses myself—for it is for this purpose that we as children learn the sentiments (*gnomai*) of the poets, in order that when we are men we may make use of them" (3.134–135). Elsewhere, the *Erga* are explicitly cited from memory (*anamimnēskomai*) by the speaker of Plato, *Lysis* 215c; and adduced with apology for the inexact quotation by the speaker of his *Protagoras* at 340d. That no large claims may be made for rural Attica on so slender a basis will be granted, but this small dossier of classical Athenian examples might just reflect an otherwise undocumented oral tradition of Hesiod's poem.

As to any contemporary explicit claims to rural literacy, our earliest testimony is preserved at 228d-229b in the Socratic dialogue entitled "Hipparchos or Lover of Gain," anciently but probably erroneously ascribed to Plato. Peisistratos's son Hipparchos (died 514) is credited with being the first to introduce the works of Homer into the land and with the recruitment of Anakreon of Teos and Simonides of Keos, all with a view to educating the citizens. Then, having dealt with the people of the town, he turned to the education of "those in the country" (*en tois agrois*), erecting statues of Hermes "alongside the roads in the middle of the *asty* and of each of the demes" (228d). The pillars were inscribed with bits of wisdom (both traditional and of his own invention) turned into elegiac verses, in order that (as the author speaking through Socrates interprets) the people might admire his own wisdom rather than the Delphic *grammata* and "that in the second place, passing to and fro and reading and getting a taste of his wisdom, they might travel from the country (*ek tōn agrōn*) and be educated in the remaining subjects." Each Hermes bore two inscriptions, one on the left in which Hermes says that he has taken his stand "in the midst of the *asty* and the deme;" while on the right side he says "This is Hipparchos's memorial. Think just thoughts as you walk." Socrates alludes to other inscriptions, citing one on the road to Steiria reading "This is Hipparchos's memorial: Don't deceive a friend."[39] Now, what are the implications here, one way or the other, for rural literacy? That the purpose of the scheme was to "educate" (*paideuein*, 228c) countryfolk will depend in part upon the identity of the author; if he was in fact Plato, then at least we could say that the assumption of a generally low educational level among country-dwellers is consistent with the views expressed in dialogues of uncontested Platonic authorship. And what of the implication that the inscribed surfaces were actually to be read by those "passing to and fro" before them? Surely, the ability to read so brief a text—and a gnomic, perhaps already generally understood text at that—would demonstrate literacy of only a very minimal level. Besides, Socrates' statement that Hipparchos's aim was to inspire countryfolk to repair "from the fields," i.e. to the town, for the remainder (*epi ta loipa*) of their instruction presumes a continuing low level of learning. Nor is it entirely clear just who the prospective readers were to be. Given the stated location of the herms, any readers, whether intended or not, could have been urban as well as rural, since movement only between town and village is strictly implied, the point that they were meant for the countryfolk (*autois*, 228d) going beyond the immanent import of the texts themselves. Rather than imply significant rural literacy, the trend of the account is actually in quite the opposite direction.[40]

To a somewhat later time belongs the famous anecdote about the Athenian politician-general Aristeides (died ca. 467) on the occasion of an ostracism under the early democracy. According to the account twice given by Plutarch (*Aristeides*, 7.5–6; *Moralia*, 186a; cf. Nepos, *Aristides*, 1), Aristeides was approached by a countryman—"one of the *agrammatoi* and utterly *agroikoi*" (Plutarch, *Aristeides*) or "an *anthropos agrammatos* and *agroikos*" (Plutarch, *Moralia*)—who, failing to recognize the man, requested him to inscribe upon his *ostrakon* the name of Aristeides. When asked by the popular general why he wanted to ostracize Aristeides, the man answered that he was tired of hearing him called "the Just;" and so, at that, Aristeides took the shard and inscribed it as requested. While the words are seemingly straightforward in meaning, the pairing of *agram-matos* and *agroikos* has not, I think, been fully appreciated. For one thing, it is unnecessary—in fact, mistaken—to water down the literal sense of *agroikos*, "dwelling in the fields" (*agros, oikein*) in favor of the usually pejorative, and characterizing, rendering "boorish." Ostracisms were conducted only in the Agora, and if a rural dweller was to participate he had no choice but to come into town, so literal *agroikoi* will have been on hand. Plutarch's language, furthermore, recalls Plato's practice of conjoining *agroikos* with a companion negative term, as though the neutral locational reference of "dwelling in the fields" needed some sort of additional specificity—and, in Plato's case, demeaning specificity at that. Finally, the use of the plural number in the genitive case in the passage from the *Life* suggests that the writer observes a class of persons in whom agrarian residence and lack of "letters" are naturally and universally combined. Thus the anecdote may have implications far beyond those otherwise suggested by a seemingly isolated case of a single farmer casting a ballot against a single politician on a single occasion.

If we proceed from historical narrative to the Attic countryside itself, we at once run up against the previously oft-mentioned epigraphic records of the demes. Major "national" cult installations, military encampments, or sites closely linked with the town through nonagricultural activity (e.g. mining or a port) are of course not at issue here. But something must be said by way of explanation for the prima facie evidence of literacy in full public view on the ground, and frequently in the name, of many a typical extramural agrarian village. Distinctions as to type of document are, first, of vital importance. Decrees of the deme assemblies constitute a large plurality and, where the matter of literacy is concerned, in terms of length and complexity of thought and language surpass the remaining record in significance. Despite their ostentatious visibility, however, the decrees do *not* point to an appreciable measure of rural writing and reading competence among the local village populations. Execution of the texts, for one thing, required the participation of only a few persons—mover, secretary, and mason—in order to compose, record, and inscribe texts of often very formulaic official prose; and of these three, the literate abilities of one, the mason, are far from guaranteed. And what of readers? The answer must, with the aforementioned work of Rosalind Thomas and others, take into account the nonverbal dimensions of these monuments (a term used advisedly in preference to the question-begging "text")—aesthetic, honorary, archival, and so on—no one of which need imply a wide readership, not even one coinciding in extent with the corps of demesmen participating in the decree's passage. Besides, even if we are driven to concede that *some* readers must be assumed in order for a decree to fulfill its intended purpose, it does not follow that we must assume a *general* literacy. A single competent individual may communicate what he (or, conceivably, she) has read to large numbers of nonreading others. Furthermore, and to instance the evidence of the inscriptions themselves, an honorary decree often contained a clause calling for it to be read aloud to an audience assembled in the theater in the deme for a religious festival. Elsewhere I have suggested that the purpose of this rehearsal of the honors was to promulgate them to the membership of the "natural" local but non-citizen members of the community not present at the official *agora* of the *demotai* at which the decree was passed.[41] Let me now add that the announcement might have served yet another purpose, to communicate the written text to large numbers of nonliterates unable to read it in its inscribed form.

Some confirmation of this approach is afforded by two recurrent strongly formulaic elements which occur with relevant frequency at the close of the honorary decrees (by far the most common type): first, the clause requiring that the inscribed stone be placed in a location (where named, agora, shrine, or theater) which in various turns of phrase is deemed to be "best";[42] and, two, the so-called "manifesto" clause declaring that the preceding honors have been so decreed in order that others be moved to devote similar energies or resources in the interests of the deme-association.[43] Both elements, the first illusively, the second less so, seem to be motivated by a like purpose: to capture the attention, then to enlist the support, of potential benefactors—and that meant men of substance, civic pride, ambition, and (I would now suggest) literacy. Nor are arguments of this kind confined to the decrees. Leases, strictly speaking, concerned only a relatively prosperous lessee and the leasing party, the latter perhaps comprising only a village- or cult-association's magisterial or financial personnel. Security *horoi* were intended to be read by prospective lenders against the security of the property so marked—again, a prosperous elite and one by no means necessarily residing in the local rural community. *Leges sacrae* dealt largely with finances and were the primary concern of a few priests and priestesses, and in any case were not, as the misnomer "cult calendar" might suggest, necessarily intended to be read by every person who might participate in the rite(s) in question. Dedications, finally, were often recognizably the doings of a prosperous set, and although the dedicator might hope that the monument would attract the attention of a large number, there is no reason to assume that it did or that such appreciation necessarily went beyond admiration of the monument's physical beauty and perhaps decipherment of a key name or two.

Nor can we overlook the fact that, where the official acts of the village-association are concerned, the villagers, as a consequence of the presence and interventions of the demarch, were subject to the influence, or even direction, of the People in Athens town. The written records of the demes—both those executed in their names and those merely associated with them—bear an unmistakably striking similarity to their urban central government counterparts, and the relative chronologies of the two sets of documents leave no doubt as to the direction of the influence—not that there could be such doubt since the practices of the extramural demes agree strongly with each other, making it certain that in each case it was the People which had provided the paradigm. Thus not even the small circumscribed degree of literacy that I have allowed the extramural village may be authentically rural, if in fact it was, as I strongly suspect, the direct result of urban governmental intervention.

Religion: Myth, Cult, and the Town

Students of Greek mythology will recall that many a story unfolds in some wild natural setting—on a mountain side, by a stream, in a cave, amidst a grove, along a road between Bronze Age settlements, and so on. Many a deity, too, as its origins, name, or a narrative indicate, presided over various departments of the rural world such as atmospheric phenomena; plant, animal, and human fertility; social institutions pertaining thereto; and sometimes the doings of peoples bound to the land, water, or sky themselves—farmers, herders, hunters, fishers, birders, and the like. And it would be difficult to identify a god or goddess, hero or heroine, the time of whose origins or entry into Greece could with assurance be shown to postdate the rise of the classical city-state.[44] All of which is to say that, with the growth of Athens, some of these pre-urban divinities should have remained in place, retaining their primordial identities, attributes, cult titles, and functions, by which we could recognize them as "rural" in contrast with their newly created (or transformed) opposite numbers in the town. Is this expectation borne out by our evidentiary record? Consider, as a point of departure, the following selection from the imperial writer Alkiphron's atticizing *Letters of Farmers*:

Dryantidas to (his female consort) *Chronion.* You no longer care for our bed or for our children in common or indeed for life in the country (*kat' agron*), but you are "all town" (*olē . . . tou asteos*), despising Pan and the Nymphs (which you used to call Epimelidai and Dryadai and Naidai). And you are introducing to us new gods in addition to the many that are already here. Where on the farm (*kat' agron*) will I set up [shrines to] Koliadai and Genetyllidai? . . . (II.8)

As commentators note, the otherwise obscure allusion to the Koliadai and Genetyllidai is probably ultimately derived from Strepsiades' speech at Aristophanes' *Clouds,* lines 39–55 (cf. [Lucian], *Amores* 42) concerning the clash of cultures between town wife and her country husband. But the countryman Strepsiades' point must be that these are a *woman's* divinities, and not that they are urban since the seat of the cults in question (of Aphrodite and the "birthday goddesses") was Cape Kolias in the remote coastal deme of Anaphlystos. Nonetheless, for Alkiphron's agrarian letter-writer "Oakley," Pan and the Nymphs represent distinctively rural (i.e. as opposed to the *asty*) divinities. Since here, as elsewhere in the collection, the imagined setting is identifiably Attica, may I suggest that this lead may be worth pursuing, if only in the brief compass dictated by the spatial limitations of this book.

The religion of rural Attica, and of the demes in particular, is a relatively well documented and much studied subject. The documentation comprises the usual scattering of literary, lexicographical, and epigraphic sources, the last mentioned including the *leges sacrae* of about a half dozen of the village associations: Aixone, Eleusis, Erchia, Marathon, Teithras, and Thorikos. Together, the sources permit a detailed, if spotty, look into the cultic arrangements of the deme-association and, beyond that, sustain significant inferences regarding the interrelations of those arrangements with those of the urban center. The pattern, however, is not a uniform one, depending as it does upon the specific type of festival in question.

Festivals primarily concerned with females and families were duplicated in *asty* and deme,[45] the purpose presumably being to permit wives and children to remain within the home community rather than hazard a journey (perhaps unattended by adult males) into town, but whatever the motive or motives the result was clearly, in conformity with the thesis of this book, still another institutional and probable cultural sundering of the village from the town. The other major state festivals, however, were not so duplicated (although of course the divinity in question might well be the object of a lesser festival in a deme), so that if the resident of a rural deme wished to participate he or she had no choice but to make a trip to the Big

City.[46] But where the major divinities are concerned, there is in the case of one divinity a strong circumstantial case for an accommodation between town and country. The local deme festivals of Dionysos, as noted by previous scholars and discussed in chapter 4, were scheduled to take place either just prior to or just following the several urban festivals of the god. Why this apparent accommodation? Given the prevailing urbanocentric assumptions of the town's superiority, it might be assumed that no one naturally would want to pass up the "City" Dionysia, Lenaia, or Anthesteria, so the object will have been to prevent the urban celebrations from drawing off participants from their own home-demes' rural festivities. But what of apprehension that ruralites might prefer their own Dionysia and not attend the *town's* festivals should they be held at the same times? Or, since we know people from town made the rounds of the *Dionysia kat'agrous*, to ensure that such trips to the country not compete with Athens' major celebrations of the same god?

Can anything of a more comprehensive nature can be said about the cults of the demes per se? Henrichs observed that whereas (again, with Mikalson) festivals such as the Theogamia primarily concerned with the family were held independently in the demes as well as in town, the cult of local heroes and agrarian deities was a distinctive feature of deme-religion and deme-religion alone.[47] This characterization is amply supported by the calendars wherein are found, alongside the major divinities of the common Greek pantheon, a multitude of minor figures unexampled not only in the *asty* but in other rural, even neighboring, demes as well. Among major deities, Dionysos's cult may illustrate the trend in some detail, for Henrichs's analysis of the calendars, the Dionysos ode in Sophocles' *Antigone*, and the celebration of the Dionysia by Dikaiopolis in Aristophanes' *Archarnians* sets out to show "different Dionysiac articulations of the country/city contrast . . ."[48] My own reconstruction of the program of the Dionysia "in the fields" in chapter 4, which (if I am right) included two events, the wineskin-game and cock-fight, not found in the well-documented urban festivals of the god, would seem to point in the same direction.

What, then, of the deities mentioned in Alkiphron's letter, Pan and the Nymphai (the latter going by several bynames)? Taking them as specimen cases, we may ask whether, above and beyond the isolated cult figures of particular demes or other extra-mural locales, it is possible to recognize in them pan-rural divinities which were not generally found in urbanized areas.[49] Such "country" gods might be expected to have existed, given the general trend of my study to this point.

Thanks to Robert Parker's recent (1996) detailed and densely documented *Athenian Religion: A History*, it will not be necessary to rehearse
the full record of archaeological, topographic, and epigraphic evidence for
the presence of these pastoral divinities—almost invariably in conjunction
with one another—throughout Attica. But it will be well to call into question the conclusion produced by, or rather methodological assumptions
underlying, that discussion, since Parker's Pan and Nymphs reach the Attic countryside by a route not easily reconcilable with some of the findings
of the present work. Reduced to its essentials, Parker's position is that Pan
came to Attica by an official act of the Athenian state and thereafter the
cult's specific expression—in cave sanctuaries, votives, dedications, and so
on—represented not what would be in the context of the present chapter
a rural Attic "reality" but rather a "part of the pastoral dream."[50] The circumstances of the god's entry into Attica are deduced from Herodotos's
account of the battle of Marathon in 490, wherein Philippides, a runner
dispatched by the Athenians to seek help from the Spartans, was met by
Pan near the Maiden Mountain above Tegea. When, after the battle, he
told his story to the Athenians and they accepted it as true, "they [i.e., the
Athenian assembly, so Parker] established a shrine of Pan below the Acropolis and, because of this report, propitiate him with annual sacrifices and a
torch-race" (6.105). From this text, in combination with the absence of textual or physical evidence for the god in Attica prior to this date, Parker in-
fers that "the *cult* [italics mine] was introduced to *Athens* [italics mine]
shortly after Marathon," its acceptance assisted by its annexation to the cult
of the Nymphs already present in Attica and worshipped in caves (as Pan
himself was soon to be). Furthermore, ". . . the familiar notion that certain
'country' gods such as Pan were honoured only by countrymen, and countrymen honoured none but them, appears to be part of the pastoral
dream"—that "dream" represented by a long tradition about "the life of
wild nature not as it is experienced, day by day, by those who live close to
it, but as it is imagined from afar." And finally, "His caves were symbolically set away from human habitation (and sometimes in genuinely remote
spots) not because this was where his worshippers typically spent their days,
but because it was not."[51]

Granting that fault might easily be found in the unnamed persons,
writings, and traditions against which Parker directs these remarks, I must
object to the view that the Attic Pan is to be reduced to his officially recognized *cult*; that because that cult was not introduced into *Athens* until
after Marathon by an act of (an urban) legislature the god (or spirit or

power or mood) could not previously have been recognized in rural Attica; and that the fact that his worship-places (typically caves) were remote somehow compromises the cult's authenticity since it indicates the influence not of actual rural people and culture but rather of "the pastoral dream" as "imagined from afar." A divinity, whether going by Pan or some other name, may preexist (or coexist with) its officially legitimated institutionalized form—one thinks at once of Alkiphron's bynames for his Nymphai, viz. Epimelidai, Dryadai, and Naidai, as a particularly appropriate parallel case. True, there is no reported physical trace of cave-worship of Pan before Marathon, but other forms of worship or recognition are clearly possible. Are we to believe that these same caves were not previously put to use by Attic herders? And did such pre-Marathon herders not experience the "fear and danger" of wild nature, "power," and "mood" (all correctly associated by Parker with Pan's divinity) because the cult had not yet been officially introduced by a decree of the Athenian Assembly enabling the establishment of a shrine at the very heart of the urban center? Parker's belief that imitation of "the city's example" (by which I understand the new shrine on the Acropolis) somehow caused the new cult to spread rapidly through the countryside, besides concerning only cult and unjustifiably presuming an extraordinary influence for the town, begs these very questions. And, lastly, the very nature and origins of Pan's divinity, viz. pastoral (cf. Latin *pascere*, "feed," hence "guardian of flocks") and hailing from mountainous and thinly populated Arcadia, necessarily means that his worship places *will* be found in remote situations. Why, then, a "pastoral dream"? Pan's (and the Nymphs') actual worshippers will have included such persons as the dedicators instanced by Parker himself: a goatherd (*IG* I^3 1974), "the shepherds" (*IG* II^2 4833, no provenience, s.IV), a dozen male and female slave (?) "washers" to Nymphai (*IG* II^2 2934, in Panathenaic stadium, med. s. IV), another group of slaves (?) to Nymphai (*IG* II^2 4650, in cave near Vari, s. IV), and the large group which together dedicates a single relief (*IG* II^2 4832, no provenience, s. IV). Such humble folk are unlikely to have been dreamers caught up in the spell of an urban fantasy.

Over against such generalizations and speculative considerations must be set what we actually know about the actual practice of religion, i.e. organized cult, on the Attic countryside. For present purposes, I must confine myself, in addition to the bibliography already cited, to referring the interested reader to the 47 densely documented pages of David Whitehead's chapter on "Religion" in *The Demes of Attica*, published in 1986;[52]

to Emily Kearns's discussion of the heroes of the demes;[53] to Parker's and my own treatment of the local religious associations;[54] and to Parker's chapter on mountain peaks and tombs of heroes.[55] Modifications of White-head's account appear elsewhere in this book concerning the so-called "Rural" Dionysia, but let me also adduce here, as bearing significantly upon relations between rural deme and town, Kevin Clinton's argument that the Thesmophoria honoring Demeter was not (as previously believed) a "national" festival but was administered by individual demes,[56] thereby calling into question once again (as I have just done with Parker's views on Pan) the supposition of a centralized establishment of rural religion from the urban center. Demeter's cereal-oriented cult, and that cult's three-day festival's exclusive invitation to female celebrants, would speak as clearly as any evidence could of the fundamentally agrarian—and specifically repro-ductive—orientation of rural Attica's religious arrangements.

Mentalité

From the foregoing discussions it will be clear that the Attic countryman and countrywoman will have borne little resemblance to their urban counterparts as we have come to know the latter through our urban and urbanizing sources. That we have been able to discern even this much about rural "realities" we owe to the survival of some authentic extramu-ral documentation (such as the security *horoi*), to reinterpretation of sources of rural origin long known but always assimilated to the practices of the town (such as the honorary decrees of the deme associations), and to the operation of our methodology permitting in the case of literary works separation of rural context from urban orientation and message. It is now time to ask what were the core attitudes and values characteristic of the rural populations, especially where such differed, if they differed at all, from those of the town.

Perhaps the fundamental value broadly setting the country apart from the town was a nexus of responses that we may conveniently sum up as "conservatism." Again, we are dealing with small-holder farmers because they numerically constituted a large majority of our extramural populations and because, majority or no, they were the Athenians about whom we think we know something. Given a predominating farming cultural way, it is clear that our Athenians' attitudes will have been rooted in, and largely determined by, the realities governing the practice of agriculture as we now understand it in the light of the ecological studies of Garnsey, Salares, Gallant, and others. Briefly, the rural land regime seems to have been dominated by citizens whose farms had stabilized at the subsistence level due to the workings of inheritance, dowry, gift, or sale. Since production in a typical year would by definition be just sufficient to sustain the owner-operator and his household, then, also on the model, any shortfall could jeopardize the continuing well-being of that household, perhaps even, if worse came to worst, leading to indebtedness and possible loss of land through default and eventually an exit from the practice of independent, self-sufficient agriculture. Appeal for assistance might be made to family members, neighbors, and friends, but on the whole they will have occupied the same socioeconomic niche and so will have been equally subject to the same environmental forces. That left, on the position outlined in chapter 2, the Big Man, the patron, who might possess the means to stave off ruin for the small-holder, but at considerable cost in terms of honor, reciprocal obligation, and loss of independence. By contrast, the livelihoods of the resident citizen population within or near the town walls, which in the vast majority of cases were not directly involved in farming, were secured by multiple publicly funded institutional safety-nets such as paid government service, remunerative labor on public works projects, and subsidized civic religious festivals. No strings were attached here, at least not of an economically or socially oppressive kind, for even if we are to conceptualize a politician sponsoring legislation as a sort of urban patron, any debt incurred could be discharged by a favorable vote in a jury court, or by support in a plebiscite or election, or by displays of social deference. But our rural Athenian small-holder operating at the subsistence level continually faced the twin threats of an opprobrious dependency or life-altering economic ruin.

Against such a background, if the overriding reality of the agrarian's ruralite's existence was the risks posed by a hostile environment, then the predictable response will have been an attitude which is well encapsulated as "conservatism." By this term, which seems to have no close analog in ancient Greek, is meant the tendency to adhere to tried-and-true practices, routines, and methods—those which had worked satisfactorily in the past and, given the continuation of past and present conditions, would go on working satisfactorily into the future. The "given" will have been a reasonable one supported by remembered past experience in a world which had seen very little significant general environmental, climatic, technological, or ideational change. Once things had reached a comfortable stage of homeostasis, to abruptly and without visible provocation alter one's ways would be nothing other than to court disaster, and all in the service of the unlikely-to-be-realized expectation of a minimal competitive advantage over one's social and economic peers. Ancient farming did not resemble a modern stock market, where a shrewd (or lucky) gamble might reap a sudden and stupendous profit. "If it ain't broke, don't fix it," goes the American formulation of the ancient Attic rural attitude. To the contrary, to judge from the indications of actual agricultural practice, farmers preferred to hedge their bets (perhaps an inappropriate image, since not gambling but rather its opposite was the object of such maneuvers). Specific strategies are a prominent topic of the ecological studies. By diversification in choice of crop, stock, or other use of his land, the farmer could minimize risk by lessening the likelihood that an unforeseen change in environmental conditions might wipe him out. The rainless drought that devastates one crop might spare another; the hailstorm that destroys a wheat field ready for harvest might have no effect on stock animals or honeybees. Given conditions allowing for a degree of variability, diversification might be practiced on a single continuous holding (say, by training grape vines into fruit trees), but the frequently attested fragmented estates comprising far-flung plots united under a single citizen's ownership point to potentially more effective possibilities. And the strategy might assume a complementary dimension of a strictly social kind as well when, through marriage, adoption, or perhaps associational membership, owner-operators in environmentally diverse localities were brought into a cooperative alliance with one another. Exchange of labor, sharing of a surplus to make good another's shortfall, communication of new-found knowledge acquired through an experiment protected by an affine's traditional practice are examples of the kinds of response that I have in mind.

The apparent absence of a classical Greek term for our "conservatism" (unless it is to be found in the moral sphere subsumed under the more extensive *sophrosynē*, "moderation," or the like) might be due to the fact that the notion had been enveloped within, and obscured by the shadow cast by, an all-embracing ideal of *autarkeia*, "self-sufficiency." It is perhaps typical of these highly socially oriented people that a purely economic notion (as characterized here) should have given way to a conceptualization of one's relationships with one's fellows. To be *autarkēs* meant that a person had attained the capacity to secure, without reliance on others, the necessities of life for himself and his household. Needless to say, the ideal was unattainable for most. Farmers might rely for supplementary sources of labor or income not only upon household members (wife, child, and slave) but also upon outsiders—hired hands, itinerant pickers, or rent-paying tenants. When a surplus was produced through good fortune or conscious design, its sale in town gave rise to a dependency not only on buyers but also, in a way that was perhaps equally threatening, on an alien, even hostile, culture. When the opposite of surplus, a shortfall, occurred, the assumption of debt could make the farmer-borrower dependent upon a creditor, and, in the worst of all possible scenarios, a default might suddenly eject him from farming altogether and render him totally dependent upon others or, if relocation to the town ensued, upon politicians and public institutions. But shortfall could expose the small-holder (or other rural Athenian) to still another, perhaps more serious, threat to his autarky: the local Big Man, for he, unlike the hired hand, buyer in the Agora, or urban politician, posed the immediate and visible threat of a continuing humiliating loss of face before one's peers. To become dependent, or more dependent, upon the local Big Man meant to descend still another rung or two downwards on the communal ladder of social status—and remain there, perhaps permanently. The possibility of a diminution of standing on this order would have animated many an Athenian to work still harder, to limit the size of his family, to marry off his daughter in a timely and advantageous fashion, to resist still more determinedly the seductive Siren-call of experimentation or other form of risk-taking.

K. J. Dover's *Greek Popular Morality in the Time of Plato and Aristotle*, published in 1974, commenced the section "Honour and Shame" with the statement ". . . where a modern speaker would probably make some reference to good and bad conscience the Athenians tended instead to use expressions such as 'be seen to . . .', 'be regarded as . . .', and these expressions were also used where we would refer neither to conscience nor to reputation, so that an Athenian's 'I wanted to be regarded as honest' is equivalent to our 'I wanted to be honest.'"[57] No town vs. country distinction is indicated here, nor could such be maintained were our intent to eliminate "honour and shame" from the urban setting. But if the modern Greek countryside has anything to teach us, it is that residents of ancient rural Attica will have expressed the shared attitudinal repertoire in a distinctively rural (that is to say, agrarian) way. Yet, however plausible, the expectation is difficult to illustrate with specfic examples, given the alternately anecdotal and idiosyncratic or documentary and opaque nature of our sources. We are informed of the facts of, say, a betrothal involving rurally based households, the hypothecation or sale of farmland, and the selection of particular countrymen as demarchs, but we seldom if ever have any idea of the underlying motivations driving such decisions and acts. For all that, one promising line of approach, a lexical one, is afforded by the term *philotimia* ("love of honor") which, in its rural context of the honorary decrees of the deme-associations, I have associated in chapter 2 with the specifically rural matter of boundary disputes. Such a dispute might engage, as in modern Greece, a person's sense of personal honor. To stifle or redirect such impulses away from one's person (and household) and toward the greater benefit of the associational group would surely be an act worthy of commendation and permanent commemoration.

Now, finally, how did all of this play out when these same Athenians came under the influence of the town? Shame, honor, prestige stood at the apex of the Gemeinschaft so uncompromisingly threatened by the Gesellschaft of Athens's intramural conurbations, but there is no reason to suspect that the "shame culture" ceased to obtain in Agora, Assembly, or urban apartment. Rather, in Athens' particular case, it was clearly the more narrowly economical mindset of the agrarian which was likely to be undermined. The Athenian *polis*'s great wealth, patently under the fifth century empire but hardly diminishing during the fourth, rendered unnecessary any "conservatism" when silver or tribute or slaves made proof against catastrophic loss or failure any experiment in monumental public monumental adornment, subsidized popular government, social welfare, or military adventure. Such colossal commitments of resources were in fundamental conflict with the ways of an Attic farmer, even a relatively prosperous one. Aristotle represented the *polis*, in contrast with its constituent households and villages, as self-sufficient (*Politics* 1.1.8: 1252b), thereby realizing the unobtainable ideal of the Athenian citizen *oikos*, but the *polis* of Athens, through the acquisition of imperial subjects and their economic exploitation, abandoned the ideal at any level comprehensible to the manager of rural *oikonomika*. The state did not need to live—or to aspire—within the limits set by its existing resources and potentialities when a maritime *archē* offered to the hegemonial capital a spectrum of goods far outstripping the capacities of Athens herself—or of any other single Aegean polity. Analogously at the household level, extremes of personal wealth unobtainable under a relatively uniform rural regime of land ownership were now possible, while the ambitious could secure election to political offices affording broad powers not limited by the traditional parameters constricting the degree of success (or failure) in an agrarian community. And in the sphere of ideas, new ways of thinking accessible only to a prosperous urban elite such as we find in classical Athens served to undercut that agrarian mindset's moral superstructure by introducing speculation regarding the nature of human society, the relativity of cultural norms, and the ultimate values of a personal existence. All of this has long been familiar. What the present chapter has endeavored to do is to bring to the fore previously ignored or insufficiently appreciated aspects of the rural traditional and essentially agrarian order to which the prodigious, outsized *chrema* of Athens town posed so thoroughgoing a challenge.

6

Images

TO THIS POINT OUR CONCERNS HAVE BEEN with what might naively be termed the real dimensions of rural Attica under the classical democracy. Now it is time for our discussion to take a somewhat different turn. The present chapter will be concerned with whether these ostensible rural realities—spaces, populations, and cultures—were recreated with more or less fidelity in the various imaginative representations that have managed to reach us from antiquity. To apply such a test, to seek out possible "constructs" of the rural, can hardly in this postmodern age lay claim to any semblance of originality, but in this case the project takes on more than the usual significance. For the cleft between reality and image has always seemed to bear a significant relation to the topographically based and conditioned divide separating the rural from the urban. Images of the rural, so far as we are informed by surviving sources, are creations of the town—of painters, poets, dramatists, essayists, or historians of urban background and training composing for an urban, and urbane, audience of readers and viewers. Such an exploration can of course be no more than tentative, inasmuch as the field of evidence to be examined comprises a substantial selection of the most familiar of classical texts. That done, we may continue in the same vein in chapter 7 to a complementary overview of the speculative utopian orders of the Athenian philosophers in their rural dimension and attempt to bring them, too, into a meaningful association with the contemporary Attic reality.[1]

Old Comedy and Aristophanes

Comedy is perhaps the most promising for our purposes of all literary genres, in view of the multiple indications of its possible rural origins and, once fully developed, eventual orientation. The matter of origins is bedeviled by the scarcity and uncertain implications of the record pertaining to comedy and comedic productions prior to the production of the earliest extant intact play, Aristophanes' *Archarnians*, in 425. K. J. Dover took the word *kōmoidoi* to be "*kōmos*-singers," the word *kōmos* to mean "a company of men behaving and singing in a happy and festive manner," but found unanswerable the question when the *kōmos* first developed a dramatic character. At best, he could instance the animal choruses, dancers, and satyrs costumed with often enormous phalluses (and compare Aristotle, *Poetics* 1449a10) and, from beyond Athens, the "unrestrained vilification and grossest sexual humour" found in Archilochos and Hipponax.[2] Alternatively, it is not from *kōmos* but from *kōmē*, "village," that "comedy" and related terms are to be derived, as suggested by a persistent ancient and later tradition evaluated by Pickard-Cambridge.[3] The contrasting etymologies are offered as mutually exclusive, but it is obvious that, on grounds of substance, both might be combined in a single monolithic etiology. Either derivation might reflect a strong agrarian interest in, or at the very least preoccupation with, fertility—plant, animal, and human—in its communal agrarian setting. Perhaps to term such primitive interests or preoccupations "rural" when the full emergence of the town (and unified state) of Athens still lay far in the future would be methodologically ill-founded, but we are justified in supposing that comedy conservatively retained once general traits, while with the growth of the new population centers the developing urban cultures (and their attendant literary genres) assumed a rather different trajectory. That is, the "rural" came into its own as the town split off from the shared cultural base and the countryside remained as before.[4] So viewed, the "Agrarian" Dionysia studied in chapter 4, and in particular its production of comedies alongside tragedy and dithyramb, would represent in part a vestige of the preurban socioeconomic order and, as such, could arguably combine elements of both etymologies: viz. a *kōmos* festival held in a *kōmē*. The memory of such an origin could easily be lost, especially to the extent that tell-tale etymologies played a role, since with Kleisthenes' constitutional reforms at the end of the sixth century the Attic village came officially to be called not *kōmē* but *dēmos*, "deme."

The remains of Old Comedy are consistent with these speculations, for traces of a rural and specifically agrarian orientation are frequently in evidence.[5] The surviving titles by themselves speak unambiguously in this regard:[6]

TOPOGRAPHY AND/OR SETTLEMENTS: "Demes" (*Dēmoi*) by

Eupolis; "Demesmen" (*Dēmotai*) by Hermippos; "Islands" (*Nēsoi*) by Aristophanes; "Cities" (*Poleis*) by Eupolis and Philyllios; "Potamians" (*Potamioi*) by Strattis; "Prospaltians" (*Prospaltioi*) by Eupolis; and "Man of Titakidai" (*Titakidēs*) by Magnes. (Potamioi and Prospaltioi are Kleisthenic demes; Titakidai a small community within the deme Aphidna[7]).

OCCUPATIONS: "Oxherds" (*Boukoloi*) by Kratinos; "Farmers" (*Georgoi*) by Aristophanes.

ANIMALS: "Goats" (*Aiges*) by Eupolis; "Mule-Car" (*Apēnē*) by Philonides; "Frogs" (*Batrachoi*) by Aristophanes, Kallias, Magnes; "Snakeskin" (or "Old Age") (*Geras*) by Aristophanes; "Fish" (*Ichthyes*) by Archippos; "Flounders" (*Krapataloi*) by Pherekrates; "Bees" (*Melittai*) by Diokles; "Ants" (*Myrmēkes*) by Kantharos, Plato Comicus; "Donkey's Shadow" (*Onou Skia*) by Archippos; "Wine Pack Donkey" (*Onos Askophoros*) by Leukon; "Birds" (*Ornithes*) by Aristophanes, Magnes; "Fig-Flies" (*Psēnes*) by Magnes; "Wasps" (*Sphēkes*) by Aristophanes; "Beasts" (*Thēria*) by Krates, and "Plover" (*Trochilos*) by Heniochos.

AGRARIAN OR RURAL (misc.): "Savages" (*Agrioi*) by Pherekrates; "Festivals" (*Heortai*) by Krates, Plato Comicus; "Hesiods" (*Hēsiodoi*) by Telekleides; "Seasons" (*Hōrai*) by Aristophanes, Kratinos; and "Revelers" (*Kōmastai*) by Ameipsias, Phrynichos.

From the texts themselves could be gathered a plethora of fragmentary references to rural entities such as fields (fallow or under tillage), rocky patches, groves, lands, marshes, villages and villagers, and the deities Pan and the Nymphs. Among proper Attic rural place names occur Lykabettos, the Pelargikon dell, Parnes, Psyra, Salamis, and the extramural demes Acharnai, Anagyrous, Diomeia, Lamptrai, Marathon, Melite, Pambotadai, Potamioi, and Teithras.

By way of illustrating Old Comedy's handling of the rural content suggested by these particulars (leaving aside for the moment the extant plays of Aristophanes), consider the following:

From Theopompos, "Peace" (*Eirēnē*), fr. 7: "And next was set up the inscription at Delphi: 'A farmer was . . . always good, first of all by escaping famine.'" According to Photios, Theopompos had in mind (in parody?) the saying "A farmer is always rich in the coming year."

From Aristophanes, fr. 706: Chorus?: "[him] having the middle dialect of the *polis*, neither the feminine and urbane (dialect) nor the unfree and rather rustic (dialect) . . ."

From Alkaios, *Pasiphae*, fr. 26: ". . . he might become urbane in mind by residing in town."

From Kratinos, fr. 357: "To appear as golden [in the town?], but back in the country (*kat' agrous*) to be leaden again."

From Lysippos, unknown play, fr. 8: "If you haven't seen Athens, you're a blockhead. If you've seen it but weren't captivated, you're a jackass. And if you run away with pleasure, you're a packass."

The beleaguered farmer's typical mindset is rooted in his precarious existence (Theopompos) and expressed in eternally springing wishfulness (the saying). The country's dichotomous relation with the town is evidenced in palpable cultural variation (Aristophanes), potentially modified by change of scene (Alkaios), but characterized in representations of urbane superiority (Kratinos, Lysippos). Attitudes and relative valuations of this kind purporting to characterize the Attic countryside and its people, especially in the context of their interactions with the town, are among the principal themes which will now occupy our attention. Let us continue, then, with the Old Comedy poet par excellence.

Aristophanes (ca. 460–450–ca. 386), as noted at the outset of our study, bore the inheritable affiliation of the intramural deme Kydathenaion (*PA* 2090; *PAA* 175685) and presumably, in the total absence of any contrary indications, resided in this, the largest of the urban demes, throughout the forty or so years of his dramatic productivity.[8] Of that productivity eleven plays have survived intact, thirty or so others are known by title, and upwards of a thousand fragments or citations have come down to us under his name. Among the fragments is "Farmers" (*Georgoi*), the traces of which are in step with the two relevant intact "War" plays: one *georgos* prefers to work his land and will pay to be released from "the *archai*" [in town] (100); the chorus (?) wishes to repair from the *asty* to the country, there to relax while bathing in a copper tub (107); peace and a brace of oxen, they say, will bring a bath, fresh cabbage and white bread, new wine (109)—all to be set within the "dear *polis* of Kekrops, homegrown Attica, . . . glistening land, breast of the good earth" (110). About "Seasons" (*Hōrai*) we have no clue save Athenaios's excerpt of Athena's catalogue of winter fruits (9.372b, cf. 14.653f). Rare feminine forms of "villagers" and "retailers" figure in a fragment from "Plays" or "Centaur" (274), the former relevant to (and confirming) my conclusions elsewhere regarding "the women of the *demotai*."[9] From "Islands" (*Nēsoi*) (according to the *Life*, attributed by some to Archippos), an unknown speaker envisions a man freed from the affairs of the Agora, dwelling in the country on his plot, with his own yoke of oxen, listening to bleating sheep and the sound of wine straining into a vat, and enjoying a morsel of chaffinch and thrush instead of having to wait in the Agora for fish—two days old, high-priced, and weighed by the fish-monger with illegal thumb! (387). What are we to make of these represen-tations? The oppressive, hated town, imposing unwelcome (democratic governmental!) duties and economically exploitative? Land, by contrast, offers good food and drink, the cleansing comfort of the bath, the pre-ferred power source of a brace of oxen, and even (again in contrast to the town) an observable female presence. Yet, amidst this welter of detail, not a trace of the less than idyllic realities of farming life. What are we to make of this silence?

Preliminary to any answer, it should be noted that the one comedy bearing the name of a deme, *Archarnians*, is, save a scene depicting an in-terrupted celebration of the Agrarian Dionysia presumably taking place in the protagonist's deme (not Acharnai, but Cholleidai), seemingly set in the town. Nor can any other play, whether intact, known by title, or preserved in a titleless fragment, be assigned to an extraurban village or other setting. Rather it is to the hero of extramural origins, whose activity Aristophanes places in an identifiably or presumably urban environment, that we must turn for evidence of an image of rural Attica. Bias is perhaps evident from the outset. For Aristophanes, and for virtually all his successors, the coun-try must come to the town if the two, for the sake of a comic clash of cul-tures, are to interact.[10]

Acharnians (*Acharnēs*), produced at the Lenaia of 425 and carrying off first prize, is conventionally categorized as a "War" play because its plot involves the efforts, in the end successful, of the protagonist Dikaiopolis ("Just City"), a demesman of Cholleidai, to secure a private peace with the Spartans, with whom Athens had been waging the Peloponnesian War since its outbreak in 431. The characterization is not an unfair one, narra-tively speaking, for Dikaiopolis acknowledges that he himself has had vines cut down (512) in the course of the annual enemy invasions of the Athen-ian countryside. Accordingly, modern critical opinion has repeatedly asked whether Aristophanes was or was not calling for an end to the War.[11] But a second strand of criticism, downplaying the issue of the War, has con-centrated on Dikaiopolis himself and has called into question his literal dra-maturgical identity as a farmer, proposing instead that he is (or is not) Aristophanes (with the poet actually playing his part on one reconstruc-tion), or the rival poet Eupolis, or by deliberate obfuscation represents "multiple personalities."[12] Similarly departing from the practical topicality of the solution-to-current-problem approach, and thirdly, is the view that this (and some of the later) plays serve to set out utopias more or less relevant to current affairs but not necessarily confined to the War.[13] Now where, in the context of the concerns of the present study, do the "realities" of rural Athens come into play, if at all? Recently the matter has been once again reopened by Gwendolyn Compton-Engle, who has found in the unfolding of Dikaiopolis's part a progression from country persona (on display in the prologue) toward a predominantly urban persona evident, for example, in his dropping his earlier aversion to the marketplace.[14] Such an orientation (while not of course to the detriment of other readings with which it is clearly compatible) has the salutary effect of bringing discussion back around to the substance of the narrative. To what extent, and in what ways, is Dikaiopolis a fair representation of an Athenian ruralite?

The answer must begin with Dikaiopolis's name, for the obviously fictive formation suggests its pointedness, namely that its bearer's position on the War is in some sense "just" for the *polis* of Athens. But just what is the *polis*? Does it include the *chora* as well as the *asty*? And if so, by what dramaturgical device(s) is the former kept before the eyes and minds of the audience (and reader)? Dikaiopolis would presumably like to see his "cut" vines restored (or, if replanted, allowed to reach productive maturity), unless, as seems to be the case with the chorus of Acharnian demesmen, simple revenge constitutes his "justice." But when, at the beginning of the play, we first meet him, he is delivering his monologue from his seat in the assembly-place on the Pnyx above the Agora in the heart of urban Athens—far away from his country deme. That deme is identified as Cholleidai by Dikaiopolis himself when he knocks at Euripides' door (406); and even if, as commentators have always suspected, the demotic is a punning reference to the tragedian's reported lameness (*cholos*, lame; cf. 411), the datum will presumably still have had a ring of plausibility. Disappointingly, as noted in our discussion of the Rural Dionysia (ch. 4, with note 27), the deme's location has not been established, but at least we know that it was not one of the five contained by the town's fortification walls. But the point to be made here (and one in conformity with Compton-Engle's analysis) is that, save for the not clearly placed celebration of the "rural" Dionysia (202, 237–279), the protagonist's country origins are scarcely heard of (or seen) again.

For all that, the town is consistently represented by our hero as a foreign, and thoroughly objectionable, place. Some of the symptoms are of course part and parcel of Athens' ongoing military operations. The Peloponnesian invasions have, in continuation with the now-deceased general-politician Pericles' grand strategy, caused the rural population to take up temporary abode within the fortifications under most disagreeable conditions (71–72). Embassies sent out by the urban-based democratic government, instead of promoting a cessation of hostilities in conformity with Dikaiopolis's aims, instead cultivate good relations with the national enemy, Persia, for the purpose of furthering the prosecution of the War—and all the while drawing high government pay and indulging in hedonistic pleasure-seeking (61–108). Innocent allied states, like Athens' own country people, are subject to threats and maltreatment by the imperial mistress's (again) urban-based government (192–193). The town is plagued by hawkers, nerve-wracking noise, thieving merchants, and a host of other unpalatable elements. No longer is Aeschylus performed, but we get Theognis in his place, not to mention the inept musical performances of a Chairis. Sexual life is dominated by perverted practices of effeminacy, fellatio, and anal intercourse between males (117–122, 133, 716, et al.). But these cultural deviations from the countryman's rural norm, startling and graphic as they are, must take a back seat to the supposedly democratic government itself, the instrument which, from its urban hub, has inflicted war and all its unwelcome consequences on the people of extramural Attica. "Supposedly," because the Demos nominally sharing the *kratos* of political power is in practice if not in theory actually an urban-dwelling subset of self-serving misdirected deviants.

Since Dikaiopolis makes so abundantly clear his dissatisfaction with town politicians' administration of affairs of state, an inappropriately sober audience member (or reader), were this not a comedy, might expect remedy in the form of a new constitution or at least reform of the existing one—as were to come in later plays. But signs of a such an attitude on our hero's part are slight. Dikaiopolis does contemplate release from campaigning (i.e. the end of the War) (251); he voices sympathy with the Spartans, thereby implicitly contemplating future peaceful relations (303–316, 338–341, 369, 482); and, similarly, at home, his complaint that town politicians woo unsuspecting country folk with flattery and payments (370–374) again suggests the possibility of future more agreeable conditions. No such incrementally reformist approach, however, is discernible in the working out of Dikaiopolis's Happy Idea, for his intentions, far from pursuing any plan for the general improvement of the *polis* of Athens or even of Athens' farming population, are consistently personal, self-serving, and hedonistic. Substantively, life in the postwar utopia will be organized around wine-induced drunkenness, plentiful delicious food, and free-wheeling unrestrained sex (the last mentioned, again, of the acceptable country variety).

The Hymn to Phales, with which the abbreviated celebration of the Agrarian Dionysia by Dikaiopolis comes to its abrupt conclusion, artfully blends these components with one another and pointedly places the ensemble in the country deme—pointedly since, in contrast with the ostensibly urban setting of the remainder of the action, this scene alone transpires in "my deme" (266–267, ?Cholleidai). It is also a personal—though hardly private—vision, for Dikaiopolis's peace treaty will extend only to himself and his family members (130–132, 268–269, 290–291), while the requests for a share of the peace by Derketes (1018–1036) and by a Best Man (with the Bride) acting on behalf of the Bridegroom (1048–1068) are met with flat refusals. Dikaiopolis' contemplation of a peaceful future goes no further than his musings about the eventual marriage and child-bearing of his daughter (253–256).

The utopian character of Dikaiopolis's vision is variously indicated. For one, comparison of the as it were record of rural life acknowledged in this play with the documentable dossier of "realities" assembled in the preceding chapter will at once reveal the consistent avoidance of the facts of rural Attic life. Does Dikaiopolis wear an animal skin? Does he speak in a *dialektos* "rather servile" in character in contrast with the "rather feminine" speech of the *asty*? Since we have neither directions for costuming (or clues from the text itself) nor any idea how a given actor might deliver an otherwise "normal" looking standard Attic Greek part, we cannot be sure, but nothing in *Archarnians* (or *Peace* or the others) suggests striving after verisimilitude. The rigors of field labor? Discomfiture with the written word? Resistance to the artificial prytany calendar determining the day of the very meeting of the Assembly with which the play began with Dikaiopolis himself in attendance? Nothing is to be won from the text on these heads, but the hero seems to move quickly away from his rural nostalgia and address his forward-thinking vision. Thus these lines spoken by Dikaiopolis to Amphitheos:

O Dionysia! This treaty is redolent of ambrosia and nektar and of never-to-await-the-call-for "three days' rations." And, once in my mouth, the treaty says "Go wherever you wish"! I'll take it! I'll offer a libation and drink it off! While telling the Acharnians to get lost! (195–200)

Ambrosia and nektar, the food of the gods? Freedom of movement, again such as enjoyed only by gods? An earthly locus might have been found in the rural deme hosting Dikaiopolis's celebration of the Agrarian Dionysia studied in chapter 4, but the sudden onslaught of the bellicose pro-War chorus of Acharnians (280) quickly dispels any such illusion. Rather, and paradoxically at first, it seems to be the town where the hero's aspirations find their realization in the creation of a private market. At line 719, Dikaiopolis reenters the stage:

These here are the boundary markers of my market. Here may all Peloponnesians and Megarians and Boeotians trade, on the condition that they sell to me, but not to Lamachos. As stewards of the market I hereby appoint these three strapping young men from Lashes. Let no sycophant enter here nor any other who is a Bird Man. But let me go and get the stele on which I inscribed the treaty, so that I may set it up in the Agora for people to see. (719–728)

Ensuing action depicts the successful operation of the market in conformity with Dikaiopolis's substantive concerns—and for his personal and exclusive benefit. From a Megarian, previously excluded by the People's notorious decree, the rural hero capitalizes upon his newly acquired treaty by purchasing two underage girls put up for sale by their impoverished father, while the informer who attempts to interfere with the transaction is sent packing. To this solitary exemplum is added the summarizing comment of the chorus: "The man has got it made! Didn't you hear where the matter of the plan is headed? The guy will rake it in, sitting in his market" (836–838)—to be followed by a litany of the objectionable urban types who will (since this is not the real Athens) accordingly be avoided (839–859). But it is a single word, *karpōsetai* ("will rake it in," lit. "will harvest"), that signals the agrarian orientation of the fantasy and opens up the possibility of an affinity with the utopian ideal which, as we are seeing throughout this study, drove and shaped visionary contemplations of an ideal rural world: the Reign of Kronos. Neither Zeus's father nor his reign finds mention anywhere in the play, but the Chorus Leader captures the essence of the Hesiodic paradigm in a single line: "To this man all good things are provided spontaneously" (978).

With the arrival of Dikaiopolis's ambitions at this Kronian climax, it is perhaps easier to comprehend the otherwise unsettling division of opinion between our hero and the chorus of Acharnian demesmen. Cholleidai, whatever its precise location, was, like Acharnai, an extramural country deme. Although the Acharnians depend economically upon the production and sale of charcoal, they also, like Dikaiopolis (512), operate vineyards which were destroyed by the invading Peloponnesians. Yet the chorus wants war; the protagonist, peace. Why the difference? Even though the

vines cannot be brought back through counterattack, the anger and bellicosity of the Acharnians must have struck the Athenian viewers of Aristophanes' play as understandable, perhaps even dictated by a code of honor.
But Dikaiopolis, save for his ultimately futile attempt to stage in the home
deme the Dionysia (featuring, significantly for the remainder of the action,
his trinity of sex, food, and wine), has opted for a retreat from reality (especially that of the omnipresent War) and flight into fantasy—yet a fantasy,
as we have just seen, informed by the continuing tradition of a rural paradise. "Fight or flight", the two responses exhausting the human repertoire,
are being put on show for contrasting evaluation.

Two years later, *Clouds* (*Nephelai*), produced in 423 (with our version
incorporating revisions made between 418 and 416), returns to the theme,
but in a more realistic manner since the opposition of town and country is
only incidental to the dominating preoccupation with the wise man
Socrates. The country side of that opposition is embodied in Strepsiades,
the town side in his (characteristically, unnamed) wife, an unhappy union
described by Strepsiades to their son, Pheidippides:

Damn! She ought to die in misery, that matchmaker who put me up to marrying
your mother! A sweet country life used to be mine, gathering dust, unswept, just
lying around, teeming with honeybees, sheep, and olive cakes. And then I married
the niece of Megakles, son of Megakles, me a country boy, she from town,
pompous, pampered, a regular Koisyra. When I married her, I jumped in the sack,
smelling of must, fig-crates, wool, and surpluses, she of fragrance, saffron, deep
kisses, extravagance, gluttony, Cape Kolias and the birthday goddess! (lines 41–52)

After the birth of their son, they quarreled over the name, she wishing to
add *hippos* ("horse")—the consummate symbol of an aristocratic pedigree—while he preferred naming after Pheidonides ("Thriftson"), the
newborn's grandfather, the two finally settling on a compromise form,
Pheidippides. Said mother to son: "Whenever you've grown up and drive
a chariot to town, like Megakles, wearing a robe, . . ." Said father to son:
"No, it'll be the goats from Rocky Patch, like your father, wearing a
skin . . ." (60–72). Is Strepsiades wearing a skin now? We can't be sure, but
that he was is suggested by the additional specific hints of the countryman's cultural orientation which crop up repeatedly in the ensuing dialogue. On the subject of the cause of rainfall, Strepsiades opts for Zeus
urinating through a sieve (373, cf. 1278–1282); and during the lengthy exchange with his increasingly frustrated prospective teacher, his responses
reveal his familiarity with matters agrarian: measures of produce

(639–645), names of barnyard animals (658–669), witchcraft (749–756), and the kneading of groats (787–789). When Socrates erupts in anger, it is with damning characterizations: "How *agroikos* and ignorant (*dysmathēs*) you are!" (646); "you are *agreios* and gauche (*skaios*)" (655), in both cases an adjective built on *agros* being conjoined with a pejorative limiting term adding a negative nuance to the otherwise neutral denominator of rural agrarian origin. Strepsiades accepts this valuation of himself when he instances his distant residence "in the fields" as an excuse for his loud disruptive knocking on the Thinkery's door (138)—that residence presumably being in his deme Kikynna (134), situated in a genuinely rural district southeast of Hymettos. When rebuked by the chorus of clouds for his unethical pursuit of personal advantage, he pleads that he, an *agroikos* and *gerōn* ("an old countryman"), has been unwittingly led on by them (1456–1457). And, running from the house with Pheidippides in hot pursuit, it is to his neighbors, kinsfolk, and demesmen that he appeals for help (1322)—a rural farmer's instinctive (and predictable) recourse to self-help even amidst an urban environment of law, state police, and courts. True, the Age of Kronos figures once in the chorus's admiring expostulation to the Better Argument (1028–1029), but the play's prevailing mood is one of urban hostility to a recognizably real, hardly idealizing, characterization of rural experience and sensibility. Dikaiopolis had been spared such demeaning treatment. Why the difference? Dikaiopolis the protagonist had been burdened with enunciating ideals held by the poet himself or at least with which he was sympathetic. Not only is Strepsiades not a protagonist but he must play the doubly subservient role of providing the butt of humor designed to define by contrast another figure who is himself the object of ridicule. Only under such restricted dramatic circumstances could rural ways, I wish to suggest, be authentically represented on Athens' urban stage.

Still another two years later, in 421, the tendencies evidenced in *Acharnians* were once again put on show, this time at the City Dionysia, when Aristophanes produced his *Peace* (*Eirēnē*), taking second prize.[15] By now the War had worn on for a decade, but the terms of a treaty had at last been worked out and only ten days later would be formalized as the Peace of Nikias. Thus, as Dover put it, the progress of events made the play more a celebration than (as in the case of *Acharnians*) a protest.[16] Perhaps for this reason, since it would now be pointless to debate the War in any realistic setting involving contemporary politicians, the initial scene is as imaginary as one could be—the palace of the gods on Mt. Olympos. Trygaios, an Athenian farmer, despairing for the countryman's predicament (see 619–627), is transported by a dung beetle (which he has fattened himself) to the palace's door, only to learn from the doorkeeper Hermes that War has moved in, removing Peace to a deep chasm. At length, Trygaios calls upon all Greeks to help him rescue Peace from her prison and, in defiance of Zeus's edict that anyone attempting to do so will be punished with death and after successfully bribing Hermes, he and the farmers by themselves succeed in freeing the goddess along with her beautiful attendants Opora (Harvest) and Theoria (Holiday). Back on earth, Trygaios presents Theoria to the Council while he himself weds Opora amidst general celebration and minor action illustrating the contrasting benefits of peace and war.

Like Dikaiopolis in *Archarnians*, the protagonist Trygaios, a demesman of extramural Athmonon, is a farmer, specifically, as his invented name, "Grape Man", indicates, a vintner. The identification facilitates specific comment on Trygaios's particular predicament (such as the contemplated fashioning of vine poles from spears, 1262–1263) as well as some pretty imagery about the glories of peace. It motivates, or at least renders plausible, the frequent mention of wine which, with food and sex, again comprise the Aristophanic agrarian rural priorities. With reference to the War, it allows Trygaios to dramatize its effects on the extramural population since vineyards, in contrast with field crops, herds of stock animals, or the apparatus of an extractive industry, once cut can be restored only over a period of several years.[17] Finally, and no less substantively, Trygaios, once self-described as an "clever vintner" (190–191; cf. 556–559, with fig trees; 566–570, 702–703, 706–708, 912, 916), may without further ado be placed at an elevated position on the agrarian hierarchy, especially on the head of agricultural labor. Aristophanes' text identifies as actively engaged in farming or allied tasks the wife, slaves, and the "boy" (1140–1171), but only once is Trygaios himself identified as a laborer and on that one occasion it is not the act but his own expression of intent for the future which is at issue (569–570). Thus in the person of the protagonist at least may be realized the ideal in association with which imaginary portrayals of rural, and specifically agrarian, life are, once again, so consistently conceived and elaborated—the Reign of Kronos when, as Hesiod puts it, a single day's work might allow a man to store up enough for an entire year.

This is not to say that the comic figure is not plausibly grounded. The deme Athmonon (190, 918), assigned by Traill to the Inland trittys of the phyle Kekropis, lay to the southwest at the foot of Mt. Pentelikon and far removed from the *asty*. [18] Though a vintner, he may still call himself a *geor-gos* (508, cf. 511) and so appeal to his fellow farmers in the audience (296), who alone succeed where all others had failed in dragging Peace from the place of her entombment (508–519) and in the end are represented as the liberators of "the deme crowd and farming people" (920–921). Foods occasioning his comment run to Attic honey (252–254), garlic (258), and groats and cheese (368), though (a possible corroborating instance of his superior position on the agrarian hierarchy) not barley (449). Tools, though with little indication of what one is to do with them, much less of the well-established debilitating effects of their use, receive brief mention: spade (566), scythe (1200), baskets (1202). But these particular bits of rural authenticity are overwhelmed by the varied and repeated revelations of the protagonist's fantasy life. One of his "wish lists" (as they may fairly be called) comprises "sailing, staying at home, screwing, sleeping, attending festivals, feasting, playing *kottabos*, and generally living it up" (340–344); another, "harvest time, parties, the Dionysia, pipes, tragedies, the songs of Sophocles, thrushes, verses of Euripides" (530–532); another, "ivy, a wine strainer, bleating flocks, bosoms of women running through the fields, a drunken slave girl, and upturned jug" (535–538); still another, "figs, myrtle berries, wine, violets by the well, and olives which we long for" (575–579). Trygaios knows how to play *kottabos* (1242–1244) and rehearses the singers for the wedding (1265–1315); once back in the country, he foresees dancing, libations, prosperity, barley, wine, figs, wives bearing children, and recovery of all that was lost during the War (1316–1328). Similarly, the chorus's (or chorus leader's) evocation of an idyllic country scene envisions a warm fire, friends in attendance, toasting pease, roasting corn, and kissing the Thracian maid while the wife is bathing (1127–1139); and again, once the seed is in the ground and receiving a gentle rain, leisure, a busy wife, slaves engaged in manual labor, a "boy" waiter, a paternal grandfather, drinking, preparations for a feast, singing cicadas, vines, figs, the "dear Seasons," thyme, and getting fat (1140–1171). Prominent here are the themes of select and delectable foods, the means of intoxication, the heterosexual (if not fully approved) pursuit of females other than one's wife, and aesthetic delights extending even to the principal dramatists of the later fifth century (to be contrasted, perhaps, with Dikaiopolis's preference for Aeschylus, *Archarnians*, 10–12). True, familiarity with the plays may as naturally be referred to a local Dionysian festival (although Athmonon is not among the demes for which the "Rural" Dionysia is so far attested) as to the town productions; and allusions to the certifiably oral *logoi* of Aesop (129–130) and

Iliad of Homer (1096–1098) are likewise consistent with listening to oral performances rather than reading. Nothing, then, intrinsically implausible for an Athenian farmer, it must be conceded, but the total absence of even a grudging acknowledgment of the documented risks, hardships, and generally miserable condition which were the usual fate of the ancient Greek farmer rather suggests the operation of an urban idealization.

Nostalgia might produce such an idealization. Since both Trygaios and the chorus,[19] despite their conflicting positions on the matter of the peace, claim destruction of their vineyards by the Peloponnesian invaders, they—or rather an outlook grounded in their collective experience—are its likely source. Once relocated in the town "from the fields" (as Hermes puts it, 632), they will have remained for the duration until such time as their stock could be replanted, for what would be the point of the costly and laborious setting out of new roots if they were only to be cut (or ripped out) the following campaigning season? After a decade of subjection to a hostile, generally incomprehensible, and even offensive urban culture, a rural demesman's mind might well have turned to a wistful longing for long absent pleasures not easily obtainable under the even more than normally cramped and suffocating conditions of the *asty*. It is this vision, distorting primarily by virtue of its extreme selectivity, which Aristophanes has put into currency. Trygaios himself gives explicit expression of the situation: "So now I myself am eager to go back to the country and at long last with my mattock hoe my little plot. Gentlemen, let us recall the antique way of life that the goddess [Peace] once provided to us: the dried fruit, the figs, the myrtle berries, . . ." (569–581).

Despite these longings, however, Trygaios's vision for the countryside does not exclude urban Athens. True, the town is the venue of sycophants, "affairs" (*pragmata*, in its usual illusive but unmistakably pejorative sense, 190–191) and unscrupulous orators (632–648), as well as of numerous other noxious elements compared unfavorably by the chorus with their rural opposite numbers (1172–1190), but Trygaios will make sure to purchase salt fish before returning to the country (562–563) and imagines with anticipation the day when the Agora will once again fill up with the imported luxury goods unobtainable on his farm (999–1015). Nor does his rejection of Dikaiopolis's insularity end with his partial acceptance of things urban. From the lips of this farmer, in striking contrast with his protagonist counterpart of four years earlier, emerges not only an acknowledgment of the indispensable necessity of the town of Athens but even a determined panhellenism. Save for a short-lived display of antagonism towards the farmers who had cut down his fig tree (628–631), Trygaios sees beyond his own personal self-interest, even representing himself as the liberator of "the deme crowd and farming people" and eventually as savior of all of Greece (865–870, 913–915, 918–922). So while his call remains one of a return "to the country" (583–600, 1316–1331), where he may once again enjoy the pleasures of wine, good food, and (as it seems to him, see 446 on Kleonymos) wholesome sex, this particularist ambition is appropriately overlaid by a contemplation of the momentarily emergent Peace of Nikias and its hoped-for welcome consequences.

Whereas the locale of Trygaios's visionary village is his farm below Pentelikon, the avian Cloudcuckooland sketched in the *Birds* (*Ornithes*), which took second prize in the City Dionysia of 414, is a different matter.[20] Although repeatedly, and at length, described and characterized (see especially 822–844, 993–1044, 1125–1167), the utopia, to the extent that it has a topographic component at all, seems to be utterly lacking a rural dimension.[21] This comes as a surprise following on the hoopoe Tereus's summoning of the birds from a varied landscape comprehending farmland, gardens, mountains, and other nonurban spaces (lines 227–262) and the bird chorus's evoking of the "woodland" Muse with its mountains, sylvan glade, ashes, Pan, and the like (737–752). Even the Athenian protagonist Euelpides—who owns two oxen (585) and whose deme affiliation is with extramural (but as yet unlocated) Krioa (645) but who apparently resides in Halimous (496) on the coast to the southeast below Hymettos—is a ruralite, for he recounts his mugging by a clothes-thief when he was exiting the walls after a visit to the town and on the way back to that deme (lines 492–498). According to Jeffrey Henderson, Peisetairos's fantasy fits the utopian mold of *Archarnians* and *Peace* wherein a hero expels all that frustrates personal happiness or impedes the common welfare, and in this respect is "a cosmic avatar of Dicaeopolis' marketplace, a utopian counter-Athens."[22] I have no quarrel with this assessment, but if it is right, are we to conclude that in a perfect world, and one fashioned utterly without the restraining influence of contemporary realities, we are all to be urbanites? Or is a rural topography (especially one envisioned in Aristophanes' avian context), with its attendant society, economy, and culture, simply an unspoken given in the design of any commonwealth imaginable in the real world of Greek antiquity?

Wealth (*Ploutos*), Aristophanes' latest extant play, produced in 388, perhaps illustrates the impossibility of an authentic presentation of the countryside or its people, at least before an urban audience.[23] Chremylos, an Athenian citizen, has a house in town where he lives with his wife and son (227–251), but he is a farmer, too, and early on orders his slave Kario to summon "my fellow farmers" whom, he says, he'll find toiling in the fields (223–224)—and in due course they appear as the chorus. The farmers are characterized by Kario as eaters of thyme, friendly demesmen, and lovers of work (253–256, cf. 322–327) but later he acknowledges their "cold and disagreeable life" (263). That life's most disagreeable aspect seems to be "breaking the surface of the earth with ploughs and reaping Deo's harvest" since this item climaxes Poverty's catalogue of tasks people won't want to perform if wealth is ever evenly distributed to all (507–516). Chremylos responds that by contrast all such tasks will be done by slaves (*hoi thera-pontes*), but Poverty counters that No, you, Chremylos, will have to do them yourself, significantly (for my argument) specifying just ploughing and digging, and adding that his life will be "much more painful than now" (522–526). Even etiquette will be characterized in its rural dimension, as when farting without excusing oneself is identified as the mark of an *agroikos* (696–706). The portrayal reaches its conclusion when the Just Man asks "Are you a farmer?" and the Informer replies "Do you think I'm crazy?" (903). We have been brought back to Strepsiades' farm in Kikynna where, prior to futilely seeking to uplift himself through relocation to town and hypergamy, Socrates' victim had herded goats while dressed in an animal skin.

Xenophon

The writings of the Athenian citizen Xenophon, son of Gryllos, of the deme Erchia (*PA* 11307) provide a substantial yet unidimensional representation of the contemporary rural scene, reflecting but not necessarily limited by his personal Attic experience. Attention to biographical detail is essential to its appreciation. As to position on the social hierarchy, while Xenophon's later life gives clear indications of a comfortable prosperity, neither the careers of his forebears nor his own early years in Athens (initially, from birth to 402 or 401) have left any trace of liturgical service, so his evident upper-class status must be otherwise established. As to place of residence in Attica, the inherited affiliation with extramural Erchia (Diogenes Laertius, 2.48) in the absence of additional testimony by itself of course tells us nothing about the setting, urban or rural, of his activity, notwithstanding Pomeroy's assertion that Xenophon "grew up in a rural deme."[24] J. K. Anderson put his birth a little after 430 and on that basis inferred that Xenophon was actually born in town during the wartime confinement, conjecturing that the family, like others, moved back into the country following the Peace of Nikias.[25] At all events, following Xenophon's departure from Athens at century's end, services to Sparta, and consequent exile from Athens, he was settled by the Spartans on a farm-estate ("land and house") in Skillous near Olympia in Elis (*Anabasis* 5.3.5–13, Diog. Laert. 2.52, Plut. *de Exil.* 605c, Paus. 5.6.5). The decree of banishment has been dated by Rahn to soon after the battle of Koroneia, in late 394 or early 393.[26] According to Diogenes' account, the property was accoutered on a lavish scale with a view to leisure activities, for here, writes Diogenes, "he spent his time hunting, dining his friends, and writing histories"—that is to say, if a negative inference is justified, "but not farming" in any active, direct sense of that term. After the Spartan defeat at Leuktra in 371 and an attack on Skillous by the Eleans, Xenophon relocated to Corinth where he was probably to remain until around 365 when the Athenians revoked the decree of banishment. While it is impossible to fit any of the writings with exactitude into this chronology, it is likely with Pomeroy that the work of principal relevance here, the *Oikonomikos*, was completed in its entirety during the years of exile in Skillous, then afterwards, at Corinth, Athens, or elsewhere, revised or expanded at least once before his death ca. 354.[27]

Twenty-two or three years (sc. 394 or 393 to 371) would have sufficed for the composition of a great many writings such have come down to us under Xenophon's name, especially including all those with rural subject matter, orientation, or reference. Nonetheless, where indications are forthcoming in these visionary writings, the setting is not Skillous (nor Asia Minor, nor Corinth, nor elsewhere in the Peloponnese) but Athens. "Revenues" (*Poroi*) contemplates enhanced exploitation of the resources, physical and human, of greater Attica. "Cavalry Commander" (*Hipparchikos*) calls for processions starting from the Herms, proceeding in a circle back to the point of departure, followed by a gallop to the Eleusinion (3.2–5) and full-dress displays at the Lyceum (3.6–9), Hippodrome (3.10–13), Academy (3.14), and perhaps at Phaleron.[28] The preamble to "On Horsemanship" (*Peri Hippikēs*) acknowledges the similar work of a predecessor, one Simon, the dedicator of an equestrian bronze in the Eleusinion (with his *erga* recorded on the base), but no explicit indication of setting is given save for repeated reference to a hilly topography consistent with much of Attica. Similarly, "Hunter" (*Kynegetikos*, "dog-leader") is placed in no specific locale, although, like "On Horsemanship," its setting is wild and rugged rural spaces. Significantly perhaps, extramural Attica is to the fore in the second of the three chapters of the "Constitution of the Athenians" ascribed to the *rhetor* Xenophon (2.11–12, natural resources; 13–16, topography; 14, farming population), and in this respect at least the treatise does reflect the interests and perspective of the more securely attributed writings.

For last I have reserved "Household Manager," where the *oikos* in question is a landed estate deriving its principal revenue from diversified agriculture. Represented as a complex web of reported remarks and conversations (thus "Socrates" relates a conversation of Kyros which he, Socrates, learned of variously through a story, a Megarian, and Lysander), the "dialogue" addresses the question why, when identical plots are worked by two different farmers, one prospers and the other fails (3.5, 20.1–29)—that is, proper agricultural practice. Except for a digression on Persian parallel usage (4.4–25), the setting is uniformly Greek (though not recognizably Athenian), with comparable coverage of both narrowly agrarian and domestic "household" management strategies. Understandably, the prominence of women's and gender studies in recent decades has resulted in sustained attention to the domestic sphere, but Pomeroy's more recent characterization of the monograph as "among the first prose treatises to be written on agriculture"[29] is equally faithful to its actual content and emphasis. Chapters 13–19 (about one-quarter of the whole) are concerned with selection of a foreman (13–14); introduction to farming (15); soil and cultivation (16); sowing, ploughing, and hoeing (17); reaping, threshing, and winnowing (18); and arboriculture and viticulture (19). To what extent and in what ways Xenophon's exposition is grounded in the realities of Greek agricultural practice has been well addressed by Pomeroy's commentary. Our concern here is rather with any tendency implicit in the work's general characterizations of the rural, and specifically agrarian, world confronted by "the household manager." The text will speak for itself:

V.1 SOCRATES. . . . I shall tell you this, Kritoboulos, because not even the most blessed ones are able to abstain from farming. For its tendence appears to be at once a sweet sensation and increase of the household and exercise of bodies for the purpose of making possible all that is appropriate to a free man. (2) First, all that on which humans depend for life, this the earth provides to those who work her; and all that from which they derive pleasure, this she provides as well. (3) Next, all that with which humans decorate altars and statues and with which they decorate themselves she provides—and at that with the sweetest smells and sights. And then there are the many delicacies, some she grows, some she nourishes. For the art of breeding livestock is attached to agriculture so that people can satisfy the gods by sacrificing and utilize (the victims) themselves. (4) But although offering the goods most unstintingly, she does not allow (us) to take (them) with softness but she accustoms (us) to endure colds of winter and heats of summer. . . . (8) . . . And what occupation more suitable than agriculture is at hand for running and throwing and jumping? And what occupation reaps greater dividends in return for those who work in it? What occupation welcomes the practitioner more sweetly, offering to him upon his arrival whatever he needs? . . . (14) Moreover, agriculture also joins in training people to help each other. For one must advance against the enemy with the assistance of people, and the working of the earth is with the assistance of people. . . . (16) And no less often must the farmer urge on his workers than the general his soldiers. And slaves need good prospects no less than free people do, indeed even more, so that they may be willing to stay. (17) The person who said that farming is the mother or nourisher of the other occupations spoke well. When farming is doing well, all the other occupations prosper too, but wherever the earth is forced to lie fallow, the other occupations too, both on land and sea, are all but extinguished.

VI.8 SOCRATES. We determined that for a gentleman (*kalos kai agathos*) the best kind of work and the best kind of knowledge is farming, from which human beings obtain the necessities.

XI.14 ISCHOMACHOS. Well, Socrates, Ischomachos said, I am accustomed to rise from bed when, if I should need to see someone, I could still find him at home. And if something needs to be done in town, while transacting the business I use this opportunity for a walk. But if there is nothing pressing in town, the slave boy leads my horse to the farm, and I perhaps make better use of the trip to the farm as a walk, Socrates, than if I should walk laps in the arcade. And when I arrive at the farm, if they chance to be planting or working the fallow or sowing or bringing in the harvest, after examining how each task is being performed, I urge a change of method if I have something better in mind. (17) Afterwards, on many occasions I mount my horse and I practice equestrian maneuvers as closely as I possibly can to the maneuvers required in war, . . . (18) When this is done, the slave boy rolls the horse and leads it home, at the same time bringing from the farm to town anything we need. Part walking, part running, home, I scrape myself with a strigil; and then eat just enough lunch as not to be either empty or too full for the rest of the day.

Socrates responds approvingly to this last speech, with comment on Ischomachos's success in using "farming" as a means for improving his health and physical strength and training for war, while deservedly being known as one of the most skillful equestrians and wealthiest people (19–20). Nothing is said about farming per se. To the contrary, among Ischomachos's most pressing problems is to find a good bailiff—that is, he, Ischomachos, functions as an overseer of overseers of others' work. Slaves, so often as we have seen associated with agrarian labor, will afford access to a Kronian paradise of livelihood without one's own personal effort. Far from enduring the rigors of country life, even the proprietor's occasional trip *eis agron* (which simultaneously serves additional purposes unconnected with agriculture) will be relieved by retreat to town, with needed provisions from the farm in tow. In fact, not only is the town the point of departure and return for this rural excursion but more importantly it also represents Ischomachos's, the dialogue's, and (let me now suggest) Xenophon's perspective. So much is implicit in the choice of Socrates as interlocutor. As the discussion of the philosopher's background and outlook in the following chapter will make clear, any interest in matters agricultural on Socrates' part would be most unconvincing on the points of both urban sensibility and aversion to manual labor—and could be no more substantively informed than in the more familiar cases of flute playing or pottery throwing. Socrates merely quotes the authority of a reputed expert, and it is Ischomachos who speaks on practical matters of agricultural technique, whereas the philosopher's contribution is chiefly methodological and ethical.[30] And Xenophon himself? While there is again no reason to believe he actually grew up in the rural Attic deme of his affiliation, his residence on the estate at Skillous for over two decades, rendered comfortable by his Asian booty and secure by friendly Spartan arms, does leave open the prospect of a leisured and enlightened engagement with the rural not unlike that of the proper *oikonomikos* himself.

Theophrastos

Successor to Aristotle at the Lyceum and, also like Aristotle, a non-Athenian residing in Athens, Theophrastos, a citizen of Eresos on Lesbos, concerned himself across much of the disciplinary ground already covered by the Peripatetic, with human behavior represented by works on friendship, marriage, and personality. The last-mentioned category includes his *Charakteres*, a collection of at least thirty sketches of objectionable traits, among which are several relating directly or indirectly to life beyond the walls.[31] Pride of place in the direct category belongs to no. 4, *Agroikia*, "Rusticity":

Rusticity would seem to be an unbecoming ignorance, and the rustic the kind of man who takes a purge before he goes to the Assembly, who declares that thyme smells every bit as sweet as perfume, who wears shoes too large for his feet, and who talks at the top of his voice. He distrusts his friends and kinsfolk, but confides matters of great importance to his slaves, and tells everything that went on in the Assembly to the hired laborers who work on his farm. He will sit down with his cloak above his knee, so that his private parts are showing. Most things this man sees in the streets do not strike him at all, but whenever he sees an ox or an ass or a billy goat, he stops to inspect it. He is skilled at eating while in the very act of taking food from the larder, and he mixes his wine too strong. On the sly he makes a pass at the slave girl who bakes the bread, then helps her grind the day's flour for the whole household, himself included. He feeds the draft animals while he is eating his breakfast. When someone knocks, he actually opens the door himself. When he puts on a feast, he calls the dog, takes him by the snout, and says: "This chap guards my house and farm." When he receives a coin, he bites it and, saying that it is lead, demands that it be exchanged for another. And if he has lent out his plough, or a basket, or a sickle, or a sack, he will remember it as he lies awake at night and get up and go out to look for it. On his way to town, he will ask anyone he meets the price of hides or herring, and whether it's a new moon festival day. If the answer is Yes, he announces that he'll get a haircut and buy some herrings at Archias's shop on the way to the barber's. He is also inclined to singing in the baths, and loves to drive hobnails into the soles of his shoes.

To comment briefly on the significance of all this, our rustic farmer is, first, a citizen (for otherwise he could not attend the Assembly), and he does (contrary to my general position) visit the town (on foot, as it happens), and for the purpose, among other reasons, of exercising his citizen's right of attending the Assembly. But before we allow to be called into question our portrayal of the rural Athenian as a farmstead-residing isolationist with at best perfunctory association with his country deme, much less with a remote town, let us remember that farming was practiced near, even within, the walls (see chapter 1); and that, as is consistently clear throughout our little sketch, his trip to town (15) is something of a special event: He is out of touch with prices, has lost track of the calendar, needs to have his hair cut and shoes repaired, and before departing picks up some salted fish—not of course for on-the-spot consumption but to take back home where, since it is preserved, it will keep until the next such—long distant?—outing. True, the Assembly is in his thinking (2, 6), but the fact that he tells "everything" that went on in the meeting to his hired hands suggests an isolated event rather than regular attendance four times per prytany. Be that as it may, however frequent his visits to town, the *agroikos* does actually reside on his farm—the *oikia* on the *chorion* which his dog defends (12).

Despite the prevailing tone of disapprobation, our anonymous (with respect to both name and deme) rustic is relatively prosperous, to judge from his ownership of slaves, farming equipment, willingness to lend out that equipment, ability to purchase food and services from retailers, and the possession of sufficient leisure to take in a festival in town. Perhaps this is what we should expect if, as is likely, the reader is also a man of prosperity, possibly a citizen, and is expected by the author to compare the rustic to himself. The entertainment value of the passage probably resides in the implicit comparison of a rural farmer of means with a townsman of means—the reader. But the specific form of that entertainment value, humor, remains merely implicit. The author seems to assume that all readers are urban, and that the urbanite's attitude towards ruralites is such that the specific behaviors ascribed to them are so laughable as to require no explicit characterization or commentary. That the author's intent is a demeaning one is in any event suggested by the titles of the other 29 *characteres* of Theophrastos's collection: arrogance, backbiting, buffoonery, cowardice, ill-breeding, stupidity, tactlessness, and so on. To be *agroikos*, to evidence *agroikia*, is self-evidently laughable, indeed contemptible. These words denote simply "rustic" and "rusticity", but the denotations had by Theophrastos's day been replaced by connotations of boorishness— hence the traditional English title of this passage.[32]

Much the same seems to apply to passages in less straightforward *characteres* wherein extramural persons or activities surface amidst an indeterminate mélange of scenes not clearly urban or rural.

"Garrulity" (no. 3, *adoleschia*, lit. "talking to satiety"), illustrated by anecdotes across a multitude of persons (in contrast to the foregoing apparently single *agroikos*), is exemplified in the man who remarks on the price of wheat in the Agora and exclaims that many *xenoi* are in town (3)— if a farmer, therefore, one in the *asty* at the time; by the man who says the crops need rain and reveals what he'll be planting next year (4); and by the man who, like the *agroikos*, must ask what day it is (although he can name the months of the Mysteries, Apatouria, and "Rural" Dionysia) (5). Again, also like the *agroikos*, the *adoleschēs* is full of wonder at the sights of the Big City—exclaiming that Damippos dedicated the largest torch at the Mys-

teries, asking about the number of pillars in the Odeion, and so on (4)—
from which it is once more easiest to imagine a rustic making a relatively
rare visit to an unfamiliar urban environment. But it is the very fact that
these utterances should be regarded as superfluous that betrays the essentially urban and urbane orientation of the sketch, for no *farmer* would la-
bel garrulous repeated remarks upon market prices for farm produce, the
need for rain, or next year's planting plans.

"Absent-Mindedness" (no. 14, *anaisthesia*) is illustrated by the man
who, scheduled to appear as defendant in court, absent-mindedly goes to
the farm (*agros*, 3)—another probable but not absolutely certain indication, incidentally, of town-residing commuting farmer. And again by the
man who, when boiling lentils on the farm (*agros*, 11), forgetfully salts the
pot twice and renders them inedible—the point of "on the farm" perhaps
being that under usual circumstances he is *not* on the farm.

By now a pattern is emerging: that the characteristic traits of the rustic can be portrayed *only* in relation to analogous or contrasting urbane
traits—and invariably to the detriment of the former. Furthermore, and
crucially, since the two spheres, rural and urban, are spatially defined and
constituted, *movement* between one and the other will normally be necessary in order to create the required dramatic interaction.[33] This inference
may, let me suggest, go far towards mitigating the general impression left
by these sketches of a mobility between country and town which is otherwise at odds with our findings concerning the "realities" of the classical Attic situation. Visits to town occurred, but these tableaux may leave a false
impression that they were more frequent or regular than they actually
were. Rather may I suggest that it was something more like the visits to the
zoo in Pittsburgh by local Amish or Mennonite rural families—a relatively
rare occurrence likely to attract stares and musings on cultural differences.
But just as it is difficult, except through serious study, for the "English" to
acquire authentic information about the "realities" of the "Plain" people,
so our Theophrastan rural types may, like the Pennsylvania Dutch of the
media, be the products of an active urbane curiosity and imagination as
much as faithful depictions of ancient Athenian "realities."

Middle Comedy

Middle Attic Comedy, conventionally spanning the outgoing "classical"
century 404 to 322, i.e., from the end of the Peloponnesian War to the

Macedonian seizure, carries forward some of the rural subjects and themes of the Old Comedy, but in ways not easily described since, after Aristophanes' intact *Ekklesiazousai* and *Ploutos*, we have only fragments until we reach New Comedy and Menander. Furthermore, the likelihood that these fragments will preserve a representative glimpse into our (or any other) subject is, when measured against Old Comedy as a standard, conditioned by three salient variables. One, the decline of the chorus was attended by a corresponding decline in the titling of plays after the chorus, but it was precisely the chorus-title which in Old Comedy so often reveals a focus germane to the concerns of this book. Two, the disproportionate preservation of the "literary" fragments in Athenaios's *Deipnosophistai* will have skewed the record on the side of food and drink, a tendency which, depending on specific circumstances, could result in either the under- or over-representation of matters rural. There is also, thirdly, the impact of the general reorientation of comedy away from controversial political questions towards "contemporary types, manners, and pursuits"[34] to be considered. True, a war with its players and victims—politicians, generals, and farmers—is no longer available for critique, caricature, or sympathy, but at the same time new, compensating possibilities are opened up when the playwright turns from topical event to the imaging of generic situations and types. Among these latter are certainly to be numbered the ruralite in his or her various dramatic incarnations.

Possible rural Attic subject matter is suggested by the titles[35] of Antiphanes' "Phrearrhian" (*Phrearrhios*, 222), Timokles' "Marathonians" (*Marathōnioi*, 24), and "Icarian Satyrs" (*Ikarioi Satyroi*, 15–19). To these may be added an allusion to the demesmen of Phaleron and Otryne as sources of gobies in Antiphanes' "Timon" (*Timōn*, 204) and a bare mention of unspecified *demotai* in Antiphanes' "Omphale" (*Omphalē*, 174–176). Among the four placed demes, Phrearrhioi, Marathon, and Ikarion are conspicuously far removed from the *asty*, thereby suggesting an interest in a clash of rural and urban cultures. "Thyme of the Hymettians" (i.e. on Mt. Hymettos, 18) and the legendary Kekropidai sallying out to Hymettos against ants (19) figure in Euboulos's "Glaukos" (*Glaukos*). "Rustic(s)" (*Agroikos/oi*) is the title of dramas by Anaxandrides (1–3), Antiphanes (1–12), Anaxilas (1), and Augeas, providing clear enough indication of a Middle Comedy "type" (and precursor to New and Roman treatments), although the fragments of text assigned to these plays are not sufficient to justify (or rule out) the traditional disparaging rendering "boor(s)." Specific rural occupations or pursuits are represented by Philetairos's "Huntress" (*Kynagis*, 6–9); Anaxandrides' "Hunters" (*Kynēgetai*, 25); Euboulos's "Mill Girl" (*Mylothris*, 65); Antiphanes' "Girl Who Went Fishing" (*Halieuomenē*, 27–29), "Gardener" (*Kēpouros*, 114), "Mill" (*Mylon*, 160), and "Sheep Man" (*Probateus*, 191); Amphis's "Vine-Dresser" (*Ampelourgos*, 3–5); Mnesimachos's "Horse-Breaker" (*Hippotrophos*, 4); Alexis's "Goatherds" (*Aipoloi*, 8), "Vine-Dresser" (*Ampelourgos*, 1–12), "The Woman into the Well" (*Hē eis to Phrear*, 85–87), and "Miller" (*Mytothros*, 157); and Timokles' "Farmer?" (*Georgos?*). Like Kratinos and Aristophanes before him, Anaxilas is represented by "Seasons" (*Hōrai*); and (recalling a mute character in Aristophanes' *Peace*) both Amphis and Alexis (169–170) put on a "Harvest" (*Opōra*). Amphis staged a "Pan" (*Pan*).

Thus a suggestive accumulation of fragments, but do we have any idea how our rural subjects were handled? Three happily preserved snippets of text reveal themes conscientiously avoided in Old Comedy but which will be staples of the New Comedy to come: the debilitating hardship of field work; the painful anxiety imposed by the realities of farming; and, by way of compensation for the ruralite's awful lot, an isolation which, in contrast to the absence of privacy in the town, shields his or her poverty from observation by others.

From Anaxilas's "Lyre-Maker" (*Lyropoios*), fr. 16: A. "How are you doing? How emaciated you are! B. Yes, I'm wasting away. For I tend a plot in the country."

From Antiphanes' "Women of Lemnos" (*Lemniai*), fr. 142: "And there could hardly be a sweeter craft or other source of income than to flatter skillfully. The painter labors—and is embittered; the farmer . . . all those risks again! There's anxiety and pain in everything! . . ." (lines 1–6).

From Amphis's "Wool Workers" (*Erithoi*), fr. 17: "And so is solitude not a thing of gold? For humans, the country (*agros*) is the father of life and alone knows how to hide poverty. But the town (*asty*) is a theater brimming with visible misfortune."

New Comedy and Menander

New Comedy, conventionally taking the genre down to the middle of the third century, continues some of the tendencies of the Middle: while Athens (and its topography and place names, laws, and customs) remains the recognizable geographical and institutional setting, the break with the topical present is complete, and stock characters acting out stock situations replace the here-and-now concrete particular with universal themes. The themes themselves are often organized around some common polarity, including the frequent opposition of town and country, which accounts in large part for the medium's considerable attention to Attica outside the walls and its peoples and ways. Non-Menandrian titles include a "Men of Erchia" (*Erchieis*) by an unknown writer,[36] a "Men of Lakiadai" (*Lakiadai*, 13–14) by Philippides, plus "Demesmen" (*Dēmotai*, 10) by Poseidippos. Both named demes lay well outside the walls, suggesting either a distinctive rural setting or collision of cultures in the town. The "rustic" type-study *Agroikos* (1) of Philemon, the occupational "Donkey-driver?" (*Onagos?*) of Demophilos, and "Fowler" (*Ornitheutēs*) of Nikostratos point in the same direction, as does the ostensibly rural "Pan" (*Pan*, 3) of Timostratos. Titles apart, numerous fleeting references to arable, farming, agricultural produce, and attendant imagery could easily be compiled, although, as with several of the titles, an actual extramural setting is by no means certain.

For an idea of New Comedy's handling of rural subjects we are dependent upon a few, but fortunately quite explicit, more substantive fragments, especially from speeches delivered out of the mouths of ruralites themselves. One farmer complains bitterly of a plot so stingy that it yields only one ass-load per year for sale at market (Diphilos, 89). Another opines that while some farms produce the vinegar-fig, his produces vinegar-vines (Apollodoros of Karystos, *Proikizomenē* or *Himatiopolis*, fr. 30). A husbandman in a fragment of Philemon laments that his farm nourishes him as though he was an invalid and, he fears, may one day turn him into a corpse (100). The dimensions of one's arable might be smaller than the proverbial "Lakonian telegram" (Adespota, 456). Incorporating the image of the Diphilos fragment's single ass-load, an unattributed speech by a farmer states his predicament in full (Adespota, 895, 896):

I farm the land not in order that it nourish me but in order that it secure nourishment *from me*. For I dutifully dig it, always sow it, and do everything with a view to giving-and-taking. But while it takes, it gives back nothing. Without knowing it, I bought a played-out field. I sowed twenty minas of barley, but it yielded not even thirteen all told. The Seven Against Thebes marched against me, it seems. Land keeps to the women's saying "May she be fruitful," but that and no more. For what the land is now producing a single ass can carry.

At the same time, such negativism is elsewhere countered by the optimistic *sententia* "Farmers are always rich in the coming year" (Philemon, *Hypobolimaios*, 85). In the same vein, Philemon in an unknown comedy celebrated the ideal of self-sufficiency (105):

> A farm (*agros*) is the most prayed-for possession for humans;
> It affords with care all that our nature demands—
> Wheat, olive oil, wine, dried figs, honey.
> But silver and goods of royal purple
> Are well suited for tragic actors but not for life.

A pair of lines attributed by Kock to Philemon makes a similar point but couched in the imagery of money-lending, adding an echo of Hesiodic spontaneity (Philemon 231K, but see *PCG* VII Adespota, p. 317):

> It's better to lend to the land than to mortals—
> The land, which yields interest even though not asked.

The former passage explicitly (viz. "tragic actors"), the latter by a reasonable surmise prompted by the reference to lending, point a contrast with a luxurious but unproductive or exploitative city. From an unattributed play, antipathy towards matters urban is implicit in a farmer's expression of indifference to a slave's report of the terms of a new peace treaty (Adespota, 726). And, although a reference to the town is lacking, the following from Sosikrates' *Parakatathēkē*, fr. 1 (with commentary for comedic parallels), may also be applicable:

> Whenever, I suppose, a pale, fat person,
> Lazy, knowing only luxurious living, takes up a hoe,
> A five-pounder, his breath starts heaving.

The Athenian citizen Menander (?344/3–292/1) was the son of one Diopeithes, one of the two *diaitetai* or public arbitrators—and hence in his 60th year—of the Kephisieis in the year 325/4 (*IG* II² 1926, lines 17–19).[37] According to an ancient dissertation on comedy,[38] the family was distinguished and wealthy as well, although the latter claim is not yet supported by documented membership in Davies' liturgical class. But it is the affiliation with the deme of Kephisia to the northeast of Athens on the southwestern flank of Mt. Pentelikon that suggests the possibility of a rural perspective for this most prolific New Comedy dramatist. The expectation is not disappointed. To be sure, where information is available, the great majority of the plays are set in Athens town, usually on a street with a house facade to left and right, but the *Perikeiromenē* is with probability placed at Corinth, and the more than a dozen titles of non-Athenian reference (*Andria, Boiotia, Chalkis, Ephesios* or *Ephesioi, Karchedonios, Leukadia, Lokroi, Messenia, Olynthia, Perinthia, Samia, Sikyonios* or *Sikyonioi, Thettalē* or *Thettaloi*) at least illustrate an interest in persons of foreign origin.[39] Within Attica itself are several certifiable examples of rural mises en scène. Whether *Halaieis* (sc. Araphenides) was set in the deme cannot be ascertained, but four others, while lacking a significant title, are shown by their own internal evidence to have been set in demes outside the walls: the *Dyskolos* in Phyle (lines 2, 3); the *Epitrepontes* in a well-wooded part of Attica, perhaps about halfway between Athens and Halai Araphenides;[40] the *Heros* in Ptelea (lines 21–22); and the *Sikyonios* in Eleusis (lines 187–188). To these may be added a number of references made en passant to these and other demes: Aixone (*Kanephoros*, fr. 222 Koerte), Cholargos (*Dyskolos*, line 33), Euonymon (*Kitharistēs*, lines 96–97), Halai Aixonides or Araphenides (*Heauton Timoumenos*, fr. 127 Koerte), Paiania (*Dyskolos*, lines 407–408), Potamioi (*Didymai*, fr. 108 Koerte), Skambonidai (*Sikyōnios*, lines 347, 350), and Trikorynthos (unknown play, fr. 652a Koerte). Names of "constitutional" demes represent only one aspect of rural Attica, but these examples, along with the author's Kephisian antecedents, are sufficient to indicate an interest extending beyond the walls of the *asty*. Indeed, some of these demes lay *far* beyond those walls; only one is intramural (Skambonidai) and three (Halai Araphenides, Phyle, and Trikorynthos) were particularly distant from the *asty*. Furthermore, several, to judge from their bouleutic quotas, were communities of fewer than average citizens, with six of the thirteen having quotas of four or fewer: Cholargos, Phyle, Ptelea, Potamioi (any of the three demes by this name), Skambonidai, and Trikorynthos.[41] When the two factors converge, as with Phyle (the scene of the *Dyskolos*) and Trikorynthos, we are at the antipodes of intramural Athens. Menander's own deme was of modest remove and size,[42] but even so in this author it is clear that we have legitimate reason to expect to find a mirror, and perhaps even exponent, of typical Athenian rural life.[43]

Initially encouraging is the fact that the corpus reflects a comprehensive view of rural Attica, at least as defined by occupational-lifestyle categories. This fact might easily go unnoticed, for the best preserved individual play, the *Dyskolos*, has a predominantly agricultural setting. But the truth is that, in addition to it and to the ostensibly agrarian "Farmer"

(*Georgos*), we have fragments of a "Fisherman" or "Fishermen" (*Halieus* or *Halieis*); a charcoal-burner (lines 257, 465) and shepherd (lines 243, 256, and 299) play conspicuous roles in the *Epitrepontes* as does another shepherd in the *Heros* (lines 21, 26–27); and the chorus of the last-mentioned play may have consisted of hunters from town in and around the tiny deme (quota 1) at Ptelea (line 22, with hunters at fr. 1 Koerte). A fleeting allusive appearance is made by goat-herding *aipoloi* in the *Epitrepontes* (lines 328 and 333). Nor is the scope of the drama confined to Attica, for a speaker in the *Aspis* relates the looting of villages, destruction of crops, and selling of booty by him and his fellow soldiers in Lykia (lines 30–33, cf. 67–68). Even when the setting is the town, contact with the countryside is made with the arrival of a character *ex agrou: Georgos* (line 32); *Kitharistēs* (lines 54–57); and *Perikeiromenē* (lines 364–365). Characterization as well as description is of course part and parcel of any comedic portrayal, and so the lost *Agroikos*—the title as always indicating the insider's representation of the Other—might, for all we know, have brought the "rustic" into collision with his urbane counterparts in an urban setting. All told, Menander's New Comedy may have been generically concerned with urban manners, but even these exiguous indicators bespeak a lively presence of the rural countryside, whether arable plain or slope, pastoral mountainside, or maritime fishery, its denizens, and returning urban visitors.

Against this larger background, we may now consider our one intact comedy and the larger fragments, beginning with *Dyskolos*, produced in 317/6. The play speaks directly to our concerns, but in order to see how it does careful attention must be given to its qualified and nuanced indications, initially in respect to the residence of the misanthropic protagonist Knemon. The god Pan, who speaks the prologue crucial for understanding the very atypical scene (as well as the complication) presented to the audience, asks us to imagine that the place is Phyle and that the shrine of the Nymphs from which he has emerged belongs to the "Phylasians—people able to farm the rocks here—a very celebrated sanctuary" (lines 1–4). Doubly remote by dint of its distance from Athens and its relative inaccessibility on the folded slopes of Mt. Parnes, Phyle was also, as just noted, a settlement of very small citizen population. To Pan's right (that is, the audience's left, the "country" side), "Knemon inhabits this farm before you" (lines 5–6), that is, in keeping with the findings of chapter 1, he actually resides on his land rather than in any supposed nucleated village center. Similarly, across the stage (the audience's right, the "town" side) dwells Gorgias (Knemon's estranged wife's son by her former husband) on his "little plot" (*choridion*) with his mother and loyal family slave (lines 23–27). Since, then, the two farmers reside on their own ground, the stage does not represent a village but rather two contiguous farms adjacent to the *nymphaion* of Pan.

The point is important, for it affords a clue as to what Pan means when he says of Knemon "he lives alone by himself" (line 30; cf. 331). These words cannot mean that he is the only occupant of his house, for the very same lines tell us that he has with him his daughter and old slave woman (lines 30–31). Nor are we at liberty to invoke a cultural explanation and suppose that females were simply invisible and did not merit notice, notwithstanding the occurrence of the phenomenon in other contexts and even with acknowledgment of the misogyny at various points in Menander's corpus. The daughter is legitimate and socially valuable as a counter in marriage; she plays a vital role in the working out of the plot; and she is in any case too visible to ignore. Indeed, if Knemon's loneliness were to be referred to the absence of a single person, that person would be a woman— his estranged wife Myrrhinē, for in a similar situation in the "Farmer" Kleainetos, described as "lonely and old," will remedy his predicament with marriage (lines 73–74). Rather, from the audience's perspective—that is, from an urban perspective—residence in the countryside, however hermetic or gregarious the person in question, of necessity entailed a certain amount of physical isolation whenever (as, in Attica, I have argued was normally the case) farmers lived on their land. The point is easily lost in the face of Knemon's misanthropy. "Not delighting in the crowd" (an extreme case of litotes), "he is ornery to everyone" (line 7); and, as Gorgias explains to his son Sostratos, "he works the farm all by himself, without the help of other people—whether family slave, hired hand from the area, or neighbor—his greatest pleasure being to see no human being" (lines 328–333). But the man's deviant unsociability should not cause us to lose sight of the very real and significant isolation that was part of the typical Attic farmer's life when compared to the dense settlement of the urban center familiar to the play's audience—indeed, partly visible from their seats as the play unfolds.

That Knemon's isolation is not to be reduced to mere personal idiosyncrasy is explicitly indicated elsewhere in Menander's text. Says Chaireas: "A poor farmer is exceedingly sharp, not just this man, but nearly all of them" (lines 129–131). Getas adds commentary on that poverty: "O this miserable creature! What a life he leads! This is unadulterated Attic farmer. Warring with rocks sprouting savory and sage, he garners pains, getting nothing good" (lines 603–606). Bitterness, then, is endemic to the Attic farmer, and it is perhaps only the form of its expression which in the present case renders Knemon quixotic and memorable. Eventually, he will bemoan his isolation (*ēremia*, lines 596–598) and, in a speech to Myrrhinē (his estranged wife) and Gorgias (her son), he will renounce his ill-conceived quest for independent self-sufficiency (lines 711–729). But even so we must continue to be careful not to mistake what I maintain is the typifying representation of a class with an individual's particular eccentricity. Isolation, impoverishment, uncertainty and anxiety, distrust and suspicion, bitterness expressed as anger—these are all qualities of Menander's generic representation of the Attic rural farmer, a representation which in the present case probably corresponded closely to the reality.

Comment on these harsh realities and, sometimes with them, the redeeming virtues of a rural existence is frequent. Set in one or the other Halai, "Self-Tormentor" (*Heauton Timoumenos*) presents a woman hanging on her loom, an old hag spinning thread, and a slave weaver-woman in wretched condition (129 and 130K-T). "A real man must excel in war; but farming—that's the work of a slave," says a character in an unknown play (560K-T). The slave in the "Farmer" tells two different, contrasting tales. First, one of Kleainetos's mattock-inflicted wound and resulting infection, inattention by barbarian house-slaves, and rescue by his future son-in-law (lines 46–62). But of that same farm he had just previously, and secondly, said: "I figure no one farms a field that is holier. For it produces myrtle, fine ivy, and such flowers! But if you sow other crops, it directly yields a fair return, no more, but in just measure" (lines 35–39). Similarly, a number of the maxims (excerpted from fuller texts in antiquity) point to compensating rewards or pleasures, sometimes vaguely ascribed to a divine-like Mother Earth. "The life of farmers possesses pleasure, consoling pains as it does with hopes" (559K-T, cf. *Gn. Mon.* 620). "The bitterness of farming has something sweet about it" (558K-T; *Gn. Mon.* 262); so also, in a pastoral setting: "The shepherd is pitied and then called 'sweetest' " (676K-T). "Peace nourishes a farmer well even on rocks, but war ill even on the plain" (556K-T). "Earth is the mother of all and communal nurse" (*Gn. Mon.* 511), but, like all Greek divinities, she may taketh away what she giveth: "Earth gives birth to all, then takes it back again" (*Gn. Mon.* 145).

Marking the climax of the agrarian ideology, suggestions that there is a moral dimension to the farmer's existence are sometimes encountered as well. "All that is gathered in season is goodwill repaid" (*Gn. Mon.* 9).

"Even among the rustics there is love of enlightenment" (*Gn. Mon.* 401).
"Plots producing poorly make people brave" ("Cousins," *Anepsioi*, line
57). Another speaker calls the country (*agros*) "the teacher of excellence
(*aretē*) and a free person's life (*biou . . . eleutherou*) for all people" ("Neck-
lace", *Plokion*, 338K-T). The adjective "free" may have been meant to suggest for the benefit of town-dwellers accustomed to equate farm labor with
servility, that as a matter of fact the country does offer something to free
people after all. Be that as it may, there is no denying that for Menander
the evaluation of the rural is inextricably bound up with complementary
valuations of the town, although, perhaps reflecting the complexities of
Athenian life, not always with consistent result. It all depended on who,
male or female, young or old, rich or poor, was doing the talking and in
what specific set of circumstances:

Any poor man (*penes*) who chooses to live in the town (*asty*) makes himself even
more dispirited. For whenever he gazes upon the luxurious man able to live in
leisure, then he can see how miserably he lives and how wretched his life. ("Neck-
lace," *Plokion*, fr. 336, lines 1–5)

The same sentiment is voiced by the slave in "Farmer" when he explains
to Myrrhinē that Kleainetos's decision to marry her daughter will improve
their present sorry lot:

Soon, they'll go there; he'll go back to the farm, taking her with him. You all will
cease battling poverty—that ill-willed and ornery beast—and at that, in the town
(*asty*). For I suppose you should either be rich or live in such a way that there
aren't lots of witnesses to your misfortune. For in these circumstances the solitude
of the country (*agros*) is something to be prayed for. (lines 76–82)

And, again, from "Water-jug" (*Hydria*), still another passage provides
contrasting commentary on the "loneliness" of the *dyskolos* Knemon:

How sweet is solitude for the man who loathes wicked ways! And how satisfying
a possession is a farm (*agros*) for the man not practicing a single evil thing—it will
nourish him well! From the masses comes only zealous competition. This luster of
the city (*polis*) does shine, I admit, but only for a brief time. (401K-T)

Both sides of the conflicted love-and-hate rural attitude are neatly illustrated, summarized, and reduced to their psychological essentials, in a
fragment of "Rustic" (*Agroikos*, alternatively titled *Hypobolimaios*, "Sup-
posititious Child"), preserved by an admiring Quintillian (1.10.18;

10.1.70). The text opposes to the "crowd, agora, thieves, dice, and hang-
outs"—whence one is bound to take away only lost money, enemies, and
plots—that man, counted most fortunate by the unknown speaker, "who
quickly returns whence he came, having gazed upon those magnificent
sights—the sun common to all, stars, water, clouds, and fire. Whether you
live a hundred, or just a few, years, you'll never see sights more magnificent than these" (416K-T).

An ideology so explicitly opposing rural excellence to the town's cor-
rupting influences might be thought proof against any potential feelings of
inferiority on the countryman's part, but Menander's *dramatis personae*
testify otherwise. Unidentified speakers from unidentified plays declare to
unnamed parties: "You pretend to be *agroikos* when in fact you're *poneros*"
(557K-T), with the evident meanings of the italicized words being "simple-
ton" and "rascal;" and "It takes a man to excel in war, for farming—that's
the work of a slave (*oiketēs*)" (560K-T). Elsewhere, we have some context.
From "Brothers" (*Adelphoi*), the fragments of which reveal a preoccupation with issues of goodness or wickedness, wealth or poverty, comes the
first person confession: "I, a rustic (*agroikos*), worker, sullen, embittered,
stingy. . . ." (11K-T). With similar diffidence, from *Georgos* the farmer
Kleainetos seems to have remarked: "I'm a rustic (*agroikos*) (and I won't
deny it), and I'm not entirely experienced in the ways of the town, but the
passage of time is making me more knowledgeable" (fr. 5 Arnott = 97K).
Thus Menander's ruralites, far from exuding a confidence born of any feelings of superiority towards the town, are disposed to allow themselves to
be measured and judged by the town's own standards. Since the word
agroikos had, by the classical period, already acquired pejorative connotations, it is particularly telling for the rural self-image that these speakers are
made to apply the term *to themselves*. Real farmers would not term themselves "rustics," much less "boors"—that is, they do not use the town's
representation of themselves as "Other." Menander's stage may have given
us a realistic portrayal of the Attic farmer in terms of the record reviewed
in the previous chapter, but this portrayal must also be conceded to contain elements of self-condemnation—whether true to the actual facts or
not we shall perhaps never know.

If we search for a single play exemplifying some of these themes in
more or less connected and intact form, then we must return to the *Dyskolos*. Pan's prologue introduces a rich man "farming property of many talents" whose young son, Sostratos, resides in the *asty* and has now by
chance arrived on the scene with some hunting friend (lines 39–43). For

the son, Phyle is a place neither to live nor to work in but to return to on occasion for pleasurable but nonproductive activity.[44] Upon his arrival, he finds Knemon's daughter, attended by a slave woman, drawing and heating water for a sacrifice—tasks which, in an Athenian urban setting, would have been executed only by slaves to the extent that, as usually is the case when visiting a well, one was required to venture out of doors. Accordingly, when Sostratos falls in love with the girl at first sight (at Pan's instigation), he remarks in an aside (not heard by her) that, though a rustic (*agroikos*), she is so *eleutheriōs* (lines 201–202). Thus the term "rustic" is opposed not by an expression meaning urban or urbane (say, *astikē*[45]), but by an adverb meaning, *au pied de la lettre*, "in the manner of a free person." Thereby Sostratos seems to implicitly ascribe a condition of servility to the countryside. The girl's gender may have disposed this male speaker to expect inferiority in her, but I rather suspect that the point is one of an urban conceit on the town-dwelling speaker's part that may be reduced to a simple syllogism: to reside in the country is to engage in manual labor; to engage in manual labor is to be servile; therefore, to reside in the country is to be servile.

7

Philosophy

THE ESTABLISHMENT OF A SIGNIFICANT cleft separating urban and rural in the formal administrative apparatuses of Greek city-states, and particularly Athens, leaves unanswered the questions how, and why, this state of affairs came to be. Should an answer be sought in explicit ancient testimony, no better beginning could be found than in the Aristotelian report regarding the tyrant Peisistratos's agrarian policy, with its ulterior motivation of keeping the rural population from venturing into the *asty* (*AthPol* 16.2–5). With the present chapter, we will continue the search, but with reference to a more speculative source, one which is uniquely rich but surprisingly heretofore untapped: the writings of the philosophers of Athens under the classical democracy.

The field of study now known as philosophy accounts for only a small segment of the range of activity of Greek *philosophoi* conducted in the name of *philosophia*. The "love of wisdom" embraced much of what in modern times is classified under several disciplinary rubrics relevant to the present study—history, political science, sociology, and economics. Furthermore, within its broad scope, *philosophia*, when its object was the structure of the state, encompassed a fundamental distinction as to the intent, latent or expressed, driving the business of speculation. Was the intent idealizing, to construct what since Thomas More has been known by his fanciful Greek formation a utopia (from Greek *ou*, "not," and *topos*, "place" and evidently punning on "*eu*topia")—a polity which certainly did not ever exist and which perhaps even the author himself would have conceded could not have existed? Or was it reformist, to bring about the improvement of actual, living polities, perhaps even with the purpose of providing guidance to a living ruler of an existing regime? To mention only the major Athenian works of the genre, to the former project would correspond Plato's *Republic*; to the latter, the same philosopher's monumental last surviving work, the *Laws*; the predecessors of Plato critiqued by

Aristotle in Book 2 of his *Politics;* and the 7th and 8th books of the *Politics* itself. But however different in approach, content, and result, the two genres of speculation seem to embody a similar overriding goal: to bring about the creation, on paper or in practice, of an orderly and stable commonwealth. Disorder and upheaval had been the legacy, and continuing bane, of the Greek historical experience. To effect a cure never ceased to be uppermost on the agenda of those who attempted to bring about improvements in the design of the classical city-state.

Not surprisingly, we are here concerned with a literary production evidencing considerable variety. The personal circumstances of the author (as, we shall see, obtain in the case of Plato); the favoring or avoidance of accepted paradigms (Cretan, Spartan, Athenian, or otherwise); the latent consequences of more fundamental, narrowly "philosophical" premises— all play roles in shaping the outcome of these utopian or revisionary explorations in the architecture of the *polis.* But underlying and unifying the varied urban-rural regimes now to be discussed are three recurrent themes:

(1) The new *polis*'s gross physical components—urban center, outlying countryside, mountain slope, and coastal harbor—will, I shall argue, be found to possess distinctive characteristics in keeping with their contemplated human populations. Topography, in other words, will acquire a characteristic human dimension as a consequence of its economic potential, military importance, or distinctive cultural milieu. The rural will be found to bear the stamp of deeply seated notions regarding the nature of its assumed or prescribed residential population and above all its agricultural work force.

(2) The specific treatment of rural spaces and populations will be found to be informed, and driven, by the ideal of the mythical Reign of Kronos. First expressed by Hesiod in the *Works and Days,* the notion of an agrarian rural paradise remains in currency throughout the lifetime of the Athenian utopian/reformist tradition. Applied to a strictly human setting, the Reign above all embodied the ideal of a spontaneously bountiful Earth that gave up its fruits with little or no toil.

(3) In the final analysis, rural spaces and populations will be systematically subordinated to the *asty.* The new city will boast a single principal conurbation, with agora, temples, and citizen residences, and adjacent to it will be situated a relatively sparsely populated countryside clearly marked as the source of the population's foodstuffs. It will be the countryside which will through its productivity render the ideal *polis* self-sufficient by removing the need for imports from abroad. It is the countryside that will

bring about the high level of civilization—usually (and paradoxically) portrayed as distinctly and uniquely urban—for the enjoyment of an elite class
occupied with non-agricultural pursuits such as military service, government, and the arts.

Reign of Kronos, Hippodamos of Miletos, and Phaleas of Chalkedon

Perhaps it is a measure of the Greeks' continuing lively inclination towards
utopian vision that the earliest surviving literature preserves just such a rural paradise. At the beginning of his Myth of Ages, Hesiod paints a vivid
portrait of the "golden" generation of mortals living under the Reign of
Kronos (*Works and Days* 109–120). Since Baldry's work on the invention
of the Golden Age, we know that the descriptor "golden" was a later ac-
cretion (perhaps an original contribution of Hesiod's own) and that the
Reign of Kronos, since it was independent of the scheme of a devolution
of metal-races, possessed a life of its own as *the* archetypal bygone age of
leisured happiness.[1] Here is Hesiod's text:

First of all, the immortals who have houses on Olympos made the golden race of
articulate humans. They were of the time of Kronos, when he ruled in heaven.
They lived like gods, with sorrowless hearts, far apart from toils and grief. Nor was
miserable old age upon them, but a match in feet and hands they rejoiced in feasts,
removed from all evils. They died as if overcome with sleep. All good things were
theirs. The grain-giving earth provided fruit on its own, in quantity and without
stint. At their pleasure and at peace, they lived off their fields with many good
things, rich in flocks and dear to the blessed gods. (*Works and Days*, 109–120)

The meaning of this vision for our subject requires that we distinguish
the visionary but unattainable from what might conceivably be realized
within the parameters of ancient Greek civilization. To be free from sor-
row, to escape the ravages of old age, in short to live like the gods themselves—these are aspirations of many a wish-fulfilling popular myth. But
the earthly, substantive content of the vision turns on agricultural labor:
the soil gave up its bounty spontaneously, so that humans, spared the debilitating effects of work in the fields, remained sound of limb and able, in
their leisure, to partake of "feasts, removed from all evils." In its essentials,
this was an attainable goal, if only the problem of work could be solved, if
only humans could devise or discover an alternative source of labor.

Because of its real-world relevance and potentiality, I believe, the Reign of Kronos, in its specifically agrarian aspect, remained in currency in later Greek antiquity. Athenian farmers extolled the tyranny of Peisistratos by comparing it to life under Kronos, according to *AthPol* 16.7. Since the same account sets out at considerable length the tyrant's agrarian policy which inter alia had resulted in increased prosperity (16.2–5), it is natural to associate with this policy the mention of "the life under Kronos" following in section 7. Much later, in the fifth century, the period of Kimon's ascendancy, prior to the rise of urban-based democratic politicians operating through governmental institutions, could be described by Plutarch as a return to the "communism" of the time of Kronos (*Kimon*, 10.6). Again, there is a link with rural agriculture, for Plutarch's comment is immediately preceded by his (second) mention of Kimon's practice of leaving his fields in the deme of Lakiadai open for anyone who wished to help himself to the harvest (10.6, cf. 10.1–2). Kimon's *megalophrosynē* (10.5, citing Kritias's word) has realized Hesiod's vision of a spontaneously bounteous earth (*aurora . . . automatē*, lines 117–118), by the provision of agricultural produce to the poor, who, free from labor, now have leisure for "public affairs alone" (10.1). Also in the fifth century, an Attic festival called Kronia, with Baldry a relic of the early worship of Kronos as the harvest god,[2] will continue to crop up in Old Comedy (usually as a symbol of obsolescence).[3] From these and other classical survivals, Dawson concluded that the legend of Kronos did no more than to provide "serious utopists" with a stock of metaphors,[4] but I am not so sure. The following discussion will reveal that this deeply seated and recurrent notion of an agrarian paradise, with its realistic focus of attention on manual agricultural labor, did more than Dawson suspects to shape the vision of the architects of the Greek "No-Place," and specifically its rural component.[5]

HIPPODAMOS OF MILETOS

Thanks to Aristotle's discussion and critique in Book Two of the writings in political theory preceding his own efforts in the *Politics*, we can identify at least one early figure whose contributions seem to have borne positively upon emerging conceptualizations of the urban, the rural, and their interrelations, Hippodamos of Miletos.[6] According to Aristotle, Hippodamos actually invented "the division of cities"—a rather vague formulation glossed and given more specific meaning by the immediately following reference to his "cutting up" (from *katatemnein*) of Peiraieus (2.5.1: 1267b). The plan is echoed in a later book when Aristotle writes of the disposition of private houses as "well cut (*eutomos*) in accordance with the newer and Hippodamian fashion" (7.10.4: 1330b). Scholars, however, have disagreed about just what it was that Aristotle is saying Hippodamos "invented." A once popular view was that he had in mind a checkerboard grid system, but archaeological discoveries in the Near East and Magna Graecia, where cities of greater antiquity long predate Hippodamos's work, prove that he could not have been the actual "inventor" of the rectilinear street and block arrangement, and it is unlikely that the well-traveled polymath Aristotle could have been mistaken on so fundamental a point. But the matter is worth pursuing further in the hope that "the Hippodamian fashion" will be found to include the articulation of rural spaces.

Perhaps the answer is to be found in the observable remains of the cities reported to have been designed by the Milesian? Thourioi is said by Diodorus Siculus (12.10.6–7) to have been laid out on a grid of four *plateiai* crisscrossing three *plateiai*, with the narrow spaces thus enclosed (*stenopoi*) filled with houses. But the association of Hippodamos with this plan lacks reliable attestation, since it depends entirely upon an emendation of an entry in Hesychios (s.v. *Hippodamou nemesis*). Nor, even if we could be sure of Hippodamos's role, are we able to test Diodorus's text, to judge from the remains reported on the site.[7] The case of Rhodes is more secure, for Strabo writes (14.654) that the city was founded during the Peloponnesian War "by the same architect as Peiraieus, so they say." Study of the site of the town (that is, of Rhodos, to be distinguished from the island as a whole) from the air and on the ground has revealed, according to McCredie's report, a grid consisting of three orders of division, a one stadion square quartered into half-stadion squares, these in turn each divided into six parts 100 by 150 feet.[8] The only obstruction to a Hippodamian Rhodos is a chronological one. Given the traditional association of the planner with the rebuilding of his city of citizenship, Miletos, soon after 479 (when he would presumably have been a grown man), he would have been too old to participate in the founding of Rhodos in 408/7. But, as Burns observes, no ancient testimony actually links Hippodamos to the rebuilding of Miletos (which, in any case, he suggests, may have been of later date); and, if one insists that it was the renewal of Miletos that somehow set Hippodamos on the path of city-planning, it is not necessary to assume that he actually participated in the project himself, only that he spent sufficient time there to become aware of the problems of planning and their solutions.[9] As for Peiraieus, while Aristotle's reference to Hippodamos's laying out of the town may never be confirmed by excavation since the classical site remains largely hidden by modern structures,[10] we are fortunate to have illuminating epigraphic evidence in the form of a series of *horoi* of the fifth century.[11] These stones originally marked boundaries between public and private land, defined specific public areas and structures, and, pertinently for the present discussion, indicated the limits of the Hippodamian "cutting up." The two texts in question read: "Here, up to this street, the town (*asty*) has been laid out (*nene/metai*)" (*IG* I² 893) and "Here, as far as this street, is the layout (*ne/mēsis*) of Mounichia" (*IG* I² 894). The Greek verb and noun at once recall Aristotle's statement that Hippodamos "cut up" (from *katanemein*) Peiraieus.[12]

But if these, and perhaps inferentially the other, *horoi* may therefore be taken as evidence for Hippodamian planning, it is evident, as commentators have realized, that *nemesis* (which may now be taken as the technical term represented by Aristotle's *diairesis*), far from simply indicating the establishment of a checkerboard rectangular grid, actually embraced a more comprehensive plan. McCredie writes of "a *system* with theoretical basis;" Burns, more concretely, of "the overall functional plan of the city;" and Gorman denies outright that the "division" has anything to do with literal urban planning.[13] Historiographically, it is such a "system" or "functional plan," not the checkerboard grid, that Hippodamos may, with Aristotle, be said to have invented. After all, the philosopher's point that Hippodamos was the first of "those not engaged in political activity" to speak on the subject of the "best" constitution (2.4.1:1267b) suggests activity transcending the mere laying out of streets. Nor is this all. Note that Aristotle's statement about the invention of *diairesis* refers not to *astē*, but to *poleis*, i.e. to the city-states in their entirety. The question for us to address now is whether Hippodamos's activity extended to rural as well as to the urban spaces which have occupied our attention up to this point. The possibility that it did is prompted by still another *horos*, *IG* II² 2623, which, if Kirchner's restoration is accepted, will have marked the limit of the deme-association's *chora*.[14]

Hippodamos's "best" constitution was to be based on a *polis* of very considerable dimensions (his term *myriandron* means a conventional 10,000) and divided into three classes (*merē*): artisans (*technitai*), farmers (*georgoi*), and "the military component in possession of arms" (2.5.2: 1267b). Aristotle continues that Hippodamos also divided the land (*chora*) into three parts (*merē*): sacred (*hiera*), public (*dēmosia*, later *koinē*), and private (*idia*). There follows a partial, but only partial, representation of the coordination of these two tripartite arrangements of people and territory. The sacred land lacks any assignment of population, for "they," Aristotle says (without specifying who "they" are), "will derive from it whatever is customary and appropriate for the gods." Aristotle adds nothing more on the nature of the sacred land, but contemporary practice suggests that it need not have been limited to sanctuaries and their architectural installations. If the sacred apparatus is to be self-sufficient, land for grazing or fodder will have been needed to produce a steady supply of sacrificial animals or, as historical practice would again suggest, to generate income through leases to outsiders. Be that as it may, the other two divisions of land are expressly of a preponderantly or even exclusively agricultural nature: the public land will provide the soldiers with their livelihood and the private land will be worked by the farmers. These latter distributions may strike us natural and unexceptional, but Aristotle, who presumably has the full text of Hippodamos's writings at his disposal, directs criticism at the theory's latent implications. For one, because only the soldiers will possess arms, the farmers, who will possess none, and the artisans, who will lack ownership of land as well, will be rendered powerless. So, he asks, what is the point of making them part of the Demos? They will become disaffected once they realize that, though formally enjoying the privilege of citizenship, they are without influence in a polity dominated by its soldiers (2.5.5–6: 1286a).

But it is a second criticism that bears more pointedly upon our concerns. For it was not clear at all to Aristotle of what use the farmers would be in Hippodamos's model state. The artisans, though landless, would provide goods needed by the state and make a living while doing so. But Hippodamos's farmers will work their private land only for themselves, since the soldiers' livelihood will be taken from the public (or common) land. The farmers stand outside the state, *ex hypothesi* not even (as in the case of a subsistence farming class removed from the economy) providing intermittent military service. Did Hippodamos imagine them as functional reproducers, supplying with excess population new artisans and soldiers? No less pressing a question concerns the workforce of the public (or common) land, for it manifestly does not consist of the soldiers themselves: if it did, Aristotle says, the military segment would be no different from the agricultural. (That the soldiers do not, on Aristotle's understanding of the plan, work that land themselves anticipates a salient feature of the imagined polities of both Plato and Aristotle). Commentators who, like Dawson, find in Hippodamos's scheme an imitation of Spartan arrangements, are naturally inclined to posit a servile population bound to the soil.[15] But Hippodamos evidently wrote nothing on this topic, since Aristotle's surmise that a work force corresponding neither to the soldiers nor to the farmers of the private land would constitute a "fourth segment (*morion*)" of the *polis* evidently had no basis in the text before him. Nonetheless, a "fourth segment" of slaves would make excellent sense here. The utopian writers do, as Dawson argues, consistently betray Laconizing tendencies,[16] and the failure to mention nonfree laborers would comport quite well with the usual historical invisibility of all population groups outside the citizen elites.

Artisans, farmers, and soldiers will together constitute the Demos in Hippodamos's *polis*, Aristotle observes, and from all three groups will be chosen the magistrates (*archontes*) (2.5.4: 1268a). So much is hardly surprising in the light of historical arrangements, above all those of classical Athens (whose port town, again, was laid out by Hippodamos), but (to look ahead to our discussions of Plato and Aristotle) the idea that the full franchise should be enjoyed by artisans and farmers can by no means be regarded as a given of utopian speculation. True, Aristotle finds domination by the soldiers, making impossible full participation by artisans and farmers, but for all we know (and we do not have before us, as Aristotle evidently did, the full text of Hippodamos's plan), the alleged imperfection is merely a latent and unforeseen consequence of his primary postulates.

Given such a societal order, can anything be deduced of a topographical nature? What about the seat of government, for example? Aristotle's discussion of the Milesian's legal, judicial, and constitutional recommendations is consistent with the supposition of a unified urban center, but that is all we can say. Possibly, as Dawson hazards, Hippodamos's plan was meant for Thourioi, but, as already noted, excavation to date has told us very little. Surely the man who laid out the town of Peiraieus was, or would become, familiar with urban spaces. Rhodos, we know with certainty, was founded as, and remained, a distinct conurbation and the hub of a vast main island, dependent island, and peraeic hinterland. Aristotle's only clue is that the three divisions segmented the *chora*, but this term may signify a state's entire territory, urban as well as rural.

The leading idea of Hippodamos's scheme, and perhaps his principal contribution to city planning, seems to have been a significant linkage between land and social/political class. But the precise nature of that linkage remains obscure. Dawson proposed that Hippodamos's first principle might have been the division of the territory into three parts corresponding to three orders of citizenry.[17] Were this true, the advance would have been momentous, not least in its possible influence on later theory. But no population is assigned to the "sacred" land, and the artisans are expressly said by Aristotle not to have possessed any land at all. Aristotle is unlikely to have misunderstood his source so badly as this. Besides, any assumption of a linkage solely on the grounds of numerical agreement is undercut by the report that Hippodamos recognized only *three* kinds of law (2.5.2: 1267b). If the number had, as it seems, special significance for the author, the three population groups and the three classes of land may well have been quite independent of one another. Nonetheless, it remains true that soldiers are to be assigned to one topographic division, nonmilitary farmers to another, while artisans, perhaps anticipating Plato's treatment of the *banausoi*, own no cultivable land, but are seemingly to be assigned to the *asty* presupposed by Hippodamos's provisions for legal, judicial, and governmental functions. This final assignment does, admittedly, go beyond Aristotle's text, but a landless artisan class domiciled in an urban center lacks no confirmation from classical Athens.

PHALEAS OF CHALKEDON

Similar thinking is detectable in another of Aristotle's predecessors, Phaleas of Chalkedon, the critique of whose scheme precedes the discussion of Hippodamos (2.4.2–13: 1266a–1267b). Nothing is known of Phaleas beyond what Aristotle tells us, but it is clear that his projected polity (perhaps, with Dawson, to be referred to some colonial venture)[18] amounted to an essentially agrarian rural regime. The underlying organizational principle (addressed to a problem recognized by the classical utopian writers as a prime seed of civil discord) was to be equality of the "estates" (*ktēseis*) of the citizens. Towards the end of his discussion, Aristotle expressly acknowledges that this rule applied only to the ownership of *land* (2.4.12: 1267b). To judge from the drift of the discussion, other types of property—his examples are slaves, cattle, and furniture—were not to be likewise subject to the principle of equality. As for groups outside the citizen class, the artisans (*technitai*) are to be public slaves (*dēmosioi*) and as such are not to count towards "the complement of the state" (that is, they are not to be citizens) (2.4.13: 1267b). Now, if the landed estates of all citizens are to be equal, if nonlanded property is so inconsequential as to be excused from the rule of equality imposed upon "estates," and if nonfarmers are to be debarred from citizenship and indeed are to be slaves, it is clear that what Phaleas envisioned was an egalitarian agrarian regime founded on land-ownership. But how do these slender hints of Phaleas's agrarian order relate to topography? Nothing Aristotle reports bears on residence, unless the choice of the term *ktēsis*, "farm," "estate," was intended to distinguish arable occupied by its owner from a mere "plot" (*chorion*). Again, as with Hippodamos, the *technitai*, disqualified from land ownership by their slave status and from an agricultural function by their occupational title, will have been residents of an *asty* to be presumed in any Greek polity, even a visionary one.

Both these predecessors of Plato's, it may be conjectured, were concerned with the design and peopling of the rural spaces of their utopian cities. To make the point may require some teasing of Aristotle's text, yet since we are dealing not with the intact writings of Hippodamos and Phaleas themselves, but with a commentator's necessarily highly abbreviated representation of those writings, a fair amount of room for conjecture is justified. At the very least, we are entitled to conclude that both theorists, while concerned primarily with sociopolitical issues, nonetheless perceived their hierarchies as significantly related to topography, urban and rural.

Plato: Deme, Place of Residence, and Urban Outlook

A third predecessor of Aristotle's is of course Plato, and it is to Plato himself that we must first come before addressing the Peripatetic's own utopian prescriptions. Whether Plato actually had a first-hand acquaintance with the writings or ideas of Hippodamos and Phaleas we cannot be sure, since he neither mentions them by name nor, on Aristotle's evidence, betrays any obvious intellectual debt. But this hardly matters, for what is most striking about Plato is the innovativeness, indeed the idiosyncrasy, of his agenda of topics and of his solutions to the set of problems underlying and prompting all Greco-Roman utopian schemes, not to mention the peculiar expression of his ideas in the form of "dramatic" dialogues. Therefore, how can we hope to appreciate his proposals unless we first understand Plato himself—or at least those elements of his background, personal circumstances, and guiding assumptions that might have conditioned his thoughts about the rural in his various utopian communities? We cannot. Only once these preliminaries have been addressed will it be possible to engage again the themes already present in the tradition and broached in the writings of his forerunners.[19]

Plato belonged to a family line extending from Dropides, archon of 645/4, down to Plato's own death nearly three centuries later in 348/7. Although, according to Davies' statement, only the philosopher's *choregia* in the boys' dithyramb formally qualifies the line as liturgical (and even it was supported by a subsidy from Dion: Plutarch, *Aristeides* 1.4, *Dion* 17.5; Diogenes Laertius, 3.3), it is clear from numerous indications, including Plato's own personal financial circumstances, that on the whole the families of Kritias, Solon, and Plato were "propertied."[20] For our purposes, the first question is what form or forms that property took, especially residential property.

An initial clue—one strangely passed over lightly in modern accounts of Plato's life—is that his deme was Kollytos (Diogenes Laertius, 3.3). Kollytos, according to Traill's most recent assignments, was one of the five demes situated within the circuit wall and probably lay to the south of the Acropolis.[21] To its west stretched Koile and Melite. Melite we know bordered on Kollytos, since Eratosthenes (cited by Strabo 1.4.7: 65), illustrating a point about the absence of marked boundaries, instances Kollytos and Melite, where there were "no accurate *horoi*" such as "*stelai* or *periboloi*." Some clues about the deme's character, urban or otherwise, are also available. Kollytos—and Kollytos alone of the central intraurban demes—is reported to have celebrated *ta Dionysia kat'agrous* ("The Dionysia in the Fields").[22] But in Plato's case, perhaps greater significance may be found in the proximity of the so-called Industrial District, although Rodney Young, in his detailed study of the physical remains, while leaving Kollytos open as a possibility, inclined towards Melite as the deme of its location.[23] "Industrial" is not of course a term of ancient origin and is in fact misleading, because it obscures the fact that much of the infrastructure of the district was residential. Several of the "shops" seem to have doubled as the residence of the shopkeeper.[24] But the presence of residences in no way compromises the fact that the area was as thoroughly urban as an ancient Greek space can be. Assignment of the District to the one deme or the other (or both), furthermore, is congruent with, indeed strongly supported by, the fact that Melite and Kollytos rank first and third respectively in the total number of metics of known deme-affiliation, metics being probable candidates for a labor force in any industrial setting.[25] As for citizens, while Melite, with a bouleutic quota of 7, boasted a substantial population, Kollytos, at 3, nominally stood fully one-half below this level. These figures suggest that industrially employed resident aliens probably accounted for a sizable fraction of the residents of Plato's deme.

Since Eratosthenes testifies that the boundary between the two demes was not marked, a more or less continuous settlement of the area might render insignificant for our purposes whether the Industrial District actually lay in Plato's Kollytos. Doubtless this is precisely Eratosthenes' point: that the development of a continuous urban infrastructure had obliterated any natural (or even human-made) boundary between the two demes. A resident of Kollytos might well have imagined himself as part of the District even if it was actually situated or centered in Melite. Be that as it may, much of significance follows for our deeper appreciation of Plato's writings. We can understand his frequent mention of craftspeople and use of crafts metaphors and images throughout his opus. We can find a new dimension of his attachment to Socrates, the son of a stoneworker (Diogenes Laertius, 5.18) and himself an acquaintance of various *demiourgoi*.[26] But, contrariwise, it is also difficult to escape the conclusion that these facts are somehow linked to the philosopher's well-known antipathy to banausic labor. Had familiarity bred contempt? And we may wonder about a possible connection with Plato's negative evaluation of the agricultural labor characteristic of the rural settings in the utopian polities which we will soon be examining.

More of significance could be learned if we could be sure of the location of Plato's actual residence or—equally likely in the case of a man of his wealth, social connections, and leisured intellectual activities—residences. Nothing whatever stands in the way of his being a inhabitant of the deme of his affiliation once we rid ourselves of the notion, now exploded by John Dillon, that he must have lived at the site of his "school," the Academy, situated to the northwest outside the walls in the outer Kerameikos.[27] A sticking point might seem to be the necessity of frequent commutes by foot between Kollytos and the Academy. But the difficulty is only apparent. For one thing, as the dialogues show, lengthy walks, even by philosophers in old age, were not uncommon;[28] and the ambulatory activities of the "Peripatetics" in particular cement the tight connection between movement on foot and intellectual cogitation. Given a route along the relevant streets and through the Dipylon Gate, the one-way distance for a foot-traveler between Kollytos and the Academy would be only about 2 1/2 kilometers. Frequent walks back and forth between deme and "school" are certainly not beyond the realm of possibility.

The Academy itself is in any event not a promising candidate for the primary residence at any time, since only minor structures are associated by the sources with its grounds. Dillon instances a tale about Xenokrates, who Diogenes says "spent most of his time in the Academy," how the notorious courtesan Phryne once sought refuge in his *oikidion* in which there was but a single small couch (*klinidion*) (4.6–7)—"not, one would think, proper lodgings for the Scholarch of the Academy."[29] An additional argument is suggested by the record of Plato's movable financial resources at the time of his death. The philosopher's estate is reported by Diogenes to have been worth three minas—a silver phiale weighing 165 drachmas, a cup weighing 45 drachmas, a gold ring and gold earring (together worth four drachmas, three obols), a debt of three minas owed Plato by Eukleides, five slaves (Artemis, now enfranchised, and four *oiketai*), furniture, and no outstanding debts (3.42–43)—hardly what one would expect to find in a one-room hut in a public sanctuary. And even if Plato did at some point adopt such a mode of living, the change will not have antedated ca. 385 when, upon his return from abroad, he acquired the property in the Academy and set up his "school." Plato was now about 45 years of age, leaving more than sufficient time for the formation of any attitudes in response to residence in or near the Industrial District. Nor, at the end of his life, do the reported circumstances surrounding the location of the philosopher's tomb alter this conclusion. Diogenes' statement (3.41) that the grave was located at the Academy, "where he spent the greatest time in philosophical activity," even if the point about the length of his time at the Academy is literally true (and it is difficult to imagine how such a fact could have been ascertained by Diogenes), need imply nothing regarding Plato's *residence* during this time. Burial in the sanctuary may have had as much to do with sentiment (such as burial in Arlington National Cemetery or a church columbarium) as with his (or anyone else's) place of residence. Supporting these particular considerations, too, is the now well-established fact that, while relocation from rural Attica to urbanized areas was relatively common, the sources, and especially the tombstones, fail to document any significant movement in the opposite direction.[30] Relocation of Plato's residence from Kollytos to Academy, though conceivable, is therefore statistically improbable.

An urban residence for Plato is also strongly favored by Socrates' reference in his trial of 399 to his supporter Krito, the father of Kritoboulos, whom he describes as a man of his own age and fellow demesman (*Apology* 33e). The demonstrated intimate bond between the two men makes better sense on the supposition that Socrates (*PA* 13101) and Krito (*PA* 8823) actually resided in the deme of their shared affiliation, Alopeke. Since, furthermore, Alopeke was a suburban deme, lying only a short distance outside the walls to the southeast of Kollytos, Socrates' relationship with my urban Plato would become more comprehensible into the bargain. Besides, if Socrates could be said to have a metier, it was *demiourgia:* His father had been a stoneworker (*lithourgos*, Diogenes Laertius 5.18), and since a law of Solon attached a severe penalty to the father who had failed to teach his son a trade,[31] it is probable that stoneworking was to have been Socrates' profession as well. Accordingly, when Diogenes reports that Krito "removed" Socrates from the *ergasterion* (5.21), he very likely refers to his father's own workshop. And later it was in *ergasteria* as well as in the Agora that Socrates subsequently carried on his philosophical discussions, for visits by the philosopher to a reinmaker's and a cobbler's—the latter strikingly illustrated by the excavators' discoveries in the Industrial District—are recorded in trustworthy sources.[32] Not surprisingly, therefore, the dramatic settings of the "dialogues" selected or invented by Plato not infrequently, as we shall soon see, belong to identifiable places in the heart of urban Athens, although they do not, whether by conscious design or not, include the shops mentioned in the literary sources. Socrates, as a famous passage in the *Phaidros* (227a–230a; see below) explicitly reminds us, appears to have been thoroughly urban with reference to place of domicile, work, movements, and even the final days leading up to and including his death. We might expect the same to have been true of his principal disciple.

But, if Plato resided in the town, he also, as we know from his will, was the owner of two plots (*choria*) outside the walls: one, of unknown size, in the deme Iphistiadai (Diogenes Laertius, 3.41); the other, also of unknown size, in the deme Eiresidai (3.42). According to Traill's latest map reflecting his placement of the deme-centers, Iphistiadai, situated on the road to the temple at Kephisia (to the NNE of the urban center), lay about 8 kilometers from the *asty* as the crow flies, probably too far to permit a regular commute by foot between the Agora area and the Academy. Eiresidai, to the NNW, was much closer, about 2 kilometers as the crow flies, and indeed Dillon suggests it as the location of Plato's residence during the time of his activity at the Academy.[33] But no evidence, direct or indirect, favors this surmise. For one thing, the will, our sole source on the properties, fails to mention a dwelling or structure of any description on either *chorion*. Note, too, that, again according to the will, the plot at Iphistiadai was bounded by properties of men of Phrearrhioi and Cholleidai, the plot at Eiresidai by properties belonging to two Myrrhinousioi and a Xypetaion. Since none of these are demesmen, the suspicion naturally arises that some or all, including Plato, resided elsewhere than on these lands. Like many of his social peers, Plato may have been an urban-dwelling absentee landlord.[34]

An inner-city residence and home base, if obtaining during the period of the composition of the dialogues, might be expected to have left discernible traces in those writings. Since the dialogues are in many cases fitted out with a so-called "dramatic" setting, it is here, at the highest level of literary organization, that one could reasonably begin the search for such influence.[35] By my count, just nineteen of the forty dialogues of the canon can be said to possess such a setting, although in several instances it is slight, mentioned in passing, and only incidental to the topic under discussion. If there is a single generalization that may be applied across the board (actually, to every case but one), it is that, to the extent that "Socrates" is involved as an interlocutor, the mise-en-scène necessarily concerns events of the more or less recent past—or at least during the philosopher's lifetime—and is set somewhere in or around his city of citizenship and residence, Athens.

About half of the positive cases with certainty or probability fall in or in close proximity to the urban center. Let us briefly review these examples. The four dialogues set in the time of Socrates' trial and execution are predictably situated in appropriate locales in and around the Agora: the Stoa Basileios (*Euthyphro*, 2a),[36] an unspecified courtroom (*Apology*, 17d, 29a, 40b), the state prison house adjacent to the Agora (*Kriton*, 43a, 53d; *Phaedo*, 57a, 58c, 59d, e, 114c). The *Symposium* recreates a dinner party at the house of Agathon (174a, e) located somewhere in or near the town by internal textual evidence.[37] The *Gorgias* is placed by Dodds initially out of doors, perhaps at the entrance to a gymnasium (*palaistra* at 456d) or other public building where the famous sophist has been lecturing, later within the building itself.[38] Similarly public (as well as urban) in setting are four dialogues staged at a site of military or gymnastic exercise: *Laches* (fighting in hoplite armor, 178a), *Theaitetos* (*palaistra*, 162b, 181a), *Charmides* (the palaistra of Taureas opposite the shrine of Basile, 153a, 155d), and *Lysis* (a *palaistra* just outside the northern wall, 206d-e).[39] About the school of

Dionysios that figures in the spurious *Rivals* (132a) we have no clue as to location, textual or otherwise.

Similarly with the explicitly extramural settings. The *Lysis* opens with Socrates walking directly from the Academy to the Lyceum, by the road skirting the outside of the walls, until he meets a group of men at a little gate at the source of the Panops, where a newly built *palaistra* is pointed out to him (203a–204a). The *Euthydemos* is set in the Lyceum itself (271a). The bank of the Ilissos River, which extends from the northeast to the southwest just outside the southeastern segment of the walls, provides a memorable venue for the philosophical saunter of the *Phaidros* (227a–230e) and, perhaps less memorably, for another ambulation towards the gymnasium at Kynosarges in the *Axiochos* (364a, 372a). Polemarchos's house in Peiraieus (1.327a–328b), the setting of the *Republic*, appears merely to parallel the domestic scene of the *Symposium*, but may equally well be viewed as a special case of what might be termed the "harbor motif." Several examples are at hand. In the initial speech at the beginning of the *Symposium*, Apollodoros recalls from the day before yesterday his walk from Phaleron up to the town (172a). Similarly, at the opening of the *Theaitetos* Eukleides reveals to Terpsion that (from the vantage point of their present situation in town) he had, when Terpsion had looked for and could not find him, been on his way down to the harbor (presumably Peiraieus) when he met Theaitetos being carried to Athens from the camp at Corinth (142a). Another spurious fragment, the *Halcyon*, is placed on the beach at Phaleron (M. D. McLeod, *Luciani Opera* IV, Oxford 1987, §1 and 8); and although the dialogue is not the work of Plato's own hand, at least this detail preserves someone's idea of a setting that Plato might have thought appropriate. Why harbors? Besides the creation of an aura of verisimilitude by the mention of known places, the device may serve to impart a sense of movement. But the destination, or at least the point of reference, of any such movement tends, as the examples illustrate, to be a town, and in particular the town of Athens.

The dialogues' settings are commonly termed "dramatic" and that they may be in some cases, but they are also, we now see, conspicuously topographic, monumental, public (save the odd private residence), occasionally out of doors (or nearly so, as the Royal Stoa in the *Euthyphro* illustrates), Athenian, and above all urban. With regard to the last point, we must never lose sight of the fact that every Athenian reader appreciated (without explicit comment from Plato himself being necessary) that the

Academy, the Lyceum, the road between them, the Ilissos River, even a private house in Peiraieus were out and out elements of the built, inner-city environment or so closely proximate to that environment as to render impossible any illusion of open spaces, wildness, or rusticity. This result, I suggest, is to be attributed in part to the urban origins, residence, and likely ambulatory habits of the author explored at the outset of our discussion. Save for his properties in Iphistiadai and Eiresidai, Plato may well not have been familiar with rural spaces outside his own apparently circumscribed urban experiences. But it is also of course a consequence of the essentially urban—and more specifically *Athenian* urban—nature of the philosophical enterprise, for only the residential center of a wealthy state like Athens could provide the necessary critical mass of educated and leisured listeners and disciples, adequate centrally located public and accessible places for groups to gather for debate and instruction, and the reservoir of experience with which to inform discussion of topics such as politics, the arts, and education. Plato himself may have journeyed at various times in his life to Pella, Mytilene, Thourioi, and Syracuse, but he did not (as he might have) set his dialogues in these places. Rather, paralleling the operation of the "harbor motif," foreigners such as the Sicilian Gorgias must come to Athens, to the Agora and its environs, and to Socrates.

But is nothing to be said of the vast expanses of rural Attica outside the walls and the immediate suburban appendages? The rural did not entirely escape Plato's attention, not even in his overtly urban productions. While no dialogue other than the *Laws* is set in a genuinely rural locale, Plato does as it were bring the country into his urban settings by a dramatic device that might be called the "arrival motif." Mention has been made already of Apollodoros's journey from his house at Phaleron up to the town in the *Symposium* (172a), to which may be added from the *Republic* the story of Leontios's sighting of corpses on his way up from Peiraieus under the outer face of the northern Long Wall (439e) and Hippokrates' late arrival in town "from Oinoe" in the *Protagoras* (310c).[40] At the opening of the *Theaitetos*, set in Megara (142c1), Terpsion the Megarian (the same man present at Socrates' death, *Phaidon* 59c), has just arrived in town "from the country" (142a, 143a) only to fail to find in the Agora Eukleides who, on his way down to the harbor, had met Theaitetos being carried to Athens from the camp at Corinth (142a). But this is mere preliminary staging; the dialogue that follows is a secondhand rendition based on Eukleides' notes of his interviews with Socrates *in Athens* (142c–d, 143a).[41] Plato permits extraurban arrivals (and of course references), but his subject, and its setting, are usually urban, whether Athens or, presumably in the case of the uniquely non-Athenian prologue of the *Theaitetos*, Megara. Only at the end of his life, in his final dialogue, will he place the massive reappraisal of his utopian vision of the ideal polity in a significantly non-Athenian and nonurban setting.

But before we address that ultimate vision, let us try to exploit further Plato's handling of his otherwise exclusively Athenian settings. Athenian scenes, Athenian interlocutors, Athenian subject matter—all should lead one to expect references to Attic topography, perhaps rural as well as urban, and specifically in the form of Athenian demes and demotics. The expectation is not disappointed. Twenty-three of the 139 constitutional demes receive mention in some form:[42] Acharnai (demotic, *Gorg.* 495d), Aixone (demotics, *Lach.* 197c; *Lys.* 204e), Alopeke (demotic, *Gorg.* 495d; cf. *Apol.* 33e, where Kriton is said to be a fellow demotes of Socrates), Anagyrous (*demotai* honor demesman, *Theag.* 127e), Aphidna (demotic, *Gorg.* 487c), Cholargos (demotic, *Gorg.* 487c), Eleusis (place, *Menex.* 243e, cf. [*Ax.*] 371e), Erchia (place, *Alc.* I 123c), Kephisia (demotic, *Apol.* 33e), Kydathenaion (demotic, *Symp.* 173b), Marathon (ten references to battle of 490), Melite (place, *Parm.* 126c), Myrrhinous (demotics, *Protag.* 315c, *Symp.* 176d, *Phdr.* 244a), Oinoe (place, *Prot.* 310c), Paiania (demotics, *Euthyd.* 273a, *Phdo.* 59b, *Rep.* 328b, *Lys.* 203a), Peiraieus (five references, three to harbor, two in connection with late fifth century upheavals), Phaleron (place, *Symp.* 172a; demotic, *Symp.* 172a), Pithos ("he is a Pitheus of the demes," *Euthphr.* 2b), Prospalta (demotic, *Cratyl.* 396d), Rhamnous (demotic, *Menex.* 236a), Sounion (place, *Crit.* 43d; demotic, *Theaet.* 144c), Sphettos (demotic, *Apol.* 33a), Steiria (toponymic adjective, *Hipp.* 229a). At first glance, the most impressive dimension of these toponymic references is their geographical breadth, for a mapping of the twenty-three demes reveals a surprisingly uniform distribution over the entire expanse of Attica, no region, urban or rural, being without example. But the initial impression is illusory. Simply consider the 17 demes (accounting for a dozen of the 23 demes) for which a demotic occurs. Notoriously, all are agreed that a demotic by itself is of little meaning absent some indication of the bearer's place of residence. That many of these Athenians with rural demotics may well have been urbanites of long standing is amply supported by recent studies demonstrating considerable relocation from rural demes to the urbanized areas.[43] Besides, Plato's use of the demotic was long ago suspected to be subject to literary motivations;[44] and in any event his variable and inconsistent use (or non-use) of demotics, patronymics, or simple unadorned *praenomina* in lists of names reveals an absence of serious interest in the demotic *qua* indication of place, rural or otherwise.[45]

Rather, if Plato has an interest, it is in the deme as a social entity. Of the 74 occurrences of the word *demos* in the Platonic corpus, while the great majority have to do with the Demos of the Athenians, a few do acknowledge the deme in its capacity as internally organized communal association. Historically, references are made to the daughter of the deme's founder-archegete (*Lys.* 205d) and to "the herm which he (Hipparchos) placed along the roads in the middle of the *asty* and the demes" (*Hipp.* 228d-229a). In the utopian future, the city of the *Laws* will be organized by demes alongside *phratriai* and *komai* (5.746d) and a citizen will be officially known by his "father's name, phyle, and the deme to which he belongs" (6.753c). Where Plato alludes parenthetically to his own contemporary world of fourth-century Athens, the allied term *demotes* (-*ai*) fairly consistently suggests close association, even intimacy: at *Apology* 33e, Socrates characterizes Kriton as "my age-mate and *demotes*"; at Laches 180c, Laches says that it would have been natural for Lysimachos to call upon his *demotes* Socrates to educate his son; at 180d, Lysimachos observes that one's *demotes* is a particularly suitable person to give advice to; at 187e, Nikias avers that sons of fellow *demotai* are likely to meet one another at deme functions; at *Theages* 121d, age-mates and *demotai* are to join in a trip to the *asty*; and at 127e, Demodoros is said to be the most respected by his *demotai* the Anagyrasioi. Throughout these examples, Plato is obviously not concerned with the deme as place, but rather with the cultural phenomenon that fellow demesmen (who are not necessarily, it must be kept in mind, residents of the deme of membership) naturally develop bonds of familiarity and reciprocity.

All such thinking might well have developed within, and been applied exclusively to, an urban environment. Not once in all the corpus of Platonic writings prior to the *Laws* can be found an attempt to portray a rural subject—place, settlement, community, culture, or personality—from other than an urban perspective. Even the celebrated stroll along the Ilissos in the opening scene of the Phaidros (227a–230e), far from betraying an awareness of or interest in the rural, explicitly indicates the opposite.[46] Socrates has found *Phaidros* walking outside the wall. Phaidros has just spent a long time with Lysias at Epikrates' house near the Olympieion "in the town" [47] and on Akoumenos's advice has sought out the roads (*hodoi*) in preference to the streets (*dromoi*). At length, they decide to turn aside and follow the Ilissos and find a place to sit. Both barefoot, they pick a grassy spot two or three stades further along underneath a tall plane tree (and a shady willow) at the crossing to the precinct of Agra, where there is an altar of Boreas. The cicadas are singing. Yet, although it is Socrates, not Phaidros, who is said to be familiar with this location made famous as the scene of the abduction of Oreithyia by Boreas, Phaidros remarks: "You appear to be a most out-of-place person (*atopotatos*, from *a-*, "without"; *topos*, "place"). For you quite resemble a foreigner (*xenos*) who is being led around and not a local (*epichorios*). You don't venture outside the town (*asty*) or go abroad beyond the borders (*hyperoria*); in fact to me at least it seems you don't go outside the walls at all." Socrates responds: "Forgive me, my friend, but I am fond of learning. Now, while the countryside (*ta choria*, literally "places") and the trees aren't likely to teach me anything, the people in the town (*asty*) do." As if this bald declaration were not clear enough, he then underscores his resistance to leaving by accusing Phaidros of administering a drug to him, comparing the use of a branch or fruit to lead a hungry animal. "Just so," he closes, "you will apparently lead me around all of Attica, to any point you wish." This final remark resumes the spatial hyperbole of Socrates' own vow that he is so determined to hear Phaidros's account of his conversation with Lysias that he will extend the *peripatos* to Megara (and, in the words of Herodikos, "go to the wall and back") (227d). But, in the event, at no point do the two venture significantly beyond the outer face of the wall. Topographically, the location is precisely in accord with the extramural but still suburban situations of the philosophical schools housed in the Academy, Lyceum, and gymnasium at Kynosarges—a spot sufficiently removed from the distractions of the inner city as to make secluded philosophical contemplation possible, while at the same time giving ready access to stoas and other public buildings, to a large pool of potential listeners and disciples, and to the private home of an Agathon.[48] Thus in this at first glance idyllic rustic setting, Socrates, a demesman of Alopeke (situated just a short distance outside the walls to the south), despite initial appearances here of wildness and solitude, has remained true to the urban orientation of his speculative calling: philosophy, as he says, is the business of "the people in the town" (230d).

Plato's Social Topography: Rural Spaces and Society in the *Republic*, *Kritias*, and *Laws*, Book 3

Such urban origins, associations, and locales, it seems to me, should have left their mark upon Plato's thinking and writing about varying topographical spaces and the peoples and cultures which occupy them. To look ahead, I shall argue that Plato's exclusively urban personal experience caused him, in his initial effort at *polis*-design, the *Republic*, not to fully appreciate the crucial role of topography and of the rural in particular. At a later stage, however, we shall find in his quasi-historical explorations of past polities in the *Kritias* and *Laws* an awareness of the necessity of conceptualizing institutions in spatial terms and of bringing his stratified populations into significant relation with the lay of the land and its distinctive resources.[49]

To begin, and in order to keep control of a large and widely scattered body of Platonic passages, it will be necessary to adopt a rough threefold categorization:

(1) Literary descriptions of imagined primordial or prehistoric polities: the warring lost civilizations of Atlantis and of antediluvian Athens in the *Kritias*, and the recapitulation of the growth of human civilization embedded in book 3 of the *Laws*. Since these constructions are largely or entirely the products of Plato's imagination, their detailed handling of their subject matter is highly relevant to any appraisal of his conceptualization of the rural.

(2) A sizable miscellaneous scattering of passages across a large number of dialogues, including many merely illustrative or metaphorical allusions to farmers, villagers, town-dwellers, etc. Because virtually all this material is incidental to the topic under discussion, the judgments it entails are likely to represent deeply seated attitudes resistant to change over time and thereby justifying combination of passages from dialogues widely separated in subject matter and date.[50]

(3) The comprehensive master blueprints of the *Republic* and the *Laws*.

With this categorization in mind, we shall now attempt to construct a crude "social topography," in which the various components of Plato's physical topographic landscape will be found to be significantly (or not) related to elements of his imagined, prehistoric, contemporary, or envisioned societies. Passages relevant to this concern occur across a wide range of the dialogues, but the more or less self-contained, free-standing visionary polities are confined to just three: the *Republic*, *Kritias*, and *Laws*. Because, fortunately, internal evidence establishes the relative chronological order of these works, it will be possible to take them up in sequence in the hope of uncovering a process of development. And to anticipate one my conclusions, this is precisely what we shall find. Let us begin, then, with the *Republic*.

THE REPUBLIC AND OTHER DIALOGUES BEFORE THE LAWS

The *Republic* is a virtual topographical blank, and what little Plato does give us concerning the rural component is largely confined to brief characterizations of mere topographically appropriate occupational categories. Rather, the concerns of the dialogue are with more fundamental organizational—constitutional, institutional, and political—matters. To the problem of internal instability, endemic in the historical city-state before and during Plato's time, he responds by moving boldly to remove the sources of discord. This is accomplished primarily by elimination of the family, the abolition of private property, and the institution of a hierarchical system of castes. But it is only incidentally to these larger projects that a few hints come our way of what Fair City (Kallipolis, 7.527c) would have ended up looking like at the level of specific societal and cultural—not to mention topographic—detail. But even hints may acquire significance when considered against the background of our second category of textual evidence—the author's attitudes as revealed by a scattering of passages across the entire corpus (excepting the *Laws*, which I reserve for separate treatment at the end of our discussion).

Any reconstruction of a city-state topography is rendered well-nigh impossible when, as in the case of the *Republic*, the word for town, *asty*, has not a single occurrence in the actual description of the envisioned polity.[51] The opposing term, *chora*, has occasional use of a state's entire territory (3.388a, 414e; 4.423b) and in the abstract sense of "place" (6.495c, 7.516b), but only one occurrence with reference to rural lands per se: at 2.373d, where in the course of a discussion of the expansion of the *chora* with a view to increasing food production, it is suggested that a portion of a neighboring state's land be appropriated in order to have enough for "pasture and plowing." Nor is the situation improved if we look for "the rural" in the form of rural settlements. In the *Republic*, the Athenian Plato never uses *dēmos* in the Athenian technical sense of constitutionalized vil-

lage (or village of any description); and the nontechnical companion term
for rural nucleated settlement, *kōmē*, has only one use. At 5.475 "the
Dionysiac festivals . . . in towns or in the country villages" were probably
brought to Plato's mind by the Atticawide celebration of the *Dionysia
kat'agrous* familiar to residents of Athens, even a town dweller like Plato,
since his own intramural deme, Kollytos, as we observed earlier, is exceptionally known to have hosted the festival. Rather, when the author of the
Republic wants to say something directly about the countryside, his term
of preference is *agros*, "field," sometimes in the singular but more often in
the plural: the sort of foods they boil "in the country" (2.372c), the piccolo
used by shepherds "in the fields" (3.399d), and trips "into the country"
(8.563d, singular; 7.541a, plural).[52] But while these few passages offer us little help, one major, though indirect, source of insight remains: the author's
extensive references to the countryside as the scene of a distinctive type of
occupation and of a corresponding set of behaviors—that is, to farmers and
rusticity.[53]

And how do these workers and these behaviors fare in Plato's hands?
The farmer (*georgos*) is sufficiently characterized in the *Republic* to reveal
his role in the utopia's economy and society. Farmers will comprise one of
the four or five irreducible components of the economically self-sufficient
polity (2.369d). Farmers, like other workers in Plato's state, are to pursue
only a single occupation (2.369e, 374b; 3.397e; 8.547d). Farmers will produce goods for the nonfarming population (2.371a), an inevitable consequence of the mandated absence of imported foodstuffs. Farmers, because
they will stick to farming, will not make their own tools (2.370c). Nor will
they have time to waste selling their produce in the marketplace, thereby
necessitating the emergence of a (despised) retailing class (2.371c). At the
same time, however, removal from the urban center will not mean that the
farmers will escape the watchful attention of the authorities. The farmers
are not to be "clothed in robes and gold"—that is, they are not to be allowed to become too happy, lest they cease to be farmers and so threaten
the welfare of the state (4.420e-421b). They are in any event unlikely in
Plato's ideal state to be so clothed, since farmers are clearly marked as a distinctly inferior class. Deserters, cowards, and other such malfeasants are to
be reduced to the status of artisan or farmer, says the text (5.468a). The
farmer's inferiority implied here is reflected in the hierarchy embodied in
the tale aired in Book 3, that the god mingled gold in the generation of
rulers, silver in that of helpers, and iron and brass in "the farmers and other
craftsmen" (4.415c). Does topography, i.e. removal from the preferred

space of the town, account for this low evaluation? Evidently not, for the herders (*aipoloi, boukoloi, nomeis, poimenes*, and *subotai*—"goatherds," "cowherds," "herders," "shepherds," and "swineherds")—despite their frequent mention in various contexts, seem to have escaped entirely the pejorative characterization of the farmers with whom they share the rural countryside. The explanation, I suspect, is literary: that Plato's frequent metaphorical styling of kings, rulers, and statesmen as "shepherds of men" or the like required that they be handled in at least a neutral manner, whereas the farmer plays no such figurative role. Socially, too, since herders will have ranked well below citizen *georgoi*, their status may have placed them out of reach of, and immune to, Plato's general disparagement of menial laborers.

Not surprisingly, the divinely sanctioned and legally defined social inferiority of the farmer is repeatedly reinforced in the *Republic* and other dialogues by Plato's handling of the conceptual field of rusticity (*agroikia*, "rusticity"; *agroikos*, "rustic", etc.), the quality emblematic of the farmer and his work and, significantly in view of Plato's preference for the word *agros/oi* as a locution for "the rural", derived from the word for "field." Nearly every one of the uses of *agroikia* (five), *agroikizomai* (one, "to be rustic"), and *agroikos* (22) is pejorative, with the demeaning intent often driven home by the author's coupling with the word a second term of explicitly negative meaning or connotation. For example, from the *Republic*, "they call moderation and orderly expenditure rusticity and servility" (8.560d), the soul of the ill-adjusted is "cowardly and rustic" (3.411a), and "even if my language is somewhat rustic and brutal" (2.361e). As this final item illustrates, the point often has to do with behavior or deportment, and particularly speech. It seems that Plato has peopled his at first glance invisible countryside with a socially inferior class of laborers whose manners are to be despised, notwithstanding the presumable value of their *technē* and the expressed acknowledgment of their vital role in feeding the nonfarming population.

Astonishingly in view of its prominence in the prehistoric polities shortly to be studied, a plain (*pedion*) nowhere figures in fleeting topography of the *Republic* (save the Plain of Lethe at 10.621a). Perhaps Plato thought that, as with the very notion of the countryside itself, it went without saying that a plain was the scene of his farmers' activities. Similarly mountains (*orē*), which, like the plain, will play a prominent a role in the prehistoric polities, receive not a single mention as a distinct topographical entity in the design of the Fair City. But as with the farmers of the invisi-

ble countryside, a montane topography is indirectly implied by the occupational classes of "cowherds, shepherds, and the other herders" (2.370d).
Elsewhere in the dialogue, allusions to flocks, herders, and the herders'
technē are merely metaphorical, figurative, or illustrative and tell us nothing definite about any contemplated legal or social status, role in the economy, and so on. What, finally, of the sea, its coast, and harbors? Despite,
with considerable irony, the fact that the discussion recreated in the *Republic* is placed in Athens' own principal port town, Peiraieus, it is the last
mentioned, the harbors, that particularly capture Plato's attention—and
disparagement. Alongside an innocuous reference to legislation concerning
markets, harbors, and such (4.425d) and the innocent anecdote about
Kephalos's discovery of corpses under the walls on the way up from
Peiraieus (4.439e), Socrates is made in the *Gorgias* to decry the democratic
politicians who "filled our city with harbors and dockyards and walls and
revenues and similar rubbish" (519a), a sentiment absent in the *Republic* itself but later to be taken into account in the city of the *Laws*. There may
be deeper meaning than is at first apparent in Kephalos's observation that
Socrates does not often come down to Peiraieus to visit him and his family (1.328c).

If Plato's views regarding the countryside, even if only implicitly expressed or latent, are so uncompromisingly negative or slighting, perhaps,
the uninformed reader might suspect, he has more positive things to say
about the town. Surely his occasional use of the term *asteios* (the adjective
of *asty*) in approving contexts involving wit, charm, elegance, and the like[54]
would suggest the existence of a constellation of laudable urban qualities
over against the corresponding deficits of the country and countryfolk?
But it is unlikely that such a favorable estimation is to be bestowed in
Plato's name upon the preponderance of the urban population of his
Kallipolis. The reason is methodological. Given everything that has been
said about Plato's silence on matters of topography up to this point, the
town can only be regarded as a kind of default location for everything that
the author writes in the absence of any indication to the contrary. Thus,
with the exception of patently rural farmers and herders, a characterization
of, say, a commercial or industrial occupational group can only be taken as
reflecting upon a presumed urban scene of operation. The despised condition of retailers reselling farmers' produce in the marketplace has already
been mentioned. To these *kapeloi* may be added, famously and notoriously,
the *banausoi* (from Greek *baunos* "furnace," *auein*, "to light a fire"), the
craftspeople consistently associated by Plato with servility (*Laws* 1.644a,

5.741e) and opposed to the intellectual pursuits of "good" men (*Alkibiades* 1.131b, *Epinomis* 976d). "Souls are bowed and mutilated by vulgar occupations even as their bodies are marred by their arts and crafts", says Plato in Book 6 of the *Republic* (495e). Wherever else Athenian *technitai* plied their craft, their workplaces certainly included the very neighborhood of Plato's own deme-affiliation, as will be recalled from our discussion at the head of this chapter. While the harbors, too, may, on a simple dualistic town vs. country model, count as part of the country, the port town of Peiraieus visited by Socrates during the festival of Bendis was, with its large compact settlement, undeniably urban. Plato's sympathies, negative or positive, are not to be reduced to any simple topographic formula.

Atlantis, Antediluvian Athens, and the Recapitulation of Civilization

But the transition from topographic blank to the rich detail of the Cretan city was not an abrupt one. For the intermediate stages of development between the *Republic* and *Laws* we have the evidence of Plato's prehistorical, and in part devolutionary, utopias. These may be arrayed in a substantively meaningful sequence: (1) the fantastic description of the island civilization of Atlantis (*Kritias* 113a–121c); (2) the contrasting recreation of Atlantis's eventually victorious opponent, Athens, 9000 years before the literary present (*Kritias* 109b–112e); (3) and the more securely grounded from-beginnings-to-present *archaeologia* of civilization in book 3 of the *Laws* (677a–683a). Each is a kind of prehistory, but while Plato's Atlantis is a creation of the imagination, the descriptions of antediluvian Athens (*Kritias*) and postdiluvian Greece (*Laws*) are recreations founded on survivals allegedly still discernible in the author's own time, especially in the former case. To the extent that they are in whole or part fictional, these histories express some of the tendencies to be expected in the light of the philosopher's background, place of residence, and movements just reviewed. To the extent that they are based on visible evidence, they represent in the latter two instances his best attempt to recover actual conditions of Athens' (and Greece's) primordial past. And it was the study of the past that finally allowed Plato to look beyond the urban center and to appreciate the crucial role played by the rural in any viable polity.

Atlantis in the Kritias *(113a–121c)*. The unbridled fantasy infusing the design of the island civilization of Atlantis might reasonably be thought sufficient justification for disqualifying it from consideration in this context.[55] After all, Plato's text permits elements of more advanced cultural development which turn out to be expressly prohibited in the utopian orders of the *Republic* and *Laws:* imports from abroad made possible by imperial rule (114d); the availability of precious metals (114e); and, in keeping with the nesiote situation (rather than the interior mainland siting preferred in the *Laws*), the presence of harbors and docks (115c).[56] Perhaps such deficits were regarded by Plato as appropriate in a prehistoric, and ultimately defeated, adversary of Athens. Be that as it may, it will, as we shall see, repay our efforts to notice some rather striking tendencies in the island empire's design, for they will emerge later as guiding assumptions underlying the design of his more historically based polities.

The principal topographic components of the island polity may be summarily rehearsed. At the center of "the whole island," a plain borders on the sea, and at the edge of the plain at a distance of 50 stades stands a mountain gently sloping on all sides (113c). Within a series of concentric rings of land and water were situated the central island, five stades in diameter, and the Acropolis, on which stood the royal palace and temples 116a, c; 117e). To the temple of Kleito and Poseidon were brought each year the offerings of agricultural produce (*horaia*) from all the allotments (116c). Fifty stades from the largest circle and harbor, a wall ran in a circle from the sea to the mouth of the channel; on it were constructed many closely spaced dwellings (117e). Beyond the *asty* lay the rest of the *chora* comprising the plain and mountains (117e–118b). The plain was crisscrossed by a system of channels used to transport goods, such as timber and seasonal produce, from country to town as well as to irrigate the crops with runoff from the mountains (118d–e). Crops were harvested twice a year (118e). Encircling the plain were the mountains, which surpassed by their repute all mountains known to exist in Kritias's own day in number, size, and beauty—dimensions, the text makes clear, of their productive potential: many rich villages of *perioikoi*; rivers, lakes, and meadows providing sufficient nourishment to all the wild and domesticated animals; and timber varied in size and type and adequate for all the crafts (118a–b).

What are we to make of all this? Random fantasies devoid of significance, as the reader might well think at first? Certain of the plan's details suggest otherwise. There are, for example, unmistakable reminders of the mythical Reign of Kronos, with which this chapter began. That the countryside of Atlantis—plain and mountain—represents an era of Kronian plenty is signaled in two ways. First, Kritias's account of Poseidon's arrangements at the foundation mentions two springs, the one warm, the other cold, providing "out of the earth sufficient and varied nourishment" (113e). Second, the remark that, over and above the aforementioned imperial imports, the island's endowment of metals, timber, animals, and every category of desirable plant was, taken together, adequate for the needs of temples, royal dwellings, harbors and docks, and "all the rest of the country" (114e–115c). Spontaneous self-sufficiency is the underlying idea. Plato is following in the utopian tradition of Hesiod's *Works and Days*.

And what does all this mean for Plato in human terms? Military personnel were to be drawn from the allotments (*kleroi* at 118e–119b, ten *lexeis* at 116c). These soldiers were 60,000 in number (119a) and—to mark the vital, topographical point—according to the text of 118e confined to "the men in the plain fit for warfare." From the mountains and "the rest of the country," men "limitless in number" were, in accordance with their village location (literally and paratactically, "places and villages"), to be assigned to "these allotments" (i.e. of the plain) under the (i.e. their) leaders (119a). These mountain villagers can only be the *perioikoi*, "dwellers around," specified as the occupants of the "rich villages" of the mountains (118b). Thus, for purposes of military organization, the mountains were to be subject to the central plain, with its *asty*, acropolis, and royal palace. Not only is this, in economic terms, a "consumer city" in terms of the reallocation of the resources of the countryside to the urbanized center. It is also, in societal terms, a regime in which the peripheral *perioikoi*, expressly reflecting the Lacedaemonian antecedents underlying so many features of the Greek utopias, were as well to offer their bodies in service of the state.

Antediluvian Athens in the Kritias *(109b–112e)*. According to the program of the *Kritias*, the Atlantid civilization, 9000 years before the narrative present of the dialogue, eventually turned out to be the opponent of the primitive state of Athens (108e–109a). In comparison with the island civilization, the Athens of the *Kritias* represents a decided advance towards the utopian vision of the *Laws*. But before we notice its design in detail, note should first be taken of a preliminary remark of Kritias's regarding sources, for its implications bear substantively upon the deeper significance of that account. Following each prehistoric destruction, he says, the surviving population consisted of "an unlettered mountain tribe" (109d).[57] The speaker's point is to excuse a lack of better information, but in making that point Kritias has prefigured a vital element of an enduring utopian portrayal of the rural: that the mountains foster separation from the higher attainments of civilization; that such civilization is represented *in primis* by

literacy and such pursuits as literacy makes possible or of which it is an indispensable component; and that, with supreme irony, when a civilization
(as the Greek conceptualized it) is destroyed or disappears, it is precisely
this "unlettered" segment that alone survives and out of which alone a new
civilization (if there is to be one) will evolve.

To reverse for convenience the dialogue's depiction of town and
country, the Acropolis, prior to a disastrous erosive rainfall (the third of the
floods preceding the deluge in the time of Deukalion, the text adds) attended by earthquakes, was originally level and rich in soil (111e–112a). A
spring, serviceable in both summer and spring, gushed forth from near the
place of the present Acropolis, providing an "unstinting stream for all the
people at that time"—still another reminiscence of Kronian spontaneous
plenty. Beneath the height's slopes dwelt the craftspeople (*demiourgoi*) and
such farmers (*georgoi*) as farmed nearby, while atop the Acropolis, which
was ringed by a circuit wall, resided the soldierly class (*to machimon*)
around the temple of Athena and Hephaistos. At the Acropolis's summit,
communal dwellings, winter mess halls, and other fixtures served the needs
of both the soldiers and the priests.[58] In conformity with Plato's utopian
prescriptions, the early Athenians made no use of gold or silver, maintained
a steady population of men and women (at a nominal 20,000), and transmitted their property unaltered to each succeeding generation. Guardians
of their own citizens and leaders of the other Greeks (who, the text is careful to add, were willing to be so led) is how Kritias sums up the role of the
soldierly component at the close of his narrative (112b–d). Thus "the military class," ensconced on the summit of the Acropolis, graphically anticipates the urban ascendancy everywhere discernible in Greek utopian
visions and, more generally, once again illustrates the decisive role of topography.

In contrast with other visionary polities, Plato subsumes under the
rubric *politai*, "citizens," all of his functional occupational categories—
demiourgia, "provisioning from the soil," and the "fighting element"
(110c) (to which, on Hermann's emendation, we may add the priests)—but
their economic interrelations hardly prove to be equitable. "But the fighting element, segregated in the beginning by divine men, lived apart, having all that was suitable for nourishment and education, no one of them
possessing any private property, but regarding everything as in common
for all and expecting to receive from the others nothing beyond adequate
nourishment (110c-d)." They were, that is, as must have immediately occurred to every contemporary reader, prehistorical Attic analogues to the

classical Spartiate citizen caste, a solider-elite sustained by the labor of *perioikoi* and helots. The ensuing depiction of the countryside renders fully plausible such a dependency: the soil was so rich that it supported a large army (*stratopedon*), which was thereby freed from the toils of agriculture (110e, again at 111c); in place of true (barren, in Plato's time) mountains it had (presumably fertile) "high earthmounds" (111b–c); tall, old-growth timber, both wild and domesticated, was to be found in the mountains (111c); pasturage for flocks existed in unlimited quantity (111c); and the as yet uneroded deep loam held the rainwater, supplying all the districts of the land with streams and springs (111d).

Along the way, Plato punctuates this narrative with evidences of past but now, due to the workings of natural forces and human overuse, lost or nearly lost abundance. Specific reference is made to rafters in still-standing buildings which had been carved from once-great forests (111c), to shrines situated at the sites of once flowing but now dry springs (111d), and, on the Acropolis itself, to the trickling remnant of what was once a generous stream issuing from the citadel's rock (112d). The effect of these Thucydidean *tekmeria* is to link the past with the present, thereby sowing the seeds for the larger project of marshaling a bygone sociopolitical order in the service of a utopian reconstruction of the present. This is not Atlantis, this antediluvian Athens. Rather it is a fully real stage of prehistoric development which, though belonging to the remote and irrecoverable past, continues to be detectable in telltale trace evidence still observable by the discerning investigator.

But taken in its own terms, Kritias's Athens is manifestly yet another variation on the Reign of Kronos with which we began our exploration. The earth yielded its bounty unabated, true to Hesiod's yearnings for that age when a day's work might be sufficient for a year (*Works and Days*, lines 42–46). Thereby, the elite military caste is freed from toil by dint of the (relatively diminished) toil of others. Thanks to the absence of gold and silver, great wealth could not be accumulated, with the result that people pursued the middle path between ostentation and servility (112c). Similarly, farmers (genuine farmers, it is added, because they do nothing else) were "tasteful and well endowed" (111e)—euphemistic language, I suspect, meaning that, as would have been expected in a true-to-life setting, agricultural labor had neither obliterated interest in higher pursuits nor deformed their bodies. Thus the natural resources of the land of Attica, of which only traces remained at the time of the dialogue's present, had sustained a comfortable, if not luxurious, mode of living for all, exploiters and

exploited alike. But a deeper significance of this polity resides in its organization according to occupational castes and in each caste's topographically
distinct (if not in every case unique or exclusive) place of abode, making
for a hierarchy of dependency in which a rural (and, in part, suburban)
population of farmers and crafters materially supported a literally ascendant
"fighting element" domiciled atop the citadel.

    The Recapitulation of Human Civilization in the Laws *(3.677a–683a)*.
Major signposts of Plato's social topography and important clues regarding its evolutionary development are graphically set out in the account of
the aftermath of the *kataklysmos* in Book 3 of the *Laws* (677a–683a). This
account describes the destruction of high civilization, then its rebirth
through a sequence of progressively more advanced constitutional/politi-
cal/economic orders, culminating in Plato's own classical city-state. At the
same time, the process of evolution, Plato is at pains to emphasize, is attended by a concurrent devolution of morality, with the result that it is precisely in the most advanced polity that the conditions exist for discord and
warfare. But, for our present purposes, the matter under scrutiny is the
manner in which the stages of human society's evolution—and devolution—are tied to its relationship with characteristic forms of land and sea.

    The two interlocutors, the Athenian and Kleinias, share a belief in the
occurrence of many destructions by flood, plague, and other calamity
whereby only a small part of the human race in each instance survived. Following the Cataclysm (by the definite article, a reference is evidently made
to Deukalion's Flood), the Athenian explains, the only survivors were
"some mountain herders"—"small embers," he says, of the human race
preserved on mountain tops (677b). Plato's recapitulation of the reemer-
gence of human civilization will thus commence with an aboriginal association of montane habitation with low-density pastoralism. These survivors
were unskilled in arts (*technai*) and devices (*mechanai*), a deficit which, in
the moral dimension, had the advantage of depriving them of the stuff of
greed, rivalry, and other villainies that men "in the cities" devise against
one another (677b). Significantly, the Athenian adds that the cities (*poleis*)
situated on the plain and near the sea had been totally destroyed (677c),
thereby reaffirming the crucial role of topography (as well as forecasting
the end result of the evolutionary/devolutionary process). Along with the
cities were lost tools and all traces of skill, political organization, and science (*technē, politikē,* and *sophia*) (677c). The land ceased to produce, but
fortunately a few herds of cattle and flocks of goats survived in order to
provide sustenance to the pastoralist survivors (677e). Because the mines

had been flooded, metals were not available to make tools, with the result that tall timber could no longer be cut; and what few tools had survived in the mountains soon wore out through excessive use (677d, 678e). The means of transportation, by use of which visits could be made by land and sea, no longer existed. But, along with the herds and flocks, the arts of making ceramics and textiles, which required no metals, survived and there was an abundance of the necessities of life (679a). Because, thanks to the country's rich resources, there was no poverty and, thanks to the absence of gold and silver, there was nothing over which to quarrel, hybris, injustice and envy failed to develop. Rather, an old-fashioned simplicity (*euētheia*) allowed the people to accept as true whatever was said about gods and men, so that peace and harmony reigned over this primitive human society (679b–c) and *stasis* and war were unknown (678e).

It was from these slender beginnings that cities, constitutions, arts and sciences, and laws were to evolve again. Paradoxically, in the course of doing so, they had the effect of introducing evil as well as goodness into the lives of people until that time "ignorant of the good things of town life (*kata ta astē*)" (678b). But advance was slow, for, the Athenian declares, there still rang in their ears a fear of descending from the heights down into the plains [i.e. to the location of the cities prior to the Cataclysm] (678c). Eventually, once literacy had been reacquired, it became possible to advance beyond customary law (*patrioi nomoi*) to written legal codes—at which point the interlocutors of the *Laws* return to the proper topic of their discussion (679e–680a)—the mention of written law prompting a brief account of societal evolution from the humble beginnings of a preliterate *dynasteia*. By *dynasteia* Plato means the rule by the male elders over the still scattered clans and households of the pastoral mountain communities (680d)—the "first" of the historical modes of government. Next, with coalescence into larger communities came agriculture and permanent settlements situated on the hillsides (*hyporeiai*) and ringed by rubble walls to keep out the wild beasts (680e–681a). The convergence of the once isolated clans brought about a comparison of customs, resulting in turn in the rejection of some and the adoption of others deemed superior and, eventually, to the emergence of aristocracy or monarchy (681c–d)—Plato's "second" evolutionary polity. From these antecedents, next, emerged a "third" form of constitution, a mixture of a variety of forms and illustrated famously by Homer's verses on Ilion, when people migrated from the heights (*hypseloi*) down onto the plain (*pedion*). True, Ilion, like its archaic and classical descendants, was situated on a hill (*lophos*), but it was of no great height, the Athenian remarks. By relying on low hillocks for defense and by placing the settlement under a number of rivers descending from the mountains, the settlers seem to have entirely forgotten the earlier Cataclysm (682b–c). Many other cities were founded, too, as populations multiplied, and attacks were made upon Ilion by sea as well as by land, since by now "all were making use of the sea fearlessly" (682c). At length, the final and "fourth" polity, a confederacy, brings Plato back to the present (683a).

Plato has given us much here. From his recapitulation of *polis* society out of the wreckage of the Cataclysm, we are implicitly and in passing (his subject, after all, is the emergence and rise of legal systems) given a hierarchy of social topographies corresponding to the successive phases of that linear process of development: mountains, foothills, plain and, with the development of the "means of transportation" (*poreia*), access *by sea* from the settlement on the plain to other lands. Thus to each dominant geographic situation corresponds a distinct evolutionary phase of societal and cultural development. But we must not forget that, for Plato, a concurrent devolutionary process, issuing in strife and warfare, has attended these advances in political organization, for, along the way, Plato has isolated the factors involved in regressive decline and has linked them to topography: namely, poverty alongside prosperity, possession of precious metals, and—particularly to the point of our study—"the ways of the cities" and access to the sea. Topography is emerging, if not as the engine driving the process, then as a key determinant governing the character of each successive stage of civilized life.

The Cretan City in Plato's *Laws*

The *Republic* had opened on a note of dramatic tension between urban civic center and urban port town, finally finding its mise-en-scène in the latter in the home of an industrial resident alien family. The *Laws* records a conversation conducted on a summer day's walk on the island of Crete from Knossos to the cave of Idaean Zeus, with shade trees and meadows serving as stage props along the way (1.625b–c; 4.704a–705c, 722c). This setting, though never fleshed out (as we might have hoped it would be) anywhere in the course of Plato's gargantuan text, is ripe with implications, if only latently. Unlike every other dialogue (save the all but entirely obscured acknowledgment of a Megarian setting in the *Theaitetos*), the

scene is not Athens. Unlike most of the dialogues with an identifiable location, the scene is not urban but almost ostentatiously rural. And, in contrast with the *Phaidros,* it is not a mere token ruralism in the shadow of a
town wall. Nor does Plato stop here. As if to disavow the maritime associations of Athens, the interlocutors are expressly directed away from the
sea as they climb upwards to their mountain destination (4.704a–705c).
Among these interlocutors, furthermore, are counted alongside the
Athenian stranger a Cretan (Kleinias) and a Lacedaemonian (Megillos).
These places of origin are clear hints to the ancient reader of the potentially archaic, even regressive, agrarian character of the design of the Cretan "Magnesia" that will emerge from their lengthy colloquy. As it will
work out, no more striking example is to be found in the Greek utopian
tradition of the rural orientation exemplified so famously by the inland
polity of classical Sparta. Accordingly, it is here that we shall find the
philosopher's clearest and fullest statement on the potentialities, for good
or for ill, of rural participation in the life of the Greek city-state.[59]

Because the city of the *Laws* represents a plan for the future, it of
course does not follow that Plato's vision is a progressive one. Rather, that
vision may be characterized as a retreat to a rapidly disappearing era of isolation and self-sufficiency embodied in an agrarian community of villages
loosely organized around an inland town center. Where Plato innovates is
primarily in the provision for a comprehensive regulatory apparatus, but
even so the social structure underlying that apparatus is recognizably a realistic replication of inherited agrarian traditions. Given this general assessment, it will be our task to situate Plato's Cretan city within the larger
context of Greek utopian speculation.[60]

The fundamental, nonderivative, independent role of topography in
the design of the Magnesian *polis* is straightforwardly indicated by Plato.
This role involves the recognition of a fundamental cleft between town and
country, with internal segmentation and a curious interrelation between
urban and rural sectors brought about by the imposition upon the state's
territory of a characteristic, though at the level of specific detail highly innovative, "public organization." Since I have examined this organization in
detail elsewhere,[61] it is necessary to rehearse here only the fundamental features of the layout. Following the selection of the site and the placement
as close as possible to its center (hereafter to be called the "acropolis") of
a sanctuary sacred to Hestia, Zeus, and Athens, the oikist is to erect
"twelve divisions of the city (the *polis*) and of all its territory (the *chora*)"
(5.745b–c). From this urban hub, so Plato seems to suggest, will radiate the

twelve wedge-shaped divisions after the fashion of a sliced pie. Each of the
cunei will be consecrated to, and named after, one of the Twelve Gods and
henceforth be technically designated a phyle (5.745d-e). Segmenting the
phyle, furthermore, will be twelve constitutionalized villages, technically
(in good Attic fashion) called *dēmoi* in their external public statewide role
as a fraction of a phyle but otherwise, in respect to their internal quasi-
private role as village associations, called *kōmai*. Complementing and presumably cutting across this network of regional divisions will be the
phratries (5.746d), about which Plato tells us very little, and Spartan-style
syssitia, "common messes," which are to be distributed, says the text, "in
each and every place" (6.762a).

   Despite the imposition of this advanced, and artificial, administrative
superstructure, the gross topography of the state remains discernible. For
one thing, with recent commentators, the boundary between town and
country is intended to be marked and preserved by the functional wall of
semi-detached dwellings described at 6.779a–b.[62] The urban-rural dichotomy is then to be applied to the distribution of the colony's 5,040
allotments over the citizen households. Each allotment will be cut in two,
with each household receiving a half parcel from the town and a half parcel
from the countryside. Equity in value is to be assured by two strategems:
the undivided lots will be large or small according to the value of the land;
and each combined lot is be equal in terms of its aggregate distance from
the geographical center. That is, the closest-in parcel will be paired with the
most distant rural parcel, the next closest-in with the second most distant,
and so on, resulting in a parity of urban access or rural isolation. Following the assignment, presumably by sortition, of the citizen households to
the 5,040 allotments, each household will be required to establish dual residences, one urban, the other rural, in the two divisions of the split holding (5.745c). Plato does not provide further detail, but it is a tempting
surmise that occupation of the two residences will alternate on a periodic,
and specifically agriculturally determined, seasonal basis.

   This scheme of allotment may in its essentials be viewed as the utopian
response to the revolutionary's call for confiscation and redistribution of
the land. The care with which Plato arranges for the relative *equality* of the
combined urban and rural plots (recalling the equal *ktēseis* called for by
Phaleas) acknowledges that the seeds of civil discord reside in gross imbal-
ances of wealth (especially landed wealth) and finds the solution to that
problem in the centrally enforced equalizing of property holdings. By this
late time in his career, however, Plato is enough of a realist to appreciate

that human acquisitiveness will eventually assert itself, so in order to brake the processes which will eventually lead to the consolidation of large estates in the hands of the few, he makes his *klēroi* indivisible and inalienable (5.741b) and fixes the population for ever at the 5,040 instituted at the foundation of the colony, thereby freezing the original regime of owner-ship.[63] Nonetheless, with the apparent concession that even these measures must sometimes end in frustration, Plato establishes a factor of four as the maximum difference between the most valuable and least valuable *kleros* (5.744e-745a).[64] But it is the ordaining of ownership (and perhaps residence as well) in both the urban and rural sectors which, from the perspective of this study, is the truly revolutionary innovation. Because, however, the measure is innovative does not mean necessarily that it is without prece-dent or other form of living inspiration. The consolidation of scattered holdings into a single estate was a well-established fact of life in ancient At-tica and was to remain the pattern for rural Greece down to the present day. Typically, too, the holding of extraurban farmland might be combined with residence in a nucleated village center or in the town itself. What Plato does is to formalize, institutionalize, and perpetuate such an arrangement by combining urban and rural components in every household's property holdings, although the sketchy description of private dwellings along the wall (6.779a–b) leaves unclear the spatial relation of the property holder's residence to his *klēros*.

It is primarily through these means that Plato will provide for the unity of his new Cretan Magnesia. Every household will, as it were, have a foot in both town and country. To the same unifying end, the crafts work force is to be divided into multiple contingents, one for the *asty*, twelve others for each of the twelve (partly urban, but mostly rural) phylai, thereby precluding a sort of industrial domination by the town (8.848e-849a). Unity, however, might in historical cities, and demonstrably so in Plato's own Athens, be complemented by a pronounced degree of decen-tralization—that is, by the more or less enforced isolation of rural districts from the urban center. It is appropriate, then, to interrogate the text of the *Laws* on this vital dimension of urban-rural relations.

There can be no question but that, as in most dimensions of its de-sign, the territory of the new Cretan city and its population are to be sub-ject to the workings of an authoritarian regulatory apparatus. Its structure, individual components, and functions are to be set out in a code of Agrar-ian Laws (*nomoi georgikoi*, 8.842e).[65] While a number of the elements of this apparatus are not expressly related to any specific topographical entity (and so must, on the "default" principle introduced earlier, be referred to the town), Plato does observe a trifold division among *asty*, *agora*, and *agros/oi* (town, civic center, and countryside), a separation of function and jurisdiction illustrated most graphically by his policing boards of *astynomoi*, *agoranomoi*, and *agronomoi* (6.763c; 9.881c; 11.914a, 920c, 936c). Each board is charged with the maintenance of order and the enforcement of the laws within its own prescribed topographically defined bailiwick. Plato is explicit regarding the specific powers of the *agronomoi* (sometimes in combination with those of the other two boards, to which corresponding powers in their own districts are assigned): to punish malfeasance, especially theft and unjust distributions (6.761e); to act as inspectors, judges, and evaluators (8.843d); to manage rainwater runoff and to issue water rations (8.844b–c); to regulate the craftsmen (8.848e); to punish persons guilty of injuring their parents (9.881d); to prosecute animals accused of homicide (11.873e); to inflict punishments (11.881c); to impose penalties (11.914a); to regulate the retail market (11.920c); to expel beggars (11.936c); and to receive from the *phyletai* a record of the preceding year's produce (12.955d). But what do these powers have to do with decentralization? Indeed, are they not evidence for quite the opposite tendency, precisely to *centralize* all powers of legitimate coercion within the central authority itself? The answer is implicit in Plato's instructions for the selection and ongoing replacement of the members of the board: each phyle is to provide five *agronomoi* (and *phrourarchoi*), each of the five then selecting twelve young men of his own phyle between the ages of 25 and 30. The term of service will be two years, the outgoing members selecting their replacements for the third year, and so on. Each phyle-contingent of 60 is to be assigned to each of the twelve phyle-districts for a period of one month, progressing in a clockwise direction; during the second year, the direction is reversed (6.760b–e). Rotation through all twelve (rural) segments of the territory will, as I have suggested elsewhere, serve to work against any excessive sectional loyalty to one's home district.[66] But the critical point here is that these "rural police" (as one commentator has labeled them), though of course themselves subject to the oversight of the central authority, appear to be intended to operate independently of their fellow boards, the *astynomoi* and *agoranomoi*. Such independence of jurisdiction both reflects and reinforces the separation of country, town, and marketplace.

Should there be any doubts on this head, they may perhaps be allayed simply by referring to Plato's contemplated judicial apparatus. Three tiers of tribunals are ordained: (1) "arbitrators and neighbors" (i.e., arbitrators who are neighbors); (2) a "tribal court" of villagers organized within a single phyle; and (3) a mixed panel of magistrates with no expressed relationship to the public organization. Most disputes will presumably be settled at one of the two lower levels, in either case within the local community—in the case of rural residents, within the village. Even at the highest level of jurisdiction, no reference is made to a "supreme court" or other centralized authority.[67] To be sure, if Plato had been following an Athenian model, he might have hearkened back to the tyrant Peisistratos's celebrated *dikastai kata demous*, dispatched from Athens to dispense justice on the spot in rural communities (*AthPol* 16.5). But the selection of neighbors and fellow villagers as judges can have the same decentralizing effect. Indeed, they posses the added advantage over circuit riders of being members of one's own rural community.

To what extent is this preliminary finding supported by Plato's representation of the economy, society, and culture of his rural communities? Again, isolation of the rural local community seems to be the underlying objective, achieved by a combination of alternately regressive and progressive measures, the former type represented graphically by the economic arrangements and regulations. Farming alone will be permitted as a means of earning a livelihood, no provision being allowed for money-making through "illiberal" commerce, for "contemptible industrial labor (*banausia*) subverts a free person's character" (5.741e). Nor does Plato stop at the (for him) predictable suppression of nontraditional *chrematismoi*. He banishes gold and silver, giving new life to the premonetary conditions prevailing in prehistoric Athens on Plato's own account in the *Kritias* (112c). Only such coins will be permitted as required by craftspeople and for paying wages to slaves or immigrants (5.742a). The diminished status of the parties concerned is sufficient indication of the social stigma that will naturally devolve on such mercenary exchanges. The domestic currency shall be valueless elsewhere; foreign coin brought into the country shall be exchanged for the coin of the realm. No one shall give or receive a dowry. Deposits and lending at interest shall be effectively prohibited because the law will not require a person to pay back either interest or principal (5.742b–c).

Plato has done his best to recreate the agrarian conditions prevailing in archaic Sparta, with its *kleros*-holding citizens, iron spits as the sole medium of exchange, and the crafts relegated to a subservient class of free (but noncitizen) *perioikoi*. True, there is a market, and market stewards (*agoranomoi*) to monitor it, but nothing Plato has told us about his farmers would give us any reason to think they spent much time there. They are not included in the stigmatized classes involved in money-handling, and in any event the legally enforced modest dimensions of their plots would seem to preclude the assumption of a marketable surplus. Probably self-sufficient break-even farming operations are what Plato had in mind for his *georgoi*. Even the periodic need to purchase a plough or hoe need not require a trip to town, since Plato has taken care to assign craftsmen to each of the twelve districts in addition to the thirteenth contingent for the *asty* (8.848e–849a). The annual produce will be divided three ways, one part for the free citizens, one part for the slaves, and one part for the craftspeople and foreigners (8.847e–848c), but nothing in Plato's text implies or suggests trips to a centrally situated market by the farmer-producer himself. Plato's economy, in short, will give his farmer no reason or incentive to leave his farm or rural village.

The same argument could be applied to constitutional/political activity in the town, but it would remain again essentially an argument from the silence of Plato's text. An assembly, a council, boards of magistrates, and possibly a court of the final instance are expressly or on reasonable surmise seated in the urban center, but the writer provides no clues regarding any scheme of composition by region. Analogous historical Athenian counterparts nominally represented City, Coast, and Inland, and although doubts may be raised concerning the actual places of residence of nominally "rural" demesmen, at least a semblance of regional representation obtained in the Council of Five Hundred and the boards of magistrates. A similar difficulty bedevils any consideration of mass cultural spectacles in the Cretan town—corresponding to the historical City Dionysia, Panathenaia, the *herotai* of the phylai, and so on—for Plato is simply silent on such subjects; and certainly their rather liberal political complexion would hardly permit us, in the absence of textual indications, to ascribe them without textual warrant to his conservative agrarian polity. Besides, did the author of the *Republic* not warn his readers not to let the farmers be "clothed in robes and gold" (4.420e–421b)?

But *argumenta e silentio* may be beside the point when we reflect upon those passages where the village life of his rural farmers is rather graphically portrayed.[68] According to Plato's (inconsistent) text, the villages numbered 144, twelve to each phyle-district.[69] Each was fitted out with temples and a market place (8.848d), altars and shrines (10.910a), the shrines serving as meeting places for the children (7.794a). The village is to be the seat of the court of the second instance (12.956c); and the villagers are to be the recipients of the fines paid by the *agronomoi* to each district (6.762a). Elsewhere in the Platonic corpus, the tyrant Peisistratos's son Hipparchos is credited with a scheme to educate the people of the Attic countryside (*Hipp.* 228b–229a), and for all we know Plato intended (though he did not express) a similar plan for his rural Magnetes. All in all, this is a rather impressive level of communal installation, resources, and activity, especially in view of Plato's general failure to flesh out the various elements of his polity in anything like the detail the reader might wish. Why should anyone doubt but that it is precisely the rural village that the philosopher intended to be the primary locus of his extraurban citizens' lives? Besides, Plato's citizen farmer was to enjoy the benefits of higher status within the village community. The contingents of craftsmen assigned to each district were, as we have seen, subject to severe social disabilities. At least some of them (recalling Phaleas of Chalkedon's relegation of his *technitai* to the status of public slaves) will be metics, since foreigners are to be allowed to enter the state and to establish residence only on the condition that they possess a craft (*technē*) (8.850b). Since, furthermore, under normal circumstances they will be required to leave (with their property) after twenty years' residence (8.850b), it is clear that their position will approximate that of slaves purchased in adulthood with skills in place and, after a lengthy period of work, manumitted upon arrival at an age when they are no longer profitable to maintain. Be that as it may, in contrast with the notorious absence of any mention of slaves or slavery in the text of the *Republic*, the text of the *Laws* is explicit on the point of the presence of servile workers (*douloi* and *oiketai*) and on their engagement in agricultural labor (7.806d–e).[70] True, Plato's citizens are to be engaged in farming, herding, bee-keeping, and the rest (8.842d), but he gives no indication that they will suffer the physically debilitating and intellectually stultifying effects of the manual labor that he so consistently abhors in industrial *banausia*. Perhaps, at the risk of stretching a point, it is legitimate to think here again of the Reign of Kronos, when, according to Hesiod's text, the earth gave up its bounty spontaneously (*Works and Days*, lines 117–118). Plato's citizen farmer-villagers will lead a comfortable existence indeed, their holdings protected from fragmentation by the law of inalienability and the prohibition on coinage, some or all of the physical labor connected with farming consigned to aliens and slaves, a resident force of craftsmen at their beck and call, and the provision at the village home base itself of the basic amenities of a cultivated and invigorating communal life. This is Hesiod's heaven on earth. Why leave it for the town?

Commentators have always drawn attention to the general topographical parameters Plato sets for his Cretan city. It will enjoy a rich variety of plain, mountain, and forest, but, at the same time, because it is to be situated about 80 stades from the sea, its harbors, though fine, will not inflict on the utopian refoundation the alleged social and political ills openly deplored, as we have seen, by the traditionally minded philosopher (4.704a–705c).[71] For Plato, topography, to paraphrase a modern slogan, is destiny. Kleinias illustrates the principle with his point that whereas, in Thessaly, which is a level country, the people travel on horseback, the Cretans are runners because the land of Crete is rugged and conducive to running on foot (1.625d). Perhaps we may detect here a faint precursor of the environmental determinism later in vogue in Hellenistic and Roman ethnographical writings.

Be that as it may, it should be clear from the discussion in this chapter to this point that the analysis cannot end with the unadorned observation that land forms and the design, institutions, and peculiar character of a city simply have something to do with each other. The one absolutely essential refinement—essential for our appreciation of the ideological complexion of Plato's "second best" constitution—is that the competing topographical venues can be, and by Plato and others were, arranged in a linear developmental sequence: mountains, foothills, plain, and plain with access to the sea; and that to these topographic options correspond distinctive, cumulatively expanding socioeconomic regimes: respectively, pastoralism, low-level agriculture and stock rearing, intensive agriculture and monetary economy, and international trade and imperialism. Plato's reformist utopian vision in the *Laws* is, as we can recognize, regressive, but it should be added that it is so for the specific reason that Plato has attempted to arrest somewhere in the third phase an evolutionary process which had in his own native community of citizenship already run clear through the fourth and, with the imminent rise of monarchy and decline of the city-state, even beyond. But not all cities were like Athens; in fact, *no* ancient Greek city was like Athens. Perhaps he had in mind any of a number of isolated inland agrarian states with underdeveloped economies, possibly such as in his day might still be found in Crete, but if he did, it is not at clear why he bestowed upon his "Magnesia" so enormous a number of households and a highly articulated government with distinctively contemporary Assembly, Council, magistracies, courts, and so on. So let us, then, in the hope that his criticisms may place his mentor's intentions in clearer perspective, turn to the discerning witness of Plato's disciple and heir to the mantle of leadership of the Athenian philosophical movement.

Aristotle

While, unlike Plato, Aristotle, a native of Stagira on the Chalkidike peninsula, was not a citizen of Athens, he spent a considerable portion of his adult life in the city, from 367, when at the age of 17 he entered Plato's Academy as a pupil, until his mentor's death 20 years later, and again from 335, soon after the death of Philip of Makedon, until his own death in 322. Ample opportunity was thus afforded for the observation of the arrangements of the city that, as we have seen, had so influenced the development of and specific form taken by the political prescriptions and utopian speculations of his predecessor. Nonetheless, the impact of Athens on the formation of Aristotle's thinking is not as easily discernible as the considerable bulk of his extant writings on government and related subjects might lead one to expect. Ancient testimony reports the collection and publication of 158 constitutions of the Greek *politeiai*, but the one that has survived more or less intact, the Athenian, is at several points in conflict with the content of an indubitably genuine work of the author's, the *Politics*, and some have for this and other reasons questioned whether the *AthPol* is actually the product of Aristotle's own hand.[72] Nor is it all clear to what extent the *Politics* actually reflects the author's Athenian experience. Much of its content is simply generically Greek, explicit references to particular polities are not conspicuous in number or detail, and such specific references as we are given as often as not concern places other than Athens. But this should not surprise us, for, above and beyond the expected impact of the availability of 158 different *politeiai*, Aristotle's own movements had taken him from Stagira to Pella in Makedonia to Assos in Mysia to Mytilene on Lesbos and, finally, after the death of Alexander, to Chalkis on Euboia.[73] So we must be on our guard when using the Peripatetic's *oeuvre* as a source for rural Attica.[74]

Granted that Aristotle was not engrossed exclusively in the city-state of his mentor and of his own eventual school in the Lyceum, does he evidence an interest in the rural, whether a particular *polis* happens to engage his attention or the more general case is under consideration? Certainly any such interest did not recognizably dominate his researches, reportage of detail, or even theorizing. The largely intact Athenian *Constitution* preserves illuminating comment on the tyrant Peisistratos's rural policies (16.2–6), an allusion to the confinement of the extramural population during the Peloponnesian War (27.3), and a few passing references to the demes in their constitutional aspect (e.g. 21.2–5, 62.1), but is otherwise silent on the subject of Attica outside the walls. As for the *Politics*, its plan of organization is topical, without significant observance of geography or topography as subjects of study in their own right. The three preliminary and foundational books concern the family (book 1), the best constitution (2), and the nature of the state (3); the next three, focused on real-life polities, treat existing constitutions (4), revolutions (5), and democracy and oligarchy with an appendage on governmental offices (6); and the final two surviving books turn more conspicuously to the subject matter of the present discussion, the utopian polity: the best constitution with reference to environmental conditions and the population (7) and, finally, education (8).[75] Much of this material is not explicitly referred to town or country, and again we are often faced with a difficult choice between the "default" assumption that anything an urban-based writer says about a city necessarily pertains to the town or, more generously, that a statement about the city or citizenship in general, barring contrary indications, concerns the extraurban as well as the urban sector. Nor does it help matters that Aristotle's intellectual proclivities lead him to eschew preoccupation with messy details. Exasperatingly (for our purposes), the author's impatience with the particular fact is once conspicuously in evidence on a topic of rural administration: in book 7, turning from the arrangements of the *asty* to that of the *chora*, he at first promisingly mentions magistrates called forest wardens and land superintendents, their guard posts and mess rooms, and the distribution of temples over the countryside, only to abruptly break off with the statement that marshaling details and discoursing on such topics is a waste of time (7.11.4: 1331b). It is therefore to be suspected that considerable awareness of matters rural may lie undetectable behind many a formulation of a general or theoretical nature otherwise lacking specific topographic reference.

Sustained contact with Plato, first as his disciple, later as his doctrinal rival, eventually issued, among other signs of lasting influence, in his extensive treatment of Platonic ideas in the opening sections of the *Politics*. At the deeper level of foundational principles, the response is negative, for Aristotle will not accept either his mentor's abolition of the traditional family or his ideas (expressed in the *Republic*) on the communal ownership of property. Rather, Aristotle's *oikos* is the fundamental unitary building block which, in combination with others like it, by a natural process coalesces into the village, with a plurality of villages by an analogous process eventually producing the self-sufficient city-state (1.1.4–12: 1252a–1253a). Aristotle finds the household as a given fact of nature. Whether understood in evolutionary, contemporaneous, or merely analytical terms, this theory obviates the possibility of a polity without traditional households. And in place of communal ownership of the land Aristotle will substitute a formula for communal exploitation of privately held plots (1.2–3: 1262b–1266a passim).[76] Nonetheless, and importantly for our purposes, it is vital to note that the work of Plato's to which Aristotle directs his criticisms is as much the *Laws* as the *Republic*[77] and that, in the main, where the rural is concerned, agreement rather than disagreement with Plato characterizes the conservative agrarian community that emerges from the *Politics*. A brief rehearsal of the key passages will illustrate the point.

Topography is destiny for the design of the city-state, it was suggested in relation to Plato's utopian blueprints. Aristotle expresses this same idea by relating to types of foodstuffs the distinctive socioeconomic regimes represented by pastoralism, hunting, fishing, and agriculture (1.3.3–4: 1256a). Foodstuffs, in turn, are explicitly linked throughout to facts of geography, natural resources, climate, and so on. Furthermore, the fact that his enumeration of forms of "wealth-getting" includes stock-raising, agriculture, beekeeping, etc., and the extraction of natural resources such as timber and precious metals (1.4.1–2: 1258b) illustrates the breadth of the philosopher's interest in rural economic pursuits and ventures. And importantly for any estimation of the dimensions of the material underlying these summary formulations, Aristotle cites the earlier writings of Charetides of Paros and Apollodoros of Lemnos on agriculture and fruit farming as well as unnamed writers on other topics, and issues a call for a collection of the scattered instances of the successful pursuit of *chremastikē* (1.4.4: 1259a), a project that will eventually be undertaken in Book 2 of the pseudo-Aristotelian *Oikonomika*. Thales' prescient cornering of the olive presses in advance of a bumper crop at Miletos and Chios provides a signal example of the potential for gain in the exploitation of the resources of the land (1.4.5–6: 1259a). Therefore, it would seem that, in a way not nearly so explicitly developed by Plato, Aristotle has sought to give specific meaning to his predecessor's largely intuitive association of topography and societal form. What he has done is to supply a suppressed premise. Plato had linked topography to the distinctive profile (political, cultural, and other-

wise) of a people; Aristotle completes the argument by specifically identifying the local economy as the topographically conditioned variable which
impresses that distinctive profile upon a population.

Nor does Aristotle fail to develop the model elsewhere in the *Politics*.[78] By 4.3.11 (1290b–1291a), farmers have been recognized (with "the
class concerned with the sea" added at 4.4.1:1291b) as a necessary sector of
the state alongside the mechanic class, the commercial class, manual laborers, and the military, although it is to be doubted whether Aristotle meant
these as mutually exclusive rather than as at least partially overlapping categories. By book 5, political discord is related explicitly to geographical
variation (5.2.12: 1303b), with a number of references to follow regarding
the divisive role played by farmland in Greece's revolutionary history.
Whereas in former times, he writes, cities were not large and people had
lived on their farms busily engaged in agriculture (5.4.5: 1305a), a bumper
crop might propel the farmers into the political fray (5.5.11: 1306b), at
Sparta dissension arose over the question of the division of the land (5.6.2:
1307a), and at Thourioi an upheaval ensued when the notables illegally
bought up the whole of the farmland (5.6.6: 1307a). If history informed the
Peripatetic's judgments (and of course it did), it is clear that his ideal polity
will of necessity have to take into account the potential destabilization originating in the rural farming lands and their occupants. The project of de-
vising a stable polity, either out of whole cloth or through reform of an
existing regime, cannot therefore fail to address the design of that polity in
its topographical dimension.

Against the background of these preliminary discussions, Aristotle
turns by degrees to the consideration of alternative polities for the future.
True to his modern-seeming proclivity to explore relations between variables, different forms of democracy are found to correspond to the preva-
lent industry of the population.[79] Among the four types, the best *dēmos* (as
well as the oldest), says Aristotle, is the agricultural (*georgikos*, lit. "pertaining to farmers"), under which rubric pastoralism (*nomē*) is included
with farming (*georgia*) in the narrow sense (6.2.1–6: 1318b–1319a). Why is it
the best? Precisely because of its stabilizing qualities. Because they do not
have much property, farmers are always too busy to meet in the assembly;
and because, conversely, they are not so poor as to be driven to covet their
neighbors' goods, they find it more profitable to work than to engage in
politics (6.2.1: 1318a). But we must be careful to note the status of this formulation. It is less prescriptive (as the utopian project might lead us to expect), more a mere empirical observation. To be sure, a certain tendency

towards the leveling of property ownership is latent in these negative characterizations of the consequences of excess of wealth or poverty, but I find no reason to find here an ideology of equality of land ownership. The distinctive, and operative, feature, of this form of democracy is not equality so much as the absence of the extremes—the abject poverty that drives a man to desperation and the excessive wealth that creates the leisure leading to a potentially disruptive participation in government.

And what is the second best democracy? Again, one with a rural base—the democracy of the herders (*nomeis*) who get their living from cattle. Not only are they absent from the assembly place, but thanks to their occupation they are physically fit and capable of living in the open and so will make good soldiers. By contrast, the artisans (*banausoi*), the market people (*agoraioi*), and the wage-earning class (*to thētikon*) are all base (*phaulos*) and without excellence (*aretē*), and because they loiter in the *agora* and *asty*, they are available for frequent attendance in the assembly (6.2.7: 1319a). Where the *chora*, Aristotle sums up, is far from the *polis*, it is easy to make a good democracy and polity, for the populace is forced (as it were) to establish "colonies" (*apoikiai*) on their fields (*agroi*), far removed from the urban center (6.2.8: 1319a).

So, we may presume, the ideal state set out in the final two books of the *Politics* will embody one of these best "farmers'" or "herders'" democracies. Not surprisingly in view of the findings of the preceding discussion, Aristotle takes pains to describe the extent and nature of the ideal territory, the site, and its proximity to the sea (7.5.1–3: 1326b), with renewed attention in a subsequent passage to the plan of the town proper, its site and aspect, water supply, street plan, fortifications, temples and other public buildings (7.10.1–11.4: 1330a–1331b). But, again, as was acknowledged at the outset, extramural arrangements are only sketchily indicated. We have already cited the passage from Book 7 (11.4: 1331b) regarding rural buildings, magistrates, and temples. Additionally, mention is made in book 6 of magistrates charged with the administration of "the country" and "the parts outside the *asty*," these variously going by such titles as *agronomoi* (interestingly, the term used by Plato in the *Laws*) and *hyloroi* ("forest wardens") (6.5.4: 1321b). And in the summary catalogue of superintendencies at 6.5.12 (1322b) occur again the boards concerned with "the *agora*, the *asty*, harbors, and the *chora*," thereby neatly (and exhaustively) comprehending the topographical components of the new polity. But what about the societal consequences? Artisans (*to banauson*) and (as Aristotle puts it platonically, cf. *Rep.* 6.500d) any other who is not "a craftsman of excellence" will not share in the *polis*, that is, will not be citizens (7.8.5: 1329a). And the farmers? Until as far along as book 7, the reader has been led to expect the *georgoi* to turn out to be free citizen landowners (so much is implied by the very raising of the question of their attendance, or non-attendance, in the assembly), but they are now revealed by Aristotle to be, in these ideal circumstances, slaves (*douloi*) or alien dwellers-about (*barbaroi perioikoi*) (7.8.5: 1329a). At 7.9.9 (1330a), this ideal arrangement is reaffirmed, with the added comment that servile workers in private employment should be private possessions, those on common land common property.

The Reign of Kronos again? Aristotle's farmer-citizen middling landowners do not have to work to bring forth the earth's bounty. Rather they have emerged as an idle landed gentry sustained by the toil of a servile workforce. At the same time, Aristotle's *georgoi* will hardly be, as Athenian practice might suggest, urban absentee landlords only loosely bound to their ground but otherwise indistinguishable from their citizen confrères in the town. To the contrary, their ideally remote remove from the seat of the democratic government will effectively debar them from participation in the affairs of the *polis*. Thus, it is here, in close (and significant) conjunction with the realization of the Kronian vision, that we now find, perhaps in its most extreme form, the combination of unity and decentralization which, it is clear, was in our period a dominant structural trait of historical rural Athens.

8

Paradigms

BY ALL RIGHTS THE RURAL IN ANY OF ITS aspects was not a thing likely to be the subject of a representation—documentary, literary, pictorial, or otherwise. To the extent that such a representation required education, training, raw materials, artistic colleagues or co-workers, and critical masses of readers, auditors, or viewers, it could emanate only from the urban center. As a formal possibility, town and country might have interacted in such a way that urbanites and ruralites could become sufficiently aware of one another as to give rise to informed, penetrating, and perhaps even sympathetic portrayals of life on the other side of—beyond or within—the walls. But in Athens' case the slight and spotty, yet consistent and convincing, testimony regarding the exclusion of countrypeople from urban spaces with which we launched our study would seem to render such contact unlikely. Details regarding the design and intent of the Peisistratid exclusionary policy are preserved for us in a trustworthy late classical source; and there is no reason to doubt that the de facto separation of rural spaces and populations remained a social and cultural reality down to and throughout the period covered by the present work, viz. the two centuries of the democracy's lifetime prior to the Macedonian seizure. Yes, of course, farmers of necessity came to town to sell their produce or to purchase items not otherwise obtainable at home; rural citizens might journey to town to exercise the option of participating in assembly, council, court, or other constitutional function; and those same citizens might be required to make that journey for the purpose of mandatory military training, exercise, or mobilization. Yes, of course, townspeople might at any time repair to the ancestral country deme or a regionally based rural phratry center; many will occasionally have participated in extramural Attica-wide festivals at Eleusis, Rhamnous, Brauron, and elsewhere; and, reversing the path of the rural recruit, town-based ephebes or soldiers were regularly assigned to a frontier guardpost or (later in our period) deme-based encampment. But these exchanges tended to be periodic, and periodic at wide intervals—from the four-times-per-prytany meeting of the assembly, to seasonal visits to market, to the annual phratric Apatouria, to the once-in-a-lifetime ephebic training and tour of Attica. Urbanites and ruralites—by which I mean the more or less permanent residents of town and country—were certainly in occasional contact and presumably had formed opinions of life on the other side of the walls, but the realities affecting town-and-country relations permit us nonetheless to continue to think in terms of spatially segregated and essentially distinct cultures for the most part beyond the reach of everyday contact with one another.

Under these circumstances, if an educated Athenian did set his mind to the task of "representing" the rural, the result was likely to resemble the ethnic *logoi* of an Herodotos: a brief sketch devoted merely to noting deviations from the writer's (and his readership's) norm, wherein, under the guise of describing "the other," what is really achieved is a running inventory, and validation, of the unspoken parallel phenomena of the unchallenged home base. To a real degree, as our chapter on "Images" should make clear, this is a fair (partial) characterization of much of what has come down to us about rural Attica under the classical democracy. At the same time, taken as a whole, our record far exceeds an Herodotean ethnography not only in volume (the Egyptian *logos* being the sole arguable exception on the Greek side of the tradition) but in depth, range, and varying attitude of treatment as well. But to what circumstances do we owe these urban (and urbanizing) observations and representations of the Athenians' own extramural subculture?

There can hardly be any doubt but that the decisive development was the enforced confinement of the extramural population of Attica within the walls, beginning with the first of the annual Peloponnesian invasions in 431 and extending down to the mid-420s. Into significant relation with these dates may be brought the evolution of the subject-matter of our primary, and potentially most illuminating source—Attic comedy. Prior to that time, comedies had for long been produced before Athenian audiences, the earliest landmark date being 488/7 or 487/6 when provision of *komoidoi* at the annual City Dionysia was made the responsibility of the relevant magistrate.[1] But for the (admittedly only fragmentarily attested) intervening half century, only scant trace has survived of a drama concerned in significant part with rural Attica in any of its topographic, institutional, or cultural dimensions. Eupolis's *Demoi* must be later than 418, his *Prospaltioi* (i.e. the Attic deme) remains undated, and his first play in any event was produced in 429.[2] Titles with potentially rural content are recorded for Kratinos (viz. "Oxherds" [*Boukoloi*] and "Seasons" [*Horai*]), but none need be placed earlier than his earliest dated play (*Cheimazomenai*) of 426.[3] Rather it is with Aristophanes' own *Archarnians*, produced in 425, to be followed by *Clouds* in 423 and *Peace* in 421, that the effects of the unnatural and sustained rural presence within the walls are first arguably noticeable—and, I would speculate, in fact first impressed themselves upon the urban Athenian literary (or other artistic) consciousness. The fact of confinement itself cannot of course be taken as in any predictable way predetermining the character of that impress, for that very properly must remain to be ascertained through inspection of the representation in the light of the reality, the partial elucidation of which has been the principal burden of this book. But we cannot doubt that, given an otherwise prevailing segregation of town and country, the cramming of the population of the lion's share of Athens' territory (and of all but six of its 139 demes) within the narrow confines of the fortification system cannot have been without significant consequences for the Attic stage. New characters, new opportunities for parody or caricature, new story lines emanating from culture clash and shock, and—not to be forgotten—a new audience of rather different composition than ever seen before.

The new interest evidently awakened by this unprecedented, numerically overwhelming, and long sustained rural presence within the walls of Athens took on, as the preceding chapters have illustrated, a range of diverse forms:

Negative critique. Written sources of urban origin and orientation preserve spotty documentation of a wide range of rural realities which contrast sharply with the ways of the town, but it is not always possible to discern whether the attitude is approving, neutral, or disapproving. Perhaps more often than is immediately apparent, disapproval was meant to go without saying whenever the urban (and urbane) audience was expected to regard as self-evidently objectionable the mere mention of, say, animal-skin garments, unpleasant body odors, a distinctively "unlettered" speech, or a general absence of sensitivity to the refinements of town living. Theophrastos's sketch of *Agroikia* is an outstanding instance, although with the recent Loeb editor it may be possible to detect hints of sympathy in the portrait of the homestead citizen farmer. But in several notable cases, the negativity of the urbanite's assessment is explicit. The clash of cultures put on stage in Aristophanes' *Clouds* is perhaps best encapsulated by Socrates' devastating rebuke of the countryman Strepsiades' failure to respond to his sophisticated teaching; it both recalls the confirmed urbanite of the *Phaidros* and graphically forecasts the documented attitude of the historical Socrates' illustrious pupil. When Plato himself pairs various pejorative terms (but never a positive one) with the otherwise neutral *agroikos*, the cumulative effect is to denigrate rusticity in all its aspects. And, no less negatively because not expressed in so many words, the only rarely broken silence which obscures the presence of the rural element across the whole spectrum of Athenian private and public life invites the inference that, as with women and slaves, to neglect corresponds a generally accepted rank of inferiority.

Negative assessment countered by selection, simplification, or idealization. A more palatable alternative to outright negativity could be obtained by various modifications of the still admittedly unpleasant facts of the agriculturist's reality. Thus Aristophanes' "farmer-hero" Trygaios is represented as "savior of the Hellenes," but his complementary role as savior of "the deme crowd and farming people" is not illustrated by any reference to the disturbing realities of Attic rural life. At best, we are given his various "wish-lists" embedded in his nostalgic and wistful evocations of country life, but their extreme selectivity (even granting the historicity of their individual items) succeeds in pruning away any element of life outside the walls that an urban audience might find repellent or merely unsettling. The tendency may even extend to the near denial of the distinctive realities of rurality, as when Dikaiopolis addresses the urban-produced and nurtured problem of war and its consequences not by an appeal to agrarian ways but through the establishment of an ideal *market*. Although the imagined location of the hero's market is not revealed by Aristophanes' text (stage sets, however, might have left no doubt), an urban audience at the Lenaia would naturally be thinking in terms of the Agora district—that is, the town itself has become the place of refuge from the War the town has created. But by and large, as the later literary record will continue to illustrate, the writer resorts to the device of substituting sex for work, festival for solitude, merry laughter for grim anxiety, blissful intoxication for depressive reality.

Negative assessment countered by conjuring of rural utopia. With Hesiod is launched the despairing typification of the agrarian's miserable lot in life, when in the *Works and Days* that life is given an historical context in terms of a declining series of "Ages" issuing in the abysmal Age of Iron of the writer's present. But if no immediate relief be in sight, at least one may seek solace in the contemplation of a bygone paradisiacal regime under Zeus's father Kronos, when an agrarian's single day of labor sufficed for the entire year. Somehow knowing that things had once been so much better in the past (however distant) gives hope for improvement in the future, at least to the extent that such improvement—which, as Hesiod's text implies, comes down to a reduction of the agrarian's investment in labor—is thereby established to be logically possible: if such conditions existed in the past, then they may exist again in the future. That the Age of Kronos could indeed be realized is variously demonstrated in the sources for classical Athens. The philosophers' utopias sought the solution to the problem of unending debilitating agrarian labor in the use of slaves, and the fact that these theorists were all associated with Athens as citizen, permanent resident, or invited city-planner accords well with the fleeting signs of servile agricultural labor in classical rural Attica. To an extent, the same thinking is in evidence in Aristophanes' farmer heroes, for the vineyard of the *Peace*'s protagonist Trygaios is worked by slaves and neither he nor Dikaiopolis of *Archarnians* is ever depicted actually laboring on his rural farm.

Glorification of the country by denigrating the town. Reduced to its essentials, this final strategy attempts to enhance rural realities by asserting or suggesting that conditions in the town are even worse. So, in this case only implicitly, the rural is subject to a latently negative appraisal but rehabilitated by juxtaposing with it an even less acceptable sole alternative option. Though already discernible in classical Attic literature, the theme does not reach full development until the emergence of the Atticizing genres of a much later age—and so, if the present analysis is to be carried further, must await a study its own.

Notes

Introduction

1. *PDAA*, pp. 537–552.

2. Pickard-Cambridge, following the evident indications of ancient literary notices, placed the Lenaion in the Agora, but reservations were expressed by Gould and Lewis, the editors of the second edition (1968, p. 37). Thompson and Wycherley seem to have abandoned this theory altogether, while continuing to regard as a possibility the region of the Theater of Dionysos in southeastern Athens (*Agora* XIV, pp. 128–129). For a fuller discussion, see Wycherley 1965, pp. 72–76.

3. Various meanings for the phrase are considered by Salmon 1984, p. 199, note 55, but none with a topographical reference such as I am proposing. For *eschatos* in a spatial sense with reference to land, see Hesiod, *Theogony*, line 731 and Sophocles, fr. 956. The substantive *eschatia* is well established in the sense of border of a country or frontierland: see *LSJ⁹*, s.v., 2, with Lewis 1973, pp. 210–212.

4. Rhodes 1981, on 53.1, p. 588.

5. For the details concerning the Greek and Latin words, see chapter 4, notes 9 and 10.

6. For the full references, see the Bibliography.

7. Humphreys 1978, p. 131.

8. Wood 1988, p. 107.

9. Jameson 1977–1978, pp. 125 ("to be fully a citizen"), 139 ("not so that he can make a fortune but so that he can be a proper citizen").

10. Osborne 1985b, p. 41, and cf. p. 185.

11. Hanson 1995, dust jacket.

12. In Cartledge, Millett, and von Reden 1998, pp. 170–190, with pp. 172 and 190 for the quotations.

13. E. Cohen 2000.

14. For Pipili's essay, see B. Cohen 2000, pp. 153–179.

15. For a succinct summary of alterity in classical studies, see B. Cohen's Introduction to *Not the Classical Ideal*, 2000, pp. 3–20.

16. For a summary of the evidence for "statewide" functions, see Jones 1987, pp. 31–47.

17. As shown by Hansen 1976.

18. See Jones 1999, pp. 151–194.

19. See Jones 1999, pp. 82–122.

20. See Jones 1999, pp. 195–220.
21. See Jones 1999, pp. 97–98.

Chapter 1. Settlement

The greater part of this chapter appeared as "Epigraphic Evidence for Farmstead Residence in Attica," *ZPE* 133 (2000) 75–90 and is reprinted by permission.

1. For full references to the states in question, see Jones 1987, Index I, pp. 387–388, s.vv. From the list of "Units originating in territorial entities" (B.2, p. 388) I omit units not clearly associated with extra-urban spaces or populations.

2. For the most recent account, with full citation of sources, see Parker 1996, pp. 328–332; and cf. Jones 1999, pp. 234–242.

3. See Jones 1987, pp. 107–111 (Epidauros), 135–138 (Megalopolis), 142–145 (Elis), 168–170 (Lokroi), 176 (Tauromenion).

4. See Traill's discussion of "spurious and late Roman demes" at 1975, pp. 81–96, with Appendix C, pp. 113–122. Among the late Roman demes associated with Aphidna, Oinoe, Dekeleia, Kolonai, and Rhamnous (pp. 87–92) are several which were certainly in existence during the classical period yet which lacked constitutional status.

5. My brief presentation owes much to the fuller treatments of Osborne 1985a; 1985b, pp. 15–46; and 1987, pp. 53–74; Burford 1993, pp. 56–66, 118–119, 198–199, 216; and Hanson 1995, pp. 50–55, 59–60.

6. Osborne 1987, p. 68.

7. Hanson 1995, pp. 50–55, 59–60.

8. The following, up to the sections on "literary evidence for rural residence" and "the nucleated village center," reproduces with minor changes my article "Epigraphic Evidence for Farmstead Residence in Attica," *ZPE* 133 (2000) 75–90.

9. Osborne 1985b, pp. 15–22, with the conclusion at p. 17: "there is no clear evidence in the literature for anyone who lives and farms out on his own in the country."

10. Thus, in reply to Osborne 1985a, Langdon 1990–1991, pp. 209–211.

11. See, for example, Boyd and Carpenter 1977 ("dragon houses"), J. E. Jones 1974 ("country houses"), J. E. Jones/Sackett/Eliot 1962 ("Dema house"), J. E. Jones/Sackett/Graham 1973 ("country house" near Vari), Langdon and Watrous 1977 ("farm" near Laurium), Wickens 1983 ("farm" of Timesios), and Young 1956 ("country estates" at Sounion). For a survey of country (as well as town) houses of classical Attica, see John Ellis Jones's 1975 paper, pp. 63–136 and 137–144. An appendix—aiming at completeness—listing isolated farms in Classical and Hellenistic Attica will be found in Osborne 1985b, pp. 190–191. In the main body of his text, Osborne gives detailed attention to the area around Vouliagmeni and Vari (pp. 22–29) and the Sounion-Thorikos region of southeast Attica (pp. 29–36). Earlier, Pečirka had succinctly reviewed Attic isolated homesteads at 1973, pp. 133–137.

12. Among several recent treatments of individual Attic demes, modern ar-

chaeological study is well represented by Lohmann 1983, pp. 93–117, 1992. Earlier, physical remains associated with the coastal demes had been described by Eliot 1962. Extensive citation of archaeological sites will be found in Pečirka's study of "homestead farms in Classical and Hellenistic Hellas," in Finley 1973, pp. 113–147 (with pp. 133–137 for Attica). Attic demes, severally and in the aggregate, are the subject of various papers in Coulson et al. 1994. For isolated farm infrastructures, see the preceding note.

13. Pečirka 1973, pp. 113–147, with pp. 133–137 for Attica.

14. Osborne 1985b, pp. 15–46, with p. 41 for the point that "The whole working of Athenian democracy demanded that the demes continued to be communities, and without modern means of communication that was effectively a demand that people continued to dwell together in villages."

15. Osborne 1985a, pp. 119–128. The Athenian material, including the leases, is discussed at pp. 122–123, 124–125, and 127.

16. Langdon 1990–1991, pp. 209–213. Security horoi are briefly mentioned at p. 211, n. 7.

17. Hanson 1995, pp. 47–89, especially 51–60.

18. Pritchett 1956, pp. 261–276, V. Real Property.

19. Osborne 1985b, p. 21.

20. Langdon 1990–1991, pp. 209–211.

21. See, for example, Burford 1993, pp. 56, 68, 119.

22. On the towers of southern Attica, their agricultural or other functions, and possible place on an isolated farm, see Osborne 1985b, pp. 31–34. Earlier, J. H. Young had associated the towers with "agricultural estates" (1956, pp. 122–146), a conclusion opposed by Osborne.

23. For the agricultural function of the klision, see Osborne's discussion (1985a, p. 122) opposing Kent's view, worked out in his study of the temple estates of Delos, Rheneia, and Mykonos, that the term denotes a "farmhouse."

24. Lambert 1997. Earlier, the stelai had been studied, but without attention to our questions, by Lewis 1973, pp. 187–212. For Lambert's item and fragment numbers, see the Table of Sales, pp. 113–147.

25. For the sale of a chorion with an oikopedon in [Thymai]tadai, see no. 79, F9B, lines 9–14, with p. 227, where Lambert suggests that the latter term denotes "a block or set of housing, a partially constructed house or, perhaps more likely, a partially ruined or abandoned one."

26. So Lambert 1997, p. 226: "In most of these cases it seems likely that what was sold was a "farm," i.e., a piece of agricultural land with associated house, or possibly other farm structure."

27. On the "garden," see Lambert 1997, p. 227, and below in connection with the leases.

28. Lambert 1997, p. 1, with chapter 6 (pp. 183–206) for the selling groups and chapter 5 (pp. 149–182) for the officials of the selling groups and the buyers.

29. Lambert 1997, pp. 226–227. At the same time, as he notes, one would not expect a group to own multiple houses of this sort in the same place, as the hypothesis would seem to require in the case of F4, wherein five chorion-and-oikia ensembles are preserved.

30. Lambert 1997, pp. 228–229. On the meaning of *eschatia*, see Lewis 1973, pp. 210–212.

31. Lambert 1997, pp. 228–229.

32. Thus I find entirely unnecessary Lambert's mention in this connection of nucleated settlements (1997, p. 242): "It was fairly common in Attica, albeit by no means universal, for agricultural holdings to lie around and [be] accessible, but separate, from nucleated settlements; . . . "

33. For the few examples, see Behrend 1970, pp. 50–55, nos. 1–4. For a full discussion of the leasing of private property at Athens, see Osborne 1988, pp. 304–319.

34. *Agora* XIX, pp. 170–207 (Agora texts). In his Preface, Walbank promises a new corpus of "all Athenian documents relating to the leasing of publicly owned real property" (p. 147).

35. For the contextual, social, and economic dimensions of these, and other Classical and Hellenistic Greek leases, see Osborne 1988, pp. 279–323, esp. 281–292 on the leasing of public and corporate property at Athens.

36. Osborne 1985a, pp. 122–123, 124–125.

37. Apud Osborne 1985a, p. 123.

38. Jameson 1982, pp. 66–74: 71–74.

39. Osborne 1985a, pp. 124–125.

40. See the editor's commentary, p. 72.

41. Burford 1993, pp. 135–137, with p. 135 for the quotation. Earlier, the garden had been the subject of Maureen Carroll-Spilleke's *Kepos: der antike griechische Garten* (1989) and of Osborne's essay on "classical Greek gardens" (1992b).

42. Plutarch, *Solon* 23.6 (= Ruschenbusch 1966, F 63 [55]).

43. A case for more extensive "artificial watering" is made by Hanson 1995, pp. 60–63.

44. Osborne 1995a, pp. 124–125.

45. The Greek, as often, inverts the expected relationship between main verb and participles.

46. Φιδάκνη is the Attic for πιθάκνη (*LSJ⁹* s.v) and the diminutive of πίθος (see the scholiast on Aristophanes, *Equites*, line 792).

47. For the derivation of the *hapax legomenon* χόνδην from χόω, giving the sense "buried or sunk in the ground," see the editors' commentary, op. cit., p. 56. Alternatively, *LSJ⁹* Supplement, s.v., refers the word to χανδάνω, giving the sense "in capacity."

48. See, for example, the descriptions of rural homes by Friedl 1962, pp. 39–42 and du Boulay 1974, pp. 15–40.

49. See Pritchett 1956, p. 265, where it is stated that in legal contexts an *oikia* is a "private residence" and that, with citation of Finley, on the *horoi* it has the meaning "personal residence."

50. Osborne observes (1985a, p. 125) that the individuals who lease temple estates on Hellenistic Delos are "men of high status who are also active in a number of other fields at the same time."

51. Thus one Hierokles, lessee in no. 1, is identified as "a man of substance" by Jameson 1982, p. 71.

52. If the restoration of the name of the lessee of no. 7 as Diopeithes, son of Diopeithes, of Sphettos is correct, he will have been *APF* 4328, p. 160.

53. The assured examples are Thrasyboulos of Alopeke in no. 4; Diognetos, son of Arkesilos, of Melite in no. 6; Diodoros, son of Kantharos, of Myrrhinous in no. 8. If the lessee in the lease from Prasiai (no. 9), Polysthenes, was himself a demesman of Prasiai, then he too is certifiably absent from the register.

54. Such as, for instance, the payment of 20 drachmas each year for 30 years in *SEG* 24.203, lines 6–9 (no. 4, above). In no. 6, the rent, payable in two install-ments, totaled 200 drachmas per year (lines 18–24); in no. 7, 50 drachmas per year due in a single payment (lines 4–6); in no. 8, 600 drachmas per year (lines 13–14).

55. Hedrick 1988, pp. 81–85, no. 1 (reproduced by Lalonde in *Agora* XIX as an addendum, H131).

56. Not included here is no. 90A, which names an *ergasterion* in conjunc-tion with a *chorion* and therefore belongs in the major category of encumbered lands (below).

57. A tabulation similar to mine will be found in Osborne 1985b, p. 205, Table 5. But his brief analysis (pp. 59–60) does not broach the question of farm-stead residence. Likewise, Pečirka's discussion of Finley's study of the *horoi* (1973, pp. 117–118) fails to perceive their relevance to our question.

58. See the "Conspectus of Deme Quotas and Locations" in Traill 1986, pp. 125–140.

59. On the complex relation between the provenience Anavyso and the an-cient deme Anaphlystos, see Eliot 1962, pp. 81–82.

60. For the assignment of Ana Voula, the findspot of this *horos*, see Eliot 1962, p. 21.

61. For the most thorough and recent roster of the documents of the deme associations, see Whitehead 1986a, Appendix 3, pp. 374–393, with the addition of a few more recent texts by Jones 1999, p. 100, n. 54 (pp. 100–101). Of the 145 doc-uments assignable to 48 specific demes, only seven originate in the five intramural units (Jones, p. 101).

62. So Finley 1985, p. 60.

63. Finley 1985, p. 60.

64. The term also occurs occasionally in the *poletai* records: see *Agora* XIX, P 17, lines 16 and 22; P 26, line 406; and P 53, line 41.

65. For the conjunction of multiple *edaphoi* with a *kaminos*, see *horos* no. 92; and of a single *edaphos* with an *oikia*, the inscription *Agora* XIX, L8, line 107.

66. Rejection of Finley's suggestion requires only that we admit in the case of no. 55 the possibility of a plot of land in Peiraieus that was "sold for redemp-tion" for 150 drachmas, a figure that Finley found exceptionally low for farming land. Naturally, a property may be used as security for a sum less than its actual value; the sum secured is not equivalent to its "fair market value" or the like. For tabulations of the *sale* prices of real properties, see Pritchett 1956, pp. 269–276.

67. Finley's text (which substitutes a *chorion* for Ziebarth's *ergasterion* in the text of line 2 in *IG* II² 2759) reads: χω]ρίο κ[αὶ κή]/[π]ου καὶ τῆς προσούσης [κρήνη]/ς τῶι κηπιδίωι (lines 2–4).

68. As an index of the deme's citizen population, one may cite its bouleutic

quota of 11? (Traill 1986, p. 138), which places it with Aixone (11?) and Lower Paiania (11) as the fourth most populous deme behind Acharnai (22, combined), Aphidna (16), and Kydathenaion (11/12). Also, with 10 known metics, Eleusis ranks eighth behind Melite, Peiraieus, Kollytos, Alopeke, Kydathenaion, Skambonidai, and Keiriadai (Whitehead 1986a, p. 83).

69. Finley 1985, p. 61.

70. Against Finley (1985, p. 253, note 50), I do not agree that Xenophon's statement at *Poroi* 2.6 that there were many vacant sites within the city walls necessarily implies that "they have no significant monetary value." Besides, contra Finley, Xenophon's remark (4.50) that an influx of population into the Laureion district would render the *choroi* no less valuable than those "around the *asty*" seems to imply quite the opposite of his position.

71. For the law, see above with note 42.

72. For the *kopron* at classical Athens, see Owens 1983, pp. 44–50.

73. The "sub–agora" districts, especially to the southwest, provide some clear examples of the phenomenon: see *Agora* XIV, pp. 173–185.

74. No. 2, from the area of the Ilissos, marks, as restored, a "*chorion, kepos,* and the *krēnē* adjacent to the *kepidion,*" but no reference to an *oikia* or other structure is preserved in the acephalous text. No. 8, from Arkesine on Amorgos, marks, as restored, *choria, oikia,* and *kepoi.*

75. Again, as noted above with note 42, the Solonian law regarding access to wells suggests that they, at least in some cases, were used to meet small demands, such as those of a household garden, and not for the irrigation of acreage.

76. Hanson 1995, p. 52.

77. Langdon 1990–1991, p. 210.

78. Langdon 1990–1991, p. 210.

79. Contra Langdon (1990–1991, p. 211): "It is as clear a statement as we could wish for in showing residence on the farm in Attica." The passage is also treated by Roy 1988, pp. 57–59.

80. Similarly, *demotes* "villager" (sg. and pl.) sometimes has local reference (*Clouds* 210, 1322; *Eccl.* 1115; cf. *Peace* 920), but without implication as to the configuration of the settlement. The other common word for village, *komē*, is not exampled, while the masculine (*Clouds* 965) and feminine (*Lysistrata* 5; fr. 274) of *kometēs* "villager" have isolated and (for our problem) uncommunicative occurrences.

81. Among two dozen or so straightforward examples, *Peace* 562–563 is of particular interest: "And then let's slip away *eis ta choria,* after we've bought some good salt fish *eis agron.*" Two chances missed to mention a village!

82. For a succinct collection of the evidence, see Jones 1987, pp. 61–65, especially 63, with notes.

83. The *agora* of the deme as the place of assembly is well treated by Whitehead 1986a, pp. 86–90. For the extraurban deme as independent administrative center, see Jones 1999, pp. 86–94, with pp. 87–89 on the *agorai.*

84. For an example, see the lease from Prasiai (*SEG* 21.644) discussed above. But nothing in the text associates this structure with any village "center."

85. Buford 1993, p. 57.

86. So Millett 1985, p. xi: "The world of the *horoi*, then, is that of the relatively wealthy landowner from the upper reaches of Athenian society, and not that of the small-scale peasant farmer."

87. Mussche et al. 1975.

88. Stainchaouer 1994, pp. 175–189.

89. Andreou 1994, pp. 191–209.

90. See above, with note 11 for references to the literature.

91. The dated examples (that is, those bearing an archon's name) compiled by Millett in his 1985 appendix to Finley (pp. ix–x) range between 363/2 (no. 127) and 184/3 (no. 137A).

Chapter 2. Society

1. On the historicity of Hesiod's *Works and Days*, see Millett 1984, pp. 84–115. More recent treatments touching on themes relevant here are Petropoulos 1994 and Tandy and Neale 1996.

2. Thuc. 2.46.1, with Plato, *Menex.* 248d–249d and Arist., *Pol.* 2.5.4: 1268a. The practice was ascribed to Solon by Diog. Laert. 1.55. See Lacey 1968, pp. 140–141, with note 60.

3. Aesch. 3.258; Plut. *Arist.* 27.4; *SIG*³ 496 (229/8), line 18, with Lacey 1968, p. 109 with note 63.

4. Plut. *Solon* 22.1, with Lacey 1968, p. 117 with note 116.

5. For γόνεων κάκωσις, see *AthPol* 56.6, with Rhodes 1981 ad loc., p. 629.

6. Harrison I 1968, pp. 122–162; MacDowell 1978, pp. 92–99.

7. Harrison I 1968, pp. 61–70; MacDowell 1978, pp. 67–68.

8. Cox 1998, pp. 52–60 (rural areas), 60–63 (inland demes of the Mesogeia and the north).

9. Osborne 1985b, pp. 127–138.

10. Cox 1988, pp. 185–188, and, more fully, 1998, pp. 38–67 ("town and country, marriage, and death").

11. Harrison I 1968, pp. 130–132; MacDowell 1978, pp. 92–95.

12. See, recently, on the subject of "Oriental seclusion" of females, Schnurr-Redford 1996; Patterson 1998, pp. 40, 125–129.

13. Damsgaard-Madsen 1988, p. 66. Cf. Hansen et al. 1990.

14. Whitehead 1983. A later study of the language of public approbation (1993, pp. 37–75) took up the "cardinal virtues" in their wider context.

15. Whitehead 1986a, p. 244, with notes 100–103, where the count excludes restored instances of the key word or phrase and documents not demonstrably those of demes.

16. Whitehead 1983, pp. 59–60 for the thesis. The argument is extended to the Attic demes at 1986a, pp. 241–252.

17. Whitehead's discussion does admit "unbridled personal ambition" (p. 242), "his innate inclination to seek prominence and acclaim" (p. 250), and "the Few either abusing property-power and hereditary influence for their own ends or

else disdaining local involvement in favor of more potent satisfactions to be found elsewhere" (p. 251). Any of these formulations might pertain to either an urban or rural setting.

18. For a reading of the poem, with an attempt to place the quarrel in its narrative and agrarian context, see Jones 1984, pp. 307–323.

19. For a recent discussion of the Attic rupestral *horoi*, with recent bibliography, see Jones 1999, pp. 59–64. The free-standing pillar *horoi* from the Agora are newly edited by Gerald V. Lalonde, in *Agora* XIX, pp. 5–51. None of the many examples edited, cited, or studied in these two publications can with certainty be associated with the boundary of an agricultural plot.

20. For the possibility, however, that the inscriptions were cut to mark the boundaries of grazing lands, see Stanton 1984, pp. 299, 304–305.

21. For discussion of the legal aspects of the dispute, see MacDowell 1978, pp. 136–137.

22. The continuum is framed on a wider scale, but with the omission of the household, in the language of a decree from ?Eupyridai, *IG* II² 1362, honoring the deme's priest of Apollo Erithaseos for his conduct "on behalf of himself and the *demotai* and the Demos of the Athenians" (lines 3–5).

23. Jameson 1977–1978, p. 138, note 79, citing P. Herfst, *La travail de la femme dans la Grèce ancienne*, diss. Utrecht 1922, pp. 16–17.

24. Fitton Brown 1984, pp. 71–74.

25. For the inside vs. outside division of space by gender, see Xen. *Oec.* 7.25–28; [Arist.], *Oec.* 1.1343b30–1344a4, with many modern discussions.

26. For a more recent (and fuller) discussion of female agricultural labor, but without addition to our slender fund of evidence, see Sheidel 1995 and 1996.

27. See Golden 1990, esp. pp. 32–36. For the painted *chous*, see p. 193, note 44. Knemon's daughter can be made to join her father in the fields for the purpose of agricultural work only by combination and inference (p. 193, note 46).

28. Jameson 1977–1978, p. 137.

29. Wood 1983, pp. 1–47.

30. Jameson 1977–1978; de Ste. Croix 1981.

31. For the details, see below on the metics.

32. Jameson 1977–1978, p. 135.

33. Jameson 1977–1978, pp. 135–136. For the references, see chapter 1, "Security Horoi."

34. But Jameson (1977–1978, pp. 136–137) suggests, inferentially, that "the passage as a whole does imply significant losses in farm labor." All Thucydides reveals is that "a" or "the" "great part" were *cheirotechnai*, i.e. skilled and not farm workers (with p. 136, note 72, on the reading).

35. For approving evaluations of the use of hired labor, see Jameson 1977–1978, p. 132; and de Ste. Croix 1981, p. 593, note 59.

36. Cox 1988, pp. 185–188, with pp. 185 and 187–188 for Plato's sister.

37. Osborne 1985b, pp. 127–138.

38. Burford 1993, p. 183.

39. Jameson 1977–1978, p. 134.

40. Jameson 1977–1978, pp. 133–134.

41. Burford 1993, p. 192.

42. For the zones, see Jones 1999, pp. 102–103.

43. Whitehead 1986a, pp. 223–234, esp. 231–232.

44. Damsgaard-Madsen 1988, p. 62. For a recent assessment of the use of sepulchral inscriptions for the demography of the demes, see Hansen et al. 1990.

45. Burford 1993, pp. 68–69.

46. Burford 1993, p. 67.

47. Hanson 1995, pp. 181–201, esp. 186–189.

48. Modern opinion on the problem is well represented by Connor 1971, pp. 18–22; Finley 1983, pp. 39–49; Millett 1989, pp. 15–47; and Whitehead 1986a, pp. 305–313. On reciprocity in ancient Greece, see Seaford 1994, Gill/Postleth-waite/Seaford 1998, and Schofield 1998.

49. For a thorough collection of instances of the word and discussion, see Rhodes 1981 on *AthPol* 2.2, pp. 90–91. Since Rhodes, "Pelatai und Klienten" have been discussed by Hahn 1983, pp. 59–64.

50. For the legal position of the *prostates*, see Whitehead 1977, pp. 89–92. For discussion of the word and its abstract substantive, *prostateia*, see Millett 1989, pp. 33–36.

51. Millett 1989, pp. 34–35.

52. By contrast, Herman in his study of ritualized friendship maintains (1987, p. 38) that the Greek language did not give rise to a pair of hierarchical status designations analogous to the Roman *patronus-cliens* (and cf. Edlund 1977, p. 132). While the linguistic point may be debatable, my position is less concerned with language than with practice and in any event I will shortly offer an explanation for the absence of appropriate specialized vocabulary.

53. Saller 1982, pp. 8–11, with p. 10 for the quotation.

54. Whitehead 1986a, pp. 305–313 at 307, with note 62, citing H.T. Wade-Gery, *AJP* 59 (1938) 131–134 (= *Essays in Greek History*, Oxford 1958, pp. 235–238); W.R. Connor, *Theopompus and Fifth-Century Athens*, Washington, D.C. 1968, pp. 30–37; and Rhodes 1981, p. 340.

55. Finley 1983, pp. 39–40, 45.

56. Whitehead 1986a, pp. 305–308, with p. 308 for the guarded conclusion that "a writer (perhaps Critias) . . . represented Kimon as having provided a species of poor relief for his fellow demesmen of Lakiadai."

57. Millett 1989, pp. 23–24.

58. Although Kirchner catalogues nearly 100 demesmen in *Prosopographia Attica*, only nine Lakiadai are registered among Davies' propertied Athenians and these nine include three members of Kimon's family (*APF*, pp. 613–614).

59. If one were to understand the reference to be to Pericles' *deme*, it may be noted that Phrearrhoi had a quota of nine, larger than the quota of Kimon's deme by a factor of four and one-half. But the run of the passage clearly suggests that the reference is actually to Pericles' prospective *clientela* in the *asty*.

60. Similarly, Davies 1971, p. 311, finds a contrast between "local dynast and national politician." For a disapproving view, see Finley 1983, p. 47, note 58.

61. See, for example, the several choregies associated with the local celebration of the Dionysia discussed in ch. 4.

62. Whitehead 1986a, p. 312.

63. Millett 1989, pp. 26–28 (Isokrates), 29–30 (Menander).

64. Millett 1989, pp. 25 (democratic revolution), 37–43 (alternatives to patronage).

65. Saller 1982, pp. 3–4, with reference to A. Blok, "Variations in Patronage," *Sociologische Gids* 16 (1969) 365–378.

66. Jones 1999, p. 100, note 54 [pp. 100–101], updating the annotated catalogue of deme inscriptions in Whitehead 1986a, pp. 374–393.

67. The 94 include five from inscriptions recording, in three cases, two, in one case, three, decrees. Accordingly, when calculating the percentage of honorary decrees against the total, I have added five to the number of inscriptions, 157, to yield 162. Additionally, to the honorary decrees I have added several dedications that in one way or another acknowledge the previous bestowal of honors upon the dedicator.

68. Demes within fortifications: Koile, none; Kollytos, none; Kydathenaion, one (*Agora* 16, no. 54); Melite, two (*SEG* 22.116 and *Hesperia* 11 [1942] 265–274, no. 51); Skambonidai, none. Peiraieus, one (*IG* II² 1214).

69. As, for example, from Acharnai, *SEG* 21.519.

70. Whitehead 1986a, pp. 238–239.

71. Whitehead 1986a, pp. 238–241.

72. *IG* I³ 250 (ca. 450–430), lines 11–14. The text itself does not specify whether "the *demotai*" are those of the Upper (quota one) or Lower (quota eleven) deme (that the deme is one or the other is proved by the stone's discovery at Liopesi), but a quorum of as many as 100 is obviously compatible only with the larger bouleutic quota (Whitehead 1986a, p. 385, no. 83).

73. Acharnai: *AE* 131 (1992)[1993] 179–193, lines A 3–5, B 4–5. Aixone: *IG* II² 1199, lines 1–6. Athmonon: *IG* II² 1203, lines 1–6. Eleusis: *Hesperia* 8 (1939) 177–180, lines 8–10; *IG* II² 949, lines 32, 34–35, [36]. Halai Aixonides, *AD* 11 (1927–1928) 40–41, no. 4, lines 5–6. Ikarion: *SEG* 22.117, lines 1–2. Lower (Coastal) Lamptrai: *IG* II² 1204, lines 3–5. Melite: *Hesperia* 11 (1942) 265–274, no. 51, lines 3–4, 6–7. Sounion: *IG* II² 1181, lines 3–4. Teithras: *SEG* 21.520, lines 7–12. Cf. Kydantidai and Ionidai: *SEG* 39.148 (41.71), lines 6–8 (superintendance of festival of Herakles).

74. *Choregia* at Acharnai: *IG* II² 3092 and 3106; Aigilia: *IG* II² 3096; Aixone: *IG* II² 1198 and 1200; *MDAI(A)* 66 (1941) 218–219, no. 1; Eleusis: *IG* II² 1186 and 3090; Ikarion: *IG* I³ 254; *IG* II² 1178, 3094, 3095, 3098, 3099; Paiania: *IG* II² 3097; Rhamnous: *IG* II² 3108 and 3109; Thorikos: *SEG* 34.107 and 40.128. For the *choregoi* of the Rural Dionysia in various demes, see ch. 4; the *choregia* in all its aspects is now the subject of a modern study by Wilson 2000.

75. Gymnasiarchy at Rhamnous: *IG* II² 3109.

76. Halai Araphenides: *AE* 1932 *Chronika*, pp. 30–32, lines 1–7: "Since Philoxenos well and honorably served as chorege for the *pyrrhichistai* and served in all the other *leitourgiai* in the deme well and honorably. . . ."

77. See ch. 4, passim.

78. Acharnai: *SEG* 21.519 (altars, with lines 17–19 for the advance of funds); *IG* II² 1207 (*anathemata*). ?Erikeia: *IG* II² 1215 (*hiera* and *anathemata*). Halai

Aixonides: *AD* 11 (1927–1928) 40–41, no. 4 (*hieron, agalmata*). Melite: *Hesperia* 11 (1942) 265–274, no. 51, lines 4–6 (*naoi*). Peiraieus: *Hesperia* 3 (1934) 44–46, no. 33 ("some public work of construction," Merritt). Sounion: *IG* II² 1180 (new agora).

79. Some explicit examples, from Eleusis: *IG* II² 1186, lines 11–12; *Hesperia* 8 (1939) 177–180, lines 8–12; *SEG* 22.127, lines 8, [18]; *IG* II² 949, lines [35], 37; ?Erikeia: *IG* II² 1215, lines 12–13; ?Sphettos: *SEG* 36.187, line 1; Teithras: *SEG* 24.153, line 3.

80. A partial listing of this common formula would include: Acharnai: *AE* 131 (1992)[1994] 179–193, lines A4, B6–7. Aixone: *IG* II² 1198, lines 11–13; 1199, lines 11–13, 27–28; 1202, lines 7–8, 17–18; *Hesperia* 8 (1939) 177–180, line 11. Athmonon: *IG* II² 1203, lines 15–16. Cholargos: *IG* II² 1184, lines 18–20. Eitea: *SEG* 28.102, lines 6–9, 13–15. Eleusis: *IG* II² 1186, lines 3–6, 6–10; 1187, lines 2–3, 14–16; 1188, lines 5–6; 1192, lines 7–9; *SEG* 28.103, lines 11–12, 15–16; 1192, lines 3, 8–9; 1193, passim; *SEG* 22.127, lines 19–23. Halai Araphenides: *AE* 1925–1926, pp. 168–177, lines 3–5. Kephisia: *AD* 24 (1969) 6–7, lines 8–9; *AE* 1932, Chronika, pp. 30–32, lines 17–20. Peiraieus: *IG* II² 1176+, lines 33–34.

81. For some contexts for such activity, see the section above on rivalry between households within village communities.

82. *IG* II² 1191 (Eleusis; 321/0 or 318/7), lines 19–21: [καὶ] οἱ τὸ προάστ/ιον οἰκοῦν[τ]ε[ς καὶ] οἱ γεω[ρ]γοὶ / σώιςωνται.

83. *SEG* 22.117 (ca. 330), line 3: καρποὶ καλοὶ κατὰ πᾶσαν τὴν χώρα[ν] γεγόνασιν .....

84. *IG* II² 1217 (263/2 or 262/1), lines 3–4: διέδωκε] / τῶν τε καρπῶν τὰ μέρ[η τὰ ἐπιβάλλοντα? _ _ _ _]. For a more conservative text, see Pouilloux 1954, no. 6.

85. *SEG* 36.187 (ca. 350–300), line 2: [....8.... τῶ]ν περιοικο[ύντων ....].

86. The Eleusinians' honoring of a Sphettian is of course an exception. For a discussion of the relatively few cases of non-demesman honorands, see Jones 1999, pp. 118–120.

87. *IG* II² 1201 (317–307).

88. *SEG* 22.127 (med. s. III), lines 12–14: τῆς τε [σωτηρίας τοῦ χωρίου] / καὶ τῶν οἰκούν [των ἐν αὐτῶι πολιτῶ]/ν·

89. *IG* II² 1299 (dated by mention of archons of 238/7, 237/6, and 236/5), lines 66–67: ἐπεμελήθη δὲ καὶ ὅπω[ς ἐκ τῆς χώρας οἱ σῖ]/τοι μετ᾽ ἀσφαλείας εἰσενεχθῶσιν·

90. *SEG* 24.154 (either 268/7 or 265/4).

91. *SEG* 25.155 (236/5): ἐπεμελήθη / τῆς τε τοῦ φρουρίου φυλακῆς καὶ τῆς ἄλλης χώρας τῆς Ἀττι/κῆς (15–17); τοῖς ὑπεκτεθημένοις τὰ βοσκή/ματα διὰ τὸν πόλεμον διασώιςων καὶ βοηθῶν...(19–20).

92. For the latest listing of the phyle documents, see Jones 1999, pp. 321–323.

93. Jones 1999, pp. 174–194 (= Jones 1995, pp. 503–542).

94. Millett 1989, pp. 30–33 (the *kolax*), 41–43 (the *eranos*).

95. Millett 1989, p. 36.

96. Millett 1989, p. 37.

97. Finley 1983, pp. 46–47.

98. Millett 1989, pp. 40–41.

99. For the notion that "public pay might act as a practical antidote to personal patronage," see Millett's discerning discussion, 1989, pp. 37–41.

100. Aixone: *IG* II² 1202, lines 1–2. Besa: *Hesperia* 26 (1957) 4, no. S2, lines 31 and 40; 15, no. S6, lines 6–8; 17, S14, lines 33–34; *Hesperia* 19 (1950) 237, no. 14, line 34. *Eleusis: IG* II² 2500; *SEG* 28.103, lines 23–24. Erchia: *SEG* 21.541, lines E 50–51. Halai Aixonides: *IG* II² 1174, lines 13–15. Otryne: [Demosthenes] 44.36. Peiraieus: *IG* II² 1176+, line 27. Skambonidai: *IG* I³ 244, lines A 9, 20–21; C 9–10. Sounion: *IG* II² 1180, lines 21–25.

101. For the inscription, see Sherwin-White 1978, p. 83, citing (for her quotation) a portion of the unpublished text reproduced by L. Robert at *REA* 65 (1963) 305, note 3.

102. *IG* I³ 250, lines 11–14.

103. The quota of Upper Paiania was only 1, implying a membership too small (e.g. 60, given an Athenian citizen body of 30,000) to demand a quorum of 100.

104. Whitehead 1986a, pp. 90–92.

105. The particulars of deme assembly business are collected at Whitehead 1986a, pp. 111–119.

106. Whitehead 1986a, pp. 219–220; Jones 1999, pp. 91–92. For the grants of *proedria*, see chapter 4.

107. Jones 1999, p. 92.

108. See chapter 4.

109. *AD* 24 (1969) 6–7, lines 4–7.

110. *IG* II² 2492, line 23.

111. See above, with note 78.

112. For the deme documents erected in agora, theater, or shrine, see Jones 1999, pp. 89–91.

113. Aixone: *IG* II² 1197, lines 15–18; 1198, lines 22–28; *MDAI(A)* 66 (1941) 218–219, no. 1, lines 6–8. Eleusis: *IG* II² 1193, lines 25–27. Myrrhinous: *IG* II² 1182, lines 11–16. Peiraieus: *IG* II² 1214, lines 33–36. Rhamnous: *SEG* 38.127, lines 3–4.

114. See, for example, note 73 above, where decrees recording sacrifices underwritten by deme honorands are listed.

115. See ch. 4, with note 94.

116. See ch. 4, with note 79.

117. Isaios, 3.80 (unknown deme); Theophrastos, *Characters* 10.11 (deme unknown); Menander, *Sikyonios*, lines 183–191 (Eleusis).

118. Aixone: *IG* II² 1199, line 22.

119. Halai Araphenides: *AE* 1932, *Chronika*, pp. 30–32, lines 3–7.

120. Whitehead 1986a, pp. 199–204, with p. 202 for the number of sacrifices.

121. *IG* I³ 244 (ca. 460), lines C 7–9.

122. For the case of the Dionysia, see chapter 4. For the general subject of female participation in deme cults, see Jones 1999, pp. 123–128.

123. Hanson 1995, passim.

Chapter 3. Village

1. For the documents, see the annotated list of Whitehead 1986a, Appendix 3, pp. 374–393, with the modifications at Jones 1999, p. 100, note 4 (pp. 100–101). Where relevant, i.e. where one of the four demes shortly to be examined is concerned, more recently published inscriptions will be cited and discussed.

2. Traill 1986, pp. 133–134.

3. *PECS*, s.v. "Acharnai," p. 6.

4. For the interpretation, see ch. 1, "Security *Horoi*."

5. See Whitehead 1986a, Appendix 5, "Acharnai," pp. 397–400, for various proposed remedies. Earlier, Gomme, on 2.20.4, had calculated the maximum possible hoplite strength of Acharnai at 1,200 and suggested that a manuscript error may be responsible for the transmitted numeral (1956, pp. 73–74).

6. My position, that the figure represents not the familiar manuscript error in the transmission of numerals, but exaggeration, is in fundamental agreement with Sterling Dow's case for "gross overstatement" (1961, pp. 66–80).

7. Travlos, *PDAA*, p. 159, VI, with fig. 219.

8. Whitehead 1986a, p. 399.

9. See, besides the Aristophanes, Pindar, *Nemean* II, line 25; Seneca, *Hippolytus*, line 22. Milchhöfer, s.v. "Acharnai", *RE*, I.i (1894) 209–210, suggests that "the nature of the most defiant and rough mountain of Attica" had been transferred to the demespeople.

10. *PCG* VIII Adespota, fr. 498, citing Photios δ762, Etym. Gen. AB (Etym. Magn. p. 288.15), Souda δ1515 (compound) and Hesychios δ2415 (compound).

11. *CPG*, vol. II, p. 16, no. 90: Ἀχαρνικοὶ ὄνοι· ἐπὶ τῶν νωθρῶν καὶ μεγάλων.

12. Whitehead 1986a, pp. 399–400.

13. On the methods of "agricultural destruction," see Hanson 1983, pp. 37–63, with pp. 56–58 on vines.

14. I translate here the Teubner text of F. Blass, *Andocidis Orationes* (Leipzig, 1906), p. 109, letting stand the lacuna following the mention of "women." K. J. Maidment, in the Loeb edition of the *Minor Attic Orators*, vol. 1 (Cambridge, Mass. 1941), pp. 582–583, eliminates the lacuna by transposing "and the wagons" to follow "the charcoal burners," but without any obvious textual or palaeographic justification.

15. For the attribution of this decree to Acharnai, see Whitehead 1986a, p. 374, no. 2.

16. *Agora* XIV, pp. 162–165, with p. 165 for the quotation.

17. Milchhöfer, s.v. "Acharnai," *RE* I.i (1894) 210, for the sources.

18. *IG* II^2 1176+, with Stroud 1974, pp. 290–298.

19. Traill 1986, p. 136.

20. Eliot 1962, pp. 21.

21. Eliot 1962, pp. 17–20. For a map illustrating some of Eliot's findings, see Figure 1, p. 18.

22. Eliot 1962, pp. 7–16, with conclusion at p. 16.

23. *PCG* VII Plato, fr. 175; Athenaios 7.325d–f; Hesychios, s.v. Αἰξωνίδα τρίγλην.

24. For pasturage and related subjects, see Burford 1993, pp. 77, 102 (conversion to arable), 123–124 (on fallow), 21, 72–75, 122, 149, 152 (public control and restrictions).

25. *APF*, p. 603.

26. *APF* 9574, p. 274.

27. Stroud 1984, pp. 355–360 at p. 357.

28. *APF*, p. 359

29. *APF*, pp. 560–561. For the identification of Cape Kolias with the promontory of Hagios Kosmas, see Eliot 1962, p. 7, note 6. Eliot places the northern boundary of Aixoneis (a short distance) south of Hagios Kosmas (p. 21).

30. *APF*, pp. 275–276.

31. Fr. 222K–T.

32. Plato, *Laches* 197c with scholia; Steph. Byz. s.v. Αἰξώνεια; Hesychios and Souda, s.v. αἰξωνεύεσθαι; Harpokration, s.v. Αἰξωνῆσιν.

33. Whitehead 1986a, pp. 218–219. Consistent with, but obviously not materially supporting, this theory is the conjecture that the five comic masks engraved above the decree in no. 9 indicate five productions and five pairs of *choregoi* (p. 219, note 252).

34. Eliot 1962, pp. 25–34, with pp. 33–34 for the conclusion.

35. Eliot 1962, pp. 32–33.

36. Stainchaour 1994, pp. 175–189.

37. Andreou 1994, pp. 191–209.

38. Eliot 1962, pp. 26–27.

39. Fr. 127K-T; Edmonds, *FAC*, Menander, Οἱ Ἁλαεῖς, p. 552, with the citations for the identification of the deme.

40. For the emendation of the transmitted subject "fishermen" (Halieis) to the plural demotic, see Eliot 1962, p. 25 with note 1.

41. Kourionotes 1927–1928 and Stauropoullos 1938.

42. Whitehead 1986a, p. 112 with note 130.

43. Whitehead 1986a, pp. 239–241.

44. Davies, *APF*, p. 603.

45. Davies, *APF*, pp. 537–538; Whitehead 1986a, p. 433, no. 199.

46. Davies, *APF*, pp. 183–184 (Epichares), 238 (Thrasyboulos).

47. Traill 1986, p. 128.

48. *PCG* VII, Theopompos, *Eirene*, fr. 12 (quoted by Athenaios 14.652).

49. If so, the joking reference would comport with Old Comedy's, and specifically Aristophanes', tendency to restrict obscene humorous references to demes of more remote remove from the urban center: see Jones 1999, p. 111.

50. Hesychios, s.v., with Souda, s.v.; scholiast on Aristophanes, *Frogs* 477.

51. *Agora* XIX, pp. 156–157.

52. *APF*, p. 620.

53. Jones 1995, p. 535, with note 151; 1999, pp. 189, with note 85.

54. Jones 1999, p. 189, with note 85.

55. Jones 1999, chapter 3, pp. 82–122.

56. Friedl 1967, pp. 75–91; du Boulay 1974, pp. 41–69, 73–99.

57. As argued in Jones 1999, chapter 3, pp. 82–122.

58. *IG* I³ 250 (ca. 450–430), lines 11–14. The bouleutic quota of 11 implies 2.2% of the Athenian citizenbody or, given a population figure of 30,000 for this time, a deme membership of 660.

59. *SEG* 21.541, ca. 375–340. According to Traill (1986, p. 127 with note 15), Erchia's quota was normally six, increasing to seven when the small deme Ionidai failed to provide its proper complement of two. Again, I assume an Athenian population of 30,000, which, however, may be too large if the *fasti* are only a single generation later than the end of the Peloponnesian War.

Chapter 4. Dionysia

1. Deubner 1932, pp. 134–138, 251.

2. Pickard-Cambridge 1962, pp. 145–147; 1968, pp. 42–56.

3. Whitehead 1986a, pp. 212–222.

4. For full references, see the Bibliography.

5. The City Dionysia is Διονύσια τὰ ἐν ἄστει (Dem. 21.10; Aesch. 1.43, 2.61, and 3.68; *IG* II² 851, lines 11–12; 1496 A, col. IV, line a80) or τὰ ἀστικά (Thuc. 5.20.1). The Lenaia is Διονύσια τὰ ἐπὶ Ληναίωι (*IG* II² 1496 A, col. IV, line a74). The Anthesteria is τὰ ἀρχαιότερα (ἀρχαιότατα, Π8) Διονύσια (Thuc. 2.15.4).

6. Thus schol. Plato, *Republic* 475d: Διονυσίοις· ἑορτὴ Ἀθήνησι Διονύσῳ ἤγετο, τὰ μὲν κατ᾽ ἀγροὺς μηνὸς Ποσειδεῶνος,... The same information is preserved in schol. Aesch., 1.43, §95 Dilts; I. Bekker, *Anecdota Graeca* 1.235.6–8; and Hesychios, s.v. Διονύσια (δ 1887 Latte).

7. "... as if they had hired out their ears to listen πάντων χορῶν, περιθέουσι τοῖς Διονυσίοις, οὔτε τῶν κατὰ πόλεις οὔτε τῶν κατὰ κώμας ἀπολειπό-μενοι."

8. For Plato's usage, see the discussion of the contrasting meanings of *komē* and *dēmos* in the *Laws* at Jones 1999, pp. 273–274. The expected (and correct) *ta kata dēmous Dionysia* is found later in association with the festival in the lexicographer Harpokration, s.v. Θεοίνιον (Θ7, p. 127 Keaney).

9. English "rural" descends from Latin *ruralis*, the adjective of *rus*, "the country (opp. the town; often w. implication of its more cultivated parts)," and only secondarily "land, or a piece of land, owned in the country, country estate" (*OLD*, s.v., 1 and 2). Modern American usage of "rural" extends beyond farming land to include small towns and villages, mining operations, abandoned fields, residential trailer parks, and maritime and lacustrine districts having nothing or little to do with the practice of agriculture.

10. Χώρα, the usual term opposed to ἄστυ (or a synonym), embraces all of a state's territories outside the walled central conurbation. However, its adjective, χωρικός, -ή, -όν ("rustic," "rural," *LSJ*, s.v.), seems not to occur in classical texts. Hesychios, s.v. ἀρουραῖος Οἰνόμαος, with reference to Aeschines' acting performance in the festival at Kollytos (Dem. 18.242; and see below), volunteers that

he was κατὰ τὴν χώραν περινοστῶν, but, writing in Alexandria in the fifth century A.D., it is unlikely that he had even the slightest idea of the intramural deme's actual location.

11. Demosthenes, 18.242, with reference to Aeschines' performance in the festival at Kollytos, labels his adversary an ἀρουραῖος Οἰνόμαος. Since the orator expressly mentions the deme and presumably knew of its intramural location, his use of the adjective carries considerable weight. The noun ἄρουρα means "tilled or arable land" etc. (*LSJ*[9], s.v.) and does not, any more than *agros/oi*, necessarily imply a situation in the "country" in opposition to the town.

12. Pickard-Cambridge 1968, pp. 43–51. Similarly, Mikalson, writing before the appearance of Whitehead's 1986 study, gives eleven demes plus Brauron and Salamis, with one deme cited by Pickard-Cambridge, viz. Rhamnous, not appearing (1977, p. 433, with note 14). Earlier, Deubner's account (1932, pp. 134–138) had instanced Acharnai, Aixone, Eleusis, Ikarion, Kollytos, Myrrhinous, Peiraieus, Phlya, Rhamnous (theater only), Thorikos (theater only); Brauron and Salamis; and the Athenian cleruchy at Hephaistia on Lemnos (with expression of uncertainty regarding its urban or rural orientation).

13. Whitehead 1986a, pp. 212–213, with the list at p. 213, note 212. Later, Parker, to whom Whitehead's study was available, gave "roughly a dozen demes" (1987, p. 141).

14. On the deme assembly in all its aspects, see Whitehead 1986a, pp. 86–120. For the agora as the site of the display of the deme's official acts, and therefore a likely venue of the meeting (called the *agora*) from which those acts emanated, see Jones 1999, p. 90, with note 26.

15. For the latest catalogue of the documents of the demes (supplementing the exhaustive catalogue published by Whitehead at 1986a, pp. 374–393), see Jones 1999, p. 100, note 54 (pp. 100–101).

16. Traill 1986, pp. 125–140.

17. Actually, Traill has suggested (1986, pp. 133–134, with references) that this enormous deme fell into two sections on two sites with quotas of 7/6? (City) and 15/16? (Inland). However, since we are dealing with a festival that demonstrably drew participants and visitors from outside the deme and since the two sites were in close proximity to one another, the point will have no bearing on our discussion.

18. Pickard-Cambridge 1968, pp. 49–50. For the *choregia* in all its aspects, see now Peter Wilson's exhaustive study (2000), with pp. 244–252, 282–283, 374–376, 386–387 on practice in the demes.

19. Hagnous is assigned by Traill to a site "SW Markopoulo, Dardiste" (1986, p. 132) and Prospalta to a site "NW of Kalyvia" (loc. cit.). Aigilia is tentatively assigned on independent evidence to a deme-site at Phoenikia near the coast due south of these two demes (1986, p. 139, with map at end).

20. For the arguments, in my estimation decisive, for disassociating the choregic monument from Vari, *IG* II[2] 3091 (ca. 400–375), from our Dionysia, see Pickard-Cambridge 1968, pp. 54–56. The victories of the demesmen were probably won in urban festivals and then, at a later date, commemorated in the deme by their family or fellow demesmen.

21. Traill 1986, p. 126.

22. εἶναι δὲ αὐτῶ[ι καὶ προεδρίαν τραγωιδῶν τῶι ἀγ]/ῶνι ὅταν ποιῶ[σι τὰ Διονύσια καὶ καλείτω αὐτὸν ὁ δή]/μαρχος εἰς τὴ[ν προεδρίαν - - - - - -] (lines 4–6).

23. Starkie 1909, p. 52.

24. Starkie 1909, p. 59.

25. Dover 1972, p. 79; Dearden 1976, pp. 43 and 44; and Fisher 1993, p. 34, with citation of ill-founded conflicting opinions at p. 46, note 19.

26. Starkie 1909, p. 90. For a recent discussion of Aristophanes' punning demotics, see Jones 1999, pp. 111–112.

27. Traill 1986, p. 130, assigns the deme to the City trittys of the phyle Leontis, citing his discussion at *Hesperia* 47 (1978) 99–100. But I fail to see the justification for his comment that "Aristophanes, *Archarnians*, 406, suggests location north of the city." Nor do the scattered locations of the demes of this trittys with known location (see Traill's map at end) provide any clues regarding orientation relative to the *asty*. Note should also be made of the fact that Traill, whose works are regularly cited by commentators on the point, changed his assignment between his 1975 and 1986 publications. In the 1975 roster, Cholleidai belongs to the Inland trittys of Leontis (p. 46 with note 18bis); in the 1986 roster, to the City trittys with location given as "unknown" (1986, p. 130, with map, where Cholleidai is placed at the foot among the demes of unknown location). The earlier assignment is reflected in the argument of Sommerstein 1980, p. 174 (on line 406) that the deme, because it belonged to the inland division (of the tribe Leontis), was "probably therefore situated not far from Acharnae (though Acharnae itself belonged to a different tribe, Oeneis;" but even if the earlier assignment remained in force, this inference would not follow. Similarly, the statement in Bowie's 1993 book that Cholleidai is a deme "which seems to have been next door to Acharnae" (1993, p. 43) depends on Traill 1975 and other works derived from it (cited in his note 107). The fact is we do not have even an approximate idea of the deme's situation.

28. Pickard-Cambridge 1968, pp. 47–48, with p. 48 for the quotation.

29. Pickard-Cambridge 1962, p. 57.

30. Traill 1986, p. 132.

31. Wilhelm 1906, pp. 238–239.

32. To the south of Loutsa (*AE* 1932, *Chronika*, p. 30), with Traill 1986, p. 128, for the site and its identification.

33. For the explication of *protochoroi*, see Buck 1886–1890, pp. 103–104.

34. For *IG* II² 1183, formerly assigned to Myrrhinous, see above on Hagnous.

35. For the identification, see Davies 1971, p. 104; Pickard-Cambridge (1968, p. 50) had regarded him as "possibly a relation of the orator."

36. For a recent concise summary of the evidence, see Garland 1987, pp. 124–126.

37. For comment, see Pickard-Cambridge 1962, pp. 4 and 57.

38. For the classical theater, see Garland 1987, p. 161. For the theater at Zea, constructed ca. 150 B.C.E., see p. 158. For discussion of the terms of the lease, see Stroud 1974, pp. 296–298.

39. Garland 1987, p. 126, with the relevant inscriptions catalogued at p. 234, nos. 54–59.

40. According to the decrees, the ephebes are credited with: sacrifice to Dionysos at the Peraia and introduction of the god while standing by in good order in Peiraieus for four days (*SEG* 15.104 [127/6], lines 24–26, as restored); leading of a bull for Dionysos at the Peraia . . . introduction of the god from the [hearth into the theater] . . . "for the *pompē*," and obtaining of good omens when sacrificing (*IG* II² 1008 [118/7], lines 13–16); introduction of Pallas and Dionysos in Peiraieus and in the *asty* and sacrifice of a bull in each of the cities (*Hesperia* 16 [1947] 170–172, no. 67 [116/5], lines 19–20); introduction of Dionysos from the hearth with a sacrifice and dedication of a phiale to "the Dionysos in Peiraieus" with a sacrifice (*IG* II² 1011 [106/5], lines 11 and 12); sacrifice of a bull to Dionysos and, at the Dionysia, leading of a bull in the *pompē* and its sacrifice in the shrine (*IG* II² 1028 [100/99], lines 16–18); similar to the foregoing in heavy restoration (*IG* II² 1029 [95/4], lines 10–12); sacrifice at the Dionysia and announcement of a crown at the new *agōn* of the Great Dionysia (*IG* II²: 1039 [83–73], lines 55 and 62).

41. Here I follow Wyse's interpretation (1904, p. 600).

42. Pickard-Cambridge 1962, p. 57.

43. Jones 1999, p. 59.

44. As indicated by his quotation marks: "at the 'rural' Dionysia in the inner-city deme of Kollytos" (1986a, p. 220).

45. Thus Young, in the course of his definitive study of the Industrial District (1951, pp. 142–143), followed later by Thompson and Wycherley in their summary account of the Agora excavations (*Agora* XIV, p. 174, note 32).

46. Finley 1985b, nos. 2, 43, 48, 53, 54, 60, 60A, 66B–D, 82B, 90A, 114B, 122, 123, 126A–C, 141A, 158, and 175B.

47. Finley 1985b, nos. 1, 18A, 21A, 33, 35, 36, 39A, 101A, 120, 120A, 139, and 176.

48. According to Whitehead's tabulations (1986a, p. 83), Eleusis, with ten known metics in residence, ranks eighth among the demes.

49. Finley 1985b, nos. 40, 57, 125, 126, and 126E.

50. See, for the most recent statement, Whitehead 1986a, pp. 212–213, where, with recognition of the generally large size of the demes in question and admission of doubt whether every deme observed the festival, it is nonetheless conceded that "many [demes] did so in modest ways which have gone unrecorded."

51. For the quotas, see Traill 1986, pp. 125–140. Where the number is queried (Aixone, Eleusis, Peiraieus, Phlya), I follow Traill's conjecture. In the one case of a variant quota, 4/5 at Ikarion (1986, p. 127), I have used the former, lower number. Where it is unclear which of two homonymous upper or lower demes we have (Lamptrai, Paiania), I have taken the larger quota on assumption that the larger deme is the more likely to have mounted the festival, although, for all we know, the festival might well have been a joint venture of both demes.

52. Jones 1999, p. 213.

53. That is, a deme with a quota of 1 (the quota of 36 of the 139 demes),

with one councillor representing 40 (on the assumption of a citizen population of 20,000) or 60 (30,000) demesmen.

54. For all except Sphettos and Eleusis, see Whitehead 1986a, p. 219, with notes 253–259. For the more recently discovered epigraphic testimony for *proedria* at Sphettos, see my catalogue above, s.v. In response to Robin Osborne's claim of archaeological evidence for a theater at Eleusis, Whitehead maintains that only indirect epigraphic evidence for it exists (p. 219, note 260 [pp. 219–220]), but the fact is that the inscriptions cited in my roster above make explicit reference to a *theatron*.

55. Alternative explanations for the absence of the festival on the Erchia calendar, none of them convincing, are summarized by Parke 1977, p. 180. Daux's suggestion there that, in addition to the stone's Greater Demarchia, there may have been a (now lost) list of lesser sacrifices obligatory on the demarch, though attractive, is not applicable here since our festival could not have been regarded as "lesser" in any obvious sense. Parke's own suggestion that certain cults may have been left to private landowners or families of the locality overlooks the patently inclusive community-centered character of the festival.

56. *IG* II² 1243 (med. s. III), lines 21–22: shrine of Dionysos (restored).

57. See, for example, from Lamptrai: *IG* II² 1204 (fin. s. IV), lines 6–7; from Peiraieus: *IG* II² 1177 (med. s. IV), lines 2–12; and compare, from Kephisia: *AD* 24 (1969) 6–7 (ca. 350–300), with Jones 1999, p. 122 with note 155.

58. Acharnai: *IG* II² 1206, lines 4–7; Peiraieus: *Agora* XIX, L 13 (= *IG* II² 1176+), passim, with Stroud 1974, pp. 296–298.

59. Dionysion at Eleusis: *IG* II² 1186, lines 32–33; Halimous: *SEG* 2.7, line 23; Ikarion: *SEG* 22.117, line 8; Thorikos: *Hesperia* 19 (1950) 264, no. 20, line 15. *Temenos* of Dionysos at Gargettos: *MDAI(A)* 67 (1942) 7–8, no. 5, lines 4–5; and Peiraieus: *Agora* XIX, L13, line 4. *hieron* of Dionysos at Marathon: *IG* II² 1243, lines 21–22; Rhamnous: *SEG* 3.122, line 16. *oikia* of Dionysos in Kerameikos (i.e. the deme Kerameis): Paus. 1.2.5.

60. Ikarion: *IG* II² 2851.

61. Eleusis: *Hesperia* 8 (1939) 177–180, lines 8–10.

62. Eleusis: *Hesperia* 8 (1939) 177–180, lines 20–21; Ikarion: *IG* I³ 253, passim.

63. Anthios at Halai Aixonides: *IG* II² 1356, line 9; Myrrhinous and Phlya: Paus. 1.31.4. Kissos at Acharnai: Paus. 1.31.6; note, however, the crown of ivy (*kissos*) in the decree from Acharnai honoring deme officers for their conduct of the festival, *SEG* 43.26, B, lines 10–12. Lenaios at Rhamnous: *IG* II² 2854, line 2. Melpomenos at Acharnai: Paus. 1.31.6; and in the Kerameikos (i.e. the deme Kerameis): Paus. 1.2.5.

64. For the text, see Keaney 1967, p. 210, no. 24.

65. Dübner 1877, p. 382.34–36: Ἑορτὴν οἱ Ἀθηναῖοι ἦγον τὰ Ἀσκώλια, ἐν ᾗ ἐνηλλοντο τοῖς ἀσκοῖς εἰς τιμὴν τοῦ Διονύσου….(**51**): Ἀσκώλια ἑορτὴ Διονύσου.

66. Its existence is doubted by Pickard-Cambridge 1968, p. 45, note 6.

67. non aliam ob culpam Baccho caper omnibus aris / caeditur et veteres ineunt proscaenia ludi, / praemiaque ingeniis pagos et compita circum / Thesidae posuere, atque inter pocula laeti / mollibus in pratis unctos saluere per utres.

68. *Theologiae Graecae compendium*, p. 60.22–24 Lang: ...καθὸ καὶ ἐκδέροντες αὐτὸν (sc. τὸν τράγον) εἰς τὸν ἀσκὸν ἐνάλλονται κατὰ τὰς᾽ Ἀττικὰς κώμας οἱ γεωργοὶ νεανίσκοι.

69. Pickard-Cambridge 1968, p. 45, note 6.

70. Whitehead 1986a, p. 214, note 225; p. 215, note 227.

71. Dübner 1877, p. 382.43–45: ἐν μέσῳ δὲ τοῦ θεάτρου ἐτίθεντο ἀσκοὺς πεφυσημένους καὶ ἀληλιμμένους, εἰς οὓς ἐναλλόμενοι ὠλίσθανον, ...

72. καὶ πρός γε τούτοις ἀσκὸν εἰς μέσον / καταθέντες εἰσάλλεσθε καὶ καγχάζετε / ἐπὶ τοῖς καταρρέσουσιν ἀπὸ κελεύσματος. With the exception of the point regarding "the middle," I follow Hunter 1983, pp. 93–95, for the interpretation.

73. Hunter 1983, p. 94. For the handling of the passage by other editors, see the apparatus to *PCG*, loc. cit.

74. Hunter 1983, p. 93. For Latte's point, see 1957, p. 388.

75. I therefore call into question Whitehead's statement, made with reference to these same articles of evidence, that the "link" is not "cogent" (1986a, p. 214). Because he does not, as here, acknowledge the role of the *theatron*, the vital evidence for that "link" was not available to him.

76. For the case that the Dionysia began as a fertility festival, with special reference to the phallos as designed "to promote or encourage the fertility of autumn-sown seed or of the earth in general," see Pickard-Cambridge 1968, pp. 42–43. With reference to the Aristophanic scene, Habash (1995, p. 567) sees Dikaiopolis as promoting "the vegetative fertility harmed by the war."

77. See 1986a, pp. 220–222, where he contrasts the worship of Dionysos, a deity associated with primitive rites and rituals contributing to the religious content of the rural Dionysia, with a secular component that came into existence "as the deme drew upon all its communal resources for the creation of an annual display of pomp and circumstance."

78. 1995, p. 561: "Thus there seem to have been two types of Rural Dionysia: the more elaborate festivals, consisting of procession, sacrifice, and dramatic productions, and the simpler ones which lacked the dramas." At p. 567 (with note 28 on the relevant literature), she airs the possibility that the games would have followed the phallic song in Dikaiopolis's aborted festival.

79. *de cupiditate divitiarum* 527d: ἡ πάτριος τῶν Διονυσίων ἑορτὴ τὸ παλαιὸν ἐπέμπετο δημοτικῶς καὶ ἱλαρῶς, ἀμφορεὺς οἴνου καὶ κληματίς, εἶτα τράγον τις εἷλκεν, ἄλλος ἰσχάδων ἄρριχον ἠκουλούθει κομίζων, ἐπὶ πᾶσι δ᾽ ὁ φαλλός. There is no reason to suspect in δημοτικῶς a reference to demes (and hence to Athens, where the deme made its most conspicuous mark). For the suggestion that not only is the reference to Athens but also that Plutarch is drawing upon Dikaiopolis's *ta kat᾽ agrous Dionysia* in Aristophanes' *Archarnians*, see Habash 1995, pp. 561–562.

80. Dübner 1877, p. 382.52–53.

81. Always to be kept in mind, too, is the living religious setting of the scene in the Theater of Dionysos. Writes Edmunds 1980, pp. 6–7: "To the spectators of *Archarnians*, who are participating in a Dionysiac festival, Dikaiopolis presents in this ritual performance the epitome of another such festival, the Rural Dionysia." This observation may be taken, furthermore, as suggesting the essential fidelity of

the ritual acts in our scene to actual practice, despite whatever elements of condensation or parody the comedic version may contain.

82. For which, see Cole 1993, p. 26.

83. Thus, in the Erchia calendar, *SEG* 21.541, a kid on the 2nd of Anthesterion (Γ 42–47); a goat on the 16th of Elaphebolion (Δ 33–40); cf. the goat for Semele on the 16th of Elaphebolion (A 44–51). A goat is also prescribed for Dionysos on the 12th of Anthesterion in the Thorikos calendar, *AC* 52 (1983) 150–174, lines 33–34.

84. Starkie 1909, p. 59, on line 242.

85. Thus Parke 1977, p. 101, and Habash 1995, p. 562. For a brief overview of sacrificial procedure, including the various phases of the "beginnings," see Burkert 1985, pp. 55–59, esp. 56.

86. For the epigraphic record of sacrifices in late Hellenistic times, see above, under Peiraieus.

87. *non posse suaviter vivi secundum Epicurum* 1098b: καὶ γὰρ οἱ θεράποντες ὅταν Κρόνια δειπνῶσιν ἢ Διονύσια κατ᾽ ἀγρὸν ἄγωσι περιιόντες, οὐκ ἂν αὐτῶν τὸν ὀλολυγμὸν ὑπομείναις καὶ τὸν θόρυβον, ὑπὸ χαρμονῆς καὶ ἀπειροκαλίας τοιαῦτα ποιούντων καὶ φθεγγομένων.

88. 1968, pp. 59–61 (preliminaries), 61–63 (the *pompē*), 63–67 (the order of events), with pp. 65–66 for the conclusions.

89. Thus Parke 1977, p. 102. Pickard-Cambridge (1968, p. 51) sees the festival as affording the demes an opportunity to "mimic" the town.

90. Pickard-Cambridge 1968, p. 54, with note 2 for the literature and fig. 29 for a photograph; Biers and Boyd 1982, p. 14 with fig. 6 (p. 15) and pl. 5b.

91. Pickard-Cambridge 1968, pp. 53–54, with p. 53, note 2 for the literature and fig. 28 for a photograph. The seats bear the dedicatory inscription *IG* II² 2849 (s. IV).

92. Pickard-Cambridge 1968, pp. 51–52.

93. Whitehead 1986a, p. 222, note 273.

94. For an *agōn* celebrating not Dionysos, but Artemis, compare Ἀμαρυσίων τῶι ἀγῶνι at Athmonon, *IG* II² 1203 (324/3), line 17.

95. Since the Law of Euegoros quoted at Demosthenes 21.10, which has the appearance of a legally comprehensive enumeration, mentions only tragedy and comedy in conjunction with the Peiraieus festival, it may be, with Pickard-Cambridge 1968, pp. 51–52, that dithyramb was not on the program in this deme.

96. For the interpretation, see Pickard-Cambridge 1968, pp. 64–65.

97. Lissarrague 1990, p. 72. By his use of *askoliasmos* here, Lissarrague does in fact refer to our wine-skin game (see p. 69).

98. A conclusion already reached by Pickard-Cambridge 1968, pp. 44–45.

99. For the frieze, and interpretation, see Deubner 1932, pp. 138 and 248–254, with plates 34–40. Whitehead (1986a, p. 219, note 252) compares the five comic masks carved above a decree from Aixone honoring two *choregoi* and calling for their crowning "at the comedies," *MDAI[A]* 66 (1941) 218–219, no. 1 (313/2) and suggests that the contest may have been between five pairs of *choregoi*.

100. Deubner 1932, p. 251, no. 13, with note 1 for references to the earlier scholarship.

101. For Green's original publication of the pot, see 1985, pp. 95–118. Taplin's counter analysis appeared two years later at 1987, pp. 92–104, followed by the appendix at 1993, pp. 101–104.

102. Taplin 1993, p. 102.

103. Fowler 1989, pp. 257–259, esp. 258 with notes 2–4.

104. Deubner 1932, p. 251.

105. *SEG* 15.104 (127/6), lines 24–26, at 25–26: παρακ[αθί]σαντες ἐν τῶι Πειραεῖ ἡμέρα[ς] ν / [τέτταρ]ρας εὐτάκτως.

106. Jones 1999, p. 92.

107. According to Mussche 1975, p. 52, the classical fifth-century theatre contained 2,220 to 2,700 seats, but, with an increase of population after ca. 350, the capacity was expanded to 3,500 to 4,000 seats. The deme's bouleutic quota was 5. Since on the assumption of an Athenian population of 30,000 a single councillor would represent about 60 citizens, on the assumption of a population of 20,000, about 40, Thorikian adult male members will have stood at around 200 to 300 at these times. For a more recent account of the remains of the theater, or rather "the theatral area," see Biers and Boyd 1982, pp. 12–14.

108. According to the assumptions given in the preceding note, Peiraieus's quota of 8? would imply a roster of between 320 and 480 demesmen. While only a few traces of the structure have survived, Thucydides' (8.93.1) and Lysias's (13.32) accounts of assemblies of the Athenians in the theater testify to its very substantial capacity.

109. As Whitehead 1986a, p. 194 with note 100, observes, only two explicit indications of the day of the month are given. The point is also made by Henrichs in his discussion of the calendar entry for the Dionysia (1990, p. 262).

110. For an extended discussion of the isolation of the deme, see Jones 1999, pp. 82–122.

111. On the particularity of the demes, see Whitehead 1986a, pp. 16–30; and Jones 1999, pp. 51–53.

112. Whitehead 1986a, pp. 130–139.

113. Whitehead 1986a, p. 121.

114. For the evidence placing the *Dionysia kat' agrous* in Posideion, see Pickard-Cambridge 1968, p. 42, note 8; and Whitehead 1986a, p. 212.

115. As observed by Parke 1977, pp. 180–181; and Parker 1987, p. 141. As Cole emphasizes (1993, p. 27), the town's Dionysia did not replace the local rural celebrations in the demes, but complemented them.

116. Namely, *IG* II^2 3091 from Aixone, with Pickard-Cambridge 1968, Appendix, pp. 54–56.

117. The case of Menander may be instructive here, for the impossibility of fitting the first performances of all 105 of his plays produced during his short lifetime into the "major Athenian festivals" led Gomme and Sandbach to speculate (1973, p. 1) that "some may have been destined for country festivals, since there were theatres in several of the demes."

118. Mikalson 1977, p. 433.

119. Habash (1995, p. 560, note 8) is accordingly mistaken when she states that the law applied to "the Rural Dionysia," concluding that "these local festivals

were recognized as state festivals." They may well, indeed, have been state festivals, but Euegoros's law provides no evidence to that effect.

Chapter 5. Realities

1. West 1978, pp. 250–251.

2. On which, see now Wallinga 1993.

3. Jones 1984.

4. An additional layer of meaning, that the poem was intended to create a sense of immediate identification with the farmer and his life, has been proposed by Stephanie Nelson in her 1996 essay "The Drama of Hesiod's Farm."

5. Jones 1984, pp. 307–323, esp. 309 and 322–323.

6. Gardens of the philosophers (Strabo 9.1.17: 396); a grove, with laurels and olives, around the Altar of Eleos (Statius, *Thebaid* 12.481–482, 491–492); plants dedicated to the Phosphoroi ca. A.D. 200 (Agora I 4745). For the "Garden of Hephaistos" (on which there is no literary testimony), see *Agora* III, p. 221 with the literature cited there. Classical Greek gardens, under the subtitle "between farm and paradise," have been studied by Robin Osborne 1992a; and Nicholas Purcell provides a valuable summary of "gardens" at *OCD*³ s.v.

7. For brief overviews, see Rhodes 1981 on the *AthPol* passage and Jon Mikalson, s.v. "calendar, Greek," in *OCD*³, pp. 273–274.

8. "Seasonal considerations" are discussed in Victor Hanson's 1983 study of warfare and agriculture at pp. 30–35.

9. See especially Wilkins, Harvey, and Dobson 1995; Dalby 1996; Davidson 1997; Wilkins 2000. Notable exceptions are Garnsey 1988 and 1999.

10. Whitehead 1986a, pp. 331, 339–340; Jones 1999, pp. 110–111; 113–114.

11. Garnsey 1999, p. xi.

12. Garnsey 1999, p. 121, 140–141, with 140 for the quotation.

13. Jones 1999, pp. 97–98, with notes 42–45. Garnsey's "Grain for Athens," 1985, pp. 62–75 (= 1998, pp. 183–200), does not address this point.

14. Wilkins 2000, pp. 103–155, esp. 106–107.

15. Pipili 2000, pp. 153–179.

16. Pipili 2000, pp. 153–154, 154 (quotation), 163–178 (country workers), 178–179 (status, *pilos* as marker of inferior status vs. "the respectable citizens").

17. The costumes of Aristophanic "farmers" are briefly discussed by Stone 1977, p. 272 Cf. also Crosby 1927, pp. 180–184.

18. Cf. Losfeld 1991, p. 309.

19. Cf. the brief comment at Stone 1977, p. 167.

20. Cf. the brief comment at Stone 1977, p. 168.

21. See Stone 1977, pp. 165–166, where, however, her claim that from *Ekklesiazousai*, line 421 it follows that the garment was "rather rustic" fails to convince.

22. Whitehead 1986a, p. 334, note 49.

23. Stone 1977, pp. 166–167. Not all her inferences, however, are justified by the passages she cites from the comedies.

24. Traill 1986, p. 136 with map at end.

25. Dover 1968, pp. xxvii–xxvii, citing a scholiast at p. xxviii, note 2.

26. Losfeld 1991, p. 311, citing Pierre Waltz, "Les Artisans de leur vie en Grèce des temps homériques à l'epoque classique," *Revue historique* 141 (1922) 161–193, at 181.

27. See Pritchett 1956, pp. 203–210 (clothing and shoes).

28. The language of non-Athenians in Old Comedy as been recently studied by S. Colvin in Harvey and Wilkins 2000.

29. 1951, p. 87.

30. Besides the books of Harris (1989) and Thomas (1989, 1992), my generalization applies to work on, or including, classical Athens by Burns 1981 (literacy in the fifth century), Cole 1981 (reading and writing of women), Santirocco 1986 (literacy, orality, and thought), Burns 1983 (role of literacy), Lentz 1989 (orality and literacy), Bowman and Woolf 1994 (literacy and power), Robb 1994 (literacy and *paideia*), and Morgan 1999 (literate education).

31. Harris 1989, pp. 11–12.

32. West 1978, pp. 1–3 (description of the *Works and Days*), 3–25 (wisdom literature).

33. Edwards 1971, passim; West 1978, pp. 41–59, with p. 43 for the quotation. For a more recent expression by West of his views, see 1981, pp. 53–73.

34. A. Rzach, *Hesiodi carmina*, Leipzig 1902, supplemented by West's article on "echoes and Imitations of the Hesiodic poems," 1969, pp. 1–9.

35. Lines 240–241 (*fals. leg.* 158), 240–247 (*Ctes.* 135).

36. Lines 25 (*Eth. Eud.*1235a18, *Pol.* 1312b5, *Rh.* 1381b21), 293+295–297 (*Eth. Nic.*1095b10, and 294 in cod. rec.), 370 (*Eth. Eud.* 1242b34, *Eth. Nic.* 1164a27), 405 (*Pol.* 1252b11, [*Oec.*]1343a21), 586 ([*Probl.*] 879a28), 699 ([*Oec.*]1344a17), 714 (*Eth. NIc.* 1170b22), and 763 (*Eth. Nic.* 1153b27).

37. Lines 25–26 (*Lys.* 215c), 121–123 (*Cratyl.* 397e), 233–234 (*Rep.* 363b), 287–289 (*Rep.* 364c), 289–292 (*Protag.* 340d), 311–313 (*Charm.* 163b), 361 (*Cratyl.* 428a), and 456 (*Theaet.* 207a).

38. Lines 287–292 (*Mem.* 2.1.20), 311 (*Mem.* 1.2.56, 57), and 336 (*Mem.* 1.3.3).

39. One actual example (known, however, only from the transcription of Fourmont) survives, *IG* I² 837.

40. I am thus in substantial agreement with Harris's reading of the situation (1989, pp. 52–53). See also B. M. Lavelle's discussion of "Hipparchos' Herms" at 1985, pp. 411–420.

41. Jones 1999, pp. 91–92.

42. Jones 1999, pp. 89–91.

43. For the term "manifesto-clause," with examples and discussion, see Whitehead 1986a, p. 246, with note 110.

44. A particularly pertinent exception with respect to Athens and Attica, Pan, will be taken up in short order.

45. Mikalson 1977, pp. 428 and 431.

46. Mikalson 1977, pp. 428 and 431.

47. Henrichs 1990, p. 261.

48. Henrichs 1990, pp. 259–260.

49. Recent synoptic studies of Pan are Borgeaud 1979 (English translation, 1988), Deligiorgi-Alexopoulou 1982, and Boardman 1998. For votive reliefs to Pan and the Nymphs, see the NYU dissertation of M. Edwards (1985).

50. Parker 1996, pp. 163–168, with p. 167 for the quotation.

51. Parker 1996, pp. 165–167.

52. Whitehead 1986a, pp. 176–222. There is also a much briefer overview in Zaidman and Pantel 1992 [1989], pp. 81–84.

53. Kearns 1989, pp. 92–100, with pp. 101–102 for a table summarizing possible deme eponyms.

54. Parker 1996, pp. 328–332; Jones 1999, pp. 234–242.

55. Parker 1996, pp. 29–42.

56. Clinton 1996, pp. 111–125.

57. Dover 1974, p. 226.

Chapter 6. Images

1. Existing discussions of representations are brief and sketchy or confined to a specific author, text, or genre. The two paragraphs headed "Town and Country" in K. J. Dover's *Greek Popular Morality* (1974, pp. 112–114) are less concerned with morality than with literary portrayals of the two worlds. Passages concerning country life are assembled from Greek (as well as Roman) sources by White 1977, but no analysis is offered. The collection of essays on Old Comedy edited by Harvey and Wilkins 2000 touches on several themes relevant to the following discussion.

2. *OCD*[3] s.v. "comedy, Greek, origins of," pp. 367–368; cf. Dover 1972, pp. 218–220. See also the insightful discussion entitled "From *Komos* to *Komoidia*" by Kenneth Reckford 1987, pp. 443–451, 492–498.

3. Pickard-Cambridge 1962, pp. 156–157.

4. The phenomenon is well illustrated by the pietist agrarian communities of the United States (especially the Amish), which may appear eccentric today but actually have merely preserved the once-general ways of a preindustrial agrarian order.

5. For a recent discussion touching on rural vs. urban tensions, see the essay by P. Ceccarelli entitled "Life among the Savages and Escape from the City in Old Comedy" in Harvey and Wilkins 2000, pp. 453–471.

6. Transliterated titles correspond to entries in *PCG*. Throughout, likewise, all fragment numbers are those of the relevant *PCG* author entry, unless otherwise indicated.

7. Traill 1975, p. 88.

8. Since the classic treatment by Ehrenberg 1951 of the "people" of Aristophanes provides a detailed study of "the farmers" (pp. 73–94), there is no need here for a systematic compilation of passages on the subject.

9. Jones 1999, pp. 123–133.

10. For a modern discussion of "the real world and the fantasy world" in Aristophanes, see McLeish 1980, pp. 64–78.

11. Thus Forrest 1963, Edmunds 1980, Newiger 1980, MacDowell 1983, Carey 1993.

12. Thus Bowie 1988 (Eupolis), Sutton 1988 (confusion of personae; Dikaiopolis played by Aristophanes?), Olson 1990 (reply to Sutton 1988), Hubbard 1991, pp. 41–59 ("the mask of Dikaiopolis"), Fisher 1993 (multiple personalities), Sidwell 1994 (Eupolis, in agreement with Bowie 1988).

13. Thus Schwinge 1977 (three kinds of utopia progressing from fantastic to more practical), Zimmermann 1983 (utopias and their political function in contemporary Athens), Olson 1991 (reforms essentially economic in nature); Dobrov 1997, part 1 ("The Theory and Practice of Utopia," pp. 3–132, essays by David Konstan, Thomas K. Hubbard, F.E. Romer, Niall W. Slater, and Gregory W. Dobrov). Cf. Reckford 1987, pp. 162–196. Utopia and utopianism are studied by I. Ruffell in Harvey and Wilkins 2000, pp. 473–506.

14. Compton-Engle 1998–1999, pp. 359–373.

15. On all aspects of text, interpretation, substance, see now the commentary of Olson 1998. Earlier work includes notably Platnauer's commentary (1964) and chapters by Reckford 1987 (pp. 3–52) and Hubbard 1991 (pp. 140–156).

16. Dover 1972, p. 137. For the role played by the War, see also Blanchard 1982 and Stark 1988.

17. Granting, of course, the possibility underscored by Hanson 1983 that in some cases the plants might not have been completely destroyed by the invaders.

18. Traill 1986, p. 135 and map at end.

19. On the problem of the identification of the chorus, see Hubbard 1991, pp. 241–242.

20. All aspects of the play are now treated in the extensive Oxford commentary of Nan Dunbar (1995).

21. The utopian plan is addressed by Kenneth Reckford 1987, pp. 330–343, and by David Konstan in his essay on the Greek *polis* and its "negations" at Dobrov 1997, pp. 3–22. Neither scholar remarks on the absence of a rural topographic dimension in Nephelokokkygia.

22. Loeb *Aristophanes*, vol. III (Cambridge, Mass., 2000), p. 6.

23. No comprehensive modern commentary in English exists, but for the play's societal context, see David 1984 passim. Sommerstein 2001 became available too late to be consulted.

24. Pomeroy 1994, p. 5.

25. Anderson 1974, pp. 9–11, 14. For a fuller account of the life, see Delebecque 1957.

26. Rahn 1981, pp. 103–119.

27. Pomeroy 1994, pp. 1–8. Higgins 1977 addresses Xenophon's relations with Athens in various dimensions (especially pp. 128–143) but without particular interest in any role played by *rural* Attica.

28. Phaleron is named by the mss. in the preliminary list of venues at 3.1, but since no further reference to the place is made in the following exposition, some editors propose the deletion of this item.

29. Pomeroy 1994, p. 15.

30. Pomeroy 1994, p. 30.

31. For the history of the genre, see Smeed 1985; for rhetorical and related affinities, see Fortenbaugh 1994, pp. 15–35; for historical dimensions, see Lane Fox 1996.

32. Rusten (Loeb 1993, p. 169) interprets more generously: "This is a more subtle portrait than most of the others, and not entirely unsympathetic." More subtle perhaps, but I fail to see any unambiguous sign of sympathy. The connotations of *agroikos* vs. *georgos* are well discussed by Hanson 1995, pp. 436–437.

33. For Theophrastos's possible debt to Old Comedy in the *Charakteres*, see Ussher 1977, pp. 71–79.

34. W. G. Arnott, "comedy (Greek), Middle," OCD^3, p. 370. As Arnott emphasizes, some of the old themes (e.g. politicians, philosophers) continue to be used, but the appearance of subject matter leading to New Comedy and Menander is unmistakable.

35. Throughout the ensuing discussions of Middle and New Comedy, I deal with titles by providing my own translations followed by a transliteration in Roman letters of the Greek. All numerical references are to the fragment number (where such exists) by author entry in *PCG*.

36. *IG* II² 2323, line 97 (= *SEG* 25, 194, line 81; *PCG* VIII Adespota 7).

37. Since *PCG* has not yet progressed to Menander, I have adopted the practice of citing, for the more substantial fragments, W.G. Arnott's recently completed set of three Loeb volumes (Cambridge, Mass. 1979–2000), F.H. Sandbach's OCT, *Menandri reliquiae selectae*, (Oxford 1972, rev. 1990) and A. Koerte's Teubner *Menandri quae supersunt*, 2d edition rev. A. Thierfelder (Leipzig 1959). The *Sententiae* are cited according to the Teubner edition of S. Jaekel, Leipzig 1964.

38. G. Kaibel, *CGF* I, p. 9 §17 = Koerte-Thierfelder, vol. 2 of Teubner edition, testimonium no. 2 (with Arnott, vol. 1 of Loeb Menander, p. xiii).

39. For the titles, see Sandbach's OCT, pp. 339–340.

40. Arnott, vol. 1 of Loeb Menander, p. 386.

41. For my division of the demes into inner, middle, and outer zones with respect to Athens town, see Jones 1999, p. 102, with notes 65–67. For the bouleutic quotas, see Traill 1986, pp. 125–140.

42. Namely, "middle" zone and bouleutic quota of six.

43. On the historicity of Menander's writings, see Webster 1974, pp. 25–42, and Goldberg 1980, pp. 109–121.

44. For the hunting of lions as a sport of the nobility, see *Epitrepontes*, lines 320–325.

45. For the word, compare *Heros*, fr. 9 Koerte (= Arnott, fr. 9; OCT dubia, p. 141): ". . . you will make yourself *astikos* again." Since the play is set in rural Ptelea, the words may have referred to the transformation of a rural person.

Chapter 7. Philosophy

1. Baldry 1952, pp. 83–92.

2. Baldry 1952, p. 85.

3. On the festival Kronia, see Aristophanes, *Clouds* 398; Philochoros, *FGrH* 328 F 97 (harvest supper), Demosthenes 24.26 (state holiday), and Plutarch 1098b (slaves' holiday), with Parke 1977, pp. 29–30, 187. Elsewhere in Aristophanes, the god appears at *Knights* 561, *Clouds* 929, *Wasps* 1480, and *Birds* 469 and 582.

4. Dawson 1992, pp. 13–14.

5. Compare the similar analysis by Smolenaars (1987) of Virgil's use of the theme of agricultural labor in the Golden Age.

6. More recent scholarship, in contrast to my approach, has tended to downplay or even deny Hippodamos's role as a literal planner of cities, rather emphasizing the theoretical aspects of his work (to which I shall return in due course): see Szidat 1980, Triebel-Schubert and Muss 1983–1984, Gehrke 1987, Nachtergael 1988, and, most fully, Gorman 1995.

7. *PECS*, s.v. "Thurii later Copia," p. 919, where the archaeological evidence is said to support the conclusion that the town was built over the southern section of Sybaris.

8. McCredie 1971, pp. 98–99, with the earlier studies cited there.

9. Burns 1976, pp. 421–422.

10. *PECS*, s.v. "Peiraieus," pp. 683–684. The lines of two important streets crossing one another have been determined, but a different orientation seems to have obtained in some outlying areas.

11. *IG* I^2 887–896. For discussion, see Hill 1932, pp. 254–259; McCredie 1971, pp. 95–100; and Garland 1987, pp. 140–141. Hill's texts, with additional notations, are at *SEG* 10.376–383.

12. Cf. the information provided by the lexicographers Hesychios and Photios, s.v. Ἱπποδάμου νέμεσις.

13. McCredie 1971, p. 100; Burns 1976, p. 417; Gorman 1995, pp. 385–395.

14. For the text, with a new reading seeming to invalidate Kirchner's restoration of [χώ]/[ρ]ας in lines 2–3, see Jones 1999, p. 59.

15. Dawson 1992, p. 25.

16. Dawson 1992, pp. 21–37.

17. Dawson 1992, p. 24.

18. Dawson 1992, pp. 29–31: 30.

19. For detailed accounts of Plato's life, see Shorey 1933, pp. 1–57; and Guthrie 1975, pp. 8–38.

20. Davies, *APF* 8792 (pp. 322–335), with XI-XII (pp. 333–335) on Plato himself. For the cited characterizations, see p. 322.

21. For a sketch map of the intramural demes, see Rhodes 1981, p. 764.

22. Aeschines 1.157.

23. See *Agora* XIV, p. 174, note 32, citing *Hesperia* 20 (1951) 141–143.

24. For examples from the "sub-agora" districts, see *Agora* XIV, pp. 173–185.

25. Whitehead 1986a, p. 83. The eight highest figures are: Melite, 75; Peiraieus, 69; Kollytos, 42; Alopeke, 31; Kydathenaion, 31; Skambonidai, 28; Keiri-

adai, 16; Eleusis, 10. Melite, Kollytos, and Kydathenaion account for three of the five intramural demes.

26. The philosopher's haunts included a rein-maker's shop (Xen., *Mem.* 4.2.1 and 8) and a cobbler's (Diog. Laert. 2.13.122 and 123).

27. Dillon 1983, pp. 51–59.

28. As a perhaps extreme example, Socrates at *Phaidros* 227d declares that, in his determination to hear Phaidros's report of his conversation with Lysias, he is prepared to follow him all the way to Megara. Shortly, we shall notice several instances of philosophical movement in our rapid survey of Plato's dramatic settings.

29. Dillon 1983, p. 57–59, with p. 57 for the quotation.

30. Damsgaard-Madsen 1988, p. 66.

31. Plut. *Solon* 22.1, with Lacey 1968, p. 117 and note 116.

32. For the ancient references, see above, note 26. For the physical remains of the shop, identified as the cobbler Simon's (Diog. Laert. 2.13.122) by the discovery just outside of the structure of the foot of a cup bearing his name in the genitive case, see *Agora* XIV, pp. 173, 174.

33. Dillon 1983, pp. 58–59: "Communal meals could be held in the garden, or more probably at the house of the scholarch—in Plato's case, probably in his house at Eiresidae, which must have been in easy walking distance of the Academy."

34. For Cox's speculations regarding Plato's betrothing of his sister with a view, she argues, to consolidating the two estates, see 1988, pp. 185, 187–188. But nothing is implied or suggested here about Plato's place of residence, on the estates or elsewhere.

35. Not at issue here is the relation of dramatic form to philosophical content, on which see Krentz 1983, pp. 32–47.

36. For the significance of this setting for the interpretation of the dialogue, see Klonoski 1984, pp. 123–139 and 1986, pp. 130–137.

37. Socrates arrives freshly bathed (174a); the porch of a neighbor's house is nearby (175a); and, upon his departure, he is in easy reach of the Lyceum (223d).

38. Dodds 1959, p. 188, with the reasons for rejecting the earlier assignment of the setting to the interlocutor Kallikles' house.

39. For the precise location, viz. a newly constructed palaistra outside the northern wall of Athens, opposite the gate where the spring of Panops was located, see Stroud 1984, p. 355, with the archaeological literature cited there (note 1).

40. In the reverse direction, Eukleides reports his trip (from the town) down to the harbor (*Theaitetos*, 42a) and the *Republic* famously opens with Socrates' mention of his trip the day before from the town down to Peiraieus (1.327a–328b).

41. No mention, however, is made of the actual location of the original conversation itself.

42. Omitted here are references to well known places (e.g. Eleusis, Marathon) in a connection unrelated to the official governmental deme structure, functions, or affiliations. The mention of Peisistratos's origin in Philaidai at *Hipp.* 228b does not concern the Kleisthenic deme going by that name.

43. Damsgaard-Madsen 1988, p. 66. By contrast, it was found that there was

"little migration between the rural districts themselves" and "very little migration from town to country."

44. See, for example, the discussion of Edwards 1916, p. 59, note 12, with Whitehead 1986a, pp. 49–50.

45. Examples at *Apol.* 33d-e, *Gorg.* 487c, *Protag.* 315c, *Phd.* 59b, *Rep.* 328b, and *Lys.* 203a.

46. For the relevance of an inscription dated ca. 440–420, *IG* I³ 257, which prohibits the treatment of hides in the Ilissos, see Lind 1987, pp. 15–19.

47. On the location of the Olympieion, see *PDAA*, pp. 402–411.

48. See, more fully, Jones 1999, pp. 227–234.

49. Modern comprehensive treatments of Plato's utopian polities include Morrow 1960b (*Laws*); Piérart 1973 (*Laws*); Ferguson 1975, pp. 61–88; Guthrie 1975 and 1978 passim; and Dawson 1992. Among these, I have found Dawson's *Cities of the Gods* especially insightful and useful for the design of my own discussion.

50. For a modern study of a particular such theme, the farmer, see Fouchard 1993 on the status of agriculturists in the ideal Greek cities of the fourth century.

51. The three instances of the word in the opening pages (1.327b, c, 328c) are of course connected with the *mise-en-scène* involving movement between Athens town and Peiraieus. The "town" at 3.388c is Troy, mentioned in a passage quoted from the *Iliad*.

52. Only twice do I find the term in the literal, narrower sense of a plot of land: 4.419a, 5.470d.

53. For other occupational groups, including "cowherds, shepherds, and the other herders," see *Rep.* 1.370d–e. Only the farmers, however, are sketched out in detail sufficient to support a sustained discussion.

54. Thus, besides *Rep.* 1.349b and 5.452d, the uniformly favorable intimations in *Phdo.* 116d, *Phdr.* 227d and 242e, *Def.* 412e, *Gorg.* 447a, *Lys.* 204c, and *Laws* 3.680c.

55. For the genre, historicity, or ideological content of the Atlantis story, see Gill 1977 (genre), Ross 1977 (historicity), Forsyth 1980 (myth), Zangger 1993 (historicity), Johansen 1998 (historicity), and Morgan 1998 (ideology).

56. Evidently meant to be viewed as a later development, for upon Poseidon's creation of the island's distinctive topography neither ships nor the art of sailing were yet in existence (113e).

57. Cf. the parallel characterizations at *Timaios* 22e (herders and shepherds) and 23b (the unlettered and uncultured).

58. I follow Hermann's emendation, "priests," for the transmitted "sacred things." Obviously, the existence of a temple presupposes the presence of temple stewards of some description.

59. Among many modern discussions, particularly valuable are Stalley 1983 and Brunt 1993 [1991], pp. 245–281.

60. For the detailed interpretation of the arrangements of the Cretan city, the standard comprehensive treatments are Bisinger 1925, Morrow 1960b, Piérart 1973, and Klingenberg 1976.

61. Jones 1999, pp. 268–287, esp. 272–283.

62. Jones 1999, p. 272, citing Golding 1975, p. 364.

63. For discussion, see Morrow 1960, pp. 103–112.

64. Aristotle, citing the *Laws*, puts the factor at five times: *Pol.* 2.4.2: 1266b, cf. 2.3.8: 1265b.

65. These laws are the subject of Klingenberg's monograph (1976).

66. Jones 1999, p. 278.

67. For detailed discussion of these courts, see Morrow 1941, pp. 314–321; Jones 1999, pp. 280–281.

68. For a debate on the place of the artisans in Plato's villages, see Vidal-Naquet 1981, pp. 289–316, with the riposte of Saunders 1982, pp. 43–48. Saunders touches briefly on the pattern of land distribution, the villages and the lot-land, and the population of the villages.

69. For the textual evidence, see Jones 1999, pp. 272–276. At 8.848c, the text seems to indicate a single village in each of the twelve districts, but I am inclined to find here confusion on the author's part (the confusion originating with the two different twelves, mistakenly reduced to one).

70. On the role of slaves, and particularly in agriculture, in Plato's scheme, see Morrow 1960b, pp. 148–152; and, more recently, on slavery in the *Republic*, Vlastos 1973 and Calvert 1987.

71. For speculation concerning the actual site of Plato's Magnesia, see Panagopoulos 1986, p. 125.

72. Rhodes 1981, pp. 58–63, with pp. 60–61 on the "striking disagreements."

73. For a detailed account of Aristotle's life and works, see Ross 1949, pp. 1–19.

74. On the use of Aristotle as an historical source, see the comprehensive treatments of Weil 1960 and Huxley 1979.

75. For the contrasting approaches, especially concerning 7 and 8 vs. the preceding three books, see Rowe's 1989 essay on "reality and utopia."

76. For land ownership in the *Laws*, with reference to Plato's earlier prohibition on private ownership expressed in the *Republic*, see Morrow 1960b, pp. 103–112.

77. On Aristotle's critique of the *Laws*, see Morrow 1960a, pp. 145–162.

78. Besides the standard commentary of Newman (1887–1902), recent comprehensive studies of the *Politics* relevant to our concerns include Lord and O'Connor 1991, Keyt and Miller 1991, Nichols 1992, and Miller 1995. Dawson's handling of Aristotle in the context of the "cities of the gods" will be found at 1992, pp. 93–99.

79. On Aristotle's handling of democratic orders, see Lintott 1992, pp. 114–128; and Hanson 1995, pp. 201–214 on "agricultural government."

Chapter 8. Paradigms

1. K. J. Dover, "comedy (Greek), Old," *OCD*[3], p. 368.

2. K. J. Dover, "Eupolis," *OCD*[3], p. 571.

3. K. J. Dover, "Cratinus," *OCD*[3], p. 407.

Bibliography

Alcock, S. E. *Graecia Capta. The Landscapes of Roman Greece.* Cambridge, 1993.

Alcock, S. E. and R. Osborne, eds. *Placing the Gods: Sanctuaries and Sacred Space in Ancient Greece,* Oxford, 1994.

Ameling, W. "The Attic Demes in the 5th Cent. B.C." *Laverna* 6 (1995) 93–146 (apud *SEG* 45.215).

Anderson, J. K. *Xenophon.* New York, 1974.

———, *Hunting in the Ancient World.* Berkeley, 1975.

Andreou, I. Ο δήμος των Αιξωνίδων Αλών, in Coulson et al. 1994, pp. 191–209.

Austin, M. M. and P. Vidal-Naquet. *Economic and Social History of Ancient Greece: An Introduction.* London, 1977.

Baldry, H. C. "Who Invented the Golden Age?" *CQ* 2 (1952) 83–92.

Barker, E., tr. *The Politics of Aristotle, with an Introduction, Notes, and Appendices.* Oxford, 1946.

Behrend, D. *Attische Pachturkunden.* Munich, 1970.

Biers, W. R. and T. D. Boyd. "Ikarion in Attica." *Hesperia* 51 (1982) 1–18.

Bisinger, J. *Der Agrarstaat in Platons Gesetzen. Klio* Supplement 17. Leipzig, 1925.

Blanchard, A. "Le dessein d'Aristophane dans la Paix," *IL* 34 (1982) 74–78.

Bloedow, E. F. "Corn Supply and Athenian Imperialism," *Ant. Clas.* 44 (1975) 20–29.

Boardman, J. *The Great God Pan: The Survival of an Image.* London, 1998.

Boegehold, A. L. and A. C. Scafuro, eds. *Athenian Identity and Civic Ideology.* Baltimore, 1994.

Borgeaud, P. *Recherches sur le dieu Pan.* Rome, 1979. Tr. K. Atlass and J. Redfield, *The Cult of Pan in Ancient Greece.* Chicago, 1988.

du Boulay, J. *Portrait of a Greek Mountain Village.* Oxford, 1974.

Bowie, A. M. *Aristophanes: Myth, Ritual and Comedy.* Cambridge, 1993.

Bowie, E. L. "Who Is Dicaeopolis?" *JHS* 108 (1988) 183–185.

Bowman, A. K. and G. Woolf, eds. *Literacy and Power in the Ancient World.* Cambridge, 1994.

Boyd, T. and J. Carpenter. "Dragon Houses: Euboia, Attika, Karia," *AJA* 81 (1977) 18–215.

Braun, T. "Barley Cakes and Emmer Bread." In J. Wilkins et al. 1995, pp. 25–37.

Brock, R. "The Labour of Women in Classical Athens." *CQ* 44 (1994) 336–346.

Brothwell, D. R. and P. Brothwell. *Food in Antiquity: A Survey of the Diet of Early Peoples.* London, 1969.

Brumfield, A. C. *The Attic Festivals of Demeter and Their Relation to the Agricultural Year.* Salem, 1981.

Brunt, P. A. *Studies in Greek History and Thought.* Oxford, 1993.

Buck, C. D. "Inscriptions from Ikaria." *Papers of the American School of Classical Studies at Athens* 5 (1886–1890) 71–108.

Burford, A. *Land and Labor in the Greek World.* Baltimore, 1993.

Burkert, W. *Greek Religion.* Tr. J. Raffan, Cambridge, Mass., 1985.

Burns, A. "Hippodamus and the Planned City," *Historia* 25 (1976) 414–428.

———. "Athenian Literacy in the Fifth Century B.C." *JHI* 42 (1981) 371–387.

———. "The Role of Literacy in Ancient Greece." *Praktika tou XII Diethnous Synedriou Klassikes Archaiologias.* Athens, 1983, pp. 69–73.

Burton, J. "Women's Commensality in the Ancient Greek World." *G&R* 45 (1998) 143–165.

Calinescu, M. "Orality in Literacy: Some Historical Paradoxes of Reading." *YJC* 6 (1993) 175–190.

Calvert, B. "Slavery in Plato's Republic." *CQ* 37 (1987) 367–372.

Campbell, J. K. *Honour, Family and Patronage.* Oxford, 1964.

Carey, C. "The Purpose of Aristophanes' *Acharnians.*" *RhM* 136 (1993) 245–263.

Carroll-Spilleke, M. *Kepos: der antike griechische Garten, Wohnen in der klassischen Polis,* III. Munich, 1989.

Cartledge, P. and F. D. Harvey, eds. *CRUX: Essays Presented to G.E.M. de Ste. Croix on His 75th Birthday* (*History of Politcal Thought*, vol. 6). Sidmouth, 1985.

———. *Aristophanes and His Theatre of the Absurd.* Bristol, 1990.

Cartledge, P., P. Millett, and S. von Reden, eds. *Kosmos.: Essays in Order, Conflict and Community in Classical Athens.* Cambridge, 1998.

Castagnoli, F. "Recenti ricerche sull' urbanistica ippodamea." *Archeologia Classica* 15 (1963) 180–197.

———. *Orthogonal Town Planning in Antiquity.* Cambridge, Mass., 1971.

Clinton, K. "The 'Thesmophorion' in Central Athens and the Celebration of the 'Thesmophoria' in Attica." In *The Role of Religion in the Early Greek Polis,* ed. R. Hägg. Åström, 1996, pp. 111–125.

Cohen, B., ed. *Not the Classical Ideal: Athens and the Construction of the Other in Greek Art.* Leiden, 2000.

Cohen, E. E. *The Athenian Nation.* Princeton, N.J., 2000.

Colburn, O. C. "A Habitation Area of Thurii." *Expedition* 9 (1967) 30–38.

Cole, S. G. "Could Greek Women Read and Write?" In *Reflections of Greek Women in Antiquity,* ed. H. Foley. New York, 1981.

———. "Procession and Celebration at the Dionysia." In *Theater and Society in the Classical World,* ed. R. Scodel. Ann Arbor, Mich. 1993, pp. 25–38.

———. "Demeter in City and Countryside." In S. Alcock and R. Osborne 1994, pp. 199–216.

Colvin, S. "Aristophanes: Dialect and Textual Criticism." *Mnemosyne* 48 (1995) 34–47.

Compton-Engle, G. L. "From Country to City: The Persona of Dicaeopolis in Aristophanes' 'Acharnians.'" *CJ* 94 (1998–1999) 359–373.

Connor, W. R. *Theopompus and Fifth-Century Athens.* Washington, D.C., 1968.

———. *The New Politicians of Fifth-Century Athens.* Princeton, N.J.,1971.

Cooper, A. B. "The Family Farm in Ancient Greece." *CJ* 73 (1977/78) 162–175.

Coulson, W. D. E. et al., eds. *The Archaeology of Athens and Attica Under the Democracy.* Oxford, 1994.

Cox, C. A. "Sisters, Daughters and the Deme of Marriage: A Note." *JHS* 108 (1988) 185–188.

———. *Household Interests.* Princeton, N.J., 1998.

Crane, G. "Oikos and Agora: Mapping the Polis in Aristophanes' *Wasps*," in Dobrov 1997, pp. 198–229.

Crosby, H. L. "Aristophanes and the Country." *CW* 20 (1927) 180–184.

Csapo, E. and W. J. Slater. *The Context of Ancient Drama.* Ann Arbor, 1995.

Dalby, A. *Siren Feasts: A History of Food and Gastronomy in Greece.* London, 1996.

Damsgaard-Madsen, A. "Attic Funeral Inscriptions: Their Use as Historical Sources and Some Preliminary Results." In *Studies... Rudi Thomsen.* Aarhus, 1988, pp. 55–68.

David, E. "Aristotle and Sparta." *Ancient Society* 13 (1982) 67–103.

———. *Aristophanes and Athenian Society of the Early Fourth Century B.C.* Leiden, 1984.

Davidson, J. *Courtesans and Fishcakes: The Consuming Passions of Classical Athens.* London, 1997.

Davies, J. K. *Athenian Propertied Familie,s 600–300 B.C.* Oxford, 1971.

———. *Wealth and the Power of Wealth in Classical Athens.* New York, 1981.

Dawson, D. *Cities of the Gods: Communist Utopias in Greek Thought.* New York, 1992.

Dearden, C. W. *The Stage of Aristophanes.* London, 1976.

Delaney, C. "Seeds of Honor, Fields of Shame." In *Honor and Shame and the Unity of the Mediterranean,* ed. D. Gilmore. Washington, D.C. 1987, pp. 35–48.

Delebecque, E. *Essai sur la vie de Xénophon.* Paris, 1957.

Deligiorgi-Alexopoulou, C. "Le culte du dieu Pan en Grèce." *Arch* 171 (1982) 36–40.

———. "Attic Caves Dedicated to the God Pan." *Archaiologia* 15 (1985) 45–54.

Deubner, L. *Attische Feste.* Berlin, 1932.

Diller, A. *Race Mixture Among the Greeks Before Alexander.* Urbana, Ill.,1937.

Dillon, J. "What Happened to Plato's Garden?" *Hermathena* 134 (1983) 51–59.

Dobrov, G., ed. *Beyond Aristophanes: Transition and Diversity in Greek Comedy.* Atlanta, 1995.

———, ed. *The City as Comedy.* Chapel Hill, N.C.,1997.

———. "Language, Fiction, and Utopia," in Dobrov 1997, pp. 95–132.

Dodds, E. R. *Plato* Gorgias. Oxford, 1959.

Dover, K. J. *Aristophanes* Clouds. Oxford, 1968.

———. *Greek Popular Morality in the Time of Plato and Aristotle.* Berkeley, Calif., 1974.

———. *Aristophanic Comedy.* Berkeley, Calif., 1972.

Dow, S. "Thucydides and the Number of Acharnian Hoplites." *TAPA* 92 (1961) 66–80.

Dübner, F. *Scholia Graeca in Aristophanem*. Paris, 1877.

Dunbar, N. *Aristophanes* Birds. Oxford, 1995.

Edlund, E. M. I. "Invisible Bonds: Clients and Patrons Through the Eyes of Poly-bius." *Klio* 59 (1977) 129–136.

Edmunds, L. "Aristophanes' *Acharnians*," In *Aristophanes: Essays in Interpreta-tion*, ed. J. Henderson. *YCS* 26 (1980) 1–41.

Edwards, G. P. *The Language of Hesiod in Its Traditional Context*. Oxford, 1971.

Edwards, J. B. *The Demesman in Attic Life*, Ph.D. Dissertation, Johns Hopkins University. Menasha, Wis., 1916.

Edwards, M. "Greek Votive Reliefs to Pan and the Nymphs." Ph.D. dissertation, New York University, 1985.

Effenterre, H. van. "Préliminaires épigraphiques aux études d'histoire du droit grec." In *Symposion 1982, Santander 1–4 Sept. 1982*. Valencia 1985, pp. 1–8.

Ehrenberg, V. *The People of Aristophanes: A Sociology of Old Attic Comedy*. Cam-bridge, Mass., 1951.

Eisenstadt, S. N. and L. Roniger. "Patron Client Relations as a Model of Struc-turing Social Exchange." *Comparative Studies in Sociology and History* 22 (1980) 42–77.

Eliot, C. W. J. *Coastal Demes of Attika: A Study of the Policy of Kleisthenes*. Toronto, 1962.

Farb, P. and G. Armelagos. *Consuming Passions: The Anthropology of Eating*. Boston, 1980.

Ferguson, J. *Utopias of the Classical World*. Ithaca, N.Y., 1975.

Figueira, T. J. "The Theognidea and Megarian Society." In T. Figueira and G. Nagy 1985, pp. 112–158 (= 1985a).

Figueira, T. J. and G. Nagy. *Theognis of Megara: Poetry and Polis*. Baltimore, 1985 (= 1985b).

Fine, J. *Horoi, Hesperia* Supplement 9. Princeton, N.J., 1951.

Finley, M. I., ed. *Problèmes de la terre en Grèce ancienne*. Paris-La Haye, 1973.

———. *Economy and Society in Ancient Greece*. Ed. B. D. Shaw and R. P. Saller. London, 1981.

———. *Politics in the Ancient World*. Cambridge, 1983.

———. *The Ancient Economy*. 2nd ed. London, 1985 [1973], ch. 5, "Town and Country," pp. 123–149 (= 1985a).

———. *Studies in Land and Credit in Ancient Athens, 500–200 B.C.: The Horos Inscriptions*, with a New Introduction by P. Millett. New Brunswick, N.J., 1985 [1951] (=1985b).

Fisher, N. R. E. "Multiple Personalities and Dionysiac Festivals: Dicaeopolis in Aristophanes' *Acharnians*." *G&R* 40 (1993) 31–47.

Fitton Brown, A. D. "The Contribution of Women to Ancient Greek Agricul-ture." *LCM* 9 (1984) 71–74.

Foley, H. "Tragedy and Politics in Aristophanes' Acharnians," *JHS* 108 (1988) 33–47 (= E. Segal 1996, pp. 117–142).

Forehand, W. F. "Pheidippides and Pan. A Modern Perspective on Pan's Epiphany," *CO* 63 (1985) 1–2.

Forrest, W. G. "Aristophanes' Acharnians," *Phoenix* 17 (1963) 1–12.

Forsyth, P. Y. *Atlantis. The Making of Myth*. Montreal and London, 1980.

Fortenbaugh, W. W. "Theophrastus, the Characters and Rhetoric," in *Peripatetic Rhetoric After Aristotle*, ed. W. W. Fortenbaugh and D. C. Mirhady. New Brunswick, N.J., 1994, pp. 15–35.

Fouchard, A. "Le statut des agriculteurs dans la cité grecque idéale au IV s. av. J.-C." *REG* 106 (1993) 61–81.

Fowler, D. "Taplin on Cocks." *CQ* 39 (1989) 257–259.

Foxhall, L. "Farming and Fighting in Ancient Greece." In *War and Society in the Greek World*, ed. J. Rich and G. Shipley. London, 1993, pp. 134–145.

Friedl, E. *Vasilika: A Village in Modern Greece*. New York, 1962.

Fuks, A. *Social Conflict in Ancient Greece*. Jerusalem, 1984.

Gallant, T. W. *A Fisherman's Tale: An Analysis of the Potential Productivity of Fishing in the Ancient World*. Ghent, 1985.

———. *Risk and Survival in Ancient Greece: Reconstructing the Rural Domestic Economy*. Stanford, Calif., 1991.

Garland, R. *The Piraeus from the Fifth to the First Century B.C.* Ithaca, N.Y., 1987.

Garnsey, P., ed. *Non-Slave Labour in the Greco-Roman World*. Cambridge Philological Society Supplement 6. Cambridge, 1980.

———. *Famine and Food Supply in the Graeco-Roman World: Responses to Risk and Crisis*. Cambridge, 1988.

———, ed. *Food, Health and Culture in Classical Antiquity*. Cambridge Faculty of Classics Working Papers no. 1. Cambridge, 1989

———. *Cities, Peasants and Food in Classical Antiquity*. Cambridge, 1998.

———. *Food and Society in Classical Antiquity*. Cambridge, 1999.

Garnsey, P. and C. R. Whittaker, eds. *Trade and Famine in Classical Antiquity*. PCPS Supplement 8. Cambridge, 1983.

Garnsey, P. and G. Woolf. "Patronage of the Rural Poor in the Roman World." In Wallace-Hadrill 1989, pp. 153–170.

Gehrke, H.-J. "Bermerkungen zu Hippodamos von Milet." In *Demokratie und Architektur: Der hippodamische Städtebau und die Entstehung der Demokratie*, ed. W. Schuller et al. Munich 1987, pp. 58–68.

Gellner, E. "Patrons and Clients," in E. Gellner and J. Waterbury 1977, pp. 2–6.

Gellner, E. and J. Waterbury. *Patrons and Clients in Mediterranean Societies*. London, 1977.

Giannopoulou-Konsolaki, E. Γλυφάδα· Ἱστορικό Παρελθόν και Μνημεία. Athens, 1990.

Gill, C. "The Genre of the Atlantis Story," *CP* 72 (1977) 287–304.

Gill, C., N. Postlethwaite and R. Seaford, eds. *Reciprocity in Ancient Greece*. Oxford, 1998.

Goldberg, S. M. *The Making of Menander's Comedy*. Berkeley, Calif., 1980.

Golden, M. *Children and Childhood in Ancient Athens*. Toronto, 1990.

Goldhill, S. "Representing Democracy: Women at the Great Dionysia." In R. Osborne and S. Hornblower 1994, pp. 347–369.

Golding, N. H. "Plato as City Planner," *Arethusa* 8 (1975) 359–371.

Gomme, A. W. *A Historical Commentary on Thucydides*, vol. II. Oxford, 1956.

Gomme, A. W. and F. H. Sandbach. *Menander: A Commentary*. Oxford, 1973.

Goody, J. *The Interface Between the Written and the Oral.* Cambridge, 1987.

Gorman, V. B. "Aristotle's Hippodamos (Politics 2.1267b22–30)." *Historia* 44 (1995) 385–395.

Gottfried, B. "Pan, the Cicadas, and Plato's Use of Myth in the Phaedrus." In *Plato's Dialogues: New Studies and Interpretations,* ed. G. A. Press. Lanham, Md., 1993.

Green, J. R. "A Representation of the *Birds* of Aristophanes." *J. P. Getty Museum: Greek Vases* 2 (1985) 95–118.

———. *Theater in Ancient Greek Society.* London, 1994.

Guthrie, W. K. C. *A History of Greek Philosophy.* Vol. 4. Cambridge, 1975; vol. 5. Cambridge, 1978; vol. 6. Cambridge, 1981.

Habash, M. "Two Complementary Festivals in Aristophanes' *Acharnians.*" *AJP* 116 (1995) 559–577.

Hahn, M. H. "Pelatai und Klienten," *Concilium Eirene* 17 (1983) 59–64.

Halstead, P. "Traditional and Ancient Rural Economy in Mediterranean Europe: plus ça change?" *JHS* 107 (1987) 77–87.

Hansen, M. H. *Aspects of Athenian Society in the Fourth Century B.C.* Odense, 1975.

———. "How Many Athenians Attended the Ecclesia?" *GRBS* 17 (1976) 115–134 (= *The Athenian Ecclesia.* Copenhagen, 1983, pp. 1–20, 21–23).

Hansen, M. H., L. Bjertrup, T. H. Nielsen, L. Rubinstein, and T. Vestergaard. "The Demography of the Attic Demes: The Evidence of the Sepulchral Inscriptions." *Analecta Romana Instituti Danici* 19 (1990) 25–44.

Hanson, V. D. *The Other Greeks: The Family Farm and the Agrarian Roots of Western Civilization.* New York, 1995.

———. *Warfare and Agriculture in Classical Greece,* 2nd ed. Berkeley, Calif., 1998 [1983].

Harris, W. V. "Notes on Literacy and Illiteracy in Fifth-Century Athens." *Index* 17 (1989) 39–45.

Harris, W. V. *Ancient Literacy.* Cambridge, Mass., 1989.

Harrison, A. R. W. *The Law of Athens.* Vol. 1, *The Family and Property.* Oxford, 1968.

Harvey, D. and J. Wilkins, eds. *The Rivals of Aristophanes: Studies in Athenian Old Comedy.* London, 2000.

Haverfield, F. *Ancient Town-Planning.* Oxford, 1913.

Healy, J. F. *Mining and Metallurgy in the Greek and Roman World.* London, 1978.

Hedrick, C. "The Thymaitian Phratry." *Hesperia* 57 (1988) 81–85.

Henrichs, A. "Between Country and City: Cultic Dimensions of Dionysus in Athens and Attica." In *Cabinet of the Muses: Essays on Classical and Comparative Literature in Honor of Thomas G. Rosenmeyer,* ed. M. Griffith and D. J. Mastronarde. Atlanta, 1990, pp. 257–277.

Hereward, D. "New Fragments of *IG* II² 10." *ABSA* 47 (1952) 102–117.

Herman, G. *Ritualised Friendship and the Greek City.* Cambridge, 1987.

Higgins, W. E. *Xenophon the Athenian: The Problem of the Individual and the Society of the Polis.* Albany, N.Y., 1977.

Hill, D. Kent. "Some Boundary Stones from the Piraeus." *AJA* 36 (1932) 254–259.

Hoepfner, W. "Zu den Stadtplänen von Milet und Piräus." *KGB* 34 (1986) 20–21.

Hopper, R. J. *Trade and Industry in Classical Greece*. London, 1979.

Hornblower, S. *A Commentary on Thucydides*. Vol. 1. Oxford, 1991.

Hubbard, T.K. *The Mask of Comedy. Aristophanes and the Intertextual Parabasis*. Ithaca, N.Y., 1991.

Humphreys, S. "Town and Country in Ancient Greece." In *Man, Settlement, and Urbanism*, ed. P. J. Ucko et al. London, 1972, pp. 763–768.

———. *Anthropology and the Greeks*. London, 1978.

———. *The Family, Women, and Death: Comparative Studies*. 2nd ed. Ann Arbor, Mich., 1993.

Hunter, R. L. *Eubulus: The Fragments*. Cambridge, 1983.

Huxley, G. *On and Aristotle and Greek Society*. Belfast, 1979.

Isager, S. and J. E. Skydsgaard. *Ancient Greek Agriculture: An Introduction*. London, 1993.

Jameson, M. H. "Agriculture and Slavery in Classical Athens," *CJ* 73 (1977–1978) 122–141.

———. "The Leasing of Land in Rhamnous," in *Studies in Attic Epigraphy, History, and Topography Presented to Eugene Vanderpool. Hesperia* Supplement 19. Princeton, N.J., 1982, pp. 66–74.

———. "Famine in the Greek World." In P. Garnsey and C. R. Whittaker 1983, pp. 6–16.

———. "Sacrifice and Animal Husbandry in Classical Greece," in C. R. Whittaker 1988, pp. 87–119.

Jameson, M. H., C. N. Runnel, and T. H. van Andel. *A Greek Countryside: The Southern Argolid from Prehistory to the Present Day*. Stanford, Calif., 1994.

Jasny, N. "Competition Among Grains in Classical Antiquity." *AHR* 47 (1942) 747–764.

———. *The Wheats of Classical Antiquity*. Baltimore, 1944.

———. "The Daily Bread of the Ancient Greeks and Romans," *Osiris* 9 (1950) 228–253.

Johansen, T. K. "Truth, Lies and History in Plato's Timaeus-Critias," *Histos* 2 (1998) non-paginated.

Johnson, T. and C. Dandeker. "Patronage: Relation and System." In A. Wallace-Hadrill 1989, pp. 219–242.

"Two Attic Country Houses." *AAA* 7 (1974) 303–312.

———. "Town and Country Houses of Attica in Classical Times." In *Miscellanea Graeca: Thorikos and Laurion in Archaic and Classical Times*. Vol. I. Brussels, 1975, pp. 63–140.

Jones, J. E., L. H. Sackett, and C. Eliot. "The Dema House in Attica," *ABSA* 57 (1962) 75–114.

Jones, J. E., L. H. Sackett, and A. J. Graham. "An Attic Country House Below the Cave of Pan at Vari." *ABSA* 68 (1973) 355–452.

Jones, N. F. "Perses, Work 'in Season,' and the Purpose of Hesiod's *Works and Days*." *CJ* 79 (1984) 307–323.

———. *Public Organization in Ancient Greece: A Documentary Study*. Philadelphia, 1987.

————. "The Athenian Phylai as Associations: Disposition, Function, and Purpose." *Hesperia* 64 (1995) 503–542.

————. *The Associations of Classical Democracy: The Response to Democracy.* New York, 1999.

————. "Epigraphic Evidence for Farmstead Residence in Attica." *ZPE* 133 (2000) 75–90.

Keaney, J. J. "New Fragments of Greek Authors in Codex Marc. Gr. 444." *TAPA* 98 (1967) 205–219.

Kearns, E. *The Heroes of Attica.* BICS Supplement 57. London, 1989.

Keyt, D., and F. Miller, Jr., eds. *A Companion to Aristotle's Politics.* Oxford, 1991.

Klingenberg, E. *Platons NOMOI GEORGIKOI und das Positive Griechische Recht.* Berlin, 1976.

Klonoski, R. J. "Setting and Characterization in Plato's Euthyphro." *Dialogos* 44 (1984) 123–139.

————. "The Portico of the Archon Basileus: On the Significance of the Setting of Plato's *Euthyphro.*" *CJ* 81 (1986) 130–137.

Kondis, I. D. *Symbole eis ten meleten tes rhymotomias tes Rhodou.* Rhodes, 1954.

————. "He diairesis ton Thourion." *AE* 1956 (1959) 106–113, 216–217.

————. "Zum antiken Stadtbauplan von Rhodos." *MDAI(A)* 73 (1958) 146–158.

Konstan, D. "The Greek Polis and Its Negations: Versions of Utopia in Aristophanes' *Birds.*" In Dobrov 1997, pp. 3–22.

Kourionotes, K. Τὸ ἱερὸν τοῦ Ἀπόλλωνος τοῦ Ζωστῆρος. *AD* 11 (1927–1928) 9–53.

Krentz, A. A. "Dramatic Form and Philosophical Content in Plato's Dialogues." *Philosophy and Literature* 7 (1983) 32–47.

Lacey, W. K. *The Family in Classical Greece.* Ithaca, N.Y. 1968.

Lambert, S. D. *The Phratries of Attica.* Ann Arbor, Mich., 1993.

————. *Rationes Centesimarum: Sales of Public Land in Lykourgan Athens.* Amsterdam, 1997.

Lane Fox, R. J. "Theophrastus' 'Characters' and the Historian." *PCPS* 42 (1996) 127–170.

Langdon, M. K. "The Territorial Basis of the Attic Demes." *SO* 60 (1985) 5–15.

————. "On the Farm in Classical Attica." *CJ* 86 (1990–1991) 209–213.

Langdon, M. K. and L. V. Watrous. "The Farm of Timesios: Rock-Cut Inscriptions in South Attica." *Hesperia* 46 (1977) 162–177.

Latte, K. "Askoliasmos." *Hermes* 85 (1957) 385–391.

Lavelle, B. M. "Hipparchos's Herms." *EMC* 29 (1985) 411–420.

Lentz, T. M. *Orality and Literacy in Hellenic Greece.* Carbondale, Ill., 1989.

Lewis, D. M. "Attic Manumissions." *Hesperia* 28 (1959) 208–238.

————. "Dedications of Phialai at Athens." *Hesperia* 37 (1968) 368–380.

————. "The Athenian Rationes Centesimarum," in Finley 1973, pp. 187–212.

Lilly, K. "Artémis, Dionysos et Pan à Athènes." *Hesperia* 60 (1991) 511–523.

Lind, H. "Sokrates am Ilissos: *IG* I³ 257 und die Eingangsszene des Platonisches 'Phaidros.'" *ZPE* 69 (1987) 15–19.

Lintott, A. "Aristotle and Democracy." *CQ* 42 (1992) 114–128.

Lissarrague, F. *The Aesthetics of the Greek Banquet. Images of Wine and Ritual,* tr. A. Szegedy-Maszak. Princeton, N.J., 1990.

Lohmann, H. "Atene, eine attische Landgemeinde klassischen Zeit." *Hellenika Jahrbuch* 1983, pp. 93–117.

———.*'Ατήνη. Forschungen zur Siedlungs- und Wirtschaftsstruktur des klassische Attika*, 2 vols. Köln, 1992.

Lord, C. and D. K. O'Connor, eds. *Essays on the Foundation of Aristotelian Political Science*. Berkeley, Calif., 1991.

Losfeld, G. *Essai sur le costume grec*. Paris, 1991.

MacDowell, D. M. *The Law in Classical Athens*, Ithaca, New York 1978.

———. "The Nature of Aristophanes' Akharnians," *G&R* 30 (1983) 143–162.

———. *Aristophanes and Athens: An Introduction to the Plays*. Oxford 1995.

Markle, M. M. "Jury Pay and Assembly Pay at Athens." In P. Cartledge and F. D. Harvey 1985, pp. 265–297.

Martin, R. *L'urbanisme dans la Grèce antique*. Paris, 1956.

McCredie, J. R. "Hippodamos of Miletos." In *Studies Presented to George M. A. Hanfmann*, ed. D. G. Mitten, J. G. Pedley, and J. A. Scott. Mainz, 1971, pp. 95–100.

McLeish, K. *The Theatre of Aristophanes*. New York, 1980.

Mikalson, J. "Religion in the Attic Demes." *AJP* 98 (1977) 424–435.

Miller, F. D., Jr. *Nature, Justice, and Rights in Aristotle's* Politics. Oxford, 1995.

Millett, P. "Hesiod and His World." *PCPS* 210 (1984) 84–115.

———. Appendix to M. I. Finley, 1985 [1951], "The Texts of the New Horoi and Accompanying Statistical Tables," pp. Xxii–xxxiii.

———. "Patronage and Its Avoidance in Classical Athens." In A. Wallace-Hadrill 1989, pp. 15–47.

Morgan, K. A. "Designer History. Plato's Atlantis Story and Fourth-Century Ideology." *JHS* 118 (1998) 101–118.

Morgan, T. J. "Literate Education in Classical Athens." *CQ* 49 (1999) 46–61.

Moritz, L. A. *Grain-Mills and Flour in Classical Antiquity*. Oxford, 1958.

Morrow, G. R. "On the Tribal Courts in Plato's *Laws*." *AJP* 62 (1941) 313–321.

Morrow, G. R. "Aristotle's Comment on Plato's Laws." In *Aristotle and Plato in Mid-Fourth Century*, ed. I. Düring and G. E. L. Owen. Göteburg, 1960, pp. 145–162 (=1960a).

———. *Plato's Cretan City: A Historical Interpretation of the* Laws. Princeton, N.J., 1960 (=1960b).

Murray, O. and S. Price, eds. *The Greek City from Homer to Aristotle*. Oxford, 1990.

Mussche, H. "Thorikos in Archaic and Classical Times." In *Thorikos and the Laurion in Archaic and Classical Times*, Miscellanea Graeca fasc. 1. Ghent, 1975, pp. 45–61.

Nachtergael, G. "Hippodamos de Milet, urbaniste et philosophe." In *Aspects de l'environnement urbain dans l'antiquité gréco-romaine*. Brussels, 1988, pp. 7–18.

Nelson, S. A. "The Drama of Hesiod's Farm." *CP* 91 (1996) 45–53.

———. *God and the Land: The Metaphysics of Farming in Hesiod and Vergil*. New York, 1998.

Newiger, H.-J. "War and Peace in the Comedy of Aristophanes." *YCS* 26 (1980) 219–237 (= E. Segal 1996, pp. 143–161).

Newman, W. L. *The Politics of Aristotle.* Oxford, 1887–1902.

Nichols, M. P. *Citizens and Statesmen: A Study of Aristotle's Politics.* Savage, Md., 1992.

Nickel, R. *Xenophon.* Darmstadt 1979.

Nussbaum, G. "Labor and Status in the Works and Days." *CQ* 54 (1960) 213–220.

Ober, J. *Fortress Attica: Defense of the Athenian Land Frontier 404–322 B.C.* Leiden, 1985.

Ober, J. and C. Hedrick, eds. *Demokratia: A Conversation on Democracies, Ancient and Modern.* Princeton, N.J., 1996.

Olson, S. D. "Dicaeopolis and Aristophanes in *Acharnians.*" *LCM* 15 (1990) 31–32.

———, "Dicaeopolis' Motivations in Aristophanes' *Acharnians.*" *JHS* 111 (1991) 200–203.

———, *Aristophanes* Peace. Oxford, 1998.

———. *Aristophanes* Archanians. Oxford, 2002.

O'Neil, J. L. *The Origins and Development of Ancient Greek Democracy.* London, 1995.

Ong, W. J. *Orality and Literacy: The Technologizing of the Word.* London, 1982.

Osborne, R. "Buildings and Residence on the Land in Classical and Hellenistic Greece: The Contributions of Epigraphy," *ABSA* 80 (1985) 119–128 (= 1985a).

———. *Demos: The Discovery of Classical Attika.* Cambridge, 1985 (= 1985b).

———. *Classical Landscape with Figures: The Ancient Greek City and Its Countryside.* London, 1987.

———. "Social and Economic Implications of the Leasing of Land and Property in Classical and Hellenistic Greece." *Chiron* 18 (1988) 279–323.

———. "Classical Greek Gardens: Between Farm and Paradise." In *Dumbarton Oaks Colloquium on the History of Landscape Architecture XIII*, ed. J. D. Hunt. Washington D.C., 1992, pp. 373–391 (= 1992a).

———. "Is it a Farm? The Definition of Agricultural Sites and Settlements in Ancient Greece." In *Agriculture in Ancient Greece*, ed. B. Wells. Stockholm, 1992, pp. 21–28 (=1992b).

———. "Woman and Sacrifice in Classical Greece." *CQ* 43 (1993) 392–405.

———. "Ancient Vegetarianism." In J. Wilkins 1995, pp. 214–224.

Osborne, R. and S. Hornblower, eds. *Ritual, Finance, Politics.* Oxford, 1994.

Owens, E. J. "The Koprologoi at Athens in the Fifth and Fourth Centuries B.C." *CQ* 33 (1983) 44–50.

Panagopoulos, A. "Two Notes on Plato's Crete." *BICS* 33 (1986) 125–126.

Parke, H. W. *Festivals of the Athenians.* Ithaca, N.Y., 1977.

Parker, R. "Festivals of the Attic Demes." In *Gifts to the Gods. Proceedings of the Uppsala Symposium 1985* (= *Boreas* 15. Uppsala, 1987, 137–147.

———. *Athenian Religion: A History.* Oxford, 1996.

Patterson, C. B. *The Family in Greek History.* Cambridge, Mass., 1998.

Pečirka, J. "Homestead Farms in Classical and Hellenistic Hellas." In Finley 1973, pp. 113–147.

Petropoulos, J. C. B. *Heat and Lust: Hesiod's Midsummer Festival Scene Revisited.* Lanham, Md., 1994.

Peyssard-Milliex, L. "Xénophon, l'homme privé, le grand propriétaire." *ConnHell* 7 (1981) 24–28.

Pickard-Cambridge, A. W. *Dithyramb, Tragedy, and Comedy.* 2nd. ed. rev. T. B. L. Webster. Oxford, 1962.

———. *The Dramatic Festivals of Athens.* 2nd ed, rev. J. Gould and D. M. Lewis. Oxford, 1968.

Piérart, M. *Platon et la cité grecque: Théorie et réalité dans la constitution des "Lois".* Brussels, 1973.

Pipili, M. "Wearing an Other Hat: Workmen in Town and Country." In B. Cohen 2000, pp. 153–179.

Platnauer, M. *Aristophanes* Peace. Oxford, 1964.

de Polignac, F. *Cults, Territory, and the Origins of the Greek City-State.* Tr. J. Lloyd. Chicago and London, 1995 [1984].

Pomeroy, S. B. "Slavery in the Greek Domestic Economy in the Light of Xenophon's *Oeconomicus.*" *Index* 17 (1989) 11–18.

———. *Xenophon* Oeconomicus. *A Social and Historical Commentary.* Oxford, 1994.

———.*Families in Classical and Hellenistic Greece: Representations and Realities.* Oxford, 1997.

Pouilloux, J. *La Forteresse de Rhamnounte: étude de topographie et d'histoire.* Paris, 1954.

Pritchett, W. K. "The Attic Stelai, Part II." *Hesperia* 25 (1956) 178–317.

Rahn, P. J. "The Date of Xenophon's Exile." In G. Shrimpton, et al., eds., *Classical Contributions in Honour of Malcolm Francis McGregor.* Locust Valley, N.Y., 1981, pp. 103–119.

Rainey, F. "The Location of Ancient Sybaris." *AJA* 73 (1969) 261–274.

Reckford, K.J. *Aristophanes' Old-and-New Comedy,* vol. 1, *Six Essays in Perspective.* Chapel Hill, N.C., 1987.

Rhodes, P. J. *A Commentary on the Aristotelian* Athenaion Politeia. Oxford, 1981.

Ribbeck, O. *Agroikos: Eine ethologische Studie.* Abh. der königlichen sächsischen Gesellschaft der Wiss. 23 (1888) 1–68.

Rich, John and A. Wallace-Hadrill, eds. *City and Country in the Ancient World.* London, 1991.

Riis, P. J. "A Colossal Athenian Pan." *Aarch* 45 (1974) 124–133.

Robb, K. *Literacy and Paideia in Ancient Greece.* New York, 1994.

Roebuck, C. *The Muses at Work.* Cambridge, Mass., 1969.

Ross, J. M. "Is There Any Truth in Atlantis?" *DUJ* 38 (1977) 189–199.

Ross, W. D. *Aristotle.* 5th ed. London, 1949.

Rowe, C. "Reality and Utopia." *Elenchos* 10 (1989) 317–336.

Roy, J. "Demosthenes 55 as Evidence for Isolated Farmsteads in Classical Attica." *LCM* 13 (1988) 57–59.

Ruschenbusch, E. *SOLONOS NOMOI, Historia Einzelschriften.* Heft 9. Wiesbaden, 1966.

Ste. Croix, G. E. M. *The Class Struggle in the Ancient Greek World, from the Archaic Age to the Arab Conquests.* London, 1981, I. Introduction (iii) "Polis and chora," pp. 9–19.

Sallares, R. *The Ecology of the Ancient Greek World*. Ithaca, N.Y., 1991.

Saller, R. P. *Personal Patronage Under the Early Empire*. Cambridge, 1982.

Sancisi-Weerdenburg, H. et al., eds. *De agricultura: In memoriam Pieter Willem De Neeve (1945–1990)*. Amsterdam, 1993.

Santirocco, M. S. "Literacy, Orality, and Thought." *AncPhil* 6 (1986) 153–160.

Saunders, T. J. "Notes on Plato as City Planner." *BICS* 23 (1976) 23–26.

———. "Artisans in the City-Planning of Plato's Magnesia." *BICS* 29 (1982) 43–48.

Scheidel, W. "The Most Silent Women of Greece and Rome: Rural Labour and Women's Life in the Ancient World." I *G&R* 42 (1995) 202–217; II, *G&R* 43 (1996) 1–10.

Schmitt-Pantel, P. "Public Feasts in the Hellenistic Greek City: Forms and Meanings," in, eds., *Conventional Values of the Hellenistic Greeks*, ed. P. Bilbe et al. Aarhus 1997, pp. 29–47.

Schnurr-Redford, C. *Frauen im klassischen Athen*. Berlin, 1996.

Schofield, M. "Political Friendship and the Ideology of Reciprocity." in P. Cartledge et al. 1998, pp. 37–51.

Schwinge, E. R. "Aristophanes und die Utopie." *WJA* 3 (1977) 43–67.

Scodel, R. *Theater and Society in the Classical World*. Ann Arbor, Mich., 1993.

Seaford, R. *Reciprocity and Ritual*. Oxford, 1994.

Segal, E., ed. *Oxford Readings in Aristophanes*. Oxford, 1996.

Shear, T. L. "A Votive Relief from the Athenian Agora." *Orom* 9 (1973) 183–191.

Shepherd, R. *Ancient Mining*. London, 1993.

Sherwin-White, S. M. *Ancient Cos*. Göttingen, 1978.

Shipley, G. and J. Salmon, eds. *Human Landscapes in Classical Antiquity: Environment and Culture*. London, 1996.

Shorey, P. *What Plato Said*. Chicago, 1933.

Sidwell, K. "Aristophanes' *Acharnians* and Eupolis." *C&M* 45 (1994) 71–115.

Siewert, P. *Die Trittyes und die Heeresreform des Kleisthenes, Vestigia* 33. Munich 1982.

Silk, M. "The People of Aristophanes." in E. Segal 1996, pp. 229–251.

Silverman, S. "Agricultural Organization, Social Structure, and Values in Italy: Amoral Familism Reconsidered." *American Anthropology* 70 (1968) 1–20.

———. "Patronage as Myth." In E. Gellner and J. Waterbury 1977, pp. 7–19.

Simon, E. "Ein nordattischer Pan." *AK* 19 (1976) 19–23.

———. *Festivals of Attica*. Ann Arbor, Mich., 1983.

Skydsgaard, J. E. "Transhumance in Ancient Greece." In Whittaker 1988, pp. 75–86.

Slater, N. "Space, Character, and Apate: Transformation and Transvaluation in the *Acharnians*." In A. H. Sommerstein et al. 1993, pp. 397–415.

Smeed, J. W. *The Theophrastan Character: The History of a Literary Genre*. Oxford, 1985.

Smolenaars, J. J. L. "Labour in the Golden Age: A Unifying Theme in Vergil's Poems." *Mnemosyne* 40 (1987) 391–405.

Sommerstein, A. H. *Acharnians*. Warminster, 1980.

————. Aristophanes, *Wealth*. Warminster, 2001.

Sommerstein, A. H., S. Halliwell, J. Henderson, and B. Zimmermann. *Tragedy, Comedy, and the Polis*. Bari, 1993.

Sparkes, B. A. "Illustrating Aristophanes." *JHS* 95 (1975) 122–135.

Stainchaouer, Giorgos. Παρατηρήσεις στην οικιστική μορφή των αττικών δήμων. In Coulson et al. 1994, pp. 175–189.

Stalley, R. F. *An Introduction to Plato's Laws*. Indianapolis, 1983.

Stanton, G. R. "Some Attic Inscriptions." *ABSA* 79 (1984) 289–306.

Stark, I. "Krieg und Frieden in den Komödien des Aristophanes." *ACD* 24 (1988) 9–14.

Starkie, W. J. M. *The* Acharnians *of Aristophanes*. London, 1909.

Stauropoullos, P. Ἱερατικὴ οἰκία ἐν Ζωστῆρι τῆς Ἀττικῆς. *AE* 1938, *Chronika* 1–31.

Stone, L. M. *Costume in Aristophanic Comedy*. New York, 1977.

Stroud, R. S. "Three Attic Decrees." *CSCA* 7 (1974) 279–298.

————. "The Gravestone of Socrates' Friend, Lysis." *Hesperia* 53 (1984) 355–360.

Sussman, L. "Workers and Drones: Labor, Idleness and Gender Definition in Hesiod's Beehive." *Arethusa* 11 (1978) 27–41.

Sutton, D. F. "Dicaeopolis as Aristophanes, Aristophanes as Dicaeopolis." *LCM* 13 (1988) 105–108.

Szidat, J. "Hippodamos von Milet: Seine Rolle in Theorie und Praxis der griechischen Stadtplanung." *BJ* 180 (1980) 31–44.

Tandy, D. W. and W. C. Neale. *Hesiod's Works and Days: A Translation and Commentary for the Social Sciences*. Berkeley, Calif., 1996.

Taplin, O. "Phallology, Phylakes, Iconography and Aristophanes." *PCPhS* 33 (1987) 92–104.

————, *Comic Angels and Other Approaches to Greek Drama through Vase-Painting*. Oxford, 1993.

Thomas, C. "Between Literacy and Orality: Herodotus Historiography." *MHR* 3 (1988) 54–69.

Thomas, R. *Oral Tradition and Written Record in Classical Athens*. Cambridge, 1989.

————. *Literacy and Orality in Ancient Greece*. Cambridge, 1992.

Traill, J. S. *The Political Organization of Attica: A Study of the Demes, Trittyes, and Phylai and Their Representation in the Athenian Council. Hesperia* Supplement 14. Princeton, N.J., 1975.

————. *Demos and Trittys: Epigraphical and Topographical Studies in the Organization of Attica*. Toronto, 1986.

Triebel-Schubert, C. and U. Muss. "Hippodamos von Milet; Staatstheoretiker oder Stadtplaner." *Hephaistos* 5–6 (1983–1984) 37–59.

Ussher, R. G. "Old Comedy and 'Character', Some Comments." *G&R* 24 (1977) 71–79.

————. *The Characters of Theophrastus. Introduction, Commentary, and Index*, rev. ed. London, 1993 [1960].

van Andel, T. H., and C. N. Runnels. *Beyond the Akropolis: A Rural Greek Past*. Stanford, Calif., 1987.

Várhelyi, Z. "The Written Word in Archaic Attica." *Klio* 78 (1996) 28–52.

Versnel, H. S. "Greek Myth and Ritual: The Case of Kronos." In J. Bremmer, ed., *Interpretations of Greek Mythology*. London, 1987, pp. 121–152.

Vidal-Naquet, P. "étude d'une ambiguité: les artisans dans la cité Platonicienne." In *Le chasseur noir: formes de penseé et formes de société dans le monde grec*. Paris, 1981, pp. 289–316.

Vlastos, G. "Slavery in Plato's Thought." In *Platonic Studies*. Princeton, N.J., 1973, pp. 140–146.

Walker, S. "Women and Housing in Classical Greece." In *Images of Women in Antiquity*, ed. A. Cameron and A. Kuhrt. London, 1983, pp. 81–91.

Wallace-Hadrill, A., ed. *Patronage in Ancient Society*. London and New York, 1989.

Wallinga, H. T. "Hesiod's Farmer as a Sailor." In H. Sancisi-Weerdenburg et al., 1993, pp. 1–12.

Watrous, V. "An Attic Farm near Laurion." *Hesperia* Supplement 19. Princeton, N.J., 1982, pp. 193–197.

Webster, T. B. L. *Studies in Later Greek Comedy*. 2nd ed. Manchester, 1970.

———. *An Introduction to Menander*. New York, 1974.

Weil, R. *Aristote et l'histoire*. Paris, 1960.

Wells, B. *Agriculture in Ancient Greece*. Stockholm, 1992.

West, M. L. "Echoes and Imitations of the Hesiodic Poems." *Philologus* 113 (1969) 1–9.

———. *Hesiod Works and Days*. Oxford, 1978.

———. "Is the 'Works and Days' an Oral Poem?" In *I poemi epici rapsodici non omerici e la tradizione orale*, ed. C. Brillante, M. Cantilena, and C. O. Pavese. Padova, 1981, pp. 53–73.

Westermann, W. L. *The Slave Systems of Greek and Roman Antiquity*. Philadelphia, 1955.

White, K. D. *Country Life in Classical Times*. London, 1977.

Whitehead, D. *The Ideology of the Athenian Metic*. Cambridge, 1977.

———. "Competitive Outlay and Community Profit." *C&M* 34 (1983) 55–74.

———. *The Demes of Attica 508/7–ca. 250 B.C.: A Political and Social Study*. Princeton, N.J., 1986 (=1986a).

———. "The Ideology of the Athenian Metic. Some Pendants and a Reappraisal." *PCPS* 212 (1986) 145–158 (= 1986b).

———. "Cardinal Virtues: The Language of Public Approbation in Democratic Athens." *C&M* 44 (1993) 37–75.

Whittaker, M. "The Comic Fragments in Their Relation to the Structure of Attic Old Comedy." *CQ* 29 (1935) 181–191.

———, ed. *Pastoral Economies in Classical Antiquity*. Cambridge, 1988.

Wickens, J. M. "Deinias' Grave at Timesius' Farm." *Hesperia* 52 (1983) 96–99.

Wiles, D. *Tragedy in Athens: Performance Space and Theatrical Meaning*. Cambridge, 1997.

———. *Greek Theatre Performance: An Introduction*. Cambridge 2000.

Wilkins, J., D. Harvey, and M. Dobson, eds. *Food in Antiquity*. Exeter, 1995.

————. *The Boastful Chef: The Discourse of Food in Ancient Greek Comedy*. Oxford, 2000.

Wilson, P. *The Athenian Institution of the* Khoregia. Cambridge, 2000.

Wolf, E. R. "Kinship, Friendship, and Patron-Client Relations in Complex Societies." In Banton 1966, pp. 1–22 (= 1966a).

Wood, E. M. "Agricultural Slavery in Classical Athens." *AJAH* 8 (1983) 1–47.

————. *Peasant-Citizen and Slave: The Foundations of Athenian Democracy*. London, 1988.

Wycherley, R. E. *"Peripatos: The Athenian Philosophical Scene."* I, *Greece & Rome* 8 (1961) 152–163; II, 9 (1962) 2–21.

————."Hippodamus and Rhodes." *Historia* 13 (1964) 135–139.

————. "Lenaion." *Hesperia* 34 (1965) 72–76.

Yoshiyuki, S. "Isolated Farms in Classical Attica." *Kodai* 4 (1993) 1–19.

Young, J. H. "Studies in South Attica: Country Estates at Sounion." *Hesperia* 25 (1956) 122–146.

Young, R. S. "An Industrial District of Ancient Athens." *Hesperia* 20 (1951) 135–288.

Zaidman, L. B., and P. S. Pantel. *Religion in the Ancient Greek City*. Tr. P. Cartledge. Cambridge, 1992 [1989].

Zangger, E. "Plato's Atlantis Account: A Distorted Recollection of the Trojan War." *OJA* 12 (1993) 77–87.

Zimmermann, B. "Utopisches und Utopie in den Komödien des Aristophanes." *WJA* 9 (1983) 57–77.

Index

Acharnai, 92–100; activities of deme-
association, 99–100; demesmen and
women, 94–96; Dionysia at, 129–130;
inscriptions, 96–98; population,
92–93; relations with town, 94,
99–100; site and remains, 92, 98
Acropolis, 36, 40
Aeschines, 133, 135
agon, 80, 88, 145, 148, 149–150
Agora, 36, 40, 76
agora (of deme-association), 86–87
"Agrarian" Dionysia. *See* Dionysia
agros, 42, 44
Aigilia, Dionysia at, 128, 130
Aixone, 100–111; activities of deme-
association, 106–111; demesmen and
women, 107–109; Dionysia at, 130;
inscriptions, 101–106; population, 100,
107–108; relations with town, 107–109,
110–111; site and remains, 100–101
alterity, x–xi
Amorgos, 35
Anagyrous, Dionysia at, 130–131
apodyterion, 87
Areopagos, 40
Aristeides, 7, 178–179
Aristophanes, 1–3, 153, 194, 195–196;
Acharnians, 1, 2, 126, 131, 151–152,
196–201; *Birds*, 206; *Clouds*, 1, 2,
201–202; *Peace*, 1, 2, 202–206; *Wealth*,
206–207
Aristotle, 1–9 passim, 18, 24, 46, 51, 57,
74–77, 267–272
askoliasmos, 143–145, 150
assembly of deme-association, 86–87
asty (as technical term), 5–9, 12–14
Athens: antediluvian (in Plato's *Laws*),
253–256; organization of, 15; town: see

town and country relations; unity of,
ix–x
Atlantis, 251–253
attitudes, rural, 54–55
autarkeia/auktarky, 188–189

Bendis, 28
Brauron, 16; Dionysia at, 136

"center" of deme-association, 44–47,
85–90
children, 59–64; as agricultural laborers,
63; and religion, 182–183
Cholleidai, 196, 197, 199; Dionysia at,
131
chora (as technical term), 5–9, 12–14
choregia/*choregoi*, 80, 124–158 passim
chorion. *See* land
cliens, 72–73
clothing, 169–173
cock-fights, 150–151
comedy: Middle, 214–216; New, 216–225;
Old, 192–196
community(ies), rural, 17–19
"conservatism," 186–189
Corinth, 3–4
country. *See* town versus country; town
and country relations
cult activities of village-association, 88
decrees of deme-associations, 78–83
Dekeleia, 8
Delos, 33
diet, 166–169
demes/deme-associations: characterized,
91–92; cults of, 185–186; distribution
across Greece, 17; honorary decrees
of, 78–82; inscriptions of, 78–79;
isolation of, 15; relations with town,

demes/deme-associations (*continued*)
121–123, 124, 152–157; religion and,
182–183; theaters in, 128–129
democracy: Athenian, 11–12; ideology of,
83–84
Demosthenes, 43, 55, 58, 62, 133, 153
dikastai kata demous, 7, 8, 57, 84
Dionysia, 5, 80, 124–158; audiences, 152;
date of, 128, 153; distribution over the
demes, 127–142; duration of, 151–152;
entr'actes in, 150–151; events and their
sequence, 142–152; in intramural
demes, 136–139; in larger demes only,
139–142; name and orientation, 125–127
diphthera, 171–172
Dyaleis, 31
ecological studies, 11, 167, 186–189

Eleusis, 16, 38, 39–40, 46; Dionysia at,
131–132, 138–139
Ephoros, 3–4
Erchia, 46, 47, 88
Erythrai, 3
estates, 21
Euonymon; Dionysia at, 128, 132
Euripides, 153, 197

family, 48–55
farmstead residence, 17–47

grain, imported, 16

Hagnous, Dionysia at, 132
Halai Aixonides: activities of deme-
association, 114–116; cults, 114–115;
demesmen, 115–116; excavations
at, 46, 47; inscriptions, 112–114;
relations with town, 116; site and
remains, 111–112
Halai Araphenides, 128; Dionysia at, 128,
133
heorte, 80, 88, 145
heroes, tombs of, 186
Hesiod, *Works and Days*, 49–50, 56, 57,
60, 69, 163–164, 176–177, 227, 228
hestiasis, 88
Hipparchos, 177–178
Hippias of Erythrai, *Investigations*, 3

Hippodamos of Miletos, 229–234
honor and shame, 189–190
horistai, 58
honors granted by deme-associations,
78–83
horoi. See security *horoi*
house. See *oikia*
household, rural, 59–68

ideology: of town, 77–78, 84–85; of
village, 88–89
Ikarion, Dionysia at, 133
images of rural, 192–225, 273–277
inheritance, 53–54
in-laws. See *peoi*
inscriptions and literacy, 179–181
Italy, 72–73, 78

katonake, 4, 170–171
Kephallenia, 3
kepos, 39, 41
Kerameikos, 36, 40
Kimon, 74–77
Kleisthenes, 5–6
Kollytos: Dionysia at, 133, 138; Plato's
deme, 236–240
kome, 17, 193
komoidos/oi, 193
komos, 150, 193
kopron, 39
krene, 87
Kronos, Reign of, 227, 228–229
ktoina, 17
Kydathenaion, 46

labor, agricultural, 59–68, 161–163
Lakiadai, 72–77
Lamptrai, Dionysia at, 133–134
land, 17–47 passim, 70–71
leases, and rural residence, 27–34
Lemnos, 35
Lenaion, 2
lesche, 87
literacy, 175–181
liturgies of deme-associations, 80

marriage, 16, 53
megalophrosyne, 75

Melite, 46
Menander, 218–225
mentalité, 54–55, 186–191
metics: as agricultural laborers, 66–68; demotics of, 67–68
migration, 54
Miletos, 230
mining, 14, 16
mobility, 54, 160–161
mountain peak cults, 186
music, 173
Myrrhinous, Dionysia at, 128, 134

Naxos, 35
neighbors, 42–43, 66
Nikolaos of Damascus, 4
Nymphs, 182–185

oba, 17
occupation and rural residence, 20
oie, 17
oikia (vel sim.), 17–47 passim
orality/oral culture, 176–177
orgeones: of Bendis, 28; of Egretes, 30–31; of the Hero, 29–30; of Hypodektes, 31
ostracism, 178–179
"Other." *See* alterity

Paiania, Dionysia at, 128, 134
Paiania, Lower, 79–80
palaistra, 87
Pan, 182–185
pannychis, 88
pastoralism, 184–185
patronage, 59–85, 88, 161
patronage, Roman, 72–73, 78
patronus, 72–73
Peiraieus, 6, 8, 16, 30, 46, 230, 231; Dionysia at, 134–135, 136–138, 154
Peisistratos, 3, 7, 8, 21, 57
Pelargikon, 6
pelates, 72–73
peoi, 60–61, 65
Periander, 3–4
Pericles, 76
perioikion, 38, 39
Phaleas of Chalkedon, 234–235
philon(e)ikia, 59

philotimia, 55–59
Phlya, Dionysia at, 135
phratries, 15–16, 31
phylai, 15, 82–83
pilos, 170
Plato: and deme Kollytos, 236–240; demes mentioned in dialogues, 243–244; family of, 236; *Kritias*, 251–256; *Laws*, 256–258, 258–267; *Republic*, 247–251; residence(s) of, 236–240; settings of dialogues, 240–245; social topography, 246–267
Plutarch: on Kimon, 74–77; on Solon, 58
Pnyx, 40
poletai records (and rural residence), 24–26
pompe, 80, 145–148
Prasiai, 31–32
proedria, 148–149
prostates, 72–73
Pyrrhic dancers, 80, 88

quarrying, 16

rationes centesimarum (and farmstead residence), 26–27
real property (terminology for), 23–24
regional associations, 186
religion, 181–186
residence patterns, 19–22, 160–161
Rhamnous, 27–28, 38, 39–40, 46; Dionysia at, 135
Rhodos, 230
risk, 59–68
rivalry, 55–59
Rome. *See* patronage, Roman
rupestral inscriptions, 57–58
rural: images of, 192–225, 273–277; as technical term, 5
Rural Dionysia. *See* Dionysia

sacrifices, 80
Salaminioi, 28–29
Salamis, Dionysia at, 136
Sappho, 169–170
seasons/seasonality, 163–166
security *horoi* (and rural residence patterns), 34–42

settlement, 18–22, 160–161
shame. *See* honor and shame
Sikyon, 4
sisyra, 171
Skambonidai, 88
Skyros, 35
slaves (as agricultural laborers), 63–65
society, 48–90
sociopolitical regime (and residence
    patterns), 21
Sophocles, 133, 153
speech, 173–175
Sphettos, Dionysia at, 128, 135
spolas, 171
state, rural community and, 17–19, 51–52,
    154–158
Syros, 35

Teithras, 117–121; activities of deme-
    association, 119–121; demesmen, 120;
    inscriptions, 38, 39–40, 117–119;
    relations with town, 120–121; site and
    bouleutic quota, 117; women, 117
territory, size of, 20
theater of or in deme, 87, 128–129, 140
Theater of Dionysos, 2, 76
Themistocles, 6–7
Theognis, 169
Theophrastos, 43–44, 211–214
Theopompos, 4, 74–77
Thesmophoria (in demes), 186

Thorikos, 46, 47; Dionysia at, 135–136
Thucydides, 7–8
thysiai. See sacrifices
topography, 20, 227
town and country relations: across
    Greece, 17–18; models for, 121–123;
    paradigms for, 273–277
town of Athens: ideological climate of,
    77–78, 84–85; migration to or
    from, 54
town versus country, x–xi, 12–14, 14–16,
    190–191; clothing, 169–173; diet,
    166–169; seasons/seasonality, 163–166
traditions, 54–55
trochades, 172

utopias, 226, 228–229

values, 54–55, 186–191
village/villagers, 44–47, 50–52, 68–85
    passim, 88–89
visibility of women and children, 54
wells, 29, cf. 41, 58
women, 59–65, 161–163; of Acharnai, 94;
    as agricultural laborers, 62–63; of
    Aixone, 109; mobility of, 162; and
    religion, 182–183; of Teithras, 117;
    visibility of, 162–163

Xenophon, 207–211

DATE DUE

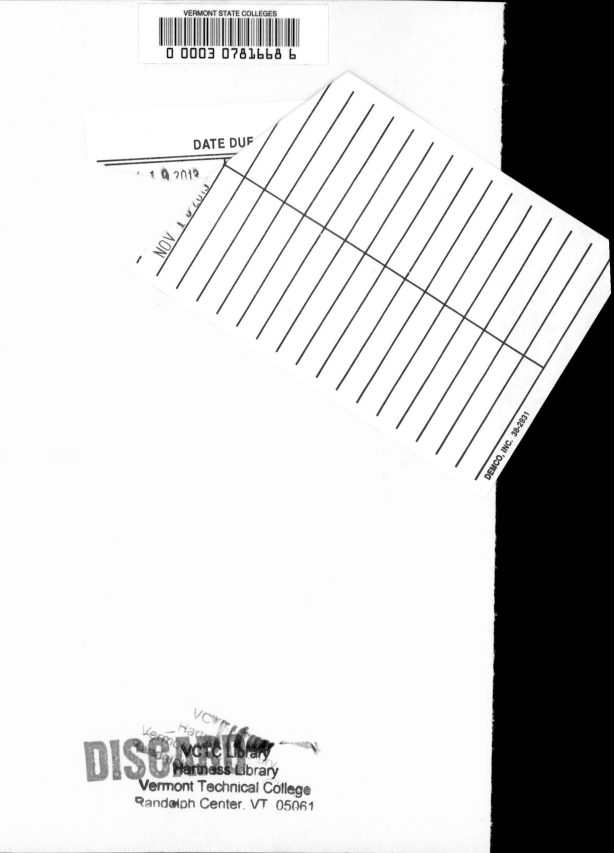

DEMCO, INC. 38-2931